# *THE* LOVE AND ROCKETS *COMPANION*

# The *Love* AND ROCKETS Companion

## 30 YEARS (AND COUNTING)

Edited by
Marc Sobel and Kristy Valenti

FANTAGRAPHICS BOOKS, INC
Seattle, WA

# CONTENTS

Edited by Marc Sobel and Kristy Valenti
Consulting Editor: Eric Reynolds
Designed by Tony Ong
Production: Paul Baresh and Preston White
Design and editorial assistance: Kristen Bisson, Matt Burke, Aidan Fitzgerald, Tom Graham, Ben
Horak, Nomi Kane, Kara Krewer, Janice Lee, Jason T. Miles, Anna Pederson and Madisen Semet
Published by Gary Groth and Kim Thompson
Associate Publisher: Eric Reynolds

With special thanks to Mark Rosenfelder (www.zompist.com).

FANTAGRAPHICS BOOKS, INC.
7563 Lake City Way NE, Seattle, WA 98115, USA
www.fantagraphics.com

ISBN 978-1-60699-579-2

First Printing: March 2013
Printed in Hong Kong

**T**he following four interviews, spanning more than 25 years, check in with the Hernandez brothers at three stages in their careers, serving as a record of their evolving attitudes toward the comics medium and industry as well as their creative concerns and processes.

The first interview, conducted by their publisher Gary Groth and *Comics Journal* staff members Robert Fiore and Thom Powers, ran in issue #126 (January 1989) of that publication. It covers Gilbert's, Jaime's and Mario's experiences in the L.A. punk scene, early family life, the origins of their characters and stories and their efforts to create a space for comics that were neither mainstream nor underground. Neil Gaiman conducted the second interview with Jaime and Gilbert for *The Comics Journal* #178 (July 1995); Gaiman was still writing *Sandman*, and he and the brothers talk about how they were starting to adapt their storytelling, creatively, to longer story arcs (i.e., "writing for the trade"). The brothers were

# INTERVIEWS

concluding the first volume of *Love and Rockets* and were planning to branch out into other comics projects (and a movie).

Author Marc Sobel conducted two new interviews exclusively for this book, in 2011 and 2012. First, he reflected with Gilbert, Jaime and Mario about the first 30 years of *Love and Rockets*, talking about what has changed in terms of exactly who gets represented in mass media, critical responses to the brothers' recent stories, digital developments, and, simply, about how they've matured as artists, both physically and artistically. This section concludes with a survey of *Love and Rockets*' publishing history with Gary Groth, who breaks down the decision-making process behind the various formats the comic has appeared in, talks about older production practices, what it means to edit *Love and Rockets* and provides some anecdotes about the early days.

Mario, Gilbert and Jaime Hernandez were born and raised in Oxnard, Calif., just north of Los Angeles. They grew up reading comic books, watching monster movies, listening to rock 'n' roll music and, most significantly, drawing their own cartoons and comics. In the late '70s they became heavily involved in punk rock, and this phenomenon opened their eyes to the possibilities of expressing themselves in comics. It was Mario who put these ambitions on a practical footing, enlisting his brothers in a self-published comic called *Love and Rockets*. They sent a review copy to Gary Groth, editor and publisher of *The Comics Journal*, who had a few ambitions of his own. He had wanted to publish a new kind of comics, and here, lo and behold, was a new kind of comics. In 1982 *Love and Rockets* became the flagship title of Fantagraphics Books.

Over the course of the first several issues the brothers' confidence steadily grew (Mario dropped out after the third issue, but contributed occasionally to later issues). Initially they thought they had to present their work in some semblance of genre trappings but these quickly fell away. Jaime began by interspersing his tongue-in-cheek science-fiction series "Mechanics" with more realistic vignettes set in the southwestern barrio Hoppers 13. Emboldened by his brother's example, Gilbert took the plunge with "Heartbreak Soup," a series of stories set in the mythical Central American town of Palomar.

On the business end of things, *Love and Rockets* was the first American comic to successfully adopt the European method of album collection after magazine serialization. The *Love and Rockets* collections allowed the brothers to make a decent living despite a relatively low circulation for the bimonthly magazine (between 18- and 19,000). Things were not going so smoothly in 1984, however, and to make ends meet they agreed to produce the first six issues of *Mister X* on a work-for-hire basis for Vortex. Mario and Gilbert plotted, Gilbert scripted and Jaime drew the artwork, scrapping all but the bare bones of Dean Motter's original concept. Unfortunately, the contract that the legally inexperienced brothers signed did not stipulate when they were to be paid (it would eventually take three years). By the time they finished the fourth issue they had not yet been fully paid for the first, so they quit the series. (The publisher would later claim that they left because they were unable to keep the schedule, although their issues came out more frequently than any subsequent team's.)

The Hernandez brothers were interviewed in several combinations in several sessions. The interviews were conducted by Gary Groth, Robert Fiore and Thom Powers, transcribed by Thom Powers, copy-edited by Gilbert and Jaime Hernandez and edited by Robert Fiore.

*Ed. Note: Some of the more dated sections of this interview have been excised in this reprint; to read what the Hernandez brothers thought of* Watchmen, *etc. digital archives are available to subscribers at tcj.com. Available back issues can be found at www.fantagraphics.com.*

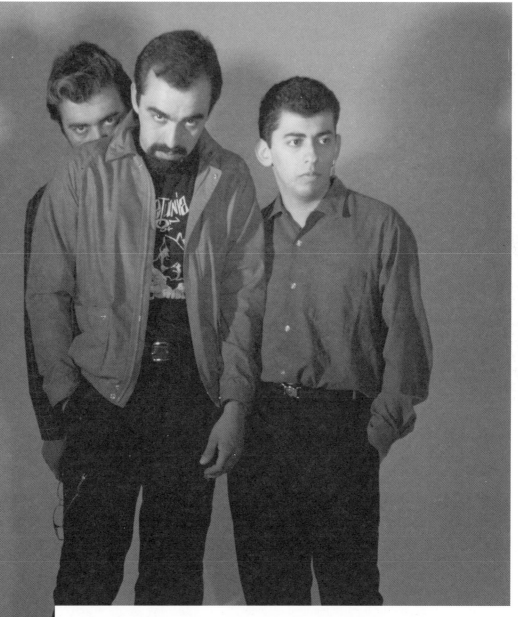

# GARY GROTH & THE BROTHERS

From *The Comics Journal* #126 (January 1989)

# PART ONE

# ORIGINS

**GARY GROTH:** I'm interested in how you grew up and where you grew up, and if you could just talk a little about your formative years spent in Oxnard. You were born in Oxnard?

**JAIME HERNANDEZ:** Yeah. Born in a Ventura hospital, but right away, driven over to Oxnard. I grew up there with my four brothers and sisters, and I grew up reading comic books.

**ROBERT FIORE:** How many relatives did you have regular contact with?

**JAIME:** We lived next door to my aunt and uncle who also had six kids, and my grandmother who was around a lot, who was always trading houses to live in. I grew up just a normal kid.

**GROTH:** Were you a close family?

**JAIME:** Sure. We were always drawing together, watching TV together: playing together. If I wasn't playing with Ismael, I was playing with Gilbert, or Richie. Mario was always the big kid, so I kinda kept away from him. It was good.

**GROTH:** You're Mexican by descent. What generation are you?

**GILBERT:** I was born in the States.

**GROTH:** How about your parents?

**GILBERT:** My dad is from Chihuahua, Mexico and like a lot of Mexicans he came over to work. And my mom is from Texas, but her family goes back all the way to when Texas was [part of] Mexico.

**GROTH:** Do you have a sense of Mexican roots?

**GILBERT:** As far as I can tell. Most of my relatives actually came from Mexico to here. It's just this generation of kids that were U.S.-born.

**GROTH:** Do you feel those roots in some way?

**GILBERT:** Yeah, because they brought a lot of those old ways, old superstitions, old ways of making food, stories of things that happened back home, simple things like that. I always felt that I was living in two worlds. One was the little Mexican world, because nearly everybody I knew, relatives and cousins and even kids in the neighborhood, were Mexican. Then school was a different world. It was pretty ethnically mixed: I had a lot of black, white, Japanese friends. One thing I can remember all the way back is that I never noticed the difference between races except skin color. That's just something I learned.

**GROTH:** Was the neighborhood that you grew up in fairly isolated in terms of its ethnic character?

**GILBERT:** The street we lived on probably had more Mexicans because the houses were inexpensive. Just a street away the kids were black or Japanese. It was a well-mixed area.

**GROTH:** Did you have any formal religious training?

**JAIME:** We were born Catholic and I did my first Holy Communion; I was confirmed. I did all that: went to Catechism on every Saturday. Boy, school on Saturday! [*Laughs.*] I couldn't believe it. Saturday

*A Mexican immigrant develops a crush on Maggie in Jaime's "Locas at the Beach" (1985), reprinted in* Maggie the Mechanic.

*Sister Mary Joseph does her part in "Roy and His Pals in Monsters and Heroes" (2003-2004) by Gilbert; from* Love and Rockets *Vol. 2 #10 (Spring 2004).*

morning was when all the cartoons were on and I had to go to Catechism!

**GROTH:** This is something that took?

**JAIME:** It didn't; I never took it seriously. It was something my mom tried to bring us up with. But she was never a real churchgoer, because she was married in court, and if a Catholic is married in court they can't go to church — I don't know exactly what it is — they can't confess or take communion. Or that was her belief. I don't know the details. There were times when we went to church every week and then we'd stop going for a long time, and then we'd start, and then stop, and then we stopped altogether.

**GROTH:** But you were never a serious practitioner of Catholicism?

**JAIME:** No, it was never really pushed. Catechism seemed like a school where the teacher didn't get mad. I never had the ruler slapped on my hand.

**GROTH:** Never got punched out by a nun?

**JAIME:** No, but there were times I thought they were going to do that.

**GILBERT:** Like a lot of Catholics, there was a point where it really, really screwed me up. Not that I thought religion was fascistic or anything like that, but it scared the shit out of me. It got to the point where I was so scared of death that I would go to the restroom and shiver. It freaked me out. I couldn't

believe that that was going to happen to me. There were two points in my life when that happened. But it was one of those things that I would keep to myself, no one else knew about it. I would watch television with my family, we'd be watching some crummy situation comedy, and I'd be sitting there breaking into a sweat because I'd remember that I was going to die someday. And I trace that back to religion, remembering that you're either going to go to heaven or to hell — and I thought, that means hell, there's no way I'm going to heaven no matter what I do. I was convinced. I don't know how it started: I just got freaked out on religion. What's weird is that I never really blamed it on religion. I blamed it on me. I always blamed it on myself, if I was nervous, or I got scared, or if something pissed me off.

**GROTH:** So eventually you became a lapsed Catholic?

**GILBERT:** Right.

**GROTH:** At what point did you break off?

**GILBERT:** Girls. I just figured I was too horny. I liked girls too much to contain myself, to follow any rigid rules: because you were only supposed to like girls in a certain way.

**GROTH:** You didn't go to a parochial school; you went to public schools.

**JAIME:** Right: all my life. I can tell you one thing; the Catholicism I was brought up with does help my imagination a lot.

**FIORE:** How so?

**JAIME:** All the fear I grew up with. It adds to my whole story.

**FIORE:** Are you afraid of hell?

**JAIME:** Yeah, I was afraid of the devil. I'm still afraid of the devil.

## AN EARLY AFFECTION

**FIORE:** You got into comics through your mother, right?

**GILBERT:** Yeah, our mom collected comic books in the '40s, and it's the old story, her mother — our grandmother — threw them out, so she didn't have any left. What she did was, she would take a small panel and blow up the face.

**MARIO:** That's how we learned about most —

**JAIME:** Golden Age characters. She would show us: "This is Captain Triumph, this is Blackhawk." To us it was really impressive.

**FIORE:** She had drawings she'd made of these characters?

**GILBERT:** Yeah, she would copy and blow them up.

**JAIME:** Luckily, she saved them.

**GILBERT:** And she'd always tell us about the old comics. [*To Mario:*] Actually, you were the one who started collecting comics.

**MARIO:** Yeah, when I was 5.

**GILBERT:** Did she encourage that or —

**MARIO:** I just started picking up comics. I'm not really sure. I just know I started collecting comics when I was 5 years old.

**FIORE:** So the rest of the family followed your lead?

**MARIO:** Yeah, because comic books got passed around, and we started drawing our own pictures.

**GILBERT:** Jaime and I were born into a world with comic books in the house. That was normal to us.

**JAIME:** I was still a baby when Mario started collecting regularly. I don't remember the first *Fantastic Four* comic that he got, which was #1, but I remember reading it. It would just be there, along with all the rest, *Dennis the Menace*, Archies, DCs, things like that. So it was never any discovery for

*Gilbert remembers Mario's review of Fantastic Four #1 (November 1961), written by Stan Lee and penciled by Jack Kirby, as: "This is great, it has monsters in it."*

me, even as far as drawing comics for ourselves. That was a natural thing to do because my brothers did it.

**GILBERT:** I distinctly remember *Fantastic Four #1* sitting on the couch, when Mario brought it home. I remember the day I picked it up, and Mario said, "This is great, it has monsters in it." We didn't know who drew it or what …

**MARIO:** Comics were everywhere. You'd go to the bathroom with comics; you'd eat dinner with comics. It was pretty lax. You could get away with something like that, just be reading all the time.

**GILBERT:** I imagine our mother let us read comics because she did. It was nostalgic for her, I guess. So, comics were always normal to us, it was an everyday thing. It wasn't until school that we realized that we were abnormal.

**FIORE:** So now you've realized you're abnormal?

**GILBERT:** Yeah, that it didn't click with any of the other school kids.

**MARIO:** Some kids liked it, but we didn't have friends that read comics. The only comic fans we knew on a regular basis were [people we met] at conventions. Up until then we were pretty much comic-book geeks.

**FIORE:** What were the comics you liked most when you first started reading them?

**MARIO:** Just the superhero stuff, *Superman*, *Adventure Comics*, all the DC stuff. And things like *Hot Stuff*, *Richie Rich*.

**GILBERT:** Almost anything that was out there, with few exceptions, like Westerns. We didn't read too many of them. The DCs, Harvey comics like *Richie Rich* and *Hot Stuff*, Dennis the Menace comics, and Archie comics. I guess the strongest influences were those. Still influence us now.

**GROTH:** Can you describe how your interest in comics evolved over the course of 10 or 12 years?

**GILBERT:** I rarely bought comics myself. Mario

From "The Mighty Diet" in Hot Stuff #38 (August 1961): The creators are not credited.

was buying them all. He was buying most of them up until the big Marvel craze. Then the DCs and the funny-animal stuff and *Mad* magazines dropped off and it was just Marvels. I liked the Kirby and Ditko stuff, but there were other things that I didn't like, like the Sub-Mariner and Hulk. I thought it was just because I didn't understand them. I didn't realize that they just weren't any good. I thought I'd grow up and understand what this means later. Kirby and Ditko I loved right away, I didn't have to think twice about them. But when the other guys started coming in, when Roy Thomas started writing the *X-Men*, things like that, I thought I just wasn't smart enough for it.

**GROTH:** When did *Archie* come in?

**GILBERT:** That was always there, too. I imagine it was because my mother suggested certain things.

**GROTH:** So there was never one kind of comic?

**GILBERT:** Never, until the Marvels came in. After Jack Kirby the old DC comics looked pretty flat in comparison.

**FIORE:** Jaime, your work is constantly compared to Archie comics. How much of an influence is there, really?

**JAIME:** I'm not influenced so much by the stories

Top: Archie cartoonist Harry Lucey was a big influence on Jaime; this panel is from "What's in a Name?" written by Frank Doyle and drawn by Lucey, reprinted in The Best of Archie. Bottom: Penny's pet dinosaur is doomed in Jaime's "Mechanics" (1983), reprinted in Maggie the Mechanic.

but the characters themselves. Believe it or not, they worked. They had a lot of sides to them because Dan DeCarlo and Harry Lucey, the two big artists, had a great way of showing body language.

**FIORE:** When did you start drawing?

**MARIO:** As far as I remember, it was about that time, when I was 5 years old.

**JAIME:** And for me it was the easiest, because I was

following three brothers, so I really don't remember when I started.

**GILBERT:** Actually, our father encouraged us …

**FIORE:** I've never heard you talk too much about your father.

**GILBERT:** Well, my mother tells us that he painted at one time. So it was already in both our parents, it was a natural thing.

**FIORE:** So your father wasn't around?

**GILBERT:** He worked at night and slept during the day, so we didn't see him a lot. He died when we were pretty young …

**JAIME:** In '68.

**MARIO:** He would get a paper bag, tear it open, and give us crayons or pencils and cut us loose.

**FIORE:** When you were very young was one of you thought of as the "good" artist, the one who was ahead of the others?

**JAIME:** It pretty much went by age. Mario was untouchable, he was the big kid; he was grown-up. I mean, the way I saw it. So he did everything better than all of us. He drew. Gilbert was the most imaginative one. He was always doing the craziest things. He always took it further than Mario. Mario didn't really get into as much as Gilbert did.

**GROTH:** Now you're talking in terms of drawing.

**JAIME:** In terms of drawing and creating. We were all drawing. All the way down to Lucinda.

**GROTH:** Would that include Richard and Ismael?

**JAIME:** Yes. They were doing their stuff. Richard less, because he was more into sports: But he did draw. He was getting good too. There was always a fight between me and him, who drew better. Of course, he'd say, "I draw better than you."

**FIORE:** Up until what age?

**JAIME:** This was about 10. Richie really slowed down on drawing when he got into junior high. He did more sports things, and hung out more. He just lost interest. I don't know why. And Mario as he got older, he started hanging out and he would just occasionally do an illustration. He didn't last long actually doing comics, like me, Gilbert and Ismael. We were constantly drawing our own comic books. He only did a few.

**FIORE:** Did you draw strips from the start? When did you start doing that?

**GILBERT:** We were pretty young. Mario did a comic book of Superman, and I did one of my own called *Spaceman*. It was really crude, of course. We did it for a while, we did it for maybe a couple of years, and then we just stopped doing it, for a long time. And then one day Jaime and I picked up and started doing it. We'd fold a piece of typing paper in half, draw a cover, and it had art on the inside and a back cover with scribbling on it.

**MARIO:** A lot of them were just covers.

**FIORE:** [*To Jaime:*] Was it the same thing with you?

**JAIME:** I must have been really young, because I remember always doing it. Just following these guys, copying big brother the whole time.

**MARIO:** The thing was, that Superman was just a lark. It was just a fun thing to do for the day, and then I dropped it, and everybody picked up on it. And then later on, I remember seeing they were still doing it. I said, "Wow, you guys are still drawing this stuff?"

**GILBERT:** What I think is really strange is that my first comic book was a character I made up. Whereas usually we did Spider-Man ...

**MARIO:** I remember my first few were copies of Captain America and stuff, Daredevil.

**FIORE:** When did you start doing your own kind of characters?

**JAIME:** When I was 7 or 8 years old, we really got hooked on the *Peanuts* cartoons.

**GILBERT:** Yeah, we started swiping those.

**JAIME:** We started swiping them, and slowly they evolved into our own thing, where we wouldn't go by the rules of storytelling, we would just go crazy, go wild. And our younger brother [Ismael] even started, and he went even crazier.

**GILBERT:** His stuff was pretty close to Crumb's, and he'd never seen a comic like that. Closer to Peter Bagge, actually.

**FIORE:** Did you generally finish what you started?

**JAIME:** Sometimes. There were a lot of times where I ended up with a bunch of half-drawn Batman comics. The last panels were "Pow!" "Bam!" "Sock!" all the way down the line until the end. Then, "Well, that's that!" But Gilbert was always the one who seemed to take it seriously.

**FIORE:** How did you get started reading underground comics?

**GILBERT:** That was a turning point.

**MARIO:** I'd always seen Bob Crumb drawings in articles — I used to get *Rolling Stone* secretly, because anything with "fuck" in it I had to hide from my mom. [*Laughter.*] I'd always wanted to read them; they looked really intriguing. As I got older, I didn't care anymore. I started smuggling these things into the house. They were a really great inspiration.

**FIORE:** Where did you get them?

**MARIO:** There was a head shop in town that I used to hang around once in a while, get records and stuff. It was interesting; it was Jim Salzer's head shop. Did you know that was the first head shop in Southern California?

**GILBERT:** Really?

**MARIO:** Yeah.

**GILBERT:** Historic.

**MARIO:** That's where I used to buy a lot of records, and pick up some underground stuff. The first ones were *Zap* #0 and #1, and Crumb's cartooning just — it's just right there the first time you look at it. It reminded you of Fleischer cartoons when they were doing really wild stuff.

**FIORE:** Did you start trying to draw like Crumb? How did that change your own drawing?

**GILBERT:** No, I think that was subliminal, because when I tried to copy Crumb, it was flat, I knew I didn't have what he had, even though it was easy to draw like that. I was more impressed with the stories, because he could get away with anything. I mean it was anything goes. And at that time, I was at the age of starting to hang around with the

teenagers and a little bit older crowd, and they had them laying around all the time. Well, even before that, it wasn't that big of a transition, because we picked up on those Wonder Wart-Hog reprints that were in hot rod cartoon magazines.

**FIORE:** It was in *Drag Cartoons*.

**GILBERT:** I'd gone from *Mad* to *CarToons* to *Drag Cartoons* to underground comics, so it wasn't that big a jump. It was pretty gradual. That's what we mean by a little bit of everything.

**FIORE:** You'd been drawing since you were kids; you took some art classes …

**GILBERT:** Well, we took the regular art classes in high school …

**JAIME:** Just so you wouldn't have to take math or something.

**GILBERT:** It was always easy for us, we always got A's in art, but then in high school it got tougher. I got a C+ and I'd say, "What is this, come on." [*Laughter.*]

**JAIME:** We got lazy.

**GILBERT:** That's because as teenagers we weren't involved in cartooning so much as music, and that's what brought us out of the geek world, because you have to deal with the real world when dealing with people who talk about music.

**FIORE:** Define the "geek world."

**GILBERT:** The comic-book guys, the guys who sit home every Saturday, watch every horror movie

*This sequence is from R. Crumb's "I'm a Ding Dong Daddy" from* Zap Comix #1 *(November 1967).*

©2013 R. Crumb

possible. Didn't really go out and play sports or anything.

**JAIME:** The ultimate fanboys.

**GILBERT:** Everybody's story. We can relate. We got beat up at school, picked on, the whole bit. I guess time is a lot slower for a kid, because I remember going through what I thought were periods of, like, months without drawing at all, which must have been just a week or two. But it seemed that we didn't draw or even think about comics for a long time.

## MOSTLY MUSIC

**FIORE:** So Mario brought in the first *Zap* comic. Who brought in the first Sex Pistols record?

**GILBERT:** Actually, this goes back to when we were little kids. I think my mother was expecting Jaime [*laughter*] — this is a true story — and next to her was a teenage girl expecting a kid, and she would listen to the radio all day long. It drove my mom crazy at first, but after a while she started getting into the songs. This was like '59. After she came home, every day she would put the radio on a major radio station, which was KRLA at the time, and we heard pop music, rock music, all day long. That was another thing. Just like comics being normal, we heard that music in the background. Then my dad would come home from work and listen to a Mexican radio station. So we either listened to Mexican music or rock 'n' roll.

**GROTH:** That would have been in the late '50s, early '60s.

**GILBERT:** Well, Jaime was born in '59, so I remember the early '60s, The Shirelles and the girl groups.

**GROTH:** The Beatles?

**GILBERT:** The Beatles hit like a ton of bricks.

**GROTH:** You must have been about 6.

**GILBERT:** Yeah, but for some reason it appealed to me. I guess their gimmick worked with the hairdos and the boots and stuff. I remember liking their music so much I couldn't stand it; I had to leave the house because I liked it so much. A lot

Peter Bagge wrote and Gilbert drew the '60s girl group-inspired Yeah! for DC Comics (later reprinted as a graphic novel by Fantagraphics). This sequence is from "Yeah! Goes to War" in #8 (May 2000).

©2013 Peter Bagge

of kids had Beatles parties and things like that. I realized when I was a kid that this music was me, it was speaking to me directly — as much as it could be at 6 years old. Then I lost interest in Top 40 music because it became repetitious and it was getting to be a formula. I guess that was the late '60s. I wasn't too much aware of the underground scene that was happening, with guys like Jimi Hendrix. Mario was a teenager, so he was listening to that, reading the old *Rolling Stone*, which I thought was a sinful magazine. I thought it was great that people were going nuts, but at the same time I thought, "That's not for me. What am I going to do? I'm 12 years old."

**FIORE:** So all through your youth all that was going on?

**GILBERT:** It was always there.

**JAIME:** And it was all normal to me.

**FIORE:** So you were also music geeks?

**GILBERT:** No, music was different.

**JAIME:** Actually, I gave up on music in the late '60s because I got into sports.

**FIORE:** Gilbert and Mario say they weren't into sports, but you were?

**JAIME:** Well, I was in it for the fun. I liked playing baseball and I liked catching. It wasn't so competitive for me, and when I actually played Little League, these guys were playing for serious, and I just couldn't get into that. So I would go for a long time without any music or comics. Or I think I did. I started getting back into it in the early '70s, when Mario and Gilbert started getting into the glitter groups: Iggy, Roxy Music, T. Rex, Mott the Hoople, New York Dolls. I would listen at Mario's door, because these guys were big guys, I was just a little guy. I couldn't hang out with them. [*Laughter.*]

Their hair was longer than mine was.

**GILBERT:** That was really strange, though, why we got into that glitter-type punky stuff, because before we were listening to Jethro Tull records, I bought the first Paul Simon record.

**MARIO:** It was pretty diverse.

**GILBERT:** But then, the one that really changed us was *Slider*, T. Rex. We listened to it and we thought it was the world's silliest record, and we kept listening to it, and our tastes were ruined forever. [*Laughter.*]

**JAIME:** Naturally, when punk came out in the late '70s, it just fit.

**GILBERT:** It was the same kind of music, except it was real fast.

**MARIO:** A breath of fresh air.

**GILBERT:** For some reason, I always thought rock 'n' roll, comics, wrestling and horror movies all sort of mixed, in a way, and when punk came out, that was all those things I suspected were alike.

**FIORE:** Before punk came in, were you involved in any kind of music thing? Did you go to shows?

**MARIO:** Yeah, we went to shows. We saw Blue Oyster Cult; we'd go once a week to the [Hollywood] Palladium.

Gilbert drew this valentine for his wife-to-be Carol Kovinick in 1980; it is reprinted in the Love and Rockets Sketchbook Vol. 1.

**JAIME:** And when disco started coming out I started backing off. And I almost gave into it before punk came along. [*Laughs.*]

**GILBERT:** The first two bands I saw were pretty nifty ones — T. Rex and Mott the Hoople. So I started out well, then I dive-bombed into Deep Purple, Queen and really shithole bands like that. Those first concerts I saw were in, like, '73.

**JAIME:** My first concert was Roxy Music.

**GILBERT:** We actually got into punk a year late. The Sex Pistols had already broken up before I bought the album.

**FIORE:** It wasn't that long between the time the album came out here and they broke up. [*Laughter.*]

**GILBERT:** That's true, but my wife Carol was into it the day the first single came out. But then again, she was around 14, and that makes a lot more sense. Because we had already gone through glitter and all that shit, through Kiss, and all that superficial stuff made us think, "Oh, here comes another one." When the punk thing came I rejected it right away because I had gone through so many different phases in music that right away I determined this was just another phase, I don't want it. This was my late teens or early 20s. Then I saw some TV special on it, the new thing in England, and I was shocked, I was appalled. But instead of pissing me off, it scared me, because it made me realize that I wasn't young any more, that things were changing, that I was one of the post-hippie era so I was part of the blank generation that they were making fun of. So it made me sit up and think, "Wait a minute, I'm not cool any more?"

**FIORE:** I remember hearing Tito Larriva, who was in The Plugz, telling about how he stumbled into the Masque [an early L.A. punk club] when the Bags were playing, and his first impression was that he was seeing the fall of Western Civilization [*laughter*] and a month later he had his own punk band.

**GILBERT:** It made me sit up and listen to it and I realized that it had all the elements that I liked about rock 'n' roll thrown into a cement mixer. It had all the trashy elements of rock that I always liked. But a lot of bands took it seriously, groups like The Clash and X. They were politically aware.

**GROTH:** Was the punk phenomenon kind of a liberating force for you, or did it clarify things for you?

**GILBERT:** Probably it confused me more because it was such a fragmented scene that nobody agreed on anything — that was another reason it sort of made itself alive.

**GROTH:** It obviously had a salutary effect.

**GILBERT:** Because it was physical. I read comics, I watched movies; I wasn't a sports guy. But rock 'n' roll was something physical. You stood up, and you sweated and ran around and did things. And punk went even further, you wore these particular type of clothes and people were either afraid of you or beat the shit out of you. There

LA."PUNKS" CIRCA 1979-1980                                    OTEB/8

was rarely any in-between. So I thought that was great.

**GROTH:** Now what year would this have been?

**GILBERT:** For me it was about 1978 to '80.

**GROTH:** Was there violence? Did you get into fights?

**GILBERT:** See, at first there wasn't. The original punk scene in L.A. was pretty much a fun thing, a lot of people just having a good time, listening to a band, bouncing around, dancing. It was more of an art scene I think; there was more of an artsy-fartsy crowd. What happened is people that came from other areas of rock music started getting interested and a lot of them were sort of stupid jocks and they participated in punk gigs the way they thought they were supposed to. They thought it was a little football game when in actuality, even though people were dancing around roughly, everybody was polite and if you fell down somebody would pick you up. Then these guys started coming in and if you fell down you got kicked in the ribs and they pretty much forced the old punks out because they weren't physical types.

**GROTH:** What was this new group?

**GILBERT:** Predominantly, they were a bunch of kids from Huntington Beach, from the beaches, surfers ...

**GROTH:** White, middle class?

**GILBERT:** Pretty much, yeah. They liked the aggressive side of punk. There were sides of punk that were experimental, brainy, pretentious. But these guys liked the meat-and-potatoes stuff, which was dying out. They had their own bands and they changed the whole scene. And since it was so physical, since it was so intense, the scene just erupted and it brought in so many other ugly elements. Right away it became sexist and racist. Look what some of it's become now, they've got the skinhead movement — all over the United States teenagers are following white supremacy bullshit. And you'll see news clips of it and they look just like the kids I used to see around. It's just become perverted, twisted. Even though punk could never merge with the mainstream because it was too exotic, too wild — all TV and record companies could do is turn it into new wave, this bouncy affectation. So where could punk go? So it just got more violent and more violent. Probably the most violent and intense concert I've ever been to was Public Image at Olympic Auditorium in L.A. Public Image is headed by John Lydon, who used to call himself Johnny Rotten in the Sex Pistols, so all these kids from all over went to see Johnny Rotten for the first time in L.A. And Lydon was into something else, into a more experimental, dance-type music, but they wanted something else, they wanted 1977 "God Save the Queen," "Anarchy in the U.K." stuff. By the end of the concert the stage was just knee-deep in spit. It was just ridiculous. That's when I knew this was not for me anymore. It was one of the best gigs I've ever been to, though.

**GROTH:** Did you like the Sex Pistols?

**GILBERT:** Oh, yeah. Like I said, they were all the elements I liked about rock 'n' roll. I don't know why but I always liked noisy music, the noisier the better. I guess it was the old teenage thing that this was my music, my way of communicating, that type of deal. So now I'm an old duffer and I don't really listen to noisy music anymore unless it's in short doses and it's usually stuff I used to listen to. I generally don't listen to that too much any more. Once you play "Louie, Louie" 16 different ways ...

**GROTH:** When you look back on that music today do you consider it good music? Does it hold up or is it something you passed through?

**GILBERT:** It's good for me and I know it's good for young people, but I don't know if it's good in

the scheme of things. I still feel 16 years old when I listen to it.

**GROTH:** I was going to ask you if there was any single performer or group that really turned your head.

**GILBERT:** At first I pretty much listened to what was around, like the Ramones, Talking Heads, Blondie, but they didn't hit me as much as the British bands. The big kahunas of that were probably the Sex Pistols. But the Sex Pistols only had one album and a number of singles, and you can only listen to the album so much. Whereas The Clash were a new band and they were strong and young and aware and they utilized all the different kinds of music that I liked, and they continued to put out album after album. Then like most good things, like Camelot, in a wink, it's over. The bands started falling apart, the music started getting shitty, ego problems, whatever. It seemed to me like it happened really fast because I was older and time goes faster for an adult than it does for a kid. When you're a kid things seem to go on forever. It seemed like the Beatles were around forever, when actually they were only around for six years. So when The Clash broke up after four years I thought, "That was quick." Now punk seems old after 10 years, but every once in a while I'll think of it as something new.

**THOM POWERS:** What was the first punk show you went to?

**GILBERT:** The first real punk show I went to was at the Santa Monica Civic, with the Ramones headlining. The Runaways opened up for them. Then I decided to go to clubs. I saw The Jam at the Starwood and The Eyes and The Dickies opened for them. The Eyes had Charlotte Caffey on bass, who later became the Go-Go's better songwriter, and The Dickies are still a goofball band.

**JAIME:** The drummer in the Eyes was Don Bonebrake, who would later be in X.

**POWERS:** What year would that be?

**GILBERT:** It was 1978 in February or March. And that was so much fun I decided I was going to go to these.

**POWERS:** How often would you go to see bands then?

*Jaime depicts punk-rock life in this "Las Mujeres Perdidas" panel (1984) reprinted in Maggie the Mechanic.*

**GILBERT:** Since we lived about 60 miles away from L.A., I guess it was every other week at first. Then it got to be every weekend. That's when we started checking out bands like X, the Germs, the old Alley Cats, the original Go-Go's, The Plugz, who are now Los Cruzados, the original Bags.

**POWERS:** Would a band like X be playing every weekend?

**GILBERT:** Yeah, you'd see X at the weirdest places, at small dives, colleges. If they were lucky they'd get booked at the Whiskey-a-Go-Go.

**JAIME:** When I first started going, X's shows were always being canceled. They were having trouble all the time. They wouldn't let them play — X was a real dangerous band.

**POWERS:** Earlier you gave a sort of chronology of the times — how it went from being strictly for fun to more rowdy. But when you were first going in early '78 it hadn't gotten rough?

**GILBERT:** Yeah. It was pretty much a fun thing: People dancing around like savages, but no violence. That continued for a long time, up to the big Elks Lodge Massacre, where for no reason cops entered halfway through the gig — it was this marathon gig with the Go-Go's, the original Zeros, X, The Plugz, The Alley Cats —

**JAIME:** A big event.

**GILBERT:** — with all the promising punk bands. And for no reason that anyone could see the cops just came in and started thumping on kids, literally came into the arena and started thumping and throwing kids down stairs. The stairs that the kids were hanging out on were pretty steep.

**POWERS:** You were at this?

**GILBERT:** Yeah. Jaime can tell you about it in more detail because as the cops came in I was leaving with two girls to go out and get drunk in the car. We came back from the car and the place was surrounded by cops and people were throwing stuff.

**JAIME:** They were coming downstairs swinging their clubs and kids were falling down the stairs. This guy Jeff from the Middle Class — his girlfriend started getting thumped on so he tried to help and they thumped on him.

**GILBERT:** But it was totally unprovoked as far we could tell. It was a civil affair: the kids pretty much behaved themselves. They may have taken too many drugs, but there was no element of tension. That began the tension between the punks and the cops. Every once in awhile the cops would pull something like that again.

**POWERS:** When was that?

**JAIME:** That was March '79, St. Patrick's Day.

**GILBERT:** It's in the *Love and Rockets Calendar*. The cops were trying to clean up something that really didn't need cleaning up. Then Jaime and I and my cousin went to a gig in Huntington Beach, which is pretty far south. We went to see The Dickies and The Weirdos, and the audience was mostly made up of drunk surfers ready for action. Everyone wanted to dance, but no one could dance at this place. When The Weirdos came on, people maintained their composure. Then The Dickies came on and played their goofy singles — like they did a cover of "Paranoid," the Black Sabbath song. Their whole point was to do this hyper-speed bubblegum music. And the audience went *berserk*. I had never seen anything like that before. Tables and chairs were flying, it was all out of fun; everybody was laughing. The bouncers were scared shitless. I got a little nervous because you want to protect your eyeballs, but at the same time it was hilarious. As violent as it turned out everybody went home happy and nobody got hurt, except maybe a couple bouncers, but they deserve it anyway.

**POWERS:** Did you like all the bands you were going to see, or did you go sometimes just to be in a place where you could drink and dance?

**GILBERT:** A lot of times we'd go to see a particular band, but there were five others playing. And sometimes we'd luck out and enjoy the bands we had never heard of. We went to hear the music because it was the only thing making us happy in our lives at the time.

**POWERS:** What did you think of the so-called new wave bands that were a little more poppy?

**GILBERT:** Some of them were pretty good actually, but we didn't like them as much as the harder bands. They weren't very important to us. I can't think of any examples now ... Go Blondie.

**JAIME:** Pre-"Heart of Glass."

**POWERS:** The Talking Heads?

**GILBERT:** Yeah. Those were considered more "new wave" bands, and college dorks listened to those.

**JAIME:** A lot of the bands were like the Talking Heads, but I couldn't get into it. They were considered "intelligent" bands, and I didn't want that kind of intelligence in my rock 'n' roll. It was almost snobbish to me. Not all of it.

**POWERS:** What about someone like Elvis Costello?

**GILBERT:** Oh, the first three albums are classics. See I was older, I wasn't as die-hard as the younger punk kids who wanted pure noise.

**JAIME:** He got into Costello at the same time we discovered the Pistols and The Clash. So there was a range.

**GILBERT:** People don't give much credit to the range, they [stereotype] punk. There was different

## LOVE & LISTS

In which the Bros list their top 15 favorite albums of all time (this month anyway!).

## JAIME

1. *Absolute Anthology (1965-1969)* — The Easybeats
2. *The Beatles (1962-1966)* — The Beatles
3. *The Clash (UK)* — The Clash
4. *Damaged* — Black Flag
5. *Fool Around (UK)* — Rachel Sweet
6. *The Great Twenty-Eight* — Chuck Berry
7. *Greatest Hits* — The Four Tops
8. *Hot Rocks (1964-1971)* — The Rolling Stones
9. *Johnny Cash at Folsom Prison and San Quentin* — Johnny Cash
10. *Machine Gun Etiquette* — The Damned
11. *Never Mind The Bollocks, Here's The Sex Pistols* — The Sex Pistols
12. *One Step Beyond* — Madness
13. *Pleased To Meet Me* — The Replacements
14. *The Sun Sessions* — Elvis Presley
15. *When I Was A Cowboy: Songs of Cowboy Life* — Various Artists

## GILBERT

1. *A Hard Day's Night (UK)* —The Beatles
2. *The Sun Sessions* — Elvis Presley
3. *Never Mind The Bollocks, Here's The Sex Pistols* — The Sex Pistols
4. *What's Going On* — Marvin Gaye
5. *The Clash* — The Clash
6. *Pleased To Meet Me* — The Replacements
7. *The Best of Dolly Parton (1975)* — Dolly Parton
8. *Raw Power* — Iggy And The Stooges
9. *Legend (UK version)* — Buddy Holly
10. *Endless Summer* — The Beach Boys
11. *His Greatest Sides, Vol. 1* — Bo Diddley
12. *Rock N Roll Animal* — Lou Reed
13. *The Band* — The Band
14. *Another Green World* — Brian Eno
15. *Greatest Hits* — The Four Tops

*[Ed. Note: These lists ran on the inside front cover of* Love and Rockets *#23 (October, 1987).]*

*Note the Middle Class band T-shirt in this panel from Jaime's "Locas at the Beach" (1985), reprinted in* Maggie the Mechanic.

type bands and they spawned a lot of other bands — If you listen to early Replacements, there's a lot of Black Flag influence there. But Jaime was more …

**JAIME:** Black Flag was one of the bands that were coming from the beach cities south of L.A., Hermosa Beach, Huntington Beach. And at first they were just another one of them, sounded like all of them, or so we thought. But as they went on they left the other bands behind.

**POWERS:** Can you put into words what separated them?

**JAIME:** They wrote better songs. And they were also notorious for riots. There was a time where you could literally find the Black Flag gig by looking for the police helicopter. That would have been 1980. For a while I wasn't really paying attention to them. When Dez [Cadena] started singing for them they really boomed, and they were writing great songs. I think even when bands like the Circle Jerks got big, they could never touch Black Flag. Then when they got Henry Rollins and came out with the album they became legitimate. Pretty soon Greg Ginn was considered the best rock guitarist by certain critics. And as the later stuff came out I liked half of it. Each album had at least one or two excellent songs.

**GILBERT:** A lot of bands start out real crude, then they learn to write songs and they keep their songs limited to four minutes at the longest and two minutes at the shortest. And I think with a lot of rock 'n' roll that works best. What happened to Black Flag was they turned into this garage band that did these endless guitar solos and repetitive nine-minute songs, and that's when a band starts losing it, I think.

**JAIME:** That's when they get the heavy metal fans, though. The thing about the Ramones is they knew they're apes and they play what they play and they are the best at that what they do.

music and sometimes different attitudes, but it was all in the same stew.

**POWERS:** Well, why don't I throw out some band names and you can tell me what your experience was with them: for instance, Black Flag?

**GILBERT:** I never cared that much for Black Flag until they put out a record. … Well, I didn't dislike them. … They came after the original Hollywood punk scene and they were trying to maintain that really aggressive, fast, hard music while the other bands started to experiment. But after a while when they started putting out records I started to like them. They put out that first album *Damaged* years later, and I liked that quite a bit. They were the last of the real evil crash-through-your-house

**POWERS:** Would they play in L.A. very much?

**GILBERT:** Yeah. I've seen them three or four times. A lot of people already consider them a dinosaur band, which is of course ridiculous. But every time they put out a single it's really good. I can't listen to a whole Ramones album, but their singles continue to be really great.

**POWERS:** What about the Go-Go's? It's hard to think of them as a part of that scene, now.

**GILBERT:** Yeah. There was a gig once with the Go-Go's and Black Flag. [*Laughs.*] There was a time when that stuff could go over, but for a short period.

**POWERS:** Did you like their music?

**GILBERT:** Oh, I loved the Go-Go's. When they first came out they were great, they were so innocent.

**JAIME:** They could barely play.

**GILBERT:** But there was real spunk there and they were real happy. That kind of music really knocks me out. I even liked the records. They weren't the world's greatest band, but they had something going.

**POWERS:** So you'd see a band like the Go-Go's before their first record came out.

**GILBERT:** Oh, yeah. We saw the Go-Go's when the band was a month old.

**JAIME:** Of the biggest bands, we saw X and the Go-Go's when they were just starting. We would see X at least once a month.

**POWERS:** What do you think of their whole career?

**GILBERT:** Well, I'm spoiled. I saw them when they were cranking in 1978-'79. The only people paying attention then were the fans, the kids going to see them.

**POWERS:** Do you think something has diminished there?

**GILBERT:** A little bit. I think the first record was a little too tight. The second record, *Wild Gift*, is better. It's actually one of the best rock records.

**POWERS:** Are The Replacements the only good band to come out in the last five years for you?

**GILBERT:** I'll be even more extreme than that. For me The Replacements are the best band since The Clash, and The Clash meant quite a bit to me when they were good. I think they're remarkable. I can't believe a band that young and —

**JAIME:** — that drunk ... [*Laughs.*] I'd say they're the only band that's knocked me out in the past five years.

**POWERS:** Is there anything you can say about what's good about them other than that they're "fast" and "fun"?

**GILBERT:** They're just everything that I loved about rock 'n' roll since I was 5 years old. They write good songs, the lyrics are funny. ... That's just it. The best of rock 'n' roll cannot be articulated. You cannot articulate why Elvis was so much fun in the early days. I just heard from Peter Bagge the other day that Robert Crumb liked the early Elvis — you're snagged on this Robert! But you can't say Elvis was good because of this or that. It's not going to work. You either get it or you don't. You have to hear it; *feel* it.

**JAIME:** A band can write any kind of song, but as long as it brings out the teenager in me, the youth

*Gilbert's "A Fan Letter" (1984) is reprinted in* Amor y Cohetes.

in me, gets the adrenaline going — that's wonderful. And The Replacements are the first band to do that in a long time.

**GILBERT:** And the balance is terrific. They'll do a bunch of fast rockers that will ruin your speakers and then they'll do some slower songs, which sometimes I think are even better than the hard rockers, and then they'll do a bouncy song like "Waitress in the Sky," and that's good too. Paul Westerberg is just remarkable — the whole band is.

**POWERS:** Probably out of both your Top 15 Records lists in *Love and Rockets* #23 the one that might be a shocker for people is Dolly Parton.

**GILBERT:** Yeah, I didn't understand. They thought it was a joke. I was dead serious. If you look at the lists, all the records here represent what I like about pop or rock and they pretty much represent me. And it's all pretty aggressive, it's all "boy" music, even The Beach Boys, and The Beach Boys is a "girl"

*The cover to the Hernandez brothers' self-published* Love and Rockets #1 (1981).

band. Do you understand the concept of "boy" music and "girl" music?

**JAIME:** Like girls didn't like Black Flag … or weren't supposed to.

**GILBERT:** Boys like the Sex Pistols, but girls like Siouxsie and the Banshees. Boys like Deep Purple, but girls like Fleetwood Mac. And I guess the Dolly Parton record to me is the girl part of me, because as much as Dolly Parton has made a complete fool of herself in the last few years, there was a time when she was actually sincere and warm about her music. On the surface the songs are really corny, but at the same time if you listen closely her vocals are very sensitive. She hasn't had a good record for 10 years, of course.

**POWERS:** How about Johnny Cash, Jaime?

**JAIME:** He's my man. I grew up watching his TV show and it was just some country variety TV show, but I kind of liked him. Then I forgot a lot about him. When we started getting into punk, guys like him were brought up a lot because Johnny Cash had some kind of punk thing about him. And I like country as well as rock because it talks about the same things.

**POWERS:** Who are some of the other country musicians you like?

**GILBERT:** Well, the greats like Hank Williams, of course.

**JAIME:** I started going further, like Jimmy Rogers. Not the "Honeycomb" Jimmy Rogers, but the old 1920s Jimmy Rogers, the Singing Brakeman.

**GILBERT:** I'm not too crazy about bogus guys like Dwight Yoakum. [*Laughs.*]

**POWERS:** I understand Bob Dylan is the new man on your list, Jaime?

**JAIME:** Yeah. I always liked his singles when I was growing up, but I never took him seriously until a few years ago. I started buying all his first albums because they were $4.99 at Tower Records. [*Laughs.*] He's one of the guys you can't ignore.

**GILBERT:** The reason we didn't get into people like Bob Dylan until later — we always liked him, but we never bought his records. We heard Dylan from the beginning. It's now that we're buying the records because we can afford decent stereos.

[*Laughs.*] But a lot of it was these goddamn hippies and their goddamn attitudes. You wanted to hate everything they liked.

**POWERS:** What did you think of the film *Sid and Nancy*?

**GILBERT:** It's *OK*. They got the look down fairly superficially, but having known the "history" of the whole thing, he actually blew the story. But it turned out OK, it was enough, and he didn't back off on any of the serious implications of being Sid Vicious. [*Laughs.*]

**POWERS:** Did you see *Repo Man*?

**GILBERT:** Yeah. I didn't think much of it at all. I think Alex Cox blew his wad with *Sid and Nancy*, though I know he did *Repo Man* before. I don't think he's much of a talent. He might come back because he does have a sense of humor, but he's not that good, and Joe Strummer should be in better movies.

**FIORE:** So punk rock had an effect on your worldview?

**GILBERT:** Yeah, I took it a little too seriously. I was real gung-ho with The Clash: it was like, "Yeah, yeah, yeah, we're going to take over the world!" After a while I realized it was just music. It was just the Johnny Rotten snotty attitude. I was never really snotty — well, I guess I was — but I didn't have anything to back it up. These guys were snotty and they sort of had something to say, and I liked that. Wow, you could be snotty and smart!

**FIORE:** Where did you fit in?

**GILBERT:** Just audience, really. We never really had hair — well, Jaime had a mohawk and stuff — but I never went out and hated my mother. I liked my mom. That's the part I never understood about rebel rock 'n' roll, you had to hate your parents.

**FIORE:** That was more of a '60s thing, wasn't it?

**GILBERT:** Yeah, but a lot of kids adopted that. A lot of kids said, "Ah, I hate hippies" but they were exactly like hippies, just different costumes.

**FIORE:** But punk rock affected your outlook on things other than music.

**GILBERT:** Yeah, it's hard to explain. I had a bad attitude about everything.

**MARIO:** Just an opinion about everything.

**JAIME:** Also, it made you realize that you could do what you want.

**GILBERT:** Yeah, it made me cocky enough to believe that I could do a comic book, and it was good and it was all right, as opposed to being intimidated by the Marvel guys. As lousy as they were, at least they could draw buildings. I couldn't draw buildings unless I made it up, and that intimidated me. And so with punk, I took that musical anarchy to comics.

## MARIO HAS AN IDEA

**FIORE:** You did the first issue of *Love and Rockets* in what year?

**GILBERT:** Was it '82 or '83?

**JAIME:** We drew it in '80-'81.

**FIORE:** So, in 1980, what were you doing?

**GILBERT:** [*Laughs*] I wasn't doing anything.

**JAIME:** You were working at the …

**GILBERT:** Was I working in 1980?

**JAIME:** During "BEM" you were.

**GILBERT:** I got a job after stalling for five years.

**FIORE:** What were you doing?

**GILBERT:** As soon as I got out of high school, I did comics for myself, vaguely similar to *Love and Rockets*, but they were just for myself. I used some of the characters from *Love and Rockets*, that would be Inez and Bang, but I got bored with that, because it didn't seem to be going anywhere. I didn't know what to do with it.

**MARIO:** Even people we asked didn't know what to do with it. There was no place to put it.

**GROTH:** At some point did you have an aspiration to draw them professionally?

**GILBERT:** No. As a matter of fact, kids in grade school, junior high, and high school said "You could get a job in comics, you could draw comics, you could work for Disney." But I thought, "What am I going to do there? I don't belong there, there's nothing that I have that they would want." And I've had that attitude all the way up to the first *Love and Rockets*.

I'VE ALREADY SKIPPED TOO MANY DAYS! OOH, I CAN'T STAND THIS SHITTY JOB! I CAN'T STAND ANY OF MY STALE JOBS! I HATE DOING STUFF I CAN'T DO!

MAGGIE! SOMETIMES YOU'RE SO DAMN STUPID IT'S PITIFUL! WHY DON'T YOU GO BACK TO YOUR MECHANIX JOB? THAT'S WHAT YOU'RE BEST AT!

*This is from the first published Maggie story, "Mechan-X" (1981), by Jaime. It's reprinted in* Maggie the Mechanic.

**GROTH:** You never thought of just putting your talent in the service of company characters or whatever?

**GILBERT:** Maybe in the back of my head I sort of dreamed that, "Maybe I can do *Spider-Man* one day, but naaah." I do what I do because that's all I can do.

**GROTH:** After you got out of high school, did you think of using your drawing skills to get a job in comics?

**GILBERT:** No, because I was lazy. That was another thing. I'm a typical cartoonist. I was already doing strips for myself. I was really naïve — I thought I was going to make it by drawing for fanzines, because I had this dumb idea that fanzines were still showcases for new artists. That was during the barbarian fad, and that's all there was in professional comics and fanzines. I drew barbarians and practiced because of course I liked drawing barbarian girls. But that was about it, just sketching.

**FIORE:** Mario, you were married, and I suppose you were working in construction?

**MARIO:** Yeah.

**JAIME:** And me, I wasn't doing anything. I was being a full-on punk rocker.

**GILBERT:** You were going to college.

**JAIME:** I was going to college, and they were paying me, so I didn't have to work. [*Laughs.*]

**FIORE:** You had a scholarship?

**JAIME:** It was some kind of Social Security deal from when my dad died.

**GROTH:** Was drawing comics professionally a goal for you?

**JAIME:** Well, I never had any drive for anything in my life. [*Laughs.*] I thought I would do everything half-assed and live, work. I rarely have ever had jobs. I mostly loafed, and hung out with friends. I never thought of reaching anything that high. Or as high as I've gotten, as far as *Love and Rockets*. When we found that we could do *Love and Rockets* and people were listening, then it wasn't too hard for me to jump in.

**GROTH:** Why do you think you didn't have any career ambitions? Was it the way you grew up?

**JAIME:** I guess. I guess nothing was that important to me.

**FIORE:** Would you say that was a fairly common feeling where you lived, among the people around you?

**JAIME:** With all my friends, yeah. They lived, worked, got drunk or high on the weekends. And that's the way I lived for years.

**FIORE:** When you left school were you considering any kind of career in art?

**JAIME:** I didn't think what I had to show was any good. I didn't think it was professional.

**FIORE:** But by the time that the first *Love and Rockets* came out in '81 it was obviously professional work.

**JAIME:** But I didn't know that.

**GILBERT:** Because it still didn't look like a Marvel comic.

**JAIME:** And because we were doing it our own way, and we thought, well, we're doing it wrong. So maybe this will be good for a fanzine ...

**MARIO:** And that's why the first *Love and Rockets* was like a fanzine ...

**FIORE:** Also, there weren't any undergrounds then that were going to publish new people.

**GILBERT:** And we weren't interested in doing the "Dealer McDope" stuff that underground comics were doing at that time. What undergrounds wanted seemed pretty narrow.

**FIORE:** Did you ever look into that?

**GILBERT:** Well, no, because we're the world's laziest human beings and we knew you'd starve if you were an underground cartoonist. I knew that right away.

**FIORE:** It makes you wonder just how much talent gets pissed away like that.

**GILBERT:** Oh, yeah. We lucked out, it's that simple. We were doing our stuff, but we were sort of not into it that much any more, and Mario says, "I have a friend that works at a college, and she works in the print shop."

**FIORE:** Why don't you let Mario tell the story: How did *Love and Rockets* get started?

**MARIO:** Like I said, we used to do our own stuff, and once in a while Jaime would let me ink some of his early stuff, his early "Mechanics," and then Gilbert would let me ink his Inez and Bang stories, and we did some things we took to conventions that nobody knew what to do with. We had a dry period for a long time, but they seemed to be keeping at it. I kind of lost touch with it, but I was starting to see that Gilbert was getting pretty good, more professional. And Jaime — you were doing "How to Kill A ... " Was that the first thing you did?

**JAIME:** That was one of them.

**MARIO:** I remember you handed me something that had your current style.

**GILBERT:** You were just preparing your little universe.

**JAIME:** Yeah, I had my little universe, but I didn't think it was going to go anywhere, so it was going to be all my own.

**GILBERT:** We'd created all these little universes before [*laughs*], and we didn't think they'd go anywhere.

**MARIO:** But the thing is that Jaime's talent went from sort of fannish-looking art to this chiaroscuro style. I picked it up and I was doing flips in my head. I thought, "This is professional art."

**GILBERT:** Jaime's talent blossomed within a year. It just went BOOM, like that.

**FIORE:** Within a year of what?

**GILBERT:** From his previous style.

**FIORE:** From little fanzine drawings?

**GILBERT:** Yeah, it was his characters like Rand Race and

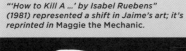

*"'How to Kill A ...' by Isabel Ruebens" (1981) represented a shift in Jaime's art; it's reprinted in* Maggie the Mechanic.

Maggie, but they were drawn in the style we came up with when we were kids, without any influence from anybody else, and his style just changed completely.

**JAIME:** And that was at the time I was taking those drawing courses.

**GILBERT:** This was a surprise to me, too. I didn't know Jaime could draw like that. That's what's really funny. He was already living outside of our mom's house; he was living with our cousin. And one day I went and saw his artwork, and I said, "Oh, I didn't know … "

**JAIME:** And when Mario asked me [to contribute] I had no idea of what I was going to do. I just did it as I went along.

**FIORE:** So it was Jaime's work that made you think it was possible?

**MARIO:** It kind of put it over the top. "If this is this good, he'll hold up the book at least. He'll hold it up for everybody else." So I told Gilbert, "We're definitely going to do this." And Gilbert started working on "BEM," and his stuff was getting really polished, and I thought, "Oh, jeez, this is going beyond." So I badgered this girl to get us into the print shop at the local college, and made up negatives of the first issue. Then we borrowed money from our brother Ismael. [*Laughter.*]

**FIORE:** How did he get money?

**MARIO:** It was from Social Security.

**JAIME:** He was the rich one at the time.

**GILBERT:** He was the baby of the boys, so he took the longest to reach 21, so he accumulated more money.

**MARIO:** So we did that, went out and got a printer to print the pages for us, and he did a lousy job of it. [*Laughter.*] We used to see ads for these little 50-cent comic books that guys self-produced, and it had been years since I'd last seen one, but I assumed it was still going on.

**FIORE:** Like minicomics?

**MARIO:** Yeah, but they were just rip-offs of superhero comics. So I just took it from there, I figured we could always sell it through fanzines. We finally got the book together …

**JAIME:** And we went to a Creation Con and everybody was telling us, "Ah, that's all wrong."

**GILBERT:** "You've got to have a color cover" … everyone was telling us it was all wrong, and we believed them. We didn't have anything to go by. And who picked it up of all people? It was one of the Schanes brothers. [*Laughter.*] We were in a Carl's Jr. [a West Coast fast-food chain], and Mario had a stack of them. Schanes looked at them, and he said, "I like these, I can sell these for you."

**MARIO:** So we sold him a bundle of them at 50 cents apiece. We didn't know what the hell he was doing; we just wanted to get it out. And so we gave him a handful of them, and he handed us some

*Gilbert occasionally uses superhero art as a counterpoint to non-superhero stories, including "Bully" (1995) from "My Love Book," reprinted in* Amor y Cohetes.

*Burne Hogarth anatomy study from* The Arcane of Hogarth.

writes a letter saying, "Wow, this is great, we want to publish our own comics, how would you guys like us to publish you?"

For a minute I said to myself, "No, we can still do it ourselves," then I said, "Am I crazy?" [*Laughs.*]

And from the beginning Gary was supportive. "Do it your way."

Everybody else had told us we had to change.

He was the first person from the beginning who said, "Do it your way, this is the way I like it."

That appealed to us, of course. We could do anything we wanted. Then we slogged out a year of adding 32 more pages to it, because he wanted to put a 64-page book out. Well, actually, it just fell into place. As soon as we got it to Gary it fell into place.

**FIORE:** What do you mean, fell into place?

**GILBERT:** Doing *Love and Rockets* as we do now. It's been the same since the first issue he published.

**FIORE:** Jaime, were you aware that Gilbert and Mario thought of your stuff as what pushed the book over the top?

**JAIME:** No, doing comics I was always the third brother. I just thought, "Good, I'm in a book with my brothers. I'm going to do the best I can."

PART TWO
# JAIME

money, and we thought, "Great, we got some money back." We showed it around this con, and nobody knew what to do with it. They said, "Yeah, you need a color cover, you've gotta be slick." And I hadn't realized this: that it had gone that far.

**JAIME:** That you had to have color covers.

**MARIO:** So I was really kind of bummed.

**FIORE:** You also sent a copy to *The Comics Journal*.

**GILBERT:** That was me. We'd been reading *The Comics Journal*, Jaime had a subscription. I thought, "God, these are the meanest sons-of-bitches in the world. [*Laughter.*] If we can take their abuse, we could take anything." See, that was my punk attitude working. I said, "Fuck these guys, I can send this to those guys, they can't do nothing to me." I got up the courage to send a couple copies straight to Gary [Groth]; I was thinking, "Well, maybe they'll review it," being really naïve about it. Two weeks later, Gary

**GROTH:** I think you once said that your drawing really flowered under the tutelage of a college drawing instructor.

**JAIME:** Yeah, when I got out of high school I didn't want to work, and I was going to get paid if I went to junior college full time. So I took all these art classes to take up all these credits. I would take art history and then I would retake it.

**FIORE:** Would you fail it?

**JAIME:** I wouldn't finish sometimes. I liked learning but I didn't want to take tests or anything like that, so at the very end I would drop out and then I would start up school again.

**FIORE:** So do you have a background in art history? Are you fairly knowledgeable?

**JAIME:** Pretty much. I forget names.

**GROTH:** I remember when you took me to the Louvre and gave me a miniature lecture.

**FIORE:** Do you think that's affected your cartooning?

**JAIME:** I think it's helped. I see beyond comic books.

**FIORE:** I don't suppose you thought it would when you took it.

**JAIME:** I didn't even think about that. Even after I knew all that stuff I didn't think it would affect anything. But I think it has.

**GROTH:** But prior to that your only real artistic font was comics?

**JAIME:** Comic books and girls. That's where I started learning anatomy. And then I took life drawing. And there was this teacher that Mario had taken, or someone that I knew had taken, the semester before. And they said, "Don't get Deitz, he's a bastard," but I needed credits and I like drawing the figures, so why not. And I took Dietz and he was a bastard, old man, glasses, growwlll. He's like a junior Burne Hogarth (is he going to read this?).

**GROTH:** He will now. [*Laughs.*]

**JAIME:** In fact, he used Hogarth a lot. He would make us draw from his books, which I found kind of interesting when I first met Hogarth. I thought, "No wonder, they're the same guy." [*Laughter.*] I took him, and he was a wonderful teacher. He taught me like no one has ever taught me anything. He taught me to draw from the inside out, what the figure is doing, not what it looks like. If a guy is running, he says, "Don't draw the hands like this, draw what he's actually doing." He had clever ways of sinking that into our brains. I still don't know how he did it. He taught me how to draw a figure sitting and then putting the chair under the person: and then the other way — having us draw a chair and then seating a person in it. And I never lost it. The only thing that I do that he taught me not to — he taught us to never start with the head. He said start with the hips or leg or shoulder, but always draw the head

Jaime says he learned "subtlety" from Kirby, who laid out this panel from "The Old Order Changeth" in The Avengers #16 (May 1965), with final pencils and inks by Dick Ayers.

last. That's the only thing I couldn't keep up. I still draw the head first.

**FIORE:** Did you pass any of that along to anybody?

**JAIME:** I wouldn't know how. I couldn't tell anybody exactly how he did it. We would go into class and he would make us look at the model for five or 10 seconds and not look at the paper and scribble the action lines of what the model was doing. And we would do about five of those at the beginning. Then we went into these one-minute drawings where we would watch her [the model] and draw. He would time it.

**GROTH:** How do exercises like that improve your skills?

**JAIME:** It's practice. It gives you confidence to put down a line. He hated chicken scratching, where you go over the same line over and over. By the end of the semester I would look at all my drawings — and we'd go through a lot of tablets because we did all that stuff — and I noticed the very first drawings were these chicken scratches: a million lines for one leg. And by the end of it I had one line.

**GROTH:** Was he big on anatomy? Was he big on the formal elements of drawing?

**JAIME:** Oh, yeah. He would kill me if he knew I

was doing comics. The way he would put it, "I hate that *Star Wars* stuff." [*Laughter.*] I don't even know if he knows that we do this comic.

**FIORE:** You don't have the nerve to show it to him?

**JAIME:** Well, he retired a few years after I had him.

**FIORE:** Is he still alive?

**JAIME:** I think he's still alive.

**GROTH:** Where else did you learn formal elements like composition and deep space and perspective and so forth?

**JAIME:** Parts of that came from other art classes. But a lot of that came from observing good illustrators, mostly good comic-strip illustrators. I was never big on illustrators outside of comics. Comics was always the thing I could relate to. Guys like Alex Toth, looking at him.

**FIORE:** While you were going to college, who was your idea of what was a good comic-book illustrator?

**JAIME:** Someone like Moebius. But then I like the painters, van Gogh and Picasso, who weren't illustrators.

**GROTH:** You obviously like Kirby.

**JAIME:** Of course, as a kid I fell in love with the dynamics of Kirby, the big machines and the power and crashing through a wall and all that. As I got older — this might sound funny, but — Kirby taught me subtlety.

**GROTH:** How so?

**JAIME:** I can even think of a panel. It was in an early *Avengers* comic when Tony Stark picks up Scarlet Witch and Quicksilver at the airport, I guess when they first join, and they're dressed as normal people.

**GROTH:** I know that, *Avengers* #16.

**JAIME:** [*Laughter.*] They're wearing overcoats and I fell in love with that kind of naturalism because I discovered that panel at the time

when everything was [John] Buscema and no one could stand still. It was Kirby who actually taught me. When someone could be standing there and lighting a cigarette it was so calm. I thought, "I like when people are standing there now," because I was so tired of the action poses.

**GROTH:** It's funny you should mention that because Kirby is so well known for dynamism and vitality, people forget he's actually quite subtle. I remember a *Fantastic Four* he did with the Thing called "This Man, This Monster" — but half of them are called "This Man, This Monster" — somebody takes over the Thing's place.

**JAIME:** The first "This Man, This Monster."

Jaime: "Hank Ketcham was the most subtle of all ... I could say that he's my favorite cartoonist": Ketcham's July 25, 1956 Dennis the Menace.

"BRING YOUR CAMERA, DAD! HERE'S SOME *REAL* CHARACTERS!"

Throw, Dukey! And remember, over the lizard's a homer!

Little girl, you're not gonna even see this one zip by!

**GROTH:** There was actually a lot of pathos in his depiction of the Thing, which is pretty amazing.

**JAIME:** And no one saw that in Kirby, and they still don't. I think it's funny that he's the one of all artists that taught me that naturalism. Then there are other guys I learned from.

**GROTH:** Hank Ketcham.

**JAIME:** Hank Ketcham. When I went back and started looking at old artists, I discovered that Hank Ketcham was the most subtle of all. He knew how to make someone droop; sit down; show body weight; everything. He's amazing. I could say that he's my favorite cartoonist of all.

## MORE LOVE, LESS ROCKETS

**FIORE:** Was there a particular point where "Locas" became more interesting to you than "Mechanics"?

**JAIME:** The first issue. [*Laughter.*]

**FIORE:** Oh, really?

**JAIME:** The 40-page "Mechanics" story that was so successful was all the "Mechanics" ideas I had at that point. I wanted them all to be in one story, and by the time I was done I was burned out on "Mechanics."

**GILBERT:** The reason we did the science-fiction things first, and I think this goes for Jaime, too, was because it's so easy. You can please the audience so easily with that stuff. Like, there's a monster in this scene, and we'd do it our way. Most people would have a monster tearing people apart; we'll have a

monster asking for change or something. It's so simple for us to do. All I have to do is draw a monster. If you draw a bum doing that it won't have the same impact with comic readers.

**GROTH:** I know a lot of what you like in that first "Mechanics" story was the fantasy element that you later eschewed.

**JAIME:** Well, actually, no, what I liked was more how Maggie reacted toward it. Sometimes Maggie worried that they were going to be wiped off the island and be killed and sometimes she just wanted to drink beer. It wasn't so much the fantasy stuff that I was having fun with, it was more how people were reacting — playing baseball and over the dinosaur was a home run, stuff like that. And that's what people didn't understand.

**GROTH:** I think there was a point where you made a deliberate decision to put "Mechanics" in the background. And I think that was because you wanted to tell more realistic stories and you were dissatisfied with "Mechanics," is that it?

**JAIME:** No, it was getting in the way. It wasn't important. The more I tried to tell more believable stories, you still wouldn't believe it if there was a dinosaur or a rocket ship in the background. I still love drawing the stuff, but it doesn't fit.

**GROTH:** You obviously made a decision to tell more realistic stories. The earlier stories have a buoyancy to them, an exhilaration, certain fantasy elements and so forth. And lately you've done more realistic stories. Now why did you make that decision?

**JAIME:** I wanted the reader to relate to the story as close as possible. So if someone had a gun and was going to shoot someone, you wanted to get out of there. Or you wanted them to get out of there. Instead of reading it, "Oh, this guy's shooting this guy!" like in every other comic. I tried to make you care, like you feel what they feel. I wanted it to get as close as that.

**GROTH:** What struck me rereading your work, in the first 12 issues or so, there was this sense of exuberance and a genuine sense of joy with life. You can see it in the line-work. It's not this Spielbergian sentimental bullshit. It's a genuine, joyous reaction to life.

**JAIME:** In the early issues I was pretty lucky because I was doing it without any thought, plan, or goal. I was doing it and it came out and people liked it. The punk mentality helped because I was sneering as I was doing it. It's like those old panels of Crumb saying, "I'll show them."

**GROTH:** I don't want to put words in your mouth, but would it be right to say that the punk phenomenon changed your own life so much that life itself became more interesting than the comic books you were reading?

**JAIME:** Oh, sure. I didn't know it at the time until someone told me. "I like your comics because your comics are realistic." "Oh, well ... I do them because I do them." Also, when I started the comics I was drawing friends. That became my inspiration instead of superheroes. Real people started inspiring me. So that helped.

**FIORE:** Are there characters that you can connect with individuals you knew?

**JAIME:** More like people I would see far away. Or a mixture of people I actually knew. But characters were never based on one person.

**FIORE:** So, say, in a story like "The Death of Speedy Ortiz," which characters in that would be the sort of people you would know, and which would be the sort you'd look at from a distance?

**JAIME:** Well, definitely Speedy's friends, the guys kicking back against the wall with the beers were my friends who I grew up with, and who I still see occasionally. The punks are punks I've known. But what I meant by "seeing people," is that, for example, I saw girls that looked like Hopey, but I never knew them, I never talked to them. I saw them from afar and heard what they were talking about from afar. I didn't know what was in their brains so I made it up. They were usually bitches. [*Laughs.*] Little brats.

**FIORE:** What made you pick this particular subject, the lives of these girls?

**JAIME:** Going to L.A. punk shows and seeing these little punk girls who I just fell in love with.

**FIORE:** What struck you about them?

*Speedy's friends are based on Jaime's. From "Vida Loca: The Death of Speedy Ortiz" (1984), reprinted in* The Girl from H.O.P.P.E.R.S.

WELL, MAG, YOU'RE OFF TO A GREAT START! WHAT ARE YOU GONNA DO NEXT? BLOW THIS WHOLE OPERATION? DAMN! THESE TAKYO WIRES SURE ARE OLD! IT'S GONNA TAKE ME HOURS JUST TO FIX THIS ONE!

*Girls with tool-belts was Jaime's high school fantasy. From "Mechan-X" (1982), reprinted in* Maggie the Mechanic.

**JAIME:** They were so full of life. They weren't like any I knew. They were cocky, they didn't give a shit about anything; they were nice.

**GILBERT:** Then again, being in Southern California, they happened to be really beautiful too, a lot of them.

**JAIME:** That helped.

**GROTH:** Now, this is the question that everyone is going to want answered, and that is, did you date girls like Maggie?

**JAIME:** I didn't date any girls for a long time. I was a dork. [*Laughs.*] I didn't date all the way through high school, even after high school for a long time. I was always too shy. That's how I started doing women in the comics. When I started discovering girls, in junior high, I started worshipping girls, holding them on this pedestal. But I couldn't touch them. I was too scared of them. And then, I started hiding my shyness to talk to them, because I wanted to be near them, they were these "visions of loveliness." Then I thought, well, I can be friends with them and I can be near them at the same time. And I guess that's how that started, how I learned to actually have friends that were girls, sometimes better than my guy friends.

**GROTH:** At some time you must have taken them off the pedestal.

**JAIME:** Oh, yeah. But at the same time I didn't tear them down. It was more like, wow, they're right here. And that's how I learned to like girls so much, actually like them as people, instead of beautiful things.

**GROTH:** It's interesting, when you said you put them on a pedestal at one time, and then of course you got to know them more as friends, but running through your work in *Love and Rockets* there's a respect for women. There's also a romanticization of them. Do you think that's accurate?

**JAIME:** Maybe it's from still liking to draw them. But I started off with the respect for them, so women were all I did. Now I try to lean it both ways, because at first I had guys who were really nothings.

**FIORE:** How did you get to putting these girls, or Maggie at least, into this "Mechanics" storyline?

**JAIME:** That was an idea I had since high school. I

thought, I'm going to draw a woman wearing a tool belt. I thought that would be really sexy — drawing a woman in a man's uniform. And I drew her on a telephone pole. Then I thought it would be good to do it in space, because at the time that's what I was interested in. At first Maggie was a middle-aged woman, but by the time the comic came out, she was 17 or 18 years old. When Mario asked me to do a comic I asked myself, what do I have to show? And so I took all these old ideas and threw them all together.

**GROTH:** The stories that were in the first *Love and Rockets* weren't the first time that you played with Maggie and the characters you'd created.

**JAIME:** No, but that was the first time that I put them in actual stories. In fact, those were the first complete, real stories that I had ever done using these main characters. I had done short stories a long time ago, but I never continued them. For years, I was doing drawings of Maggie and Hopey, and I didn't know what I was going to do with them. I wanted to put them in stories. I guess a lot of it was laziness.

**FIORE:** Were you developing the characters in your head, too, while you were doing that?

**JAIME:** They were developing as characters. When I was in high school, Maggie was a 30-year-old woman. I was going to do stories about this woman, science-fiction stories, whatever.

**FIORE:** How close would you say that this 30-year-old you're imagining would be to Rena now in the stories?

**JAIME:** I would say that Maggie was at first like Izzy. Well, Izzy, in "'How To Kill A ...' By Isabel Ruebens." A woman who views all of these weird things happening. That's what Maggie was at first. I got the name "Maggie" because I liked the name from *Dark Shadows*, the soap opera. [*Groth and Fiore: laughter.*] The girl that was named Maggie. I always liked that name, and I thought, "I want to make up a character named Maggie." It started with the name.

Hopey came about when I started going to punk gigs, and seeing all these cute little girls with short, black hair and mousy voices, really feisty and running around. First Hopey was going to be this cute, nice, perfect little character that you'd love. She was going to be adorable. But right away I thought, no, it would be perfect if she was a bitch. That would be more interesting. Or more realistic. One thing that came from our so-called "punk upbringing" was that we always turned the tables. I had this smart-aleckness, where I decided, "No, I'm going to make her a bitch and make everyone mad." And that's how a lot of the comic book is still done. We'll think, "If we do it this way, we'll really get them mad, but they'll be back for more."

*Jaime: "Hopey's the kind of character whose thoughts you're not supposed to figure out." "Ninety-Three Miles from the Sun" (1988) reprinted in* The Girl from H.O.P.P.E.R.S.

**FIORE:** Do you think that Hopey is an unlikable character in some ways?

**JAIME:** It depends on who's looking at her. I'm giving you this loud-mouthed, bitchy character. In a lot of ways, I admired that type when I saw them, and I hope people are looking at Hopey that way. Well, I know people are looking at Hopey that way. They admire her. She's probably the most popular character in the whole comic.

**GROTH:** Maggie?

**JAIME:** No, Hopey.

**GROTH:** You think Hopey's more popular?

**JAIME:** Oh, I get more response. Unless the Maggie fans just don't speak up.

**GROTH:** Well, is this since she gained weight?

**JAIME:** No, ever since the beginning.

**GROTH:** But Hopey can also be very sweet, when she's engagingly anti-authoritarian. She doesn't feel it.

**JAIME:** I just give you the facts. Because Hopey's the kind of character whose thoughts you're not supposed to figure out. So everything I give you of Hopey that's what —

**GROTH:** Well, how thoughtful is Hopey? Does she do much thinking?

**JAIME:** No, she reacts.

**GROTH:** Spontaneous.

*Jaime's "A Date with Hopey" (1986-1987) is based on a true story: reprinted in* Maggie the Mechanic.

"THE NEXT MORNING WAS LIKE I WOKE UP FROM A WEIRD DREAM. ALL OF A SUDDEN THERE I WAS IN MY BED. NO MORE HOPEY, NO MORE MAGGIE, NO MORE HANGING OUT. IT WAS BACK TO HOW IT WAS BEFORE I EVER MET THEM. STRANGE."

"IT TOOK ME DAYS TO FIGURE OUT WHAT HAPPENED TO OUR FRIENDSHIP. I GUESS THERE'S JUST SOME PEOPLE WHO YOU SHOULD NOT GET TOO CLOSE TO IF YOU WANNA KEEP 'EM, HUH? BUT, I WAS IN LOVE, MAN!"

"THREE WEEKS AFTER THAT FATEFUL NIGHT, HOPEY CALLS ME. WE TALKED AND TALKED LIKE NOTHING HAPPENED. IT WASN'T THE SAME. SHE NEVER CALLED AGAIN AFTER THAT."

"I SAW HER ABOUT SIX MONTHS AFTER THAT WHILE LEAVING AN APE SEX GIG. SHE WAS YELLING AT THE GUY WHO RUNS THE DOOR. SHE DIDN'T SEE ME, AND I COULDN'T BUILD UP THE COURAGE TO WALK UP AND TALK TO HER. THAT WAS MY LAST PUNK GIG."

**JAIME:** Yeah, she's just spontaneous. What you see with Hopey is what you get. Whereas Maggie is a different thing: You have thought balloons with Maggie all the time. I tried at a point to make Hopey that way, to go into her mind, but it failed. You're not supposed to know what's happening in Hopey's head.

**FIORE:** At times "Locas" seems like *Peanuts* grown up, in that there are very few adults in it except for the police and people like —

**JAIME:** Adults. [*Laughter.*]

**FIORE:** No, I mean except for larger-than-life, mythic characters like Rena Titañon, Penny Century and Rand Race.

**MARIO:** When you're that age, people *are* mythic.

**FIORE:** What I'm more interested in is the focus on younger characters.

**GILBERT:** Babes, that's it, Bob. Babes. [*Laughter.*]

**JAIME:** That's part of it. One reason is that you're seeing the story through Maggie's eyes. It's kind of like a normal person seeing their heroes. They see them as larger than life. Rand Race is larger than life to her. Penny Century comes from that world. You know there's another side to her that's not so glamorous. And Rena is just a legend. I just like doing it that way. Also, I want to come up with stories — I've barely touched on it before — where guys that are in love with Maggie see her the same way, that she and Hopey are these legendary punk girls and they just wish they could know them. She's this perfect thing to them. I want to show them in a different light.

**FIORE:** Is "A Date With Hopey," the story from *Love and Rockets* Book Three, an attempt at that sort of thing?

**JAIME:** Actually, it was a story that really happened.

**FIORE:** To you?

**JAIME:** Uh, yeah. [*Laughter.*] And I wanted to show someone else's view of them.

**FIORE:** I also remember a story where these kids are hanging around their parents' house when the parents aren't present, and it's almost like a world where adults have disappeared. Is that just the way it is?

**JAIME:** With these kids, I imagine. That's where I am right now with the book. Maybe later I'll show more of the adult point of view. I do want to show that Hopey's mother isn't just a bitch, that there's her side of the story, because all you hear are horror stories. Maggie says her mom's crazy. ... I don't want to make this like some John Hughes film where the teenagers know everything and the grown-ups are evil.

**FIORE:** So Maggie does have parents. I'd gotten the idea that Maggie had more or less grown up on her own.

**JAIME:** She was raised apart from the rest of her family. I got that idea from my mom's oldest sister. She might as well be a cousin, because she was raised by her grandmother rather than her mother, and she's so apart it's like she's from another part of the family.

**FIORE:** There seems to be an economic difference between Maggie and Hopey. Maggie apparently comes from a somewhat poorer background, Hopey comes from a more middle-class background, and Hopey is more of a free spirit.

**JAIME:** Yeah, it's like Maggie grew up more traditional. Traditional ways, old ways of the Mexican culture, and Hopey never had a family, really. She's reckless. There's nothing to keep her down, like family or love.

**GILBERT:** Luba and Hopey are alike, I just realized while you were talking, because they're both spoiled.

**GROTH:** One of the things I was really struck with, reading over all the published work from the beginning is how astonishingly organic it is. There was a reference, for example, to Speedy, in the very first "Mechanics" story, yet Speedy didn't really appear for any significant extent until quite a while after that. So I'm wondering, when you started the work, to what extent did you have this mapped out? To what extent did you know your characters and know how they were going to interact and so forth?

**JAIME:** Well, Speedy had been made up long before the comic. His name was Steve, though. I changed it to Speedy because I also wanted this Mexican guy, this homeboy, like guys I knew when I was growing up. I was making up people like that, because I knew I'd bring them in later. Then you'd say, "Oh, that's the guy they're talking about!" And it almost makes it like you've known that guy for a while, and you're comfortable with it. I did a lot of that because I didn't have enough room to put all those people in, so I only introduced them by word of mouth, and then later showed them.

**GROTH:** Was all this in your head? Do you have a genealogy chart at home?

**JAIME:** Sure [*to the first question*]. It's like I know my characters so well, and I know what they like, and I know what they don't like. That can become a problem.

**GROTH:** In what way?

**JAIME:** Well, like in the mid-teen issues, the story there became only characters, no stories. After "The Lost Women," when I went into the "Locas" stuff, I was so into the characters that they were writing the stories, so there was no room for a plot, and I didn't realize it until 10 issues later or so. Now I'm aware of that, now I can balance. I know my mistake.

**GROTH:** Do you consider those stories a mistake? For example, one story was a couple of guys looking for their records, which was a great story.

**JAIME:** Well, actually, that was the one where I thought I was actually starting to get things going again. But before that, issues #13-16 were really slow issues. It was "Locas" living life. I'm not sorry for those stories, but if I would have kept that up, I wouldn't have gotten very far.

**GROTH:** You can't do that forever.

**JAIME:** I don't think it really hurt. I can just say it was a slow period in their life.

**GROTH:** One thing I'm really interested in is to what extent early on did you know the trajectory of all the characters? And to what extent was it a sense of discovery for yourself as you continued to draw and write?

**JAIME:** It was all a mixture. I was discovering things as I was going along. Characters like Race, I couldn't figure out what their home life was like. That's why he failed.

**GROTH:** As a character.

**JAIME:** Yeah, as a character. So it's better to keep

him in the background as the mythical movie star, or something. I can figure out everything about Maggie. But with Race, I couldn't figure out what kind of life he lived outside his mechanics job. So you leave that alone, drop him out of the center.

**FIORE:** Do you think that's possible at all for that kind of character?

**JAIME:** Well, I was going by instinct when I was doing it. Let's put it this way, I'm not going to push a character like Race because he doesn't seem interesting with no background. I have no sense of him being my old buddy. You know, Maggie is my old buddy because I know everything about her. I know how she was as a baby. I know what she was like growing up. Hopey doesn't go below age 15 or 13. She doesn't go past what she is now, because I could never imagine what a girl like that does when she grows up.

**FIORE:** And Maggie?

**JAIME:** Maggie I can picture for the rest of her life, 'til she's dead.

**FIORE:** Aside from Race, what other major characters have been phased out?

**JAIME:** Penny should be going out real soon. There's not much left of her story. That's also the way it works sometimes. Their story is up. Like Maggie's Aunt Vicki, this was her last story. The next time you see her will be in the background where she began, maybe in a couple panels, if ever.

**FIORE:** Are you through with wrestling too?

**JAIME:** No. I love that. That's why Vicki might come back, but it won't be centered around her and Maggie anymore. Their story had been brewing since "Lost Women," when Vicki was told that Rena and Maggie were dead and she actually had to think about them.

**FIORE:** Is Rena played out too?

**JAIME:** That's a toss of the coin. She could either come back and still be active or the next time you see her she could put on 200 pounds and sit there the rest of her life. I haven't figured that out yet. I want to do a story about her origin, when she was born, how she grew up, all the way up to her winning the championship.

**GROTH:** Rena actually seems like one of the characters most filled with possibilities because of course I think you've gone into at least three phases of her life. Now she's about 48?

**JAIME:** Yeah. An old character is really great to work with because you can go backwards. With a young character you can't go very far back.

**GROTH:** Have you ever thought about jumping ahead 20 years?

**JAIME:** I've thought of it, but I'd jump back again.

**FIORE:** That's turning into science fiction. You'd have to work out the social changes of the future.

**JAIME:** And if I jump ahead the decisions I make have to be really carefully planned out because I wouldn't want to have to go back and say, "Oh well, she can't do this."

**FIORE:** How far back would you be interested in going? Would you be interested in writing stories about times before you were born?

**JAIME:** Oh, sure. Like Rena's time. I want to go back to when she's 15 when she first takes up wrestling. That's the '50s or around there.

**GROTH:** Even the time frame is ambiguous. The present is hardly the present.

**JAIME:** It's a lot closer though.

**GROTH:** Well, it's been getting closer because the stories have been getting more realistic.

**JAIME:** Rena still lives in that outer space world. Not so much with rocket ships, robots and aliens, but in the old days I had people dressing weird.

**GROTH:** Now in "Toyo's Request," was she about 34 then?

**JAIME:** That one's kind of screwed up because she's about 34 but she talks about those events as if she was 21. So she's 21 there, or in her early 20s because she talks about trying to win the championship that she won at 21. It still works. She can look like that at that age.

**GROTH:** Well, if she was around 21, that's years ago ...

**JAIME:** So it's an imaginary year before I was born. Anything before me I make up.

**FIORE:** So you're not interested in researching any periods?

**JAIME:** Not for Rena, but for someone else I would — one of the Maggie characters. But as far as Rena, it's anything goes.

**GROTH:** Why is that?

**JAIME:** It's the way it started. Rena was born in a foreign country and I make it an imaginary foreign country. The reason I used to separate Maggie's home life and her work life is because reading "Mechanics" is like going to a foreign country. Everything was weird. Just like you go overseas and you say, "We don't do things that way." That's what "Mechanics" was. They have rocket ships over there and we don't have them over here. That's why you'll never see Hopey

*"House of Raging Women"(1984-1986), by Jaime, is reprinted in* The Girl from H.O.P.P.E.R.S.

in a "Mechanics" story. She wouldn't fit. She's too much in the real world.

**FIORE:** As you were saying, you originally had this large cast of characters. Have you deliberately tried to expand it any since then?

**JAIME:** Umm. It's pretty much evolved as I was going along. It turned out that if I needed a new character I would make up one. Sometimes I have characters that I thought up a long time ago and now it's time to bring them in. Characters like Tex, Hopey's new boyfriend, he came up. I wanted Hopey to be with a total stranger, stranded out there, and he came along.

**FIORE:** In the original stories, as a mechanic, Maggie has a particular trade, something she does outside any relationships she might have. Would you say that's more or less disappeared from the character?

**JAIME:** Yeah. It's like she wasn't happy being what she was, in her trade.

**GROTH:** How much of that was a device to get you away from "Mechanics"?

**JAIME:** I found better things to do with Maggie.

**GROTH:** It does seem odd that she would give up something she was so good at to work at a hamburger shop, which she did at one point.

**JAIME:** Well, Maggie's insecure enough that she would give that all up to forget one bad memory.

She's actually trying to forget the memory of herself at that time. She's more mad at herself than anything. She's embarrassed of the fool she made of herself. That's what she's trying to forget: it's not so much Race. In the "Death of Speedy" when she says, "I don't want to want Rand Race anymore, I don't want to want you [Speedy] anymore." She was actually mad, fed up with herself and he wasn't letting her forget.

**FIORE:** The last time you brought Penny Century back, it seems like she was going nuts with her fantasy life.

**JAIME:** Penny's like the female Race, but she's a lot more fun to do because she's more fun to draw. [*Laughter.*] She always had more than Race because she was flaky; she was crazy. I guess I love screwing with perfect people. Penny's this perfect thing and I love screwing with it.

**GROTH:** This would be a good time to ask you about the fairly common observation which is that your women characters are so fully fleshed out, three-dimensional, and your male characters are so flat.

**JAIME:** I'm working on that. [*Laughter.*] There was a lot I had to tell about the women before I could get the men in there. That's why it took a while before men actually started showing up.

**GROTH:** Do you think you're better at delineating women characters? Because Rand is obviously a cipher.

*From "All This and Penny, Too … " (1987) by Jaime: reprinted in The Girl from H.O.P.P.E.R.S.*

SHIT, I PUT 'EM ON INSIDE OUT AGAIN. RAY, DO YOU REMEMBER ME WHEN I WAS SKINNY?

YEAH. BORING, SHAPELESS, LIFELESS... HEAD UP, PLEASE.

*Ray stands in for Jaime in this panel from "Boxer, Bikini, or Brief" (1988), reprinted in* The Girl from H.O.P.P.E.R.S.

**JAIME:** No. I was having so much fun with them. Like I was saying, in the 'teen issues they were running away. They were carrying me. I wasn't doing them. I was having so much fun. And while I'm still having fun, I want to do the male characters because there's a lot I can't put in the female characters from me.

**FIORE:** There's one or two male characters that are fleshed out, Doyle for instance.

**JAIME:** Doyle and Ray.

**FIORE:** Ray not so much to me. The other one that seemed to have more depth to him is Litos.

**JAIME:** He had been there since the first issue along with Speedy, but I hadn't given him a character until the "Death of Speedy." He's similar to my best friend, this really frustrated guy who wants to bust up. But he doesn't know where or how or who.

**GROTH:** You're going to be doing some stories focusing on male characters?

**JAIME:** Oh, yeah. In fact this issue [#28] I have a couple Ray stories with Doyle. And I'm having fun because I'm doing stuff that the girls couldn't do.

**GROTH:** Is there any sense in which you like drawing the girls more?

**JAIME:** [*Laughter.*] I love drawing them. Of all of them I love drawing Maggie. As soon as I made her fat it was perfect. I was 100 percent happier. She was meant to be fat.

**FIORE:** Do you think there was something missing in her character before?

**JAIME:** No, I didn't think that until I started making her fat. Then I thought, this is it, so much better, so much more realistic. She just took on a bigger personality than she ever had. I just didn't know it at first.

**GROTH:** Now you've dragged Maggie through shit for 10 issues or so ...

**JAIME:** That's why I gave you a happy ending at the end of #27. Originally, the story was leading to her leaving Ray to look for Hopey and I thought, "No, no." I made myself have her go back to Ray and at least relax for an issue or two.

**FIORE:** When Hopey comes back, is something going to be changed between Maggie and Hopey?

**JAIME:** Well, it's not going to be the same. It's almost like real life because I'm going to try to make it the same, but it still won't be, even to me as I'm doing it.

**FIORE:** Has Hopey changed any because of this trip across the country that she's made?

**JAIME:** She's mellowed out some. I mean, I haven't actually done it, but I have in my mind.

**FIORE:** Mellowed towards what?

**JAIME:** Mellowed towards just giving up. It's kind of like, they're has-been punks now, Maggie and Hopey, but they don't know it. They think they're pretty hip, but they've been out of it for a couple of years.

**FIORE:** So are you going to start playing up the people who aren't punks?

**JAIME:** Yeah. The punk thing is going to be more in the background, because I want to concentrate more on my Mexican upbringing for the next several issues.

**FIORE:** I was never particularly close to it myself, but I'd gotten the impression when I was living in Hollywood that there were ugly aspects to the lives of punks that I don't see in the "Locas" stories, and I was wondering whether that was just a difference between Hollywood and Oxnard or ...

**JAIME:** Yeah, basically. There's a lot of stuff that I don't know about Hollywood punks who live in abandoned hotels. That's how they lived all the time. Well, I went home every night. Or, if I stayed overnight somewhere, I was home the next day. It's just something I don't know that much about, so I don't get too deep into it. In the story where Hopey's living on the streets, she's having a miserable time, because where she once had all these people to support her, if not her parents, her friends. She thinks she's pretty hot, but now she's seeing what it's really like.

**FIORE:** When you were involved in punk rock, how far did you go along with the idea of "No Future," nihilism, I guess you'd call it.

**JAIME:** It was all fun to me. I went and got drunk and we listened to bands and danced and met all these crazy people. It was all fun to me. There was a future because I was actually doing something.

**FIORE:** I understand that in England punk was a reaction to this life kids were living, where there were no jobs for them and there never were going to be any jobs for them except the most menial kind, and all they had to look forward to is a life on the dole ...

**JAIME:** Here in L.A. a lot of it was just bored rich kids. It was more out of boredom than out of poverty. They just wanted something to do.

**GILBERT:** Because poor kids listen to disco. Always have.

**JAIME:** Now, it's rapping.

**FIORE:** In a way, I get the impression that *Love and Rockets* is about what you do after you've been a punk; Gilbert is reaching back to his roots and Jaime is exploring this community-in-spite-of-itself that grew out of punk.

**JAIME:** I'm just doing what I'm doing.

**GILBERT:** He's doing what's happened after punk, because a lot of people just went straight back to the mainstream, and obviously Maggie and Hopey haven't, and so they're sort of lost.

**JAIME:** Yeah, they're not hip right now. As much as they may think they are, they're not.

**FIORE:** Is there going to be some sort of collision between what they're doing and the realities?

**JAIME:** I don't know. I'm still thinking about that. Because I want to show other peoples' views towards them, the so-called hip people that look at them and say, "Oh, punkers, that's so old." I'm still working on it. That's why my work is moving slower than Gilbert's. I really don't know what punks do after punk. I'm just learning. I know what I'm doing, I'm drawing comics, but not everyone can draw comics. I'll be damned if I know what happens to Hopey types, because I've seen people like her, and I've never seen any of them after that.

**FIORE:** Earlier you were talking about wanting to "release yourself, go bonkers, but be successful at it." Have you ever done anything you think is like that?

**JAIME:** Not since the second issue, where I actually went out and didn't care 'til the very ending when I had to wrap it up.

**GROTH:** You're referring to the 40-page "Mechanics" story.

**JAIME:** "100 Rooms" had a lot of that, but it didn't have as much as the second issue where I didn't care. I was drawing it panel by panel.

**GROTH:** Do you attribute that to youthful vigor?

**JAIME:** Partly that and partly that I still didn't know what I was doing.

**GROTH:** Do you think you'd ever go back to that frame of mind?

**JAIME:** I'm getting in that frame of mind, loosening up. When I do "Izzy in Mexico" it's going to be a lot looser, wackier and more screwball.

**FIORE:** Gilbert's been saying the same thing.

**JAIME:** Gilbert I think is loosening up a lot. We got caught up in something that wasn't bad, but we like to balance it. It was almost like it got so serious that it wasn't fun. We had fun doing it, but there wasn't much fun going on. I had fun with the "Polar Bears" story with Maggie and Vicki. I'm trying to let myself go and not keep it so serious and tight. "Izzy in Mexico" is going to be closer to "How to Kill A ... ". That had weird elements in it. But weird within the context of Mexico, with superstitions, religion, Mexican ghosts, all that. I plan to get wacky in that way.

**GROTH:** In the first 10 or 15 issues of *Love and Rockets* with Maggie and Hopey and the characters there's a sense of frivolity — there are very few consequences to their actions and behavior so they can kind of roll through life. And that strikes me as being a kind of youthful perspective. Now you've gotten in the last half-dozen or so issues it's gotten much more grim and there are consequences. You can certainly see that in "The Death of Speedy." Do you think that's you getting older and wanting to face certain consequences?

**JAIME:** It's actually the characters getting older and having to face things like that.

**GROTH:** But is that a deliberate strategy on your part?

**JAIME:** No, it's working out that way. And that's why I want to loosen up again. Even if it's too late for some of the characters, I can do that with the newer ones.

**GROTH:** I want to get back to something that interests me, which is that you so much enjoy drawing the girls. Is there a conflict between the narrative values and your own preferences as to what you draw? In other words, do you have to force yourself to draw the men? Do you have to force yourself to draw stories dealing with the men rather than the girls?

*Jaime cut loose cartooning this slapstick four-panel sequence from "In the Valley of the Polar Bears" (1988) reprinted in* The Girl from H.O.P.P.E.R.S.

**JAIME:** No, I got over that in high school. In high school all I drew was women. I didn't want to draw anything else. I guess that's why I ended up with so many female characters in the beginning because I had so many. I would rarely draw men. Race was the only male I drew for years. The only normal male anyway.

**GROTH:** You don't find that true today though?

**JAIME:** No. But I sure like it when I get to those Maggie panels, or Danita ... or Terry. Terry's a lot of fun too. I guess it's because she's the only one left that's skinny.

**GROTH:** Well, Hopey's still skinny.

**JAIME:** Right. But Hopey doesn't show off her body like Terry does.

**FIORE:** In the first 16 issues or so the sexual relationship between Maggie and Hopey seemed ambivalent, or at least you didn't make it explicit. It always seemed to me they were friends before they were anything else. Then there came a point,

*Jaime often utilizes love triangles as a plot device, as in this sequence from "Locas at the Beach" (1985), reprinted in Maggie the Mechanic.*

I guess, when you decided to make it explicit. Was there a lot of thought going on there?

**JAIME:** I showed it when I found out it was a mystery to people. "Are they or aren't they?" "Are they lovers or aren't they?" "No, they aren't." "Well, maybe they are." "Come on, tell us, tell us." I didn't mean to make it this big mystery. I think something like that should be handled naturally.

**FIORE:** I think in a way that's the difference between being serious and being lightweight. If you're not doing it seriously you could keep up that mystery angle forever and ever.

**JAIME:** I showed it because I wanted to be fair. I wanted to say this is natural to them so it should be natural to the reader as well.

**FIORE:** Before you did it I thought if you made it explicit one way or the other it might be less interesting because it wouldn't have that ambivalence to it. But even when it's explicit it still has an ambivalence to it.

**JAIME:** I try.

**GROTH:** That's sort of a strategy you use through the whole strip. Things unravel slowly, gradually, but they're hinted at. Then you go back 10 issues ago and see where something was touched upon. Do you remember in that review I wrote before we published *Love and Rockets* I think I picked up on the bisexuality. The open sexuality of the characters seemed to be pretty implicit in the first story.

**JAIME:** I didn't come out and tell you, but I always figured that people would know it was there.

**GROTH:** I'm curious about your view towards sexuality. Obviously, the characters are pretty open sexually. How did you come to that perspective? Obviously, you don't have a real conservative view of...

**JAIME:** Maybe in my personal life. I have this open mind now where anything is possible. I figure, well, they're lovers. There's a lot of women who are lovers in this world. So it wasn't so shocking. That's another thing that came from my "punk background" — that anything was possible.

**FIORE:** What I was talking about in terms of ambivalence is that there's a difference between friendship and love, and even as lovers, their relationship has more of the character of friendship.

**GROTH:** What I thought is you combine the two so felicitously — love and friendship — there was really a kind of ambiguous boundary between the two. You mentioned you might be more conservative in your personal life than what your characters ...

**JAIME:** Well, I'm saying my personal life has nothing to do with what I put down as far as sex. I treat whatever turns anyone on — "let 'em." My own way is my own business. It doesn't reflect.

**GROTH:** Do you feel a need to impose your own values on the story content? In other words, do you make moral judgments on your characters?

**JAIME:** Sure. You have a certain responsibility on certain things. Like, if I have someone who's a drug addict, I have to have someone who's not, who's fighting it. I have to be fair about all this. Half my characters have been or are still on drugs. Hopey and Maggie did drugs when they were younger, like fiends. I don't know what drugs they took because I never took drugs. They did and drugs are bad, right? So I'm not trying to show anyone that drugs are great. I try to give both sides.

**FIORE:** Obviously, Izzy has done a lot of peyote.

**JAIME:** Oh, yeah.

**GROTH:** Do you think the sex in *Love and Rockets* is frivolously portrayed?

**JAIME:** Well, sex is everywhere in real life. It's something that people — or people I've known — talk about openly, freely. And that was another thing that I learned to like about girls when I was becoming friends with them and actually talking to them and finding out they're real human beings. A lot of punk girls I met would talk about anything. Sex, anything. And I liked that openness about it. So I never had anything to hide talking about that.

**GROTH:** Do you think your work expresses a permissive view towards sex?

**JAIME:** Sure. I try to portray sex as it is. People talk about it. People do it. People have their own little ways of doing it, their own ways of not doing it. I try to put it down there. And I make up a lot because I know that there are no boundaries. People will go to any lengths. It never surprises me anymore when I hear a new story on the news about some guy or

girl who did something. The way I made Hopey bisexual or lesbian or whichever she is —

**GROTH:** Are you saying?

**FIORE:** You once could win a lot of money betting whether Hopey had ever been in bed with a man in *Love and Rockets*, because most people wouldn't think of that one panel in the first "Mechanics" story. Did you ever think that that might have been a slip or a mistake?

**JAIME:** No, no. That panel was never intended to look like they had sex. That was Zero, the drummer from the band.

**GROTH:** It was ambiguous; you don't know.

**JAIME:** You don't know, but as I was drawing it I was thinking he has smudges on his face, bruises. He got beat up and ran to her house and asked to spend the night because these guys are out to kill him. I wasn't telling you what to think in that panel, that was not the intention.

**GROTH:** Now will a fact like that, that you know but no one else knows — until they read this interview — will that come out eventually?

**JAIME:** It could, it could. It depends on what story I want to tell.

**GROTH:** But you're not obsessed about tying up all these loose ends.

**JAIME:** There's some that can be left alone until I feel like it. That's the way I do it. I leave a lot of it open so I can come back, or leave it as it is.

**GROTH:** I find it incredible that you can keep all this in your head. The strip is amazingly organic. Something that is referred to in one issue can be referred to 10 issues later. It will probably be the

*Was this panel of Hopey in bed with a man in "Mechanics" (1983) a "slip or mistake"? Reprinted in* Maggie the Mechanic.

subject of many Ph.D theses because of all this.

**JAIME:** There are times that I'll go back and look at old issues and find things I've actually forgotten. "I remember this. OK. I'm going to do something about this." And it gives you a feeling that there's a time change. It makes you more comfortable in knowing the characters.

**GROTH:** You said earlier that you can't imagine Hopey being an adult. I suppose one of the challenges you face is when you start articulating your characters as adults.

**FIORE:** How much have they aged since the first issue?

**JAIME:** Only three years. It's screwing me up because when I do flashbacks they're not in the right time frames anymore. I'm beginning to worry because I'm starting to screw up. The new issues are actually happening in 1984, if you want to be technical.

**GROTH:** When your characters face adulthood it

seems to me that's going to be a challenge for you too because that's the time when most of us face a lot of decisions that we didn't have to confront when we were, say, under 21.

**JAIME:** But the way I look at life is that I'm already where I am. I don't see myself changing. I'm going to be like the way I am for a long time. I may change, I don't know. But as far as right now I am where I am. I'm there already.

**GROTH:** Do you intend to chart your characters' lives and deaths?

**JAIME:** I'd like to see it.

**GROTH:** So that's something you look forward to.

**JAIME:** Yeah. But not in the near future. I still want to keep Maggie.

**GROTH:** You reminded me of something I wanted to ask you about, which is what I consider this almost unfathomable way you work. Tell me if this is accurate and please expand upon it. You will bring in pages and you will have the first three pages completely finished, the last two pages half-finished, miscellaneous panels between the beginning and the end sort of half-finished; some panels are penciled, some panels aren't penciled at all. Can you explain how you work this?

**JAIME:** That keeps me interested. It's the way we've always done it.

**GROTH:** Can you actually describe the process?

**JAIME:** Well, it's a lot tighter now. I actually work, not from a tight script of the whole story, but tight scenes. I used to draw only what interested me at the time. It's the way we think of our universe, how we know our characters. When we're doing a story, it's the same thing — "Well, I know I can jump from here to here, because I know there's only a certain amount I can do here in the middle." Sometimes it's the result of being bored with a page. "I don't want to draw this now and if I make myself it's going to take too long and I'm going to waste time, so why don't I jump over here." Then there are times that I want to get to that Maggie panel because she's dressed a certain way and I want to draw it.

**GROTH:** Now, if I remember correctly there'd be some panels in which you literally didn't know what you were going to put in. And this would be in the middle of the story that was half-completed.

**JAIME:** I guess the best example is that 40-page "Mechanics." You should have seen it, in the middle stages. It was a mess. I was afraid that you would hate it, that you would think, "What the hell did he do here?" I thought I fucked up.

**GROTH:** There's two instances that I remember that demonstrate your talent at this organic construction. One was the very first "Mechanics" story

which you self-published; then we published it and you inserted pages without breaking the flow of the story.

**JAIME:** Two pages.

**GROTH:** Then of course there was "100 Rooms" where you added six pages of panels interspersed between panels for the reprinting of the story in *Book Two*.

**JAIME:** It's not that hard for me.

**FIORE:** When you're leaving panels, is it a musical sort of thing, where you know there's supposed to be a beat here and a beat there, but you don't know what each beat is going to be?

**JAIME:** Exactly. I know I need a page to tell a particular part of the story, but I don't know what I'm going to tell. So I leave that blank. And I still do it that way. And Gilbert still does it that way. It's like a beat. I know there's so many beats that I'm going to need for something, but I don't know what.

**GROTH:** So you generally know what's going to

An unfinished Gilbert page from "Poison River" (1988-1994) submitted for proofreading. Reprinted in Beyond Palomar.

happen on a page even if you have a few panels that are left blank.

**JAIME:** And if I don't, I fill it in with bullshit. [*Laughter.*] And that doesn't always hurt. In fact, that makes it a lot more fun.

**FIORE:** Is that what happened when Gilbert does a panel in one of your stories, or you do one in Gilbert's?

**JAIME:** Exactly. He says, put someone in there because this scene is done. And instead of showing a building far away and saying, "The next morning ... " we fill the blank that way.

**GROTH:** One of the things you do really well is small talk. You might even have a story like "Hey, Hopey" that's all small talk. But when you finish reading it you realize it meant something. It sort of accrued in some weird way.

**JAIME:** When I have all this small talk I try to wind it up with something meaningful. Not with a moral or a message, but something like, "what goes around comes around." If they start off talking about something and they go off on a tangent, maybe they'll go back to talking about to the original subject.

**GROTH:** What led you to believe that you could do that?

**JAIME:** When people liked it.

**GROTH:** No, no, no. You had to do it first before they liked it.

**JAIME:** Well, like I said, when we first started the comic I just did it and I didn't know if anyone was going to like it. We didn't know if you'd like the first issue. We thought you'd trash it. I did it and then you said, "I like this."

And I said, "Oh, good, because that's the way I do it." I try to tell a good story, but I didn't know if my storytelling was any good until I got feedback ... and an offer to be published. Gilbert one time said he asked himself in his mind, "Why is Jaime writing like that? Are they going to like it? Are they going to allow him to do it like that?"

That's why he did "BEM" and "Radio Zero" first, because he didn't think people were ready for "Heartbreak Soup." "Heartbreak Soup" had been planned since the first issue, or before. And he didn't think anyone would buy it, or allow it [*laughter*] until I started getting good reviews and he realized, "Oh, they like this stuff." I liked "BEM" and "Radio Zero," but when he did "Heartbreak Soup" I could tell that's what he wanted to do.

**GROTH:** Was there anything that gave you the idea to use the epistolary form in the "Mechanics" story?

**JAIME:** It was a way of having Maggie narrate it, because I have a very limited vocabulary and I couldn't do it in captions. At first I did single-page stories, each covering one day, and I left the date

*Gilbert "kind of came up with" how Hopey writes letters: a sequence from Jaime's "In the Valley of the Polar Bears"(1988), reprinted in* The Girl from H.O.P.P.E.R.S.

blank. Then I took all these pages and put them together. I said, "This will come before this one, wait, I need a page between this and a page between that." All I needed was the setting — Maggie in the jungle fixing the rocket ship. I would realize that there should be a little time between this scene and this scene. That's when I'd add two pages. The first page didn't come for a while. Then I saw I had a story here and I felt the responsibility of having it make sense. When it ended up and I thought, "Oh, God, I hope [Groth] likes it."

**FIORE:** In this last series, with Hopey and the band on the road, did you have trouble imagining the sort of letter Hopey would write?

**JAIME:** Well, Gilbert kind of came up with that. He said, "Why don't you have it where Hopey's letters don't make sense because she can't write."

All her words are jumbled but she understands it so she expects you to understand it. That's how that turned out. I actually threw out a story that used the "Mechanics" device with Hopey's letters this time. And it was talking about how she and the band are doing this, and they're breaking up, and they hate each other, and it went day by day, the same way. It was only a four-page story, but it didn't work out and it was moving too slow. I threw that out and started the story where they're already breaking up and Hopey and Tex are on the street. I wanted to get to that right away, so I threw out the letter part.

**GROTH:** How much stuff do you throw out?

**JAIME:** Sometimes a few pages. Well, a script never turns out the way it started. Or sometimes it goes back to the way it started after eight different changes.

**GROTH:** How much do you revise a single story?

**JAIME:** Most of the stories turn out different. I'd say 99 percent of the stuff turns out different than what I planned. You know how I jump around and draw part of a page then move on — it keeps me from getting bored. I'm as surprised as the reader. The story isn't finished 'til the last inked panel.

**GROTH:** Does Gilbert's work influence or affect yours?

**JAIME:** Oh, yeah.

**GROTH:** In what ways?

**JAIME:** I think he's so much better than me.

**GROTH:** Better how?

**JAIME:** He's more imaginative and a better writer. He always has been.

**GROTH:** Better in the sense that you think he brings greater depth to the characters?

**JAIME:** No, as far as ideas, actually writing stories. I think my stuff is pretty dull compared to his. I'm lucky when I come up with an idea that surprises me. I'm rarely dazzled by my stuff — until after it's done and published, then I think, "Wow, I did that?" That's always fun. But at the time sometimes I think, "Why am I doing this? This is so boring. No one wants to read this; no one wants to see this. Am I standing still?" It's sometimes hard to tell if I'm dying.

**FIORE:** What sort of effect does all this adulation that the book gets have on you?

**JAIME:** It helps.

**FIORE:** It doesn't make you self-conscious in any way?

**JAIME:** I really still have that innocence. I still have an innocence that when people like it or don't like it I keep thinking, "Well, I'm still going to do it, I'm still going to do it and boy, this is going to be great. I'm gonna show them." Every time I'm doing it I have that feeling of "I'm gonna show them," even my peers or guys who I think are better than me — I'm gonna show them because they don't do what I do. It's back to the old punk mentality of "I'm going to do it whether you want it or not."

**GROTH:** I remember when we were getting all the letters — the hate mail about Maggie gaining weight and I remember your reaction. It was virulent. You said she was going to stay fat and if anything it was even a more violent reaction that she was going to stay fat.

**JAIME:** Yeah.

**GROTH:** Maybe the longer you kept getting these letters, the less you were going to pay attention to them.

**JAIME:** They're still coming. The ones who have dropped the comic for those reasons — I don't need those kind of readers anyway.

*Is Hopey out of character? The last panel from "All This and Penny, Too ... " (1987) by Jaime: reprinted in* The Girl from H.O.P.P.E.R.S.

**FIORE:** Do you have readers who think they have a proprietary interest in the characters?

**JAIME:** Once in a while I'll get letters from somebody giving me the bottom line. They're telling me, "You should be doing this, there's no question about it." "Oh, wrong, I found Hopey very out of character."

A lot of women found Hopey out of character when she wore the garters in the last panel, in that Penny story. [*Laughter.*] They found her out of character. And I said, "But she wasn't, because I know."

When someone said that, Gilbert said, "It just goes to show that Hopey has a better sense of humor than some of her readers."

That's the bottom line. She did it as a joke, and she did it. I felt right doing it ... so it was.

**GROTH:** What did you think of Crumb's criticism of your work, [that it's too cute]?

**JAIME:** I don't agree, but I can see where he's coming from.

**FIORE:** I think it might have been based more on the first 10 issues or so.

**JAIME:** Well, I still think he wouldn't like it. I don't know. Crumb is Crumb.

**GROTH:** Did that bother you?

**JAIME:** Well, for a while it did bother me, coming from someone who I admire so much. That's always hard when they do something like that. You melt in your chair. You think, "God, how could he say that, I like his stuff." [*Laughter.*] After a while I felt, well, that's him. He's got a different view of women than I do. [*Laughter.*] I look at it that way. I believe what I believe about women and he believes what he believes. Like when he said that's not how women really are. Well, I happen to know some are.

**GROTH:** Do you make a distinction between what you do and soap opera? Sometimes you're accused of doing soap opera and sometimes you're praised for doing soap opera.

**JAIME:** It depends on what you call soap opera. If soap opera is a never-ending story of life that goes on, then yes, it is a soap opera. But if they're calling it a soap opera because of dopey plots and unbelievable people and stuff like that ...

**GROTH:** I think soap opera implies that it treats emotions like pornography treats sex; it's repetition.

**JAIME:** Yeah. Soap opera's a bad word, that's why I don't accept it when it's used. But if soap opera means a story that goes on like real life, then that's fine.

**GROTH:** What do you hope to be accomplishing in your work — I know that's a terribly broad question.

**JAIME:** I hope it's stuff that will still be fresh 20-50 years from now. I hope it doesn't lose anything in the long run. Even if I'm writing about contemporary things, punks and rock 'n' roll and all that, I hope people can look back at it as a piece of history instead of a gimmick: because we've never tried gimmicks in the comic from the beginning. Now when we're advertising the comic we use Maggie and Hopey because they're the biggest sellers of the comic. But there was never anything "high concept" about this comic, unlike a lot of other ones that died after 10 issues, and people wonder why.

# PART THREE
# GILBERT

**GROTH:** How were you in school?

**GILBERT:** Back in grade school I was the first person in my family to get an F and I was really surprised my mom didn't beat the hell out of me. I think she saw it coming in me. I think she knew that I was going to be this guy who wasn't going to do well in life.

**GROTH:** An F in what subject?

**GILBERT:** I don't remember actually. I think it was English or literature. The teacher didn't like me, a guy named Mr. Bergman ... and if I ever see that guy again I'm going to kick his fucking ass, I swear to God. [*Laughter*].

**GROTH:** He was a real ballbuster?

**GILBERT:** I don't know if you remember in your school, but there were a lot of teachers who didn't like you, who did treat you with a prejudice, that did fuck around with you, even in grading. And I just got the feeling that Bergman was that kind of guy. He's a child psychologist or something like that now.

**GROTH:** But your mother accepted the F?

**GILBERT:** Yeah, she accepted it. She was pissed, but I think she felt, this F makes sense, because I was always a problem. I stopped learning in fourth grade, learning properly that is. I'm surprised that I made it this far, that I can think, because I just gave up on school, got bored with it. I just wanted to draw. What year did the *Batman* TV show come out? '66? I remember since third grade all I wanted to do was draw Batman. Batman meant something to me and long division didn't mean shit. And that's the way it was with me.

**GROTH:** Are you yourself reconciled to life as a failure?

**GILBERT:** Yeah. I never thought I would amount to anything. I just

thought, this is me; I want to draw Frankenstein. There was a period when Mario used to collect the *Rocket's Blast ComicCollector* and I would check out this fan art and have a good time. It was pretty dumb, but I liked it. There was this one guy named Jim Jones who would do these really stylized cartoons. And I thought, these are fabulous. Even as a little kid I liked them. And he did a short article on Dick Briefer's *Frankenstein*. [*Snaps fingers:*] Boom! Fifth grade, that's all I drew: his Frankenstein. I didn't do my homework. The teacher would give us an assignment and I would close my book and start drawing Frankenstein. I resigned myself to a life of stupidity. [*Laughter.*]

**GROTH:** At what point did you realize that you were not going to become a failure and that you were, in fact, headed toward success?

**GILBERT:** Well, I didn't think I was going to be successful, but I had ideas. In high school I had ideas. I wanted to do the ultimate comic strip somehow. I don't know where that came from, but I remember thinking about it and telling my friends, "I'm going to do this ultimate comic strip."

Sort of like what I'm doing with "Heartbreak Soup" now, except that "Heartbreak Soup" has some substance. I think it was going to be a space opera. I wanted to cross *Gone With the Wind* with *Forbidden Planet*. I just always had this feeling that I had that epic in me. I've got a lot of notes on it, but it's really bad stuff. Actually, I thought more in terms of films, but I also thought there's no fucking way, I'm not

*A big inspiration for Gilbert: Dick Briefer's* Frankenstein. *This sequence was reprinted in* Art Out of Time.

©1949 Dick Briefer

going to be a film director. I didn't know how people did that. I didn't know how you got from being a normal guy to directing *Star Wars*. So I thought, well, I could do it in comics. And I always had an interest in comics, even when I wasn't following them too closely. In high school I didn't follow comics too closely because I was interested in [*shouts*] GIRLS! and beer and partying and stuff.

**GROTH:** That would have been in the mid-'70s.

**GILBERT:** Yeah. I don't know why, but I started doing stories about women in a more positive sense. I got into the big *Star Wars* thing — taking the barbarians into outer space — before *Star Wars*. That way I could draw rockets and women in skimpy costumes. But I started leaning towards the women characters and giving them personalities. I preferred to draw the women, so why create a male character when I can have all the good stuff — personality, intelligence, whatever — in the women characters? Then I started creating women characters who weren't barbarian girls. They lived on Earth and the barbarian girls would visit them. I did it because I just felt like drawing girls sitting around some apartment, similar things to what Jaime's doing. You'll see some of that stuff in the sketchbook, the stories about Inez and Bang. They were offshoots of the space-galactic barbarian stuff. Then *Star Wars* hit and that's what everybody did. I eventually started drawing the proper size with ink, I learned to use a nib, I learned to use a thesaurus and a dictionary [*laughs*].

**GROTH:** Was the self-published *Love and Rockets* comic the first time you actually published your work?

**GILBERT:** We had already sent things to fanzines before that, but that was just spot illustrations. I was desperate at the time. I wasn't working or anything and I wondered what I was going to do with my life.

I was in my early 20s and I thought, "I got to do something."

**GROTH:** You were living at home?

**GILBERT:** Yeah, I was living at home, starving, just drawing. I was out of high school and all my friends had moved away. I had to decide what I was going to do. And Mario said, let's put out this comic book. It took about a year to get around to it though because Jaime didn't have any work at the time that he felt was worth printing, so he came up with the Maggie and Hopey stuff. And it was the same with me. "BEM" was the only story I was working on at the time. I had abandoned it six months before because I thought it was a stupid story, but when Mario said let's do it, it was the only thing I had.

**FIORE:** Explain what "BEM" is.

**GILBERT:** "BEM" was the first story I did for *Love and Rockets*. It was a quasi-*Heavy Metal*-type story.

**MARIO:** Yeah, because we were still influenced a lot by *Heavy Metal*.

**GILBERT:** The magazine *Heavy Metal*. I just thought it was really funny ... you see I didn't know the translations were bad. I thought the stories were supposed to be funny. People tell me now that all those Moebius translations were bad. I thought they were

*From "Captain Future" by Manoeuvre and Clerc, in* Heavy Metal *Vol. III #2 (June 1979).*

Luba and two other characters dance in an attempt to capture BEM: from Gilbert's "BEM" (1980-1981), reprinted in Amor y Cohetes.

**GILBERT:** It's really clear in the first few chapters. Then I figured, "Well, I wrote all this bullshit, let me try to wrap it up somehow." I have to admit, we were always good at that. We could just get ourselves into a ridiculous situation, and somehow manage to get ourselves out of it. Not all the time, but that's how we tell stories. We get ourselves into these rotten situations — like, what am I gonna do? — and we get out of it.

**GROTH:** In your 32-page self-published comic there was about half of what eventually came to be the whole "BEM." Did you intend for it to become as long as it was?

**GILBERT:** No.

**GROTH:** Because it seems to me that the second half of "BEM" took off in even wilder directions than the first half, and I was wondering if that was planned that way.

**GILBERT:** I think it was going to be more of a straight adventure deal. Then you said we needed 32 more pages. I didn't want to junk "BEM" because I didn't know what else to do. I felt if I was going to end "BEM" I had to make it worth reading, because so far I didn't think it was.

**GROTH:** You once told me that you didn't do "Heartbreak Soup" first because you didn't think anyone would be receptive to it or interested in it.

**GILBERT:** Right. With the second issue of *Love and Rockets* I basically forced myself to do "Radio Zero" and the "Errata Stigmata" story because I was scared. I did not know what to do. Jaime had already grabbed the Maggie and Hopey thing. I could have done Bang and Inez, which was somewhat similar, but I thought Jaime had grabbed that and he was already doing a real good job at it. I really didn't know what I was doing, so I bluffed it. I postponed things with "Radio Zero."

**FIORE:** How did "BEM" turn into "Heartbreak Soup"?

being funny. I thought it was like *National Lampoon*, it was so far out there for me, that I just thought these were comic books like the *National Lampoon*, with wacky humor that's so far out that nobody's going to get it: because if you read those old *Heavy Metal* editorials you don't know what's going on. I was still pretty young. I sort of got lost along the way of doing my women characters, because I was always telling myself, "They don't want to see this. This isn't interesting. I've never seen this in comics before so it's not going to be anything. These aren't the days of undergrounds anymore where you can just do anything." I guess I was at a really depressed state and I didn't think anything I did was worth it. "BEM" was a grab bag of all that *Heavy Metal*-type of humor. I drew Luba the way I did in the first "BEM" because they always have these big-breasted women in these stories, so I thought I'll make mine with bigger breasts. Villains were always stupid, so I'll make mine stupider. I exaggerated everything. I didn't have any real thread. I didn't have any reason to be doing anything. It was almost like doodling. I wasn't really serious about it, but that was the only story I was working on at the time. That was the only thing I had, and I didn't want to start something new. That's when Mario said, "Let's do the comic," and so I thought I'd put more chapters on it. If you read the first chapter, it's all bullshit. It's just, now I'll change the scene, now I'll change the scene ...

**FIORE:** That's just what I thought! [*Laughter.*]

**GILBERT:** "Heartbreak Soup" was with me since my early teens. That was my movie geek period, when I started watching every movie made before 1950 that was on TV. I'd watch anything from before 1950, because there was a romantic feel to those films, good or bad. I had no taste; I liked them all. Then I progressed to '50s movies, and I got into foreign movies, and when I would watch Sophia Loren movies like *Yesterday, Today, and Tomorrow* or when I saw *Black Orpheus* I always thought, "This would make a great [comic] series." Sort of like *Gasoline Alley*, but use an exotic locale, so I could draw girls in tight skirts with baskets of food on their heads. It was a boyish fantasy.

**GROTH:** At what point did you start seeing foreign films?

**GILBERT:** Well, I'd go to the library a lot and look at film magazines because they had neat pictures. I would always look at the sections on foreign films and they would have a scene from *Bicycle Thief* or *400 Blows* or something. And they always intrigued me because, as I was saying earlier, I would think, I don't understand this but I will someday. I always had that attitude. But foreign films to me were a dream world where they did things differently. And they were always kind of sexy. That was before porn movies became a big deal so the closest thing you could do was see pictures of a foreign movie. There's that one shot of Marcello Mastroianni just burying himself in Sophia Loren's chest from *Marriage Italian Style* or something like that. And I thought, "These people are crazy, but what a life." Then I began actually seeing films by Fellini, Buñuel and DeSica. I didn't necessarily understand them, but I liked that world, particularly Fellini's, because it was just like a zoo with all these sexy women running around. I thought: this is the life! There was something that was charming about the people. And it reminded me of my background, my childhood. I would watch a Sophia Loren movie and I would get that feeling of recognition.

**GROTH:** Where did you see them?

**GILBERT:** On television. I remember I saw *La Dolce Vita* late at night. It was dubbed and I didn't understand a word of it, but it was crazy and sexy.

So I guess it was just out of indulgence at first, just because they were taboo movies.

**FIORE:** You've also said you'd become interested in your roots ...

**GILBERT:** That was falling into place, too. There was always great stories that we'd heard from our uncles and aunts and our grandmother. They told these great stories about when they were living in Mexico or when they were living in Texas, where my mother's folks were from. And we thought, "If we could just tell those stories somehow ... " But we figured that nobody white could understand this. We were naïve. But, then, at the same time, there were movies about white kids with elements like that, and I thought that if [white people] could get that, maybe they could get this. So, all this was in the back of my head, even though I was still churning out fantasy stories, because I figured fantasy was what people read in comics. I put that element of "Heartbreak Soup" in "BEM," when they have a big party for the solar eclipse. The reason I jumped from that to "Heartbreak Soup" was because Jaime's stories were getting really good response, and mine were getting sort of mediocre response. It wasn't because I was jealous; it was because they were right. They were pointing out things in Jaime's stories, and I was saying, "Wait a minute, I can do that."

**FIORE:** What were they pointing out?

**GILBERT:** They were talking about Maggie and Hopey's relationship, and how Maggie seemed like a real person even if she was in a strange background, and I had been doing stuff like that before with Bang and Inez. I thought, "I understand this, I know this is better, and if they're willing to accept it, I'm willing to do it." But he'd already done Maggie and Hopey, and if I'd used Bang and Inez it would have been the same thing. I had to stand on my own, I had to have something on my own that was just as good but was completely different. So all that stuff, all those Sophia Loren movies and all that stuff came back to me. I dared myself to do "Heartbreak Soup."

**FIORE:** So "Heartbreak Soup" is a combination of stories you've heard, movies you've admired, and elements from your own life?

**GILBERT:** Yeah, elements from my own life. Like, when I have the teenage guys talking, that's usually just me and my friends when we were young, talking about girls or whatever. But I understood I had to change it a bit, to make it like a Central American village.

**FIORE:** Did you study Central America at all?

**GILBERT:** No, no, if there's one thing I can't stand, it's research. [*Laughs.*] That's another reason why Palomar is an imaginary town, because I'd hate to do the research.

**FIORE:** The main holdover from "BEM" to "Heartbreak Soup" is the character Luba, who is the center of the stories in many ways.

**GILBERT:** Yes, because I was originally doing "Heartbreak Soup" as a sort of roundabout way of doing a "BEM" sequel.

**FIORE:** So what was Luba at the start?

**GILBERT:** In "BEM" she was just a voodoo woman, an island lady who wanted power, wanted to take over the world. You know, it was just bullshit. [*Laughs.*] She was sort of like Corben's queen bitch in *Den*. I just did it, I didn't think about it at all. I decided to do "Heartbreak Soup" as a sequel to "BEM." At the end of "BEM" you'll remember that Luba starts a revolution. I thought "Heartbreak Soup" would be the story of Luba after she's ousted from the revolutionary party, and she's hiding out in this little town. Then I'd reintroduce "BEM" towards the end of the story. As I was planning this I thought I've got enough here to tell a real story. And I trusted Gary and Kim to support me in this. I didn't really talk to [Groth] about it much until he saw it, but I figured from reading his views in the *Journal* that he would support it, and if not I'll just have to cut it off next issue. I took a chance on getting rid of the science-fiction elements because I knew that would be a problem with a

lot of readers that were reading *Love and Rockets* for a different reason. There actually is one panel in "Heartbreak Soup" that is from the old "BEM," that I didn't take out because it still works, where Ofelia is telling Luba, "I told you not to talk to the locals." And Luba says, "Oh, we'll be OK here." And that's because they were hiding out originally. But I threw out all the "BEM" stuff except that panel.

**GROTH:** Obviously, after you did the first "Heartbreak Soup" you decided to concentrate on that.

**GILBERT:** Yeah, it was at the period when Jaime and I and some friends had been going out to the punk rock scene in L.A. and that opened up our eyes to say, "Fuck everybody else, I'm just going to do my work, my way." I've got nothing to lose.

*The single panel from Gilbert's Palomar series that refers back to the "BEM" incarnation of Luba: from "Heartbreak Soup" (1983), reprinted in* Heartbreak Soup.

I'm not in competition with John Byrne and Chris Claremont; I'm not doing what they're doing. So my attitude was full steam ahead. I'm going to do this "Heartbreak Soup" strip and I'm going to really go for it. I had nothing to lose.

**FIORE:** How did Luba evolve from the character in "BEM" to the character in "Heartbreak Soup?"

**GILBERT:** She almost wrote herself. At the time I was very sensitive to what feminists were saying about how women were portrayed in popular culture, movies and comic books. At the time I was thinking, "How could I draw a character like this and think I'm doing something progressive?" So I had to try real hard to make her a good character. And there are still people who won't read it because Luba's tits are too big.

**GROTH:** Did you pretty much know what was going on when you first started "Heartbreak Soup," or was this as much a journey of discovery for you as the reader?

**GILBERT:** Part of it was discovery. What I needed was a protagonist. You have to see things through a particular character's eyes. But I didn't want the main character to be totally obvious. That's why Heraclio was originally just another one of the gang. I always intended him to be the protagonist but I didn't emphasize him so much as I did characters like Luba, Sheriff Chelo. I actually created a lot of these characters just to push Heraclio to the background a little bit, then I brought him out slowly.

**GROTH:** Did you learn about these characters as you drew them? Did things keep coming out and relationships start imposing themselves on you?

**GILBERT:** Sure. Usually, the next story is being written in my head as I'm doing the present one. I have the lives of a character or two planned out to their deaths.

**FIORE:** Do you have any particular themes you're working towards, or are you just telling stories spontaneously?

**GILBERT:** I'm not sure ...

**MARIO:** I wouldn't think it was that spontaneous, because I can remember that as far back as when he was starting "Heartbreak Soup," he was talking about "Human Diastrophism." I mean, he had all this stuff planned out. I couldn't believe it. He says, "One of these days I'm going to do a story about this murderer who does this ... "

**GILBERT:** I talked about the murder story two years ago.

**GROTH:** I'd like to talk about some of the characters. I think one time you said you were going to do "Heartbreak Soup" for a long, long time, over the years. Do you intend to explore all of the characters in "Heartbreak Soup?"

**GILBERT:** I plan on using most of the characters, but not necessarily going too much into their past, because some characters just work as they are. Particularly Vicente, the guy with the disfigured face. I recognized that he works best the way he is, not knowing too much about him. I'm almost sorry that I put so much emphasis on Luba, because I think she would have worked like Vicente, more of a force of nature. But then at the same time, it's worked out, because Luba has become the center of "Heartbreak Soup." As I have her kids grow up, the stories will be about her kids and their lives.

**GROTH:** Why did you jump the story between the first "Heartbreak Soup" and the second one "Act of Contrition"? It jumped dramatically from one period to another. Was that planned from the beginning or did you just choose to do that after you finished the first one?

**GILBERT:** No. When I finished the first one, I had to get away from it. I wanted it to be its own piece, just in case I got hit by a train or something. I didn't want to spoil it with stories similar to it. So I took the chance and jumped ahead a few years. That way I could utilize the first story as flashbacks.

**GROTH:** There's certainly this sense in "Heartbreak Soup" of time having passed and people having a past.

**GILBERT:** I've planned it for 20 years, and five are up. Now, you think, "Twenty years? Oh my God, that's longer than *Cerebus!*"

**GROTH:** You're talking about 20 of your years?

**GILBERT:** Yeah. When I first told people that a

couple years ago, they said, "That's ridiculous." But not really, because five years is up already.

**GROTH:** It's better than doing 62 different superheroes.

**GILBERT:** Exactly, and they go through so many different writers and artists. I plan to have just a handful of characters left at the end, and all the others will have either died or moved away. I'm not sure which characters those are, but I'm thinking that maybe Luba and Chelo can be the last two little old ladies living in this futuristic city that's Palomar. I'm just toying with ideas. I don't know who's going to be left.

**GROTH:** Did you know what was going to happen to Tonantzín?

**GILBERT:** No, that just sort of happened. I was never that happy with Tonantzín. I liked drawing her, but she didn't seem right to me. There's something missing about her. She was one of the later characters I created. Her sister Diana was a more complete character. But Tonantzín was just there. She was almost generic. I could stick her in any situation. And then the thing about her becoming confused and politically aware, that came as a surprise to me.

**GROTH:** Did you know that Tonantzín was going to kill herself when you started writing "Human Diastrophism"?

**GILBERT:** No, that was the last thing I knew. The other things I knew.

**GROTH:** It just seemed inevitable to you at that point?

**GILBERT:** Yeah, and not because I had to get rid of her. I could have had that story end, and then gone back to business as usual next issue. I had read an article [in the *L.A. Weekly*] about a man who immolated himself, and the people who knew him kept emphasizing that he wasn't crazy.

**GROTH:** Was that here in L.A.?

**GILBERT:** Yeah. And I knew, reading the article, that there are people who are serious and who can't

*Tonantzín self-immolates in "Human Diastrophism" (1987) reprinted in the volume of the same title.*

61

think of any other way of getting their message across. I could just see that some people are serious and we shouldn't dismiss them as crazy, thinking, "They just committed suicide, they just wanted to be on TV."

**GROTH:** But one did get the impression that Tonantzín was a little bent.

**GILBERT:** Yeah, that's just it. At the end of "Human Diastrophism," nobody but Heraclio knows that Tonantzín died. Of course, that's going to have serious repercussions in the future "Heartbreak Soup" stories. She's going to be talked about in the past tense.

**GROTH:** Now, will you ever go back and do stories about Tonantzín now that she's dead?

**GILBERT:** There'll be flashbacks. I have a scene in mind where somebody's walking through the town and he's thinking, "God, I miss those fried babosas. I can remember Tonantzín just whipping around the comer, singing to herself." And then I'll have her whipping around the comer. As the scene switches you'll see the guy 10 years younger. I'll use a flashback that way. Both Jaime and I decided to use flashbacks that way, because we can jump back and forth as long as we keep it clear how old the character is between the changes. We find telling it that way better than having a character or a panel with 600 words in a balloon explaining something that happened 10 years ago. It's a visual medium; it's a way of telling stories. If you'll notice, we're a lot better with flashbacks now.

That's one way I think comics work even better than movies, because in a film you've got to hire an actor who looks like that person 10 years younger. One of the best usages of that in an American movie was in *Godfather Part II*, where Al Pacino is thinking about things that happened in the first movie, and James Caan came out. And I thought that was a sweet touch because there was James Caan, he was alive again — you remember in the *Godfather* he was gunned down — and here he is again, he's happy and he's being a jerk and he's bothering his brothers. And I thought I could do that ...

**GROTH:** Is most of the stuff about village and small town life in "Heartbreak Soup" simply made up?

**GILBERT:** A lot of it is made up, and of course there's stuff from movies, too. It's a mythical town. The characters aren't necessarily Mexican. A little kid from Colombia can read it, and think that it's his town, and so maybe it is.

**GROTH:** What's the purpose of keeping it ambiguous, that it's not Mexico and it's not Colombia, and it's not really anything in particular?

**GILBERT:** Because I'd be restricted by too many rules, too many traditions, too many facts about the country. I still like the fact that it's surreal fantasy. People used to talk about it being really gritty and down to earth and banal, the day-to-day drudgery. I thought the Palomarians were having a good time. I never had anybody trudging to work. Usually, when they're digging a hole or something, they're goofing around, laughing.

**GROTH:** Do you do any research in terms of architecture, or family life?

**GILBERT:** Most of it is from what I remember when I was a kid. My momma and my aunts talking about when they were young, telling a story about where they were, "Well, we were next to the train yard and they had this big square, and there was a little market there." Things like that. I guess I retain images pretty well from films, and where I've been. Actually, Jaime's really good at it. I'm really surprised at how accurate his portrayal of a small neighborhood is. And Jaime doesn't go out and draw like Crumb and a lot of good artists who go out and they draw and get good at it. He just knocks it off and it's surprisingly close.

**GROTH:** Let me give you an example, the slugs, the babosas. Is that just something you made up?

**GILBERT:** That's something I made up, but everything I make up has to feel like it's real, or seem like it's real. Actually, my wife Carol told me a story about how her dad was working in New Guinea on oil rigs, and they hired some of the local guys. One day they all dropped their shovels, and they started yelling in whatever language it is, and one guy ran up a tree, and grabbed this huge slug, and they were all really happy, because it was a prime delicacy. Where stories like that repulse most people, I thought, "That's a great story!"

**GROTH:** Correct me if I'm wrong, but didn't you drop a line in one of the stories where you mention that Soledad is Manuel's ex-lover?

**GILBERT:** Yeah.

**GROTH:** You dropped it and left it ... is that true? Do you intend to explore that at all or is that going to be one of those ambiguous loose ends?

**GILBERT:** Yeah, you're right. I never intended it to be ambiguous. I thought it was self-explanatory that Manuel and Soledad grew up together and experimented like a lot of boys do and that was the extent of it. Manuel didn't realize that Soledad fell in love with him. And since they were friends since birth Manuel just laughed it off and that's why Soledad killed him.

**GROTH:** Because when you say ex-lovers that means to me more than just childhood experimentation.

**GILBERT:** Ex-lovers sounds better than ex-fuckers. Manuel and Soledad were bisexual. But I try to emphasize that Manuel never took any relationship seriously, although his lovers usually did.

**GROTH:** You know, when I reread the work, even though I had read it before and was aware of it all, Manuel's death almost took me by surprise again because he was such a primal force and a likable character, and of course there was something almost unstoppable about his sense of joy, and youth, and vigor. So I was wondering why you saw fit to have him killed so early in the series.

**GILBERT:** To borrow Michael Cimino's line, it was a dramatic device. I wanted the original "Heartbreak Soup" story to be a complete story. I wanted to have life, death, birth, coming of age, sexy girls, the whole kit and caboodle. I wanted it all in this first

story, funny kids, funny teenagers, funny adults and death. I was thinking in classic terms then and I try not to think that way anymore, because it becomes clichéd, but I was thinking in terms of grand stories like *Les Misérables*.

**GROTH:** Now was the death of Manuel any kind of a moral judgment on your part?

**GILBERT:** No. Not consciously.

**GROTH:** In other words, he wasn't being punished for his sexual promiscuity.

**GILBERT:** No, absolutely not. That was the problem that I had when Tonantzín killed herself — she was Miss Hotpants — so there goes two, Manuel and Tonantzín. Hopefully, that's just a coincidence,

*"Something I made up" — a page from Gilbert's "Slug Fest" (1985), reprinted in* Heartbreak Soup.

because there's no conscious effort to have my characters die because they screwed around. That means Luba should be dead any day now.

**GROTH:** I want to ask you about your attitude towards sex, because in both yours and Jaime's stories sex is very openly discussed and acted upon, there's bisexuality in the strips, there's homosexuality and God knows there's a lot of heterosexual activity in the strips. I guess I want to ask you what your own attitude towards that kind of open sexual display is? Do you impose any kind of moral judgment on sexual promiscuity, homosexuality, bisexuality?

**GILBERT:** I don't want to sound old-fashioned, but I think if it's between consenting adults then go ahead and have fun. That's become an old-fashioned attitude now.

**GROTH:** Has it? With the new conservatism that might be considered out of fashion.

**GILBERT:** You're probably right. But since I was a young teen I figured ...

**GROTH:** How did you develop such fairly liberal and progressive attitudes about sex? It would occur to me that your upbringing would have been somewhat conservative since your parents were from Mexico. Or am I wrong?

**GILBERT:** Since I was young I reasoned, "If I can expect to have what I want, then so can everybody else."

**GROTH:** Did those attitudes ever run into conflict with your parents teaching or any religious upbringing or anything like that?

**GILBERT:** I'm not sure.

**GROTH:** I'm just wondering if you expressed these fairly liberal attitudes towards sex to your parents or school authorities or religious authorities and if you ever ran into conflict.

**GILBERT:** I kept this stuff to myself. I never talked to my parents about it. Actually, my dad died when I was pretty young, so it was just my poor mom raising these kids and I never talked to her about things like that. She had enough to worry about.

**GROTH:** I was curious about that because I think I spotted it in Jaime's work immediately, this casual attitude towards bisexuality and then in your work.

**GILBERT:** If I do have all this wild sex, sexy women and horny guys, it's because I myself am a sex-crazed maniac.

**GROTH:** You're a fairly conventional guy, married at the age of 28 after dating Carol for quite a while.

**GILBERT:** Six years.

**GROTH:** There was one interesting attitude that I saw in your strip that I might have interpreted wrongly. In the "Bullnecks and Bracelets" piece it seemed to me that you were suggesting that city life represented a kind of decadence in contra-distinction to the life of Palomar — a theory that might be blown away with "Human Diastrophism," but then I also noted this story where Heraclio goes to college and his college-mates were deriding Palomar and

*City life contrasts unfavorably to Palomar in "Bullnecks and Bracelets" (1986) by Gilbert: reprinted in* Heartbreak Soup.

he stated unequivocally and pretty authoritatively that they were wrong. I was wondering, is that a strongly held point of view of yours, that attitude about small town life?

**GILBERT:** Yeah, I would lean toward Heraclio's point of view ...

**GROTH:** Because I don't want to ascribe to you what your characters are thinking, but it came across so forcefully, it seemed like it was almost an opinion you believed.

**GILBERT:** In "Human Diastrophism" the poor guy who's killed, the Swedish archeologist, sees Palomar as a place of beauty and he loves it, because of that simple lifestyle and the great scenery, and he says, "They just can't see the forest for the trees here."

And that's basically it, Palomar is a nice little place; it's dull, but it's a nice place to live. People are generally cool there, Chelo has probably only had to shoot the gun six times in her whole career as sheriff. Heraclio is us, so he can see the beauty in it.

I remember somebody once saying, why emphasize Heraclio so much because he's such a wimp, and that hit me because I thought, am I being too sensitive? Is he like Charlie Brown or something? So I had to think about it and I thought, naah, he's not a wimp.

**GROTH:** He's a good character through whose eyes you can see the town, because he's educated and he has a perspective, so he's a good observer.

**GILBERT:** And he doesn't really judge too harshly. He's not too critical of things because the guys he hangs out with are pretty much nut cases, but they're his friends and he loves his friends. When he becomes intellectual he doesn't lose that closeness to people. Heraclio loves his friends. Well, Israel he doesn't any more because of what happened with Carmen and that's going to be explored a little more, too.

**GROTH:** Now is there a difficulty in Carmen and Heraclio's relationship where Heraclio obviously has a better education?

**GILBERT:** She's intimidated by him, that's all. She doesn't want to feel stupid. She feels weird enough that she doesn't know who she is. She was found somewhere; they named her Carmen. She doesn't know what's going to happen to her next. Nobody knows anything about her; she doesn't know anything about herself, so she's already spooked. To have Heraclio reading and talking about things that she doesn't understand just spooks her more. So that thing about her rejecting *One Hundred Years of Solitude*, it's just because she's spooked.

**GROTH:** When Heraclio asks Carmen to marry him, she made a very big point of asking him if he'd ever had sex with anyone else. He said no and she married him. I think it was made fairly clear that her decision rested upon his answer; at least he thought so.

**GILBERT:** Yes, he thought so.

**GROTH:** What point were you trying to make there?

**GILBERT:** The same thing: that Carmen is spooked. I thought maybe that some women would catch it, that if he had sex before with other women, then he might have sex with another woman while he was with Carmen. I might have been too vague with that. But I think some women caught that.

**GROTH:** Because that was a fairly important point on Carmen's part.

**GILBERT:** It's just like I said, it's that Carmen's spooked constantly. She hides it by being very gregarious. She's like all my women, she's hot to trot, and she always had this crush on Israel. If I didn't explain that well enough, I will later. That's another thing good about the series that I've got, that if I screw up, I've got plenty of room and time to repair it.

**GROTH:** Right. If you think of something that supersedes something that you wrote and drew before and it doesn't quite fit into a new game plan, will you actually go back and change something?

**GILBERT:** You mean change the meaning of something?

**GROTH:** Rewrite a page, redraw a panel, so you wouldn't be burdened with something.

**GILBERT:** Oh, no. If I write something and it's printed in the book, it's there. I'll edit things for the reprint books, but it won't change what's gone on before.

WELL ... SHE DOESN'T BRING IT UP IN FIGHTS ANY MORE; NOT AFTER HER LITTLE 'THING' WITH ISRAEL.

THREE MONTHS AGO, RIGHT AFTER DINNER, OUT OF THE BLUE CARMEN BROKE DOWN CRYING AND CONFESSED TO CHEATING ON ME.

Panel from Gilbert's "For the Love of Carmen" (1985), reprinted in Heartbreak Soup.

**GROTH:** Another one of these ambiguities I found in the stories that I wanted to ask you about was, Heraclio was deflowered by Luba and was absolutely scared shitless that Carmen was going to find out. Eventually he told Carmen, but off-panel.

**GILBERT:** I just thought there were too many soapy elements in the story as it was, and to have another confrontation was just too much. I'll probably have the confrontation later, and that will lead to another story.

**GROTH:** What does Carmen have against Luba?

**GILBERT:** I don't know. It was just sort of a personality quirk. I just noticed my girl friends in high school, whenever they'd see somebody like Luba or in general a girl with a womanly look, immediately they would throw all self-control out the window and just become completely rude. It always fascinated me you could be as progressive as anybody,

but when it comes to those feelings ... it was a realistic way for a particular woman to react to another particular woman. Not all women are like that, of course. Covered my ass.

**GROTH:** One of the things I was surprised at in "Heartbreak Soup" is how much goes on between the panels, how much is hinted at and how much you don't explain, but the reader is simply faced with and accepts. One of the things of course is Pipo whose life story sort of shot through there like a rocket. First she's deflowered by Soledad, she has a kind of romantic tryst with Manuel, then she marries Gato, but the readers aren't quite sure how that came about, then Gato evidently just turns into a swine, and now she's divorcing him.

**GILBERT:** She's divorced and living in Palomar by herself.

**GROTH:** And then there was a fairly grim episode in "Bullnecks and Bracelets" where she tries to have an affair with Israel.

**GILBERT:** That was to show how bad her relationship with Gato was.

**GROTH:** Which it did. [*Laughter.*] Now you could obviously take Pipo's story and write half a dozen stories about her.

**GILBERT:** Yeah, I plan to.

**GROTH:** Is that right?

**GILBERT:** After the major story I'm doing now, "The Poison River," which outlines Luba's life, from when she's born up to the first "Heartbreak Soup" story, I'm going to go around to different characters. I might do Chelo's story, because there hasn't been too much about her. Then Pipo too. I'm just going to show parts of Pipo ... Pipo's barely there. I'm surprised people even recognize her. All that stuff Luba was saying about her in issue #24 was true, about the nose job, the breast implants. She's one of those crazy women that's already pretty and then they go and do this stuff to themselves. You ask, "What'd you do that for?" They do it because they can afford it. I haven't emphasized it, but Pipo's pretty well off — when she was married to Gato she saved a little bundle of her own.

**GROTH:** The story's so organic, do you find that

troublesome at all? That you're locked in, whatever you write and draw? You can't change if you come up with a better idea that would supersede the meaning of a previous story.

**GILBERT:** Oh, yeah, you always get better ideas all the time. One of my clunkiest stories is "An American in Palomar." If I did it now, I would be 60 percent better, just because I know what I'm doing now. I'm more confident. At the time I wasn't that confident in doing that story.

**GROTH:** Well, you know, it's funny, because I read that, the last piece of your work that I read, and I thought it was actually a little less good than I remembered it being. I think it's probably because I read a lot of stuff afterward which I think was actually better.

**GILBERT:** That was at the period where we'd pretty much settled into our little niche and we relaxed a bit. We didn't let it go, we were always concerned about making it good, but it was just a point where we slowed up.

**GROTH:** You were coasting?

**GILBERT:** I guess so. But in the case of "An American in Palomar" it was clunky because I wasn't sure what I wanted to say in it. I've got a lot of pages that I took out and redid, just to make the story clearer.

**GROTH:** Now, how much of an exploiter did you mean to make Howard Miller? Did you mean to condemn him?

**GILBERT:** No, I just really wanted to make a bad artist. He did think Palomar was lovely, but I didn't really emphasize that, I was always having him put it down: like a lot of foreigners in poorer countries.

**GROTH:** — slightly condescending.

**GILBERT:** Yeah, and just not understanding the culture because they're too busy having their vacation or whatever. Like I said, the story's clunky. But it's too late.

**GROTH:** Actually, I thought you humanized the character surprisingly in about a page and a half at the end of "Human Diastrophism."

**GILBERT:** Right.

**GROTH:** In fact, there was one panel that was exceptionally good, where he came across much more as a three-dimensional character.

**GILBERT:** As a matter fact, later on, I'm probably going to do stories about Howard Miller. See, now that Tonantzín is gone I'm going to do stories about all the people who were involved with her, what they thought of her. Howard Miller by this time has grown up. But I haven't really shown him growing up; you just get the result at the end of "Human Diastrophism." He's getting better as an artist; he's getting better as a human being.

**GROTH:** Now, Howard Miller is a white, middle-class, urban guy. Does it intimidate you to go outside the Mexican milieu?

**GILBERT:** No, because a lot of my friends are from that

background and I have no problem with it. I thought readers were getting a little comfortable with Palomar. That's why I brought in the slugs and stuff like that. They forgot that this was a different culture and a different place. Our prejudices in real life — I mean, I always joke that if Maggie and Hopey went to Palomar, Hopey'd probably just make fun of the people there behind their backs. Luba would think they were the weirdest people in the world, she'd not understand why they did that to their hair.

**GROTH:** Yes, there is a certain sense of Palomarian nationalism among the characters. I forget which characters in which stories, but occasionally a character would talk about the U.S., how the food is bad and the music is lousy. There's this odd kind of chauvinism.

**GILBERT:** Yes. And then I had Howard Miller saying the same thing. The music was lousy, the food's bad, but the beer's good. Because there's that old cliché, "Well, I don't know about blacks, but I sure like their girls." That sort of thing.

"Mexicans, I don't know, but their beer and their girls are OK."

That old thing. Even the worst racists can make an effort to like something about those they disdain.

**GROTH:** Could you tell me a little about how you actually developed your drawing?

**GILBERT:** It's organic. I've taken more time to clarify my art. I don't think I necessarily draw better, I think I just clarify my art better. You're able to look at the drawing a lot quicker, if you choose, and know what's going on. Whereas before a lot of dialogue was helping out the drawing.

**GROTH:** How do you think you've improved in the last five years in terms of drawing?

**GILBERT:** Making things more naturalistic. Not using so many crutches. Like I said, a lot of times in my stories, the dialogue is helping the drawing a lot. And now I'm using the drawing, the image and then the dialogue. I just think I'm becoming looser and more confident. And the characters are starting to look different from one another. Some of the characters used to run together; they would look

the same. That's a lot of characters, how many is it, 50? I think some fan counted once, and it was 52 or something.

**GROTH:** Do you practice drawing?

**GILBERT:** No, actually I don't. I don't know if you've talked to Jaime about this, but I don't sit around and doodle like I used to. That's all I did up until *Love and Rockets*. I love doing it, but I never do any leisure drawing, unless I force myself to do it, because all my drawing now is for getting the book out.

**GROTH:** On average, I think it takes you guys about three days a page. If you averaged it out over the course of a year.

**GILBERT:** Oh, sure, it'd be three, sometimes more.

**GROTH:** So where does the time go in doing the stories, is it more in writing or drawing or vice versa?

**GILBERT:** It's both, but the worst is rewriting. Sometimes it's the drawing that takes longer than the writing. In a way drawing is writing, because if you don't have it typed up in your head, you don't know what you're going to be drawing. The storytelling has got to be right because I only want to do it one time. If I miss something, I don't like to go back; I have, but I don't like to. I've held up stories for a week, just to get a person saying the right sentence.

**GROTH:** I know.

**GILBERT:** [*Laughs.*] Yeah, you'd know. I don't like doing it, but I'm not doing it for fun. I'm doing it because I want it right. And I've got such a nice publisher and editor who allows me this: because I know a lot of guys who don't have that privilege. Good artists, too.

**GROTH:** Well, John Byrne sometimes takes four or five minutes to get the right line.

**GILBERT:** I want that in. [*Laughter.*]

**GROTH:** You threw me off. Can you take me through a typical story of how you go about it? What is the first thing you do? What are the stages you go through to do a typical story?

**GILBERT:** Well, I usually start sketching. Sometimes I'll just draw a scene, I'll draw Luba talking to somebody or I'll have her bending over, using a shovel. Then I can write a whole scene around that. Why is she doing it? Who's talking to her? Why are they talking to her? Sometimes I can write whole stories that way. That's how I used to do it. Now, I pretty much have the next story coming together as I'm working on the present story. These last two issues have taken so long because I swear I go through 10 or 11 different stories 'til I get one. And it's ridiculous because I usually go back to the first one.

**GROTH:** But in "Heartbreak Soup" one story can act as a springboard for the next story.

**GILBERT:** Yes, because it is this whole "expanding universe."

**GROTH:** So a drawing might actually begin the creative process?

**GILBERT:** Sure.

**GROTH:** At what point do you actually sit down and write panel for panel? Or do you write an outline first?

**GILBERT:** Well, with "Human Diastrophism" I wrote an outline, and I found that that worked really well, even if a lot of the dialogue took a long time to write. I knew where it was leading to. Except for the Tonantzín killing herself. I wrote that as I was going along. That wasn't easy to do. I hate sounding corny and cliché saying, "The characters write themselves," but they do slip out of your hands, and it's hard to bring them back.

**GROTH:** Do you write an outline for everything now?

**GILBERT:** I have an outline for "Poison River" as well.

**GROTH:** How long will "Poison River" be?

**GILBERT:** It will probably be longer than "Human Diastrophism," because the chapters will be shorter and I have a lot more to tell. With "Human Diastrophism" I was pretty much wrapping up where "Heartbreak Soup" had been since the beginning. The story is a little long and a little clunky because I had to correct things. I had to make things clear. But at the same time I created more confusion for the future, so you can't win. "Poison River" is going to be new ground for the reader, because nobody knows anything about Luba before Palomar. Jaime noted something interesting about the Palomar stories, that the two main protagonists, Luba and Heraclio, are newcomers to Palomar as well as the reader. In that first story Heraclio's been there for three months and Luba has just arrived.

**GROTH:** I can understand how an outline would be essential on a story as complicated as "Human Diastrophism" or as long as "Poison River" is going to be, but what about shorter stories like "On Isidro's Beach" or "The Reticent Heart" or something like that?

**GILBERT:** Well, short stories are the hardest thing for me to do, because you've got to think about an ending within that issue, and a lot of times the endings are the hardest part. So I'm lucky if I ever pull off a story contained in one issue. Probably my slowest story is "Love Bites" with Carmen and Heraclio. That was the first one that got mediocre reviews. That was because it was a self-contained story and they're difficult to write.

**GROTH:** So do you have an outline for something like "Love Bites"?

**GILBERT:** I had an outline for that particular story, and I had one for "Isidro's Beach." But if you'll notice, those short stories just aren't that good.

**GROTH:** You don't think so?

**GILBERT:** Not for me: like "Boys Will Be Boys" in issue #13 ... "Reticent Heart" worked because it was a part of another story — it was a part of Heraclio losing his virginity with Luba. "Love Bites" was done to clarify Carmen and Heraclio's relationship as well as how Luba fits in the middle, but now that I look at it I really didn't need to do that story. I liked it, but these short stories don't work for me, they've got to be a part of a long story.

**GROTH:** How precise is an outline?

**GILBERT:** It's mostly just incidents in the story.

**GROTH:** Do you write it page by page?

**GILBERT:** I usually write it first in separate scenes and then I'll put the scenes in order. I just looked at "Human Diastrophism," and I realized there was a scene out of sequence. [*Laughs.*] It still works, but

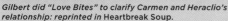
Gilbert did "Love Bites" to clarify Carmen and Heraclio's relationship: reprinted in Heartbreak Soup.

the part where the killer is chasing Diana to the beach looks like it happens in a minute where actually it happens over a longer period of time. That's because I made a mistake in putting the order together.

**GROTH:** When she's walking backwards?

**GILBERT:** Yeah. A good way to lengthen scenes is to put a scene in the middle of another scene, and when you go back to that scene it seems like a long time has passed.

**GROTH:** So how do you pace a story? Page by page?

**GILBERT:** What I usually do if I only have so many pages is, I'll spread it out to maybe 20 pages on sketch paper, then I'll realize — this happens almost every time — that I can fit a scene which took five panels into three or two. That's why my stories are very tight and it looks like, "Wow, this guy knows just what to write." Well, actually I write quite a bit and cut it down.

**GROTH:** Do you know when you write a story how long it's going to be?

**GILBERT:** Usually, Jaime and I talk about that.

**GROTH:** You have to coordinate your efforts in a 32-page comic.

**GILBERT:** Exactly.

**GROTH:** In "For the Love of Carmen," which is very text heavy, it could have theoretically been twice as long simply by spreading the text among more panels. What prompted you to make that particular story more text heavy than others?

**GILBERT:** Why did I? I guess at the time I was reading a lot of Crumb's and Lynda Barry's work and at the time Crumb was doing "My Troubles with Women." I guess I was taking a lead from there. I'd been telling stories in the same old way — "Duck Feet" is a wild adventure, then I had that gruesome Israel story, then I thought, how do I do it differently? I figured that since Heraclio is a sympathetic character, most people will like being in his head. At the beginning of the story — and I meant this for myself as well — he says, "I'm not a writer so don't ... " Even though I tried to write well in the story I knew that I wasn't that good —

**GROTH:** You were off the hook.

**GILBERT:** No, I wasn't trying to cover my ass. I was being honest with myself at the time. I was thinking, I know my limits, so I'm just going to talk it out. It worked with Jaime in "Mechanics."

**GROTH:** Well, earlier you said the drawing is part of the writing, and I wonder if you can elaborate on that.

**GILBERT:** That probably sounds really dumb. But what I'm saying is that there's so much in the panel that isn't in the words, and it's got to be different from the words but yet connect. Particularly if a caption describes a lot, and particularly if it describes a scene that moves along in time and different locations and you've got to fit it in one panel. It's very difficult to do.

**GROTH:** Now, I know you pretty well, and I think you have a sense of values when it comes to drawing, to stories, and I guess to culture in general which I happen to agree with entirely and which I think is far more sophisticated than most of the alleged sophisticated artists and writers populating the comics field — many of whom have college degrees and occasionally quote Dostoyevsky — and yet you don't have a formal education and you don't quote Kant, but it seems to me you have this rock bed of values. I'm curious as to how you think you came to those? You seem to have an inordinate respect for art and try to find an enduring value to the work you do which is very rare in this field.

**GILBERT:** I should say one good thing about my teachers is that when they told me art is good, art is something you aspire to and that was the best, all the other stuff was just diversion, I believed that. Even if I loved Batman, even if I loved comic books, there was always part of me that would say, "That Picasso stuff looks like a little kid drew it, but it sure looks good, doesn't it." I guess adults respected it, so that meant something to me as a youth. If adults respected something, that was important. I don't know why I felt that. I guess I had more respect for adults than I let myself believe. There was always part of me that was saying this serious movie is better than that horror movie, even though I liked the horror movie.

**GROTH:** You still made that distinction.

**GILBERT:** I might not have dwelled on it too deeply at the time, but I would think about it. I always expected to understand it later. And to be honest I'm not disappointed. A lot of people become disappointed that way. They say, "I was ready to grow up and for something to happen and nothing happened."

But there was a lot of things that did happen, like art and good films and good books. Those books that they told me were good, even if at the time I wasn't going to go near them, turned out to be good.

**FIORE:** Your work has a literary feel, although I understand it doesn't come from literature so much ...

**GILBERT:** To tell the truth, I'm not that well read. The things I took from movies, I tried to take farther. And my own life ...

**FIORE:** Life is what it's supposed to come from anyway ...

**GILBERT:** Yeah, it's only been recently that I've been reading a lot of good stuff.

**FIORE:** Living will get you through times of no reading better than reading will get you through times of no living.

**GILBERT:** I think I'm just lucky, I have this knack for telling stories that seem like they're literate. ... [*Laughter.*]

**GROTH:** At what point did you start making these kinds of serious aesthetic distinctions intellectually rather than just by intuiting them from the evaluations of adults?

**GILBERT:** I guess that was in the mid-'70s and late '70s when punk came around and — you're never going to believe this, Gary — I started reading *The Comics Journal*. The *Journal* spoke directly about comics, so it was something I could hold onto. The *Journal* would talk about specific things in comics, saying this is a bunch of shit. I thought, hmmmmm. But I was so paranoid I thought everything I like must be on their list too. I was very paranoid, very self-conscious. That's why I sent the original *Love and Rockets* to you, because I figured I couldn't second-guess you guys.

**GROTH:** You just wanted to see it get trashed.

**GILBERT:** I didn't know. Because sometimes you guys would like stuff, like Harvey Kurtzman; but I thought, Harvey Kurtzman draws like a funny guy. And [*Journal* critics] hated the guy from *Epic*, the guy who used to draw mashed potatoes, Tim Conrad. You'd talk about specific artists like poor Marshall Rogers or something — you'd sort of pick on him — and so I just became lost. I thought, if I can take their criticism ... They're going to bang away, maybe it's better I get it over with now.

**GROTH:** Did you ever read anything in the *Journal*

that blew one of your heroes away and you thought fuck these guys, they don't know what they're talking about?

**GILBERT:** No, because you guys pretty much stuck to ... I don't remember. I might read something like, "Neal Adams isn't that good." And I'd think, well, I like Neal Adams. Then I'd look at those *Green Lantern/Green Arrow* comics and I'd think, I guess they're right. At the time I wasn't really fighting you guys. I guess it was just the attitude that took me and most people aback. It was just so volatile. [*Laughter.*] When I look back at the letters in old *Journals*, I think the readers were attacking the attitudes behind the criticism. And I thought that was a mistake, that's why I've never been a letter writer. I thought, naaah, I'd just blow it out my ass and make a big fool of myself. But you guys never attacked anybody I really liked; Kirby was always praised, and Ditko. ... I didn't have any particular heroes at the time when I was reading that stuff, so it didn't bother me, other than the attitude.

**GROTH:** What kind of concrete effect did punk rock have on your work? Obviously, it had a real effect on Jaime's work because it's in Jaime's work, but no one's going to look at "Heartbreak Soup" and see punk ... or would they?

**GILBERT:** Well ... maybe two people out there would. [*Laughs.*] I always thought it was in there.

**GROTH:** Where would you point to the influence?

**GILBERT:** Basically I'm doing what I want to do and making a lot of the characters not terribly sympathetic. Sometimes the characters are really intense, and I don't think I would have done that if I hadn't experienced ... I'm sorry to say I never read that much. But even when I did read something it

Like Luba, the Hernandez brothers' mother enjoyed rock music. From "Human Diastrophism" (1987), reprinted in the eponymous volume.

still didn't have that ... it was still reading. As good as say, *Catcher in the Rye* was — and I read it twice when I was a teenager — as much as I loved it and as much as I could understand Holden Caulfield it didn't have that immediacy of having somebody standing up in front of you, sweat drops flying from his head. And I tried to put that in the comic. Because rock 'n' roll was the most immediate thing for me, standing up and just being mad. And I wanted to be original too. Actually, Jaime doing Maggie and Hopey and the punk scene freed me from that because I would have done the same thing or something very similar. My ego is always telling me to be original, be the guy that people say, "He did this strip, it's his strip and nobody's done one like it." That was always important to me.

**GROTH:** More of a motivational force.

**GILBERT:** Sure. You caught us at an interesting time, when I was getting away from the girl stuff and I didn't know what I was going to do, and Jaime was getting into doing the girl stuff. Now if you'd approached us a year or two before, I would have been doing the girl stuff and Jaime would have been doing superheroes. Back then Jaime was always a few steps behind me, not because I was so advanced, but because he's two years younger than me. And that's how it always progressed until now. Now we're pretty much even.

**GROTH:** Is there a political attitude expressed in your work?

**GILBERT:** Yeah. I mean I'm not hardline anything, like Harvey Pekar said he was a strident leftist. I don't have a lot of political background because I never really followed politics. Listening to people talk about politics I realized it was almost like a soap opera, it was like a game, but the stakes were very high. It seemed so ridiculous to me and horrible too, because of the serious stakes, so I kept away from it.

**GROTH:** Did you see a political content in the punk phenomenon?

**GILBERT:** Yeah, a lot of the punk bands, especially from England, leaned towards socialism. And I had a lot of friends in high school ... a lot of young people when they get into politics they wind up being Marxist for some reason. So I was exposed to politics that way. When people become Marxists they feel they're going to do it, they're going to help make this world a better place, and I sort of listened. I have a friend named Peter Garcia who's a pretty political guy. He works at a university in New Mexico in the cultural end of it where they're trying to preserve indigenous cultures in the U.S.A. He was the guy who turned me on to a lot of Mexican folk artists.

**GROTH:** One strip that I thought was overtly political is "Locker Room." Can you tell me what you were doing in the strip?

**GILBERT:** I think there was a line in *The Year of Living Dangerously* where Linda Hunt as Billy Kwan says, "Starvation makes for a great aphrodisiac." And that really hit me. It's not a good film but that line hit me. And that strip was an extension on it. I did it with goofy monsters and stuff instead of doing it seriously because it attracts people for some reason, and if it has a serious message behind those monsters it seems to be more powerful in certain instances.

**GROTH:** Yeah, I saw them clearly as a metaphor.

**GILBERT:** Right. If I had done "Heartbreak Soup" with monsters or bunnies or horses or mice — though actually I like *Maus* quite a bit — I felt that I would have lost a lot of what "Heartbreak Soup" is. I had to make them real. In my mind and in my heart these had to be my people, not rabbits and not metaphors and not symbols. That's the way it works best. That's why film is such a powerful art form. At home watching TV there's all these distractions, but when you're in the theater you've paid and you're sitting there and it's looking at you as much as you're looking at it. That's why someday, I hope, there will be a *Love and Rockets* or "Heartbreak Soup" movie, just to get it closer to people. But that doesn't look too likely the way Hollywood works. Unless I win 15 million dollars in the lottery it's not going to happen.

**GROTH:** Earlier when I asked you why Gato turned into a swine you replied, "It was business, man." Now does that betray any political attitude or were you just being glib?

**GILBERT:** Well, nowadays it sure seems that businessman equals jerk, as far as I'm concerned. If you're an artist or musician who has to deal with

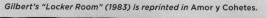

*Gilbert's "Locker Room" (1983) is reprinted in* Amor y Cohetes.

*"I couldn't ask for a better gig." "And So it Was" is part of "My Love Book" (1995), reprinted in* Amor y Cohetes.

business that's different, but if you're a businessman all you do is keep the gears working, you're pretty fucking worthless as far as I'm concerned. [*Laughs.*] Of course there's more to it. I'm not saying that just because a person's not an artist they're not worth anything, but when you're in that position of moving stuff around you better be worth a shit and a lot of these people aren't. I don't know what the deal is. You have farm workers busting their chops and they still aren't paid anything. And you got these fucking jerks that play with video games, and do lunch, play tennis, fly to Dallas and go home and that's it.

**GROTH:** Were you ever seduced by socialism?

**GILBERT:** I guess vaguely, superficially. I never read into it or anything. My friends were interested in it, and the basic things they talked about seemed logical to me — free public medical care and stuff, those ideas made a lot of sense.

**GROTH:** Do you have any kind of overriding goal or aspiration in "Heartbreak Soup?"

**GILBERT:** This sounds really corny, but I just wanted to bring us closer together. I thought it was something that was good, my childhood, my heritage; I thought it was just as interesting as anybody else's. I just needed a way to show it in an interesting and humorous way, without it being boring and academic. When I started it was at the point when "high concept" really took off. Stuff that only lasted

five minutes, it was the *Star Wars* generation, the *E.T.* generation. I wanted something that would last, and I wanted something that was worth lasting. And the story had never been told. I could go to the movies and I could not see — unless it was a Mexican movie made in the '50s by Buñuel or somebody, which nobody goes to anyway — you just weren't going to see it in popular entertainment. There were the books, the Central and South American writers that are very popular now, but those are books. People don't read books. It's almost impossible to get something truthful on television. I thought, if this comic book simply exists, hopefully it means something. If five people see these stories, maybe it'll have been worth the trouble. I was just thinking in those terms. I wanted something that would last, and something that was original. I was lucky that it was original. If I had done the punk thing like Jaime we would have just been going around in circles trying to top each other with the more realistic punk story. So, I'm really happy I did it. Deadlines are a pain in the ass, but I couldn't ask for a better gig.

## A LIE, A CHEAT AND A RIP-OFF

**GROTH:** What did you think of the whole ratings flap?

**GILBERT:** I didn't know what was going to happen. I thought we were doing the right thing having the mature readers label on our comic, because our stuff gets pretty wild and far be it for me to tell what's pornographic and what isn't.

**JAIME:** While some cartoonists were complaining that an advisory would hold them back, I think it gives us freedom. But then again I'm not worrying about that Marvel check either.

**GROTH:** Were you sympathetic to Marvel and DC artists who were worried about the political nature of that whole difficulty? I think what they were saying is that they didn't mind labels being on comics, but they objected to the reasons Marvel and DC did it. They saw this as a kind of slippery slope and the thing that would happen is the same thing that's happened to the motion picture ratings.

**GILBERT:** I thought in a way that liberated films. You couldn't see *Blue Velvet* in 1965. I don't see why that wouldn't have liberated comics. You know, they want to draw nipples on Supergirl, that's the extent of their creative desires.

**GROTH:** Are you not taking this seriously?

**JAIME:** [*Laughs.*]

**GILBERT:** Fuck it, man.

**GROTH:** It doesn't sound like you're taking these artists' freedom seriously.

**GILBERT:** Well, I wouldn't call most of them artists. I guess I would call them employees.

**JAIME:** Well, as I understand it, according to Dave Sim, we're employees.

**GROTH:** What do you think of Dave Sim's distinction, that any artist who is published by someone other than himself, is an employee?

**GILBERT:** Hemingway was an employee of Scribners, is that what he's saying?

**GROTH:** Yes.

**GILBERT:** Uh ... [*Laughs.*]

**GROTH:** Is that too self-evidently absurd to comment about?

**GILBERT:** Yeah, I guess in the '50s Fellini was an employee of Carlo Ponti. Yep, I'm just a schlepper at Fantagraphics.

**GROTH:** I was having lunch with Spiegelman today and we came to the conclusion that there just weren't enough good cartoonists to really establish a beachhead of good alternative cartooning.

**GILBERT:** Not at the moment.

**GROTH:** Then either Kim Thompson or I also suggested that we thought we could blame the publishers as well as the cartoonists because the publishers don't generally, I think, encourage adult cartooning. So I want for a minute to broach the subject of publishers. I was wondering how important you think publishers are in the profession and what your general feelings are toward publishers and toward mainstream publishers in particular. [*Pause.*]

**GILBERT:** Shit, I don't how to begin.

**GROTH:** Well, let me refocus the question. How important, for example, is ownership of your work? In other words, could you do the work you do now for a company that owned the copyright?

**GILBERT:** Absolutely not. I wouldn't be doing "Heartbreak Soup" or Errata Stigmata stories for anybody else.

**JAIME:** I would still be doing "Mechanics." I couldn't be doing "Locas."

**GROTH:** That's because "Locas" is more personal?

**JAIME:** Yeah. And it's got no hook to it. And publishers, no matter how alternative they want to get, still want that hook. A lot of the fault is the editors.

**GROTH:** When we first started publishing *Love and Rockets*, were you acutely conscious of creator's rights, of ownership and so forth and so on?

**GILBERT:** I think I was aware that the underground cartoonists owned all their stuff even if they were all poor. That was about it. There were things like *Star*Reach* and I knew that people owned their stuff on that. I talked to Mike Friedrich, we'd write to each other. I sent him my first story for *Star*Reach* and he rejected it, but it was a nice rejection. He really encouraged me. He said, this is really interesting; it's just not polished or whatever. I sent the story to somebody else in northern California and I never got a response and I don't know where that story is. My first story is out there somewhere. If anybody knows John D. Cothran, he's got my first story. Stupid me, I lost my photocopy.

**GROTH:** Then there was *Mister X*.

**GILBERT:** Dum de dum dum!

**GROTH:** Just for the record, why don't you explain how *Mister X* came about, how you were approached, and so forth.

**GILBERT:** We'd seen the advertisements for it in the *Journal* and other places, and Paul Rivoche's art attracted us right away. We read about how it kept getting postponed. And one day Ken Steacy, who was the editor, called us and asked us if we wanted to do it. I said, "We've been waiting for it to come out."

Apparently Dean Motter and Paul Rivoche had a falling-out, and that was at the time when *Love and Rockets* wasn't doing that well financially. I thought

*Mario, Gilbert and Jaime's work-for-hire collaboration was ill-fated: from* Mister X *# 1 (June 1984).*

©1984 Vortex Comics

well, this goofball science fiction would be easy to do. I actually made the decision myself and Mario and Jaime went along with it. That's how it started.

**GROTH:** You guys basically signed a work-for-hire contract or its equivalent.

**GILBERT:** Yeah, they own everything.

**GROTH:** Did you know what you were doing at the time?

**GILBERT:** We knew it was their character, we knew that we would have nothing after we were through with it.

**JAIME:** All we expected from it was to get paid —

**GILBERT:** To get paid fairly well. I figured we'd do it for fun and hopefully make some money. It sounds really stupid now — doing it for money.

**GROTH:** That'll teach you to try to be commercial.

**GILBERT:** Yeah, we tried it, we got fucked over and that's it. *Mister X* wasn't even that rewarding artistically, because Mario and I were plotting it and I was scripting it and Jaime was drawing it and we could never make a smooth connection. *Mister X* was fragmented. It could have been something if I had written and drawn it or if Jaime had written and drawn it. It would have been a whole different book, and it would have been better, I think, because that's how we work the best. Mario's a good idea man, but he's not trained particularly well in telling an entire story.

**GROTH:** I wonder if you wanted to talk about Mario's contribution to *Love and Rockets*.

**JAIME:** He was the one who pushed us, at least me. I wouldn't be doing it —

**GILBERT:** He was the one who grabbed us by the arm. We were dragging our feet and he was raring to go.

**GROTH:** Why hasn't he drawn much in the last three years?

**GILBERT:** Mario doesn't practice that often. It's a vicious circle for him — he's got a job, he's got to support himself and his family, so he doesn't have a lot of time to practice drawing, and if he can't practice, he can't progress. And Mario's not that confident either. He'll write something, then he backs off and he won't finish it. He might be intimidated by what's expected from us in the book. I don't know, I've never asked him. But there'll always be room for him in *Love and Rockets* when he's ready.

**GROTH:** How did Vortex owning *Mister X* outright affect you? Did that mitigate your effort?

**GILBERT:** We couldn't do much with *Mister X*. He

was the protagonist. If you have a comic called *Mister X*, he's got to be the main focus of things, and I found that for us a character like that didn't work. If we had done *Mister X*, our way, he would have been a background character the whole time, sort of a spook running around. Then it would have worked a lot better, and we could have focused on the other characters. Those other characters are ours, by the way. We created most of the characters aside from *Mister X*.

**GROTH:** You mean you created them and Vortex owns them?

**GILBERT:** Right. But in God's eyes they're ours. [*Laughs.*]

**JAIME:** If Mercedes is the most popular character in the comic, it's because she's Gilbert's.

**GILBERT:** I've noticed they've turned her into a Hopey facsimile in recent issues — she's in a rock band and she's even dressing like Hopey more or less. I'm just sorry we didn't flesh out the characters enough, I was never comfortable with them. And we quit by the time Jaime and I started getting warmed up to them.

**GROTH:** And you quit over a monetary dispute?

**GILBERT:** Yeah, at issue four. We were going to go up to issue six, but it never happened, never will.

**JAIME:** Gilbert had this great idea of killing off every character he created to set it up for Motter, so he could start it over with the character he originally planned.

**GILBERT:** But they knew a good thing when they saw it, and kept Mercedes.

**GROTH:** Let me ask you a question which might seem obvious, but since Harlan Ellison once told me that between *Mister X* and *Love and Rockets*, he thought *Mister X* was the real thing, how do you look at *Mister X* in comparison to *Love and Rockets*?

**GILBERT:** There is no comparison. Mister X was just something that sort of happened, like a bad zit, and now it's gone away. That's all. [*Laughs.*] There are other cartoonists who shall remain nameless who have said that *Love and Rockets* is OK but *Mister X* was the real thing. I don't know, maybe what they're talking about is Dean Motter's ideas.

**GROTH:** It seems to me that there is a lack of solidarity among cartoonists. Tell me if you think I'm wrong here, but I always had the impression that you somehow did not fit into any of the various cliques in comics. For example, as you said earlier, you were taken advantage of in the *Mister X* deal, and yet no cartoonists came to your defense —

**GILBERT:** Maybe not in the press, but we talked to a few people at conventions who told us they supported us.

**GROTH:** But publicly nobody's really come to your defense, and cartoonists continue to —

**GILBERT:** — work on *Mister X*, do covers for *Mister X*, things like that.

**JAIME:** Then they complain about creator's rights.

**GROTH:** Sure. I was wondering how you felt about that. Would you, for example, feel any obligation to support cartoonists who were in your view taken advantage of by a publisher?

**GILBERT:** We supported Kirby through the whole Marvel mess. Of course, if somebody's being dicked over ...

**GROTH:** Is there any sense in which you feel somewhat isolated?

**GILBERT:** Yeah, I guess. I see [Mike] Kaluta did the last cover of *Mister X*. ... I don't know what's going on between those artists and Bill Marks. Chester Brown seems happy at Vortex.

**GROTH:** There seems to be a prevailing ethic in this industry where, "As long as he doesn't fuck me over I'm happy."

**GILBERT:** Exactly. So you're asking if we're isolated? I think we're becoming more and more isolated, but there are people that we can talk to — the Peter Bagges and Dan Cloweses — I know they would support us if some shit ever came up, and we'd definitely support them. But as far as the mainstream goes, we seem to be getting further and further away from the whole deal.

**JAIME:** I haven't met one of those guys who has something really personal that he's trying to get out and is being fucked over. The first thing I would say is don't go to a big publisher. Some of those guys just seem to care more about getting more money than getting their vision out.

This panel is from Gilbert's "They Laughed When I Told Them I Wanted to Rock" which appeared in The Comics Journal Special Edition Summer 2002 Vol. 2.

**GROTH:** Do you feel that you have to act as an advocate or a spokesman in any way for what you see as the progressive movement in comics?

**GILBERT:** Whenever we're interviewed I try to emphasize that we're serious about this, that there are other cartoonists serious about telling stories about life, forget the *Dark Knights*, forget the yuppyized Superman, forget it.

**JAIME:** We're also doing it for those guys who aren't selling worth a shit who are serious and talented.

**GROTH:** I wonder how much you guys are a product of your times. That's the old argument Gil Kane and I always have, how much free will is a part of this and how much a cartoonist is a part of his times. And I wonder: If you were born 30 years ago would you be doing *Doll Man*?

**GILBERT:** It's been good for us because we're in a position of owning our work, of doing whatever we goddamn well please.

**JAIME:** Years ago we couldn't do what we're doing now.

**GILBERT:** We're very lucky. But that doesn't mean we would have wanted to do superhero genre stuff. If we wanted to do superhero stuff we'd be doing it.

**JAIME:** And there's plenty of alternative publishers who are welcoming superheroes.

**GROTH:** Where do you place the blame for the hegemony of superheroes and genre crap? Do you place it primarily on the cartoonists themselves or the publishers?

**GILBERT:** It's probably an equal distribution of publishers, cartoonists and retailers.

**JAIME:** The publishers want to sell something and the artists are only too happy to give them what they want.

**GILBERT:** And retailers have to survive, so they're going to go with what sells. It's a vicious circle and I'm happy to be at least partly away from it.

**GROTH:** Do you guys ever feel demoralized that you're fighting against the current?

**GILBERT:** I don't look into it that much. It drives some people crazy. I think Peter Bagge looks into it too much — he might not have any alternative because his book sells so poorly. But I talk to him about it and it drives him crazy how the market is. I try to keep away from it, because I would get demoralized, my work might suffer.

**JAIME:** I'm able to do what I want to do and I'm able to live off it, so I'm fine where I am. I would love to have more readers, but as long as I'm able to do it comfortably ...

**GILBERT:** That's the best we can do right now.

**GROTH:** So where do you see the future of comics going five to 10 years from now? Do you see those who we can comfortably call "us" still struggling to produce the kind of comics we are, or do you see a breakthrough?

**GILBERT:** It could go either way.

**JAIME:** When our comic gets a lot of press, maybe not a lot of readers, but a lot of good press, you think people are opening up. But this could just be some big gimmick and it could all fall apart and we'll have to do something else. But I try not to think about it. I'm living for the next day on this comic. Hopefully, I can do it forever, but tomorrow I may be crushed.

**GROTH:** It seems from my point of view that every time there's something that can be called a breakthrough — I think *Maus* could legitimately be called a breakthrough — it hasn't had that substantial an effect. It was almost a fluke. If *Maus*, for example, didn't have the theme of the Holocaust it might not have been a breakthrough, if *Batman* didn't have the gimmick of DC's character, it wouldn't have been a breakthrough. So these breakthroughs are not the breakthroughs we thought. Even though there's a "graphic novel" trend now — I use the term loosely — what happens is that the breach is filled with all kinds of garbage. So we're back to square one struggling against this huge tide of mediocre product that manufacturers crank out to fill up a perceived need.

**GILBERT:** If you're asking if I see myself in the same position 10 years from now ... if I got to do it, I got to do it. I don't see myself quitting.

**JAIME:** It's been going good for me. I'm really comfortable so far.

**GROTH:** When you say it's been comfortable what do you mean?

**JAIME:** Maybe comfortable's not the word. I've worked at it so long that I can't quit. If I couldn't do what I'm doing I wouldn't be cartooning at all.

**GILBERT:** Some people ask, "Is *Love and Rockets* a stepping stone to something else?" And I like to think that the "Heartbreak Soup" stories are what I've aspired to all my life. There's no end to what I can do with "Heartbreak Soup." I don't need to do "a more meaningful comic" — I can't get more meaningful. This is it.

**GROTH:** How do you feel about merchandizing? You have control over how your work is presented.

**GILBERT:** We like to keep it at some kind of minimum. But if we didn't do T-shirts and posters, somebody else would. We learned that through the rock 'n' roll, that if the band doesn't put out a T-shirt, there'll be thousands of bootlegs.

**JAIME:** Speaking of rock 'n' roll, there's a band ...

**GROTH:** You might as well go on the record. How do you feel about the band Love and Rockets?

**GILBERT:** Well, I'm not too crazy about it, because Jaime and I are musicians and we wanted to call ourselves *Love and Rockets*. After all, we came up with the name ...

**GROTH:** Have you guys been intimidated by the press and applause you've been getting?

**JAIME:** If they like it or don't like it I'm going to do it anyway. I used to look at the good reviews and say, "They're right, they're right." And look at the bad reviews and say, "They're full of shit." Now I can't just look at one side because I have to look at the other. There are enough people to support us.

**GROTH:** God bless them.

**GILBERT:** We love you all. Seriously. ∎

*Tonantzín dreams of fame in "An American in Palomar"(1985), reprinted in* Heartbreak Soup.

It was Oscar season in Hollywood, the weirdest of times in the weirdest of cities. The hotel in which I was staying had become the hotel of choice of a number of minor English celebrities, out there for the awards, which meant that while I sat in the hotel courtyard with Jaime and Gilbert Hernandez, having lunch mid-interview, our floor show was what appeared to be the final sad disintegration of the marriage of a minor British pop star and his minor British television personality wife, at the table next door. I was there because Gary Groth had called me several months before and asked me if I'd be interested in interviewing Los Bros. for the *Journal.* They had already been interviewed once, extensively in *TCJ* #126 by Gary, Thom Powers and Robert Fiore and he felt that he wanted a fresh point of view. He knew I interviewed them in front of an audience at a U.K. comic convention in 1988, and knew I was (I make no bones about it) a fan of the brothers' work. We'd met since at conventions, said our hellos, but were not by any stretch of the imagination friends. I hadn't done an interview for print for many years, and did not have the time; but there were questions I wanted to ask Jaime and Gilbert, both as a *Love and Rockets* reader and as someone who makes things up for a living. So I had agreed, and I had arrived in Los Angeles hoping that Jaime would be less taciturn than he had been on the United Kingdom Comic Art Convention stage in 1988. When the interview began we were all of us a little nervous, and a little unsure of what to expect. In the end, our only regret was that we didn't have more time. What follows careens from interview to conversation, and from art to career.

—NEIL GAIMAN, 1995

*Ed. Note: Some of the more dated sections of this interview have been excised in this reprint; digital archives are available to subscribers at www.tcj.com. Available back issues can be found at www.fantagraphics.com.*

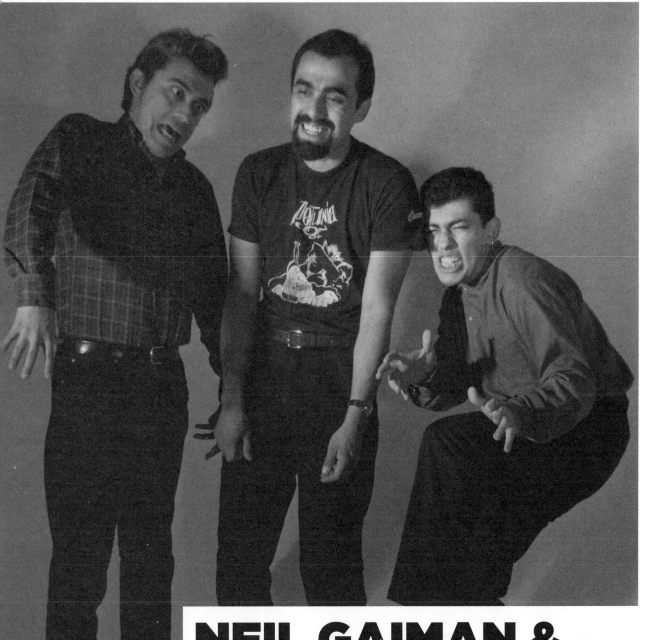

# NEIL GAIMAN & THE BROTHERS

From *The Comics Journal* #178 (July 1995)

**NEIL GAIMAN:** So what was your reaction when Gary said, "I'm thinking of having Neil do the interview?"

**GILBERT HERNANDEZ:** We said, "We're going to sell a lot of copies!" [*Gaiman laughs.*] No really, that was our first reaction! Because things are going well for you.

**JAIME HERNANDEZ:** Also it didn't hit me for a long time but Gary can't interview us anymore.

**GAIMAN:** That was why he came to me. He said, "Look, I can't do it again." He knows that I'm a fan; he knows I did the famous awkward UKCAC interview with you guys. ... And also there's a level on which, at least this way it's not necessarily seen as being incestuous.

**GILBERT:** Well, Gary can't do it again and Ezra Pound is dead, so there was Neil Gaiman. [*Laughter.*]

**GAIMAN:** You mean you really want Ezra Pound? Wonderful poet, but very strange.

**JAIME:** It is "Gaiman," isn't it? (Gay-mən)

**GAIMAN:** Yes, it's Gaiman.

**JAIME:** We've heard "Guy-mon ..."

**GAIMAN:** I hear all sorts of things.

**JAIME:** All my life I've been Jamey, Himey, Hamey ...

**GILBERT:** I don't think Gary pronounces your name right still.

**JAIME:** And he *did* the first years I met him ... Mr. Growth! [*Laughter.*]

**GAIMAN:** Yeah, somebody should do a best-selling title, "Pronunciation Guide: How to say 'Gilbert' right."

**GILBERT:** I had an easy out because my name is actually Gilberto (Heel-bear′-toe), which sounds a lot nicer than Gilbert, but it got me through.

**JAIME:** You had it a lot easier in elementary school; I had the hard part.

**GAIMAN:** Did you tend to become "James" for a while?

**JAIME:** I was James for a year, and I look back at that and hope no one noticed! [*Laughs.*] It's kind of the selling out, being the white boy when you're not, and where I come from that's kind of a no-no.

**GAIMAN:** Last time I interviewed you guys was on-stage at the UKCAC. I remember you weren't talking.

**JAIME:** It was jet lag and culture shock because we hadn't had such a warm reception in the States as

> *Gilbert provides non-Spanish-speaking readers a pronunciation guide for his characters' names; from "Heartbreak Soup" (1983) reprinted in* Heartbreak Soup.

CARMEN – CAR′MEN / GATO – GAH′TOE / AUGUSTIN′– AW GOOSE TEEN′ / LUCIA – LOU SEE′UH / PIPO – PEE′POE / CHELO – CHEH′LOW / GORDO – GORE′THOUGH

we had there. Simple as that. We filled an auditorium, and we had never seen that before.

**GAIMAN:** You were stars. I didn't realize or understand that wasn't the case out here. Yes, of course you filled an auditorium, you were the Hernandezes, this was *Love and Rockets*. Did you never get that reaction out here?

**GILBERT:** Not on a large scale like that.

**JAIME:** It just seemed like here all our fans were too "cool" to do that kind of thing. They don't come to get their books signed because "that's so geeky," that kind of thing. I'm not saying all of our fans but ... They don't like crowds, so they don't want to come where we're going to be mobbed — but then they don't know that five people came.

**GILBERT:** Another thing might be that they don't feel they have to pay to get our autograph or to hear us speak. They can go to a book signing at a comic-book store. Our fans are intelligent and independent.

**GAIMAN:** The recording will miss the facial expressions. [*Laughter.*] I wonder if to some extent that part of it, in England, *Love and Rockets* is simply perceived as being an American thing. It's an American comic. It's hipper because it's good, but it's not hip in that strange sense of, "I've discovered something small and hip and I cannot let the rest of the world discover it, or even admit that I like it because if other people find out, then I'm going to have to stop liking it."

**GILBERT:** Also in the States, there are just so many distractions. Everybody's got their interests elsewhere. It seems, as far as I can tell, that most things that do catch on in a big way are things that make a lot of money. And God bless the college student, because the college student is the one who creates the alternative music scene, the alternative comic-book scene, because they're always hungry for alternative entertainment. And the rest of America could give a hoot. They're just plugged into all the various big things out there: *big* Hollywood movies, *big* MTV bands, *big* video games, whatever is big and makes a lot of money and makes a big stink, at least superficially.

**GAIMAN:** They seem much more impressed over here by success. The other thing that is weird about success is it doesn't necessarily seem to have any correlation to what you do. It seems to have a correlation to simply how many people know your name or your face.

**JAIME:** Yeah, and they won't speak up unless the person next to them goes, "Oh, *you* do *Love and Rockets*?" Then they light up and say, "Oh! Great!" They don't know what the hell you're talking about —

**GILBERT:** — But they want to be in there, in the know.

## TIMES HAVE CHANGED

**GAIMAN:** What is the readership right now with *Love and Rockets*? Not sales necessarily, but ...

**GILBERT:** You probably know as much as we do.

**JAIME:** From the mail that we get, that's dwindled quite considerably. I think a lot of the readers just don't know what to make of *Love and Rockets* anymore. I think the old readers are still there but I think times have changed, the book has changed, we've changed, the readers have grown.

**GAIMAN:** The point at which I started having problems with *Love and Rockets* was that period during which you guys were doing "Poison River," "Wigwam Bam," "*Love and Rockets*" ... It was coming out very infrequently, so that when a *Love and Rockets* would come out, it would be an event. I would take it home, I would read it, I'd get three pages in and suddenly think, "Who are these people and what are they doing?" [*Laughter.*] It was like being handed three chapters of three different novels. [*Laughter.*] It was just far enough away for you to forget everything that had happened.

**GILBERT:** Yeah, those were the days of madness. That was total madness, but —

**JAIME:** We decided to both be mad at the same time.

**GILBERT:** Yes, we were both tearing our hair out. ... But the goal was, for me at least, to create the most dense graphic novel I could. OK, not necessarily dense, but complex, the kitchen sink, everything I possibly had going on in my head, to be put into an epic about Luba's life.

**GAIMAN:** I suppose this is part of the core of what I want to chew around a lot in this interview, which is not exactly art versus commerce, and it's not exactly accessibility versus art-house. But it's how do you do it? How does one strike a balance? "Poison River" is a remarkable achievement. I was impressed looking at *Love and Rockets* [X], what an achievement that was. It really worked, except it was hell on the readers. It was hell on the people who were buying the periodical, which would eventually be collected into something that would be a very, very easy and fascinating read.

**JAIME:** Yeah, "Wigwam Bam" was the first time I used a long-term frame of mind, where it was going to be collected as a complete book. I used to always just go issue by issue and then let it build itself. But this one, I actually had a long-term plan in mind, it just so happened that Gilbert was doing the same thing, so there wasn't that balance where you could read one half and then take a deep breath and then get to the other half.

**GAIMAN:** I remember the first of the short stories after *Wigwam Bam* was done, the one of the bus

station: I read it, and it was complete elation. It was a lovely feeling. Something began and ended. It's weird because one of the things we're doing is selling serial entertainment, selling serial fiction. It's the Dickens thing. And we don't plan it all out before we start. We start knowing sort of what we're doing and roughly where it's going and some of the characters and a few of the high spots, and maybe more than the reader knows. Then you go and see where it takes you. The last *Sandman* story has now taken 16 or 17 months to tell, over 13 issues.

**GILBERT:** Child's play.

**GAIMAN:** And what is interesting now was watching the readership shift, watching them get very uncomfortable. They were having to hold this stuff in their head. There was stuff that I did that I know is going to work perfectly when it's read as a book. When it's read as a book, they're going to be going, "Fuck! That's the same character! Fuck, how did he do that?" But right now ...

**JAIME:** Roughly how many characters do you have in that story?

**GAIMAN:** Probably somewhere in the region of 30, bopping around. But that's also partly because I went and grabbed all of the characters who have been wandering around through the seven years of *Sandman*, so everybody pretty much came on, at least for a bit.

Jaime: "Wigwam Bam *was the first time I used a long-term frame of mind, where it was going to be collected as a complete book.*": from "Wigwam Bam" in Perla La Loca. (2007)

CYCLING IS FUN - SHONEN KNIFE

WORLD WRESTLING CLASSIC - RENA TITAÑON AND MITZI KUÑO VS THE ROCK SISTERS

**JAIME:** I was only asking because, [*to Gilbert*] how many did *Poison River* have?

**GILBERT:** I don't know, I lost track after ...

**JAIME:** Because I'm wondering if it depends on how many people you're following in a given chapter.

**GAIMAN:** I think a lot of it depends on the number of people, and a lot of it is the effects that you create at the point at which somebody reads the book. Right now, I'm very rarely writing monthly comics to write a monthly comic. In the middle of the last storyline, I did one issue for them that was pretty much complete in itself, and was full of stuff they like [*Sandman #64*]. It's almost like I was saying, "You've all been very good, here's one you like. Now can we get back to ... ?"

**GILBERT:** Does that bother you at all when you do say, "All right, I want to stop for a minute and do this for the fans," and it turns out well? Does it bother you when it turns out well? Because then you think, "Well then, what am I doing the rest of the time?"

**GAIMAN:** Yes, it always does. There are things I've read in photocopied form before they were ready to go out. There was one story [*Sandman #31*] which is one of the most popular *Sandman* stories I ever wrote, and I read it and I thought, "This is just cheap, it's obvious, it's stupid," and I said, "Can't we just pull this one?" They said, "No! We can't just pull this one!" Then it came out and everybody loved it. But what is weird is now, when I go back and look at it, and I look at the issues surrounding it, and I can't see particularly why I felt that way. That's the other thing ...

**GILBERT:** This has become "the Neil Gaiman interview." [*Chuckling.*] But that's all right!

For some reason it irritates the hell out of us when we do a story they like. What's wrong with us?! [*Laughter.*] One thing that miffs me a little bit is, I think the most response I got in the last five years or so was when I did the biography of Frida Kahlo, the Mexican painter. I didn't write that story; it's based on a true story. And I had a lot of help from Kim Thompson, who helped me put the captions together, the actual writing, because it was really rough.

From *The Sandman #64 (November 1994), reprinted as Part 8 of* The Kindly Ones; *written by Neil Gaiman and drawn by Teddy Kristiansen.*

©2013 DC Comics

So it's actually written by Kim Thompson and myself. Then I just drew it in an abstract style of drawing in two weeks, I just blasted it out ... And it's everybody's favorite story of mine! I almost cut my head off doing *Poison River*, and they say, "Oh, that was hard to read." And that's it.

**GAIMAN:** Yes, that is unfair and it's a bitch. But the problem with *Poison River*, as a periodical, it was hard to read.

**GILBERT:** Yeah.

**JAIME:** Sure.

**GAIMAN:** As a book —

**GILBERT:** — It's even harder to read, as I understand. [*Laughs.*]

**GAIMAN:** I didn't think so. I thought it was magnificent as a book.

**GILBERT:** The collection's also got extra pages, so it's smoothed over a little bit.

**GAIMAN:** Did you change [*Love and Rockets*] *X*?

**GILBERT:** I added a few panels to that too, just a few.

**GAIMAN:** Why did you pick the format change? I was interested in the different rhythm of it, from a nine-panel grid rhythm, to this six-panel grid rhythm. The whole flow of the thing changed.

**GILBERT:** Yeah. I don't know. That was actually Fantagraphics' idea. They were looking for a different package, a different format, a rock 'n' rolly thing, because this was a direct "rock 'n' roll story." I believe they were looking at it that way. And it worked out. It is unusual. Hell if you can fit it on any bookshelf, but ... It's a little bit like *Big Numbers*, it's like, "What do I do with this thing?" [*Laughs.*] I'm referring to the packaging now, not the material. But that was their idea, and I think it turned out well. I'm very happy with the way it turned out.

**GAIMAN:** I thought it turned out very well, but it did have a completely different rhythm, and it had a different rhythm on the page. It's like when I was a little kid discovering Jules Feiffer cartoons. I got them in those collections, which had two panels to a page. It would take two or three pages to read the Jules Feiffer cartoon. I've never been able to get used to them as these little things covering one square box.

## WOO THE FANS

**GAIMAN:** So describe the relationship then with your fans. Because you're doing this stuff to piss them off — except you're not doing it to piss them off.

**GILBERT:** We're trying to piss off our parents, but we're trying to woo the fans. [*Laughs.*] No, too much pop psychology going around in my head. But I think we're still trying to bring them along with us on this bumpy journey, but you know, we've had a few casualties on the way and they've gone to other books. I noticed, there's the new book by Adrian Tomine called *Optic Nerve*, and I understand that the popularity of it is just due to the fact that it's a lot easier to read, and it's a lot more direct, the drawings are simple, there's not a lot of continuity, all the stuff that's driving readers of *Love and Rockets* and other books crazy.

**GAIMAN:** But if you guys had had to do 13 years of seven-page stories, funky little Hopey and Maggie

*"Love and Rockets X" (1989-1993) was first published in a nine-panel grid, as per this Gilbert page (top) from* Love and Rockets *Vol. I #36 (November 1991). Fantagraphics reformatted it into six-panel grids in the 1993 collection.*

stories in which they were being cute, you'd be mad by now.

**GILBERT:** Yeah, and rich and successful. [*Laughter.*] Yeah, the book grew as we grew and with *Poison River*, that period was a period of madness. It was crazy. I don't regret it. Actually, my only problem with *Poison River* is that it's too short. It actually should be novel length, in the true sense. It's just too short for what's going on.

**JAIME:** And after the madness of *Poison River* and *Wigwam Bam*, I felt like I was allowed to do silly little six-page Maggie-running-through-her-apartment-in-her-underwear stories, that didn't have this big climax of her life, because she already went through one, for now. And when I start doing those, I start getting itchy to do a get-her-closer-to-God kind of thing. I want to get bigger again, and then after that I just want to have her eating breakfast.

**GAIMAN:** Yeah, it's that weird rhythm thing.

**JAIME:** And I'm hoping the readers follow that; I hope they're with me as I'm doing that. I hope they're not in the mood for silly little stories when I'm doing *Wigwam Bam*, and then they're in the mood for epics when I'm not. I'm just hoping that they're going with the rhythm.

**GAIMAN:** I'd say there are two different kinds of characters: the ones who carry on living in your head while you're not writing or thinking about them, the ones you can almost check in on; and the ones who, when they're not on-stage, don't do anything. They sit around having a cigarette waiting for you to call them. They have no lives when they're offstage. Do you find that at all?

**JAIME:** Yeah, but those are the kind of people that I've always known, the people who I can go and have a beer with and then not see them for a year, and then I see them again and they're the same. And that's always a pleasant thing for me. It's not that I *expect* it from them, but there are just some people I know who I don't have to see for three years, and I'll see them again and we're starting where we left off our last joke, you know? And that's the way I treat some of my characters. A lot of times those characters become favorites, and then I get this guilt feeling like, "Well maybe I should give them more character," but then I slap myself in the face and remember, "No, they like them in the first place because they are so simple and friendly."

**GAIMAN:** Gilbert, how about you with your characters? You tend to operate on a much larger time frame.

**GILBERT:** Well, back to *Poison River*, I think what I was doing there was trying to give everybody their little bit, and when you have 75 characters, well, let's not have *everybody* have their little bit! But it was a challenge for me — and obviously for the readers. But I'm learning now to just let some characters *be*. And like Jaime says, a lot of those times those are the characters readers really want to see more of. But they have to stop and think, "Well, the reason I *do* like them is because there isn't a lot of them in the story." I'm still getting requests for Errata Stigmata. Now let me explain something to the readers out there: I don't do Errata Stigmata not because I don't like the character, it's just that I have absolutely nothing to say about the character. I like drawing her, I like sticking her in a side gag maybe, but I have absolutely nothing to say with that particular character. But the readers constantly ask: "Where is Errata Stigmata? I want to see Errata Stigmata!" And I guess that's OK. It's the life of a cartoonist. You're going to have to hear that sort of thing.

*Errata Stigmata, an early fan favorite, starred in Gilbert and Mario's "Tears from Heaven" (1985), reprinted in* Amor y Cohetes.

**GAIMAN:** This is the second time in the last 24 hours that you referred to yourself as a "cartoonist." Do you consider yourself a cartoonist? Or as a writer? Or as a writer-artist?

**GILBERT:** Isn't a writer-artist a cartoonist?

**GAIMAN:** I don't know. I'm asking.

**GILBERT:** That's what I suspect it is. A cartoonist is Charles Schulz, somebody who writes — well, I don't know if he's been writing *Peanuts* for the last 20 years, let's hope not! [*Laughs.*]

**GAIMAN:** I remember when it was good ...

**GILBERT:** Up until the mid-'70s. It was very good.

**JAIME:** I use the word "cartoonist" because it covers it all. And I basically cover it all. I do everything: I ink the borders, everything, myself. Sometimes I wish I didn't have to, but ... oh, poor me.

**GILBERT:** And you know how the words "cartoon" and "cartoonist" don't really apply to what we're doing nowadays, the modern —

**GAIMAN:** Go and see some Leonardo da Vinci cartoons.

**GILBERT:** Yeah. But at the same time I'm not embarrassed by "cartoonist."

**JAIME:** Sure. If Charles Schulz can call himself a cartoonist, I think nobody should be ashamed to call themselves a cartoonist.

## SOMETHING LASTING

**GAIMAN:** So at what point did you realize that, for want of a better word, you were in it for the "long haul"?

**GILBERT:** From the very beginning. I wanted something that lasted. I wasn't exactly sure what I was going to be doing that was going to last, but I knew I wanted something lasting.

**GAIMAN:** The "BEM," the "Radio Zero" stuff, that has a wonderful quality, it's like somebody going crazy in the basement of junk culture. And it's shot like a Russ Meyer film, and paced a lot like a Russ Meyer film. [*Chuckles.*] But as soon as you got into "Heartbreak Soup," it seemed to be much more

going in for the long haul.

**GILBERT:** With "Heartbreak Soup", I had an agenda of sorts. I'm trying to get non-Latinos, for lack of a better word, to identify with Latinos as human beings. Simple as that. I think I've felt that since I was a kid.

**GAIMAN:** Which I think may be, as a footnote, one reason why it might be easier for English, European, non-American readers to get on with *Love and Rockets* insofar as there are definitely certain American agendas and things of race that aren't over there. We have different problems. The French would have the problems with the Algerians coming in and so on. But there is a different set of problems, and it's definitely not ... I would never think of you as "Latino creators." I'd think of you as Americans.

**GILBERT:** Yeah, that's probably, like you said, the reason why Europeans would look at it differently. Right now in America, it's a black and white country. Everybody else is in the middle and has to wait their turn. It's great that the blacks have made such powerful inroads into film in the last 10 years, because they made a big stink about it. They insisted on being there. Well, right now the Asians and Latinos are gearing up in the wings, and we hope to be involved in making more of a dent in the near future as far as that goes. But right now, America is black and white.

**JAIME:** It's a black and white thang.

**GAIMAN:** It seems to be one of the texts of *Love and Rockets*, what you're both doing. Race runs through very, very solidly, as a motivating force, as a dividing force, as a uniting force. There are specific things one can look at: the gulf between people, the way people can reach out and try and touch other people, the fallacies and frailties of people in love and the cost of love and so forth. But race is definitely in there as one of the ingredients in the mix, continually.

**JAIME:** Well, race has been an issue with us since we were born. That's just a thing that's in you if you're not white here.

**GILBERT:** You're constantly reminded that you're not white in this country — by the system or

*One of the many instances in which Jaime explores racial issues: "Wigwam Bam" (1990) is reprinted in* Perla La Loca.

whatever, I'm not saying by individuals, but in television and advertising, that sort of thing. Whites are normal and then there's everybody else.

**GAIMAN:** Yes, I suppose so, but ... I would not regard you guys as not white.

**GILBERT:** Like I said, on an individual basis it's not like that, at least not often. In general it's just a constant barrage of images and role models, etc.

**GAIMAN:** I've noticed it with the English, which is something I never thought I'd notice, but coming out here, if there's an English character on a sitcom, you know everything you need to know about them:

You know they're going to be snobbish, untrustworthy and will run off with somebody's money in the end. [*Laughter.*] You'll have English bad guys in movies, a good action movie will have a good English crazy villain.

**GILBERT:** But he'd be very smooth, very suave.

**JAIME:** And even if there were an English character in an American movie, and they were the good guy, you would still know that guy was English. This movie would just tell you: "This guy is English! Look at him! Look at the way he talks! Look at the way he acts!"

And that's kind of the thing with us growing up. Like he said, we were just constantly reminded that we are not the ones running the place.

89

*Gilbert's take on race: from* Love and Rockets X *reprinted in* Beyond Palomar. *(2007)*

**GAIMAN:** In *Love and Rockets X*, the moment that I really found went into my head and changed something (one of those moments which good fiction ought to do a lot, and happens less and less as you get older), was running into Riri and Maricela in L.A., and watching them speak very, very bad English, and knowing that these were characters who were totally fluent. ... That was a fascinating little moment for me. It was a genuine moment of going, "No, of course they're not stupid! I know these people and they are not stupid people! They're in the same position I would be if I were in a foreign country and did not speak, picking up the language desperately as I went along."

**GILBERT:** Yeah, we're just hoping the readers are reading a lot of the material, other than just *Love and Rockets X* because we go into *Love and Rockets X* and you get Maricela and Riri, and you get them as these stumbling immigrants to an extent. But if you read *Human Diastrophism*, or the books before that, you know they're not that way.

**GAIMAN:** That's what I mean. There was this moment of horrible recognition: They didn't just appear here to sweep up. These are people with stories, and realizing it would have been easy to just put them into little holes.

**GILBERT:** I was able to go that route in *Love and Rockets X* because I *did* have that background. I probably wouldn't have done the characters that way if they were new characters.

**GAIMAN:** One feels one can take liberties more with characters who have been around a little bit. If the reader knows them enough to know they aren't stereotypes, you can let them act a little like stereotypes because sometimes human beings do that. [*Laughs.*] As a matter of fact, human beings do that quite a lot of the time.

**GILBERT:** Clichés come from the truth.

**GAIMAN:** Yes. But you can't do that if you're just introducing somebody for the first time.

**GILBERT:** Or it's difficult. It's a juggling act.

**GAIMAN:** But if you do that, then you're going to have to open them up later.

**GILBERT:** Yeah, you'll definitely have to go back to them, and if you don't want to do that, you better get it straight the first time.

**GAIMAN:** You two handle dialogue very differently. Gilbert: Something like *Love and Rockets X*, everybody is speaking almost phonetically through it. You're almost transcribing how the sounds sounded, or that I'm getting all the accents right. Whereas it feels like Jaime's approach to dialogue is much more, "This is what they're saying." The tendency to —

**GILBERT:** Well, in my case, I was working off the *Heartbreak Soup* stories where everybody is speaking Spanish. I have to remind my readers now and again that they're speaking Spanish *entirely* in Palomar, and sometimes the reader forgets. I guess that's a good thing that they forget because they're just reading the characters. But since that is the "normal" way of speaking in Palomar, I was paying more attention to the different way people speak.

**JAIME:** Different classes of people.

**GILBERT:** Because *Love and Rockets X* is an extension of *Heartbreak Soup*, whereas Jaime is just always dealing with the same ...

**GAIMAN:** That was the thing — your characters have voices. And they have very, very distinct voices. It would be hard to confuse three or four of your characters. But there's just a directness and an economy to the way you write dialogue.

**GILBERT:** Also it's his lettering too, have you

noticed? You have to read mine with a magnifying glass, and his is very bold and simple to read.

**JAIME:** I guess I just want to make it clear.

## NERVE

**GAIMAN:** When I did the interview with you guys in '88, you were talking at that point about the next few years. It seemed like that was pretty much what turned out to be the last eight years of *Love and Rockets*. Gilbert, you were talking essentially about doing *Poison River* at the time; whereas Jaime, you seemed more unsure about what you were going to do next, as if Gilbert had planned the whole thing, planned a huge, organic entity, and you were quite happily ... "Making it up as you go along" is the wrong thing to say to anybody who's not actually a writer or cartoonist or whatever because they get very upset with you if they think you're making it up as you go along.

**JAIME:** That's just the difference in the way we've always worked. Gilbert's always had a set plan a lot

*Gilbert revealed Tonantzín's fate in "Human Diastrophism" (1987), reprinted in the volume of the same title.*

In "Human Diastrophism" (1987), reprinted in the eponymous volume, Gilbert explores the relationship between violence and art.

farther on than mine. I just basically know how my characters act and how they're going to act later, if they're going to go through a change as they get older. But I don't know where they're headed. It's kind of like the characters write themselves.

**GILBERT:** Ahh, more pop psychology from Gilbert: Characters don't write themselves. We write them. Jaime works more from his unconscious, and I'm conscious of my plan. Jaime's got a plan; it's just not on the surface. It comes out as he's working. It's simply a different rate of appearing in his head.

**GAIMAN:** I will do things when I'm writing sometimes that I will not let myself know that I'm doing — which can be a bit of both stuff that you've planned out, and other stuff that ... It's like you don't let yourself know you're going to kill this character later on. Then when you go back, it was completely obvious that you'd set everything up; everything's there, and it was the only possible way it could have gone. But you didn't know that it was happening that way when you were doing it.

**GILBERT:** The perfect example for me would be in "Human Diastrophism," which is reprinted in *Blood of Palomar*, is I didn't know Tonantzín was going to die. Well of course I did! I knew all along — but I didn't know. It was clouded, let's say.

**GAIMAN:** That was actually an example I was

going to give you. That had both qualities: the quality of surprise, and the quality of inevitability — it was the only thing that *could* have happened, except that when it happened it was like, "What?"

**GILBERT:** [*Laughs.*] Yeah. Obviously that was my plan. It goes all the way back to "Duck Feet," which was started in *Love and Rockets* #17, and then "Human Diastrophism" ended in #26, I believe, and when you read it from #17 to #26, it's there. It's clear that's where Tonantzín is going; it's buried in my unconscious, and it comes out the way the reader will see it. That can be tricky though; that can screw you up. It's like you're driving and you go by three green lights, but you don't know how you got there: Uh-oh. It's sort of the same thing. The problem with that is sometimes you just go over the same route and you don't know you're doing that.

**GAIMAN:** The flip side of that also is writer's block, and quite possibly artist's block. The flip side of it is just the, "What am I doing here?" The getting up in the morning and not knowing what the characters will say next. Do you go through those spells of, you got up to something, everything was going fine, you get up the next morning ... and there's nobody there?

**JAIME:** Sure.

**GAIMAN:** And then suddenly something will happen a half an hour later, or a day later, or three or four weeks later, and they'll be there and start talking again.

**JAIME:** That's the scary part about the way I work,

the as-it-goes-along kind of thing. No real set plans. There have been a couple of times — and I've got it as we speak, right now — where I finished an issue and everything is going smoothly, and this issue I have absolutely no idea where it's going. It's kind of scary. It'll come to me while I'm dropping off to sleep — maybe even tonight. But those in-betweens are really scary.

**GAIMAN:** They are the scariest moments, because you really don't know if it's going to come back. You assume it will, and also if you've been doing it long enough and you've gone through enough of them, you sort of figure, yeah, you go over it in your head before you go to sleep and maybe you'll get it, or maybe you'll wake up the next morning and you'll get it in that period between sleep and waking. But you don't know. There's no certainty.

**GILBERT:** It's just not letting yourself lose your nerve. What happens to a lot of artists and writers and such is, somebody writes a great book in 1953, and you find out this great writer is still alive, but he hasn't written anything since, and they have all these excuses why they don't write, but it's really that they lost their nerve. What's kind of good about serializing the comic books is that we don't give ourselves enough time to lose our nerve.

**GAIMAN:** Part of it is the time, and part of it is the deadline. The fact that we have somebody standing there saying, "Come on, where's the next chapter? Come on."

**GILBERT:** The fact that I have to pay bills with *Love and Rockets* is also a reason to keep me going.

**GAIMAN:** I despair continually at artists who are terrific, they are really good, and they won't do anything because everything has to be perfect. And they'll never get to perfection, so they'll spend a week on a drawing and it isn't perfect, so nobody will ever see it. And they'll spend a year and a half on a 10-page comic, and maybe they will let it get printed, but it wasn't a year and a half's worth of work.

**GILBERT:** But then again you do an abstract painting and someone asks you, "How long did it take you to do that?" The answer? "All my life." But you can't live that way. [*Laughs.*] You can't survive that way, by

putting something out once a year. But also I discovered with myself, and I might be projecting here but, when an artist searches for that perfection in writing or drawing, they're just simply not admitting their great, utter fear. And they can show us the smoothest surface of being the together, the with-it guy or woman, but inside they're trembling in their boots. It's getting over the fear. You have nothing to fear but fear itself. And you can quote me on that. [*Laughter.*]

## COMMERCE

**GAIMAN:** Let's talk about commerce. Right now the comics market, which has never been anything that anybody could remotely describe as "sane" — for as long as I've known it, it's never been anything remotely sane — is now completely bugfuck. The strange contortions of the market, people got driven away in droves —

**GILBERT:** We're talking about commerce.

**JAIME:** I just don't know if the market makes much of a difference with our comic. As far as competing with what's hot and what's slick and what's out there in the big comics world, we're still in the little comics world.

**GAIMAN:** No, you're not competing with that stuff. You may be competing for dollars in the shops, it's the shops buying, but not the actual coming in and buying it. Particularly, we're talking about women readers. People say, "Oh, women just come in, they buy a copy of *Sandman*, they buy their copy of *Love and Rockets*, and they go away."

**JAIME:** [*Clapping.*] Bravo! Bravo! As it should be. [*Laughs.*]

**GAIMAN:** It seems to be how it works. They come in, buy that, and go out.

**GILBERT:** Well, there's not much for women, as far as I can tell. I look at Image comics, I look at Marvel comics, which look exactly like Image comics, and I admire their insanity in a way, what it must take to draw that way, every day! [*Laughter.*] It's a bit insane and I kind of like that, but a little bit of it goes a very

Speech bubbles in image:
- LISTEN, KID, HALF THE GUYS IN THIS *ALLEY* DID A DEAL WITH A DEVIL AT SOME POINT.
- *THEIR* DEVIL GAVE THEM POWER AND WEALTH AND LOVE AND FAME, *EVERYTHING* THEY'D EVER WANT. THEN HE COLLECTED, AND THEY HAVE TO BE BUMS IN ALLEYWAYS FOR THE NEXT HOW-EVER LONG.
- *LOOK,* SONNY. THERE'S A *LOT* YOU DON'T UNDERSTAND ABOUT WHAT'S BEEN HAPPENING TO YOU...

*Spawn #9 (March 1999) was written by Gaiman and drawn by Todd McFarlane.*

long way, and I don't see the appeal for any normal person.

**GAIMAN:** I wrote an Image comic because my son Mikey, who's 11, is a *Spawn* fan. He is a *Spawn* fan like I was a ... I don't think there was anything I was that crazy about. He found the comics, he took them all up to his room, he's got all the toys and he's been on me for years to write something he'd like. So I thought, "I can do this ..." and I wrote *each issue* in a day — which, normally, if I managed a page of *Sandman* in a day I'm kind of proud of myself.

**GILBERT:** Yeah, sure.

**GAIMAN:** That was the thing that terrified me; it was so nightmarishly easy. It was something you could do —

**JAIME:** But the nightmare is a little calmed when you get paid for three years of work!

**GAIMAN:** But I didn't mind doing it as a sort of weird little holiday thing, like, you could probably go back and do a *Birdland* thing in a day. You could do one of those and say, "That was fun!" and then go back to doing real stuff. But the idea of having to do that every day — I mean, could you imagine doing *Birdland* every day forever?

**GILBERT:** Ohhh ... *Birdland* was very difficult. I don't think I'd ever do it again.

**JAIME:** The amazing thing is the guys who are doing it love it. They absolutely adore it; they wouldn't do it any other way. Superhero comics, that is.

**GILBERT:** It's all they know, too. That's why their passions are funneled into these horribly grotesque superhero comics.

**GAIMAN:** But they love it! They really do! They have a wonderful time doing it. They want to draw big things hitting each other and women with ...

these *strange* proportions. It's not even the big breasts, it's just the *strange* ...

**JAIME:** And like Gilbert said, I kind of admire the insanity behind it.

**GILBERT:** The obsessiveness of it.

**JAIME:** I would *love* to walk into a comic-book store and buy *everything* on the rack and enjoy it.

**GILBERT:** "Water, water, everywhere, and not a drop to drink."

**GAIMAN:** I find now that I'm getting ... I don't know if it's grumpier, but when I pick up the pile of comics, I do it with less enthusiasm.

**GILBERT:** Oh, sure.

**GAIMAN:** Even the ones I'm quite looking forward to seeing what so-and-so is doing: Oh, good, a new *Hate* is out. But it can sit on the table for two days before I finally get around to reading it.

**JAIME:** Yeah, it's not that old, sitting on a Sunday morning, reading your stack of comics, and having the best time of your life.

**GAIMAN:** Exactly. And I remember the immediacy, even five years ago. If I bought comics, it was, "They're in my bag! Am I going to get onto a train or a bus? And when I get home I'm going to *read my comics!*"

**GILBERT:** We're just old. [*Laughter.*] Obviously the kids are loving it, so ... Even though the comics we grew up with are better than theirs!

**GAIMAN:** I think the magic is as much the magic of being a kid and reading comics, as, yes, a Ditko *Dr. Strange*, a Kirby *Fantastic Four* ... The stuff that was good, you look back at it now and it's still good.

**GILBERT:** Also there was a period of artists — Stan Lee wrote better than any of these new guys. Jack Kirby drew better than them: they were just better artists; they had better training.

**GAIMAN:** They also seemed to have learned to draw; these guys could draw things.

**JAIME:** That's for sure.

**GAIMAN:** One of the things I find odd and strange ... How do you feel when people do you? I see it more with you, Jaime, than I do

with Gilbert, but people who steal the way you'll draw something without trying to steal any of the stuff underneath.

**JAIME:** The way I see it is that it's like when I was 10 years old and I wanted to draw like Jack Kirby, but *knowing* I couldn't. I'd come to that realization. Because at first I would just *do* it, I'd try to draw Kirby's machinery, and then when I came to the realization that I couldn't, there was a frustration that I couldn't be that. And I see sometimes these artists who, I don't know about all of them, but they really love the stuff so much, they wish they did it. Then they try it and they do it, and maybe it's a good copy, or maybe it's a bad copy ...

**GAIMAN:** Going back to the very first couple of issues of *Love and Rockets*, one can watch you two assimilating influences all over the place. You look through, and all of a sudden there's a Wally Wood panel. Here's a Steve Ditko panel. There's something that's lit like a Kirby panel. There's something that's got a weird, Frazetta-y, classic feel to it.

**GILBERT:** There's a Tony Tallarico woman. [*Laughs.*]

**GAIMAN:** Then both of you went through that and became what you are today; nobody can confuse a panel done by either of you two with anybody else's work. There comes that point when you realize that you have your own voice.

**GILBERT:** I think what Jaime was saying is that he

*Jaime played around with drawing "[Jack] Kirby's machinery." This panel is from "Mechan-X" (1981), reprinted in* Maggie the Mechanic.

*This sequence from Jaime's "Maggie Vs. Maniakk" (1983), reprinted in* Maggie the Mechanic, *is also Kirby-influenced.*

couldn't be Kirby, so he's going to have to settle with being himself — and that always turns out better.

**JAIME:** And I was successful enough to be myself, and people like it.

**GAIMAN:** Yes, I suppose that's what I'm saying, that you did become yourself. The point I think the billions of Image clones and Marvel clones have not figured out, is that all you have to offer that makes you unique, that sets you apart from everybody else, is the stuff that only you can do. So you might as well find out what that is rather than trying to do the stuff that anybody could do, because anybody can do it. You're infinitely replaceable.

**JAIME:** I don't know if many of them care though. Like, let's say, Barry Smith used to draw Kirby badly, and then all of a sudden he decided to draw his own way. And he became him, and people wanted to be him. But I think there aren't that many. There are only a few who can come out of that. I guess that's where talent comes in. [*Laughs.*]

**GILBERT:** It's funny, the alternative cartoonists and alternative comics fans reading this interview are going to be scratching their heads going, "Why are they talking about all these mainstream guys?" Because we *learn* from the old mainstream guys. We

learn from people who could draw. They're learning from other alternative comics guys or whatever, and, like you said, in the first few issues of *Love and Rockets* you saw all our influences. Well there's a *shit-load* in there, there aren't just three guys. There are 12, or 24 people in there. And they were all good artists I like to think.

**GAIMAN:** I think they were, I think you learn from them. Like the stuff Chester Brown does, watching how Chester assimilated all these strange little things and turned it into what Chester does, and what *only* Chester does.

**GILBERT:** Definitely. He's one of a kind. It's all Chester now.

## TIME

**GAIMAN:** I wanted to ask you about the weirdness of the fact that you may have just about reached 1995 by now in your stuff. The weirdness of trying to do a comic that occurs in more or less real time, particularly when you're doing a storyline that takes place over a week or whatever, and takes three or four years to come out.

**JAIME:** Yeah, right now, the issue we just finished —

**GILBERT:** [*Laughs.*] Yeah, that's 1991! The recent past becomes almost alien, and you're not really sure how people dressed or what they were listening to, unless you have a time capsule of some sort — what was I listening to at this time? What shoes were the girls wearing? Because fashion is very important, particularly to women, and they will look at the book and say, "Nobody wore those in that year, in that month." I look at old fashion magazines ...

**GAIMAN:** But that isn't where the stuff on the street was happening, either.

**JAIME:** It's always pretty difficult.

**GILBERT:** The odd thing that I just realized is, if I'm going by any kind of time frame, I suspect Luba's about 40 by now. She seems like she's been 40 for quite a long time [*laughs*], but she just has a war-ravaged face.

**GAIMAN:** Are you setting this all down on paper, or is it all in your head?

**JAIME:** I actually have made myself a chart because I was driving myself crazy. But I've got to admit, everything worked out. Everything fits. There are only a couple of things in the earlier issues that, it's like, "Ohh! Why is she wearing that '50s outfit when it's 1972?" And recently I got a letter from some guy who said, "That *Love and Rockets* chronology that they did for you guys sucks! This is mine: I went through every single issue ... " And it was pretty dead-on. So I must be doing something right. [*Laughter.*]

**GILBERT:** Sometimes I'll do something like have someone listening to a song that didn't come out until a year later, and it really bothers me. [*Laughs.*] I mean, I'm sure the readers don't care.

**JAIME:** Yeah, I feel the same.

**GAIMAN:** Do you ever wind up making a point of not drawing anybody's attention to when things are happening, or how long it's actually taking? Even though you know and you're playing fair? I mean, *Sandman*, in theory, moves in real time, except I'm not actually pointing out to anybody that we've now reached January 1994, because we just had an 18-month storyline that took place over ...

**GILBERT:** Yeah, *Wigwam Bam* happens in a month.

**JAIME:** That's what really threw me off! I had caught up with #30, I believe, and then *Wigwam Bam* just set me back — which took almost two years to complete.

**GILBERT:** Part of the problem, at least in my case, I think more than yours, Jaime, is that if I'm doing 1956 or 1968, or 1975, or 1989, it all looks like the '50s. [*Laughs.*] It's the way I draw! And the way I dress the women. So I have to be more specific about a time frame.

**GAIMAN:** I tend to do it in your stuff just by how old people look, which is a very odd phenomenon, having seen some of these characters go from children to middle-age.

**GILBERT:** Yeah. But then there's a point where a person doesn't really age too much from age 35 to 50.

**GAIMAN:** That's the thing about how long Luba has been 40.

**GILBERT:** Exactly. She's had that face since she was 29. That was my own thing, but I'm sure the reader has difficulty. But when I do stories back in

*Getting period hairstyles right is challenging for Gilbert: from "Poison River" (1988–1994), reprinted in* Beyond Palomar.

the '50s, it looks the same [as any other era]! Even if I'm getting the clothes accurate, because I will research that. But I draw that way anyway.

**GAIMAN:** How much visual research do you actually wind up doing?

**GILBERT:** It depends on if I'm really trying to make clear a certain time without using that caption that says, "Meanwhile in 1948 ... " But sometimes you just can't tell, from 1948 to 1958, even hairstyles. Hairstyle changes are so subtle. As a matter of fact, I just finished an issue of *Love and Rockets* where I had the last story of Luba's mother and part of the story takes place in 1948, but it could be any year. Her haircut is a curly Bettie Page-type haircut. You can't look at it and say, "I know what year this is." So I put a big banner behind her head that says, "1948!" [*Laughs.*] I'm starting to do that now because a lot of readers have difficulty following the stories with when it's a flashback, and when it's not.

**JAIME:** That's why I gave the story, "Spring 1982," that title. So you couldn't possibly think this was now! [*Laughs.*]

This is from Gilbert's Birdland (1990-1994), which was released through Fantagraphics' pornography imprint, Eros.

**GAIMAN:** You both do the unannounced flashback, which can occasionally throw me for about three panels, or occasionally it can slide right past me until something happens and I'll suddenly go, "Hang on!" [*Laughter.*]

**GILBERT:** [Maybe we're being] too subtle for our good.

**GAIMAN:** But are you?

**GILBERT:** I understand it because, for instance, if Kim Thompson is editing, he'll say, "Well, I didn't catch the flashback until the end of the scene," and I'll go back and look at it and try to look at it from a different point of view, and he's right. But I'm right, too. So what's going to make it easier on the reader? I'm really trying to make it easier on the reader; it shouldn't be a battle to read our stuff.

**JAIME:** Shouldn't be a big mystery.

**GAIMAN:** I find that a lot of it has to do with how much work you want to make the reader do for what they're going to get. I don't mind making a reader work hard, but if I'm going to do that, I'd like to make them work hard for something that's actually going to pay them back in some way. Making them work hard to realize that I've just done a flashback, if it wasn't important, that is something I would tend not to do — to take pity on them.

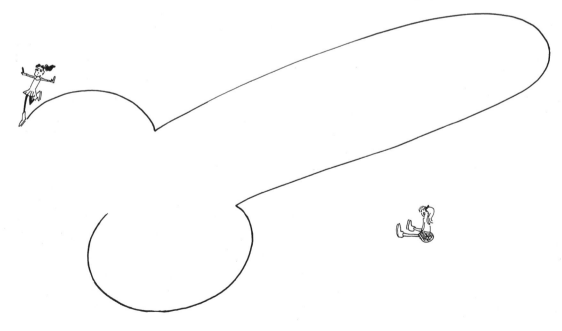

GILBERT: Yeah, why should it be difficult for them to just figure out where the character is?

GAIMAN: Exactly: What country are we in right now?

GILBERT: Yeah, it shouldn't be difficult, and I'm very aware of that now and I'm lightening up on it.

## EROS

GAIMAN: So tell me about *Birdland* and Eros, and what happened there.

GILBERT: *Birdland* came out in the midst of *Poison River*, which was madness and I was going crazy just dealing with the same characters and going through difficult creative spots in the story, because I felt I was locked into this part of the story that was difficult to have fun with. It was more of a duty than actually having fun with it. So I just needed some fun. I needed to jump off a building and land and not get hurt — brains dashed on the sidewalk and then I pick up my brains and walk home, that sort of thing. And it was the climate of the country, it was when George [H.W.] Bush was still president, and sex was once again evil — the old truism: You can stab a tit but you can't show someone kissing one. It was that sort of climate, and I said, "Let's have a go at it." A wild sex romp without any violence.

JAIME: Without anybody getting hurt.

GILBERT: Other than emotionally, which can never be avoided. But you can certainly avoid physical violence. And that was it: Just a romp, just to go wild, just to exorcise demons, whatever.

GAIMAN: I don't think I was so disappointed by *Birdland* but I was really deeply disappointed by Eros. I had had this wonderful vision of this bright, new dawn of pornographic comics in which there would be marvelous pornographic comics — and then discovering that no, it was *Birdland*, and *Birdland* was fun, and that was about it. *The Erotic Art of Frank Thorne*? [*Laughter.*]

GILBERT: Actually *Birdland* was a bit of a disappointment even to me in the way that, basically it was a sitcom with tits. And I realized that was because I didn't really care about what was going on. I liked the sex and I liked the jokes, and everybody having fun, and the women being on the top, all that's important to me. But in the end, it didn't add up to much other than just a romp. Although I had great fun with it, I still think the sex in *Love and Rockets* is much more exciting.

GAIMAN: I think partly that's because the sex in *Love and Rockets* happens to people rather than cartoons.

GILBERT: That's why I don't have much of a desire to go back to doing erotic comics other than if I have to pay some bills or something — *or* if I have to exorcise more sexual demons. It was fun, but it wasn't satisfying in the way *Love and Rockets* is because I care about everything that's going on in *Love and Rockets* — maybe too much sometimes.

GAIMAN: The sex in *Love and Rockets* — I think you guys do amazing sex.

GILBERT: I'm never sure if it's ever erotic though.

GAIMAN: I don't think it is, but I don't think that real sex ... The thing I like about your sex is it's very matter-of-fact, it's erotic insofar as you both draw wonderful women and pretty good blokes [*laughter*], and it looks like real people having sex. But it's part of the whole thing.

GILBERT: Yeah, and that's what was missing from *Birdland*. It was fun, but where's the real thing?

GAIMAN: When I was 13 or 14, going through that period of hormones, I had just discovered the whole concept of sex, and I assumed that *all* adults, at any point where I could not see them, were *obviously* having sex. Because what else would anybody want to do?

GILBERT: Because they can!

GAIMAN: Yes — wow! [*Laughter.*] I sometimes think that is the parallel universe that all pornography takes place in. It's this wonderful parallel universe in which if any man and woman are together, and if the maid comes in saying, "I have to clean the room," why, of course the three of them are going to have a sex romp! Because it's taking place in this parallel universe!

**JAIME:** Hear, hear!

**GAIMAN:** But it bears no relationship to this world. *Birdland* felt like it took place in that parallel universe.

**JAIME:** That's the approach you took, though. You set it up as a whole different world.

**GILBERT:** A different world where there's no AIDS, there's no rubbers.

**GAIMAN:** It's science fiction.

**GILBERT:** Exactly.

**GAIMAN:** I think Kurt Vonnegut said somewhere that the thing that science fiction and pornography have in common is they're both visions of an impossibly hospitable world. [*Laughter.*] And *Birdland* was set in that hospitable world. Sex obviously wasn't going to result in pregnancy or disease.

**GILBERT:** Since so much is left out of it, like I said, I don't have any strong desire to go back to it. I may do a thing here or there, but ... To tell you the truth, issues #2 and #3 of *Birdland*, I worked just as hard as I've ever done just writing that dialogue, writing funny things for them to say and clever incidents to happen. But in the end it was like coming out of an orgy, I suppose: You're exhausted, but empty. I imagine that's what it's like; I wouldn't know. Or when people live that lifestyle, people in the porn industry, say, it always turns out that the women are sad and the men are hiding their sadness so they get into drugs, blah, blah ... There's this void that is being filled with this constant sex.

**GAIMAN:** When I was 23 and I was doing a lot of interviews for English magazines, the men's magazines, I was hired as assistant editor of one of the tit magazines for a week, filling in for a guy who was on holiday. My job was to type up the readers' letters, fix the grammar and spelling and change it from scrawly handwriting to [readable], and caption the models. I quit after three or four days. I realized I was deeply, darkly, going off sex. Not just going off sex, but I was starting to hope that human beings would start reproducing by splitting down the middle. I didn't want anything to do with this stuff! [*Laughter.*] I thought, if I carried on with this, I would go crazy. So I stopped, just from self-protection.

**GILBERT:** Apparently that's one of the complaints strippers have, even if they're successful and conditions are good. They still get that feeling of constantly having men want you, constantly it's sex, sex, sex, and it's the last thing they want to think of when they get home — unless the woman is a little unstable and needs that constant superficial attention.

**GAIMAN:** Do you get accusations of sexism or exploitation?

**JAIME:** For *Love and Rockets*?

**GAIMAN:** Yes.

**JAIME:** There have been a few odd ones now and then. They'll call a particular situation a rape: "Yeah, it's a rape, but it's not a rape ... " But nothing where they were breaking down our doors.

**GILBERT:** Yeah, there have been little things here or there, but I always figure it's just a person's insecurity.

**GAIMAN:** You don't wind up self-censoring.

**GILBERT:** No. We might push it just to bother people maybe. But this is infrequent. Especially now. Nobody says anything about that. This one woman came up to me at a signing once and she looked at me with that look of, "I can't believe you did *Birdland*." I said, "Oh! *Birdland* is nonsense! You don't have to read it, big deal." But she said, "No, no, no, I can't believe you did *Birdland*." She just had to tell me, she had to control me somehow. And I thought, "So you didn't like it. So what?" So it's people's personalities.

**JAIME:** It's funny because we're treated the same way with our musical tastes: "I can't believe you didn't mention this band." [*Laughter.*] It's like they treat everything the same.

### US LOVE BEAUTY

**GAIMAN:** The music in *Love and Rockets* is obviously tied in with the whole thing. At the point where you discover why *Wigwam Bam* is called *Wigwam Bam*, the entire story falls into shape. And you understand why a dumb, trivial, sweet song, like from Sweet and Slade, and these bands —

BUT IT WAS THE SAME. SHE DIDN'T HAVE AS MANY TOYS AS SHE USED TO, BUT AS I HOPED, SHE STILL SNUCK OUT HER BROTHER'S RECORDS THAT WE DUG SO MUCH. ONE SONG THAT STOOD OUT WAS THIS ONE BY THE SWEET CALLED "WIGWAM BAM." IT WASN'T THE GREATEST SONG IN THE WORLD, BUT IT WAS OUR SONG. LETTY CALLED IT OUR SECRET ANTHEM.

*Music changes Maggie's and Letty's lives in "Wigwam Bam" (1990), reprinted in* Perla La Loca.

**GILBERT:** They mean so much to a kid because I think a different artist would have put the Bruce Springsteen song, the Neil Young song: the right song for the situation. But to me, no, we like the most dumb, vacuous thing ... but it moved us. T. Rex moved us. And it still does, when I listen to it, because of the past.

**JAIME:** That whole flashback about Maggie in *Wigwam Bam*, I knew, I was telling you that this is them; this ain't you. They just have the same emotions as you going. "Wigwam Bam" was their favorite song out of all those records. I hope I got it across that, just put your own song in there, and then you'll get it. I think I got it across. But at the time we weren't getting any letters, so I don't know.

**GILBERT:** To be honest, we don't get much response anymore.

**GAIMAN:** Yeah, but they only seem to write letters 1) if you're printing letters, and 2) if you're coming out frequently. I find if I'm doing something which has no letters column, has no expectation that anybody will ever read this letter except for me, I'll get maybe five letters on something. If there is a letters

column, and if there's some kind of implication of, "If you'll write, your letter will see print," you'll get 30 or 40 letters.

So. How's it been working with Fantagraphics? ... There's a contentious subject.

**GILBERT:** This is in *The Comics Journal*, so we have to tread lightly. [*Laughs.*] No, it's fine, I guess. To be honest, we don't have much of a yardstick, because we haven't done too much work with other people.

**GAIMAN:** You did the famous *Mister X* thing where you got badly ripped off.

**GILBERT:** I think we just got ripped off the way people normally get ripped off. I don't think it was that big an issue. We just took umbrage with Bill Marks himself. We just didn't like him after a while, you know what I mean? There are just some people you don't forgive.

**GAIMAN:** The thing about Bill is, when you meet Bill and he says, "Hi. I'm a scumbag and I rip people off," you go, "What endearing honesty this guy has!" [*Laughter.*] It comes across kind of sweet. It's really fun! He tells you upfront he's a scumbag, and you think, "Everyone else here is saying, 'I'm a great guy,' and he's saying 'I'm a scumbag,'" well ... cool! Actually, just the action of saying "I'm a scumbag" doesn't make one any less a scumbag! [*Laughs.*]

**GILBERT:** He had to do that after the fact of *Mister X* though because he wasn't that way before. He was the smiling scumbag who did not admit he was a scumbag.

**GAIMAN:** Oh. By the time I met him ...

**GILBERT:** Yeah. See now he's saying, "Oh, it's all very funny, it's all very cute," and he can be as cute to people as he wants, but there's some shit you just scrape off your shoe and just keep it off.

**GAIMAN:** Were you ever tempted to, when Dave Sim does his diatribes on —

**GILBERT:** — Women?

**GAIMAN:** No, not the woman one! [*Laughter.*] We can get into that if you like. But I was thinking of Dave's thing of, "You guys could go off and do it on your own. You could print the stuff on your own, you don't need Gary, and Gary knows that, and so forth."

**GILBERT:** Yeah, but what we need less than that, of doing it ourselves, is that it's business. Fuck business. I mean, I will work with somebody on equal terms and get something going and I'm happy. But getting involved in the business aspect, I mean, I'm an artist. I just want to create.

**JAIME:** The business thing just leaves a bad taste in my mouth, even if it's good.

**GILBERT:** Yeah, it might even be good for us, but we've never done it.

**JAIME:** Even the good stuff that comes out of it, I go, "OK, that's fine. Now let's get to work." I just don't want to get into *any* part of it. I like to watch over what's happening to me, but if they want to talk to me about numbers and being on the phone all day pushing myself, and having to act differently towards this guy to get my stuff in there, and then

*Gilbert drew Catwoman and Wonder Woman for* Bizarro Comics.

©2013 DC Comics

act differently towards the next guy, it's just total dishonesty to me. There are people who are hired for that. That's their job, to be dishonest, a whore, to be an asshole, or to be pushy. I'd rather give somebody money to do that for me.

**GILBERT:** As a matter of fact, this is a long-shot, I'm stretching it here, but I could actually see somebody like Peter Bagge eventually becoming his own boss, becoming self-published, just because of the way he works, the way he thinks, and the way he likes to be completely involved in all aspects of putting his work out. It's obviously helped him because *Hate* is, I believe, Fantagraphics' best-selling title. Fucker. [*Laughter.*] Well, that's because he's worked for it, though! He's put his butt on the line, he's been out there doing it, and that's something he likes to do. Or maybe he doesn't like to do it, but he insists on it, to make it work. So I see him self-publishing some day. But us? Nah … Well, hey, we might be making the worst mistake of our life, but …

**GAIMAN:** But your interests are sitting at the drawing table.

**GILBERT:** Life isn't business to us. I mean, I know that's really naïve to say, but our pursuit is love and beauty. The ladder to heaven, that's what we want. And money doesn't take you that way.

**JAIME:** We're the anti-Bizarros. Us love beauty, us hate ugliness.

## LOS PUNKS

**GAIMAN:** When did you get into punk? When did it actually come out over here? I was under the impression that there was a time lag, like an echo, with things crossing the Atlantic.

**GILBERT:** Yeah, but for us, there was always punk music, but it came in such bits and pieces, like OK, the New York Dolls were punk, but those bands disintegrated, were self-destructive. And even when Patti Smith and the Ramones came out, we listened to them, but we still didn't take it seriously. It wasn't until the Pistols came to America, and were on the news every day. It was hilarious — and frightening at the same time. It was one of those things where it really was unexpected. I suspect the reason the Sex Pistols and the original punk wave didn't quite happen was because it was basically ignored by the general public in the U.S. But now, from what I understand, it's just the fear of change. And the Sex Pistols represented: CHANGE. And they were marching across the U.S.

**JAIME:** And 1970s America did not welcome any sort of change at that time.

**GILBERT:** It was sort of like, "We're complacent now, we're fat and mellow, we're not going to have this again. We've gone through the '50s, we've gone through the '60s, we're not going to have this again!"

**JAIME:** We have disco.

**GILBERT:** Yeah. And then the Pistols came out and it was like, "Oh no, we're not going to have that again." You know the stories: Guys would actually go to the concerts to beat them up! Now what kind of thinking is that?

**GAIMAN:** In England, I was there, I was 16, my hair was dyed bright red and cut very ugly and I had my little dog collar on. But I know what it was about there. And I don't think that was what it was about once it crossed the Atlantic. What it was about there was partly, I think, musically a reaction against super-groups, against the huge stadiums, the light shows and the Yeses and the Pink Floyds and all the music we hated.

**JAIME:** Yeah, and that was brought over here as well.

**GAIMAN:** But socially it was the whole "No Future" thing: Yes, we have nothing to lose. We are a fucked generation.

**GILBERT:** So why did we get into punk? Well, the Pistols broke up in San Francisco and a friend of mine bought the album because I hadn't heard it yet. I was 21 years old, and my new wife and the younger punk kids were into their teens. Now a teen will take anything. And when you're old and crotchety like I was at 21 years old, I had seen it before, or thought I did: "I've seen glitter, I've seen hippies, and this is just another thing."

**GAIMAN:** You heard the New York Dolls doing "Mystery Girls."

**GILBERT:** Yeah, I liked it but I was just completely cynical and pessimistic at the time — but in the wrong direction. Instead of with the punk thing, I just didn't care. It was an apathy thing. It wasn't until I heard the music more and thought, "I like the music, I like these riffs, I like this guy yelling," and it grew on me in a musical way instead of the big statements. They simply just kicked ass. Then the actual meaning of the music came through, and there was no turning back.

**GAIMAN:** The feeling I got at the time was that the possibilities were endless. The whole idea of punk was, "Any four kids, no matter how lacking in talent, if they want, can pick up guitar, bass, drums, and somebody can yell, and they could be stars!" That was the idea, the concept.

**GILBERT:** That's definitely what happened with alternative comics. I do believe it takes a little longer to draw well than it does to play bass. It takes a week to play bass. [*Laughter.*]

**GAIMAN:** Less time than that if you're not fussy about how well you play. [*Laughter.*]

**GILBERT:** Right — it takes three notes to do an entire gig, so …

**JAIME:** It's really funny because when I was in bands I was a bass player because everyone wanted to be the guitar player, so I thought, "There will be plenty of room for me." And I think it's funny when I think back, because I basically learned from Sid! [*Laughter.*] Of all people! I mean, you hit the string and it's music! That's perfect. When I think back, I think, "Whoa, what a teacher, huh?"

**GAIMAN:** Did that carry over into creating the comics?

**JAIME:** Well sure, the whole mentality of, "We're going to do it ourselves, we can do it." But we always liked comics in the beginning, we liked our superheroes and we liked our *Dennis the Menace* comics, and with the punk mentality that we had going, I was having more fun than I had in years, since I was a little kid, doing the punk thing. Our comics were still just sitting there. We were still

From "Locas at the Beach" (1985), reprinted in Maggie the Mechanic.

just creating our superheroes for ourselves, or just creating stuff that just didn't seem like it was going to go anywhere. I never thought I'd be professional until the punk thing. Then I thought, "Oh, this is kind of the same thing." After a while I started realizing that music, comics and movies, all run the same, all are done the same way. They were all the same to me, so if you could do that with punk, you could do that with comics, you could do that with movies — but I wasn't going to go make a movie, because you do need money, no matter how cheap it is.

**GAIMAN:** Even if you're going to charge it all on credit cards, the money for the film stock and everything has to come from somewhere.

**JAIME:** Yeah, and I wasn't part of that movie community, but I was part of comics and punk.

**GILBERT:** It's the most stripped-down of the three because with movies, it's the big one, it's a large collaboration; with a band it's a small collaboration; and then with comics it's just you. This was really do-it-yourself, I mean we were doing *everything* ourselves, except publishing it. Because we've had difficulty with bands, just dealing with the other members, and we're talking about two or three people. Can you imagine in a film? [*Laughs.*] We'd have to deal with 50 to 100 people!

**GAIMAN:** And the great thing about comics is you just do them up on your own. You sit and do them. Even if you're writing them and not drawing them, you're dealing with one other person, maybe two. It's a tiny number of people. Films are huge numbers of people and lots of lots of different viewpoints.

**GILBERT:** In films, to be able to do what you want to do, you've got to prove yourself to all these people that you can do it, and that your opinion matters.

**JAIME:** That's hard when the idea of the movie industry is: Everybody's a star! [*Laughter.*] That was the thing about the punk thing that kind of started turning it around, as far as where I hung out — we all wanted to be in a band, and it's the easiest thing in the world, but we all wanted to be the singer! [*Laughs.*] We all wanted to be the star. We all wanted you to hear my drumsticks, or my bass, or you wanted to see me jump in the air higher. That got kind of out of hand, so I just couldn't stick with the band thing.

**GAIMAN:** Do you think there's a level in which comics is kind of like being a rock star without having actually to go out there and sing or sneakily turn your amp up?

**JAIME:** Well yeah, you get to do all this work and then it's out there and you're hiding in your little house saying, "You can't touch me now."

**GAIMAN:** Let me throw a weird question at you two and get whatever take you have on this: I am of the opinion that if you two broke fully formed on the world of comics tomorrow, like had you two never existed and the first issue of *Love and Rockets*, even if it were pretty much the same as the first issue that came out in 1982, came out tomorrow, it would cause a huge stir in the world of comics.

**JAIME:** You think so?

**GAIMAN:** Yes, I do. But I think there's this bizarre level on which both of you now are almost taken for granted. You've been displaying this level of competence and remarkable creativity, but it's kind of like, "Well, you're not new."

**GILBERT:** That enters my mind, just as you're saying. If it's not new, it must not be that good anymore. And of course that's not true, about anything.

**JAIME:** And nobody ever got tired of Carl Barks telling the same story over and over again.

**GAIMAN:** No, this is quite true. That's not quite what I'm getting at. I'm not talking about quality, and I'm not necessarily even talking about people getting tired of you. I'm just talking about the fact that, I think there's a level now on which you've established yourself —

**GILBERT:** Are you talking about the particular material we do?

**GAIMAN:** No, not even the material. Just the fact that you two are out there and are doing it, and have been doing it now for 13, 14 years. There comes a point where they sort of expect it to be good, you know? You're not surprising them anymore by doing good stuff. I suppose I'm talking more about the relationship with the audience. You're not new. They can't have just discovered you. You've been around for a while. They can't make a fuss about you particularly.

**JAIME:** And if they can't discover you anymore, the hipness kind of goes away.

**GAIMAN:** And you aren't doing anything different. You're still doing what you were doing ...

**JAIME:** And I'm still taking as much time to do it as I always have.

**GILBERT:** And if they picked up the comic at a certain point in their own life, their life is different by now — because we've been around that long, and they now might have different interests or might see things differently.

**GAIMAN:** That was something I noticed rereading the whole of *Love and Rockets* before doing the interview.

**GILBERT:** Wow. You've got a headache. [*Laughs.*]

**GAIMAN:** No! It was very, very pleasant. But the strange thing was sometimes turning a page and realizing what I've been doing, where I've been, how old I was when I read that page as a periodical, when I bought it when it came out. We're talking about a significant period of people's lives now. There are 15-year-old kids who picked you up when you first came out in 1982 who are going to be in their late 20s.

**GILBERT:** I know a person who was 13 when he first read the comic, and he just turned 25. Thirteen to 25, that's a lot of growing.

**GAIMAN:** You've been doing it for most of his life.

*Jaime's "Easter Hunt" (1993) is reprinted in* Amor y Cohetes.

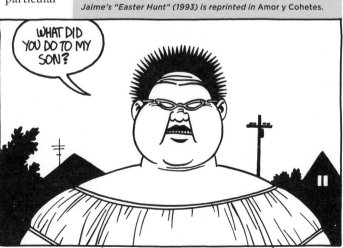

**GILBERT:** Yeah, and that's a lot of growing for that person. So it's flattering when they're still fans, definitely. Even if it's a nostalgic thing, a sentimental thing, that's OK with me. Sentiment has never bothered me. I don't know why it bothers artists and critics so much: "Oh, it's sentimental — it *can't* be good." I've never understood the anger toward sentimentality. I mean, I understand preferring better things, but I've never understood what makes them angry. It's obviously a personal thing. It makes them *angry* when something's sentimental. It's trash. Well, I'm not sure that's so. It might not be as good as something else, something more thought out.

**GAIMAN:** But I think sentiment and nostalgia are both driving human forces.

**JAIME:** And I think that's the part that bugs them. [*Laughter.*] They don't want to be human! They want to be better! Intellectual! ... Well, that's human.

**GAIMAN:** Have you ever thought about doing something that was as different from what you normally do as *Love and Rockets X* was from what Gilbert had normally been doing?

**JAIME:** Yeah, take *Birdland* for instance. My demons are just not as powerful as Gilbert's. You could call it laziness if you want. [*Snickers.*] I just don't have this thing in me that's strong enough to make me want to bust out and go crazy, become a madman. That's one thing I envy about Gilbert, is that he's this crazy man who does it because he has to. I've got this recurring nightmare where, if I didn't do this, I'd be OK. [*Laughter.*] And that scares the shit out of me! But back to your question. I've thought about it, but there's just not a big drive, there's not this demon inside me clawing away to get out. I wish there was a lot of times.

**GAIMAN:** There is the occasional time where you'll take Maggie on a road trip and just meet a bunch of different people. Does that fulfill it?

**JAIME:** Yeah, that usually fulfills it. So it's kind of a gradual thing, a mellow jump. It's not a leap. It's just this smooth walk-across-a-bridge kind of thing. I just wish someday I was that madman, like Robert Crumb. He'd be dead if he didn't do what he does. And I just wish I had that. And maybe mine is just at a different speed or set on a different temperature.

**GILBERT:** My amps go to 11. [*Laughter.*] But then again, it might not be that big a deal. Your demons may just be buried deeper. You never really know if they're there.

## DIFFERENT APPROACHES

**GAIMAN:** Where do you see yourselves going artistically? Your stuff seems to be continuing to simplify and explore the cartooning language between the representational stuff you've been doing, slightly more cartoony stuff, it seems to be pushing the edge in that direction. Do you see it going in that direction at all? Are you conscious of where it goes?

**JAIME:** The plan where I've always wanted it to go, and I guess it kind of still holds true, is to tell it as simple as possible, while entertaining myself — meaning, entertaining the fans at the same time. Instead of, you can go so simple where you have stick figures not doing anything — which is what some comics do now! [*Laughs.*] But just trying to put it down in its simplest form instead of going more complex, I'll try to make it more simple. But at the same time, doing it that way, it kind of makes it more complex. I don't know if that makes any sense.

**GILBERT:** More subtly complex?

**JAIME:** Yeah, I guess so. Are we talking about where I want my characters to go, or —

**GAIMAN:** Less characteristics, and more the look of the stuff on the paper.

**GILBERT:** Yeah, Jaime, what happened to all those little lines, man? What happened to all that detail? What's wrong with you, man?

**JAIME:** People have never forgiven me for getting rid of all of those little, tiny lines.

**GAIMAN:** I think they feel their getting their money's worth, the more little lines. It's like the Image stuff; it's got all these little lines!

**JAIME:** Yeah, but they don't know how hard it is not to put in a lot of lines. I just noticed as my art progresses — or regresses — that it's becoming more abstract in that all the lines are beginning to go somewhere. Where in the early days the lines just fit the drawing. Now I'm balancing a lot of little lines in one little corner, and putting less lines in the other corner. I'm actually paying more attention to composition, when I used to just put it down unconsciously. Now I guess with less lines to work with, the more I put them to work.

**GILBERT:** It's almost like what you set yourself up for. Obviously you drew a certain way in the early issues because that's what was coming out of you: All the lines, all the heavy detail, you put 12 panels on a page, and then on another page you'd just have

six. I noticed people like Crumb or Barks don't get any guff for that stuff, because they've always stuck to what they were doing all along. They progress as artists, but they didn't really *change* things — and if there's anything people don't like, it's change. I just saw the new Crumb book he did with Aline called *Self-Loathing*, and Crumb could care less about composition and the way a page or the story progresses or layouts. It's all completely naturalistic; he goes from panel to panel to how he *feels* the panel should look. It's more what the stories are about. Whereas Jaime gets a lot of, "Why aren't you doing this anymore? Why did you change it? Why don't you do it this way?"

**GAIMAN:** Particularly with Barks, though, a lot of the artifice is in hiding the artifice.

*Top: An example of Jaime's "many line" style from "Locas Tambien" (1981), reprinted in* Maggie the Mechanic. *Bottom: By 1987's "Jerusalem Crickets," reprinted in* The Girl from H.O.P.P.E.R.S., *his style was pared down.*

**GILBERT:** Right.

**GAIMAN:** And I think, to some extent these day, with Crumb. Part of what makes Crumb brilliant right now is it looks like anybody could do it. It's that Zen thing — I just did it. It's like watching a tightrope walker dance on a tightrope, and it looks so easy.

**GILBERT:** So that means we're fucked, Jaime. [*Laughs.*]

**JAIME:** OK, going back to my style, though, this is only one part of me talking because another part of me can't wait to get into detail. Occasionally you'll see one panel, and you'll think, "How come there's so much in that one, and not way over here?" It just depends on my mood, and sometimes I like to put a lot of lines on a jacket, sometimes I don't put any. Luckily I still work where I jump around from panel to panel, from page one to page six, back to page two, so it kind of balances it. If I did it all in order, you would see a very detailed comic go to a very simple comic, go to a very busy comic, to a very boring comic, to ... As I'm doing the comic I go from these highs and lows, or ins and outs, whatever you want to call them, just getting into certain styles or different approaches of doing it. I guess that's what still keeps me interested in doing this kind of work.

**GAIMAN:** Let me throw a question at both of you, something I go back and forth on over the years. The basic unit of comics: Is it the panel or the page? What is the unit you are giving people?

**GILBERT:** I'd say both.

**JAIME:** On any given, what's important to you at the time?

**GILBERT:** Like, say, if you're doing a fight scene, you'll use a whole page to do it. But if you're having a conversation, that can be done as a page or a panel-to-panel thing. We look at the whole story in our head as we're drawing it, so even when we're doing it panel-to-panel, we're still thinking of the entire story as we're drawing it.

**GAIMAN:** I find I still find a page as a discrete unit, even if it's just a conversation that goes over four pages and nothing much happens.

**JAIME:** Sure. Even if I paid more attention to one panel than the next three on a page, I'll still look at the page after it's done, and if it's unbalanced, I'll fix it. So I start off on single panels, but when the page is finally finished, I look at the whole thing. So I guess you'd say it's both.

**GAIMAN:** That makes sense. I think that's why I was asking about the *Love and Rockets X* reformatting. Because it had gone from a nine-panel grid — which is one thing, it has its own pace and its own look — to almost individual, discreet panels. One starts to wonder what that would have been like if it had been a panel to a page, like *Tantrum* was. To what extent it changes the reading experience.

**GILBERT:** Sometimes I wonder if it makes that much of a difference. I'll do a nine-panel grid for *Love and Rockets X*, and then we'll change it to six panels on a page. I wonder if that gives it a different read, but not necessarily an inferior one ... ?

**GAIMAN:** I don't think we're talking inferior or superior, but I think we are talking just a change in ... Well, did you notice a difference in things like *Peanuts*, the part when things got smaller — they all went from four panels to three panels? It was like a time change. The four used to get: Something, Something, Punch line, Reaction. And the genius of *Peanuts* for me particularly, but in a lot of other strips too, it wasn't the punch line. The punch line came in panel three. It was panel four where somebody would turn around and look at the narrator, or where somebody would say something that actually sort of kept the punch line. When they went to three panels, the rhythm changed.

**GILBERT:** But then you're talking about Schulz, who developed it with that particular structure. And we've always jumped around to different forms.

**GAIMAN:** That was what I was talking about. And also the fact that you have a weird visual overlap between ... You may not have looked at it yet but you sort of know what's there ...

**JAIME:** Yeah, even if I'm drawing this panel, I know that down here it's got to be either more white or more black.

## RUMORS AND CONFIRMATIONS

**GAIMAN:** What do you reckon of the whole, there seemed a while where, Chester went into that strange loop of autobiographical comics, and you got the whole Joe Matt and Seth going into it, and Julie [Doucet] ... There seemed like a point where, people had begun to feel fiction was suddenly bad. There was almost a puritan idea. It was, "How could you possibly be taken seriously when you were making stuff up?"

**GILBERT:** We didn't worry about it too much because we were going ahead with what we do. But I think it's the other way around, meaning, a lot of autobiographical stuff is done because they say it's the truth, but it isn't. Because even some of the cartoonists have told me: "I changed this character because I didn't want to offend him," or, "I refused to do this because of that." Then what are you doing, calling it autobiographical? You're turning it into fiction.

**GAIMAN:** It's also the process of selection.

**JAIME:** Yeah. And if I went and did autobiographical

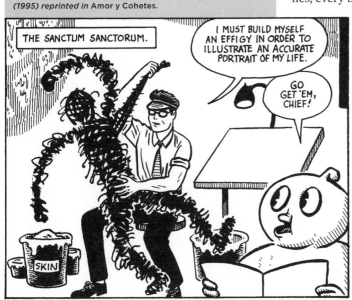

*Gilbert's version of an autobio comic: from "My Love Book" (1995) reprinted in* Amor y Cohetes.

comics, no matter how I portrayed myself, everybody else portrays me differently. They see me differently. And I don't think that would be fair of me telling about my life, because I don't see it from the outside, I can't step outside and see. And I think that's the strength of the artist: to be able to step back and watch.

**GILBERT:** I think there is more freedom in fiction because you can disguise something to a certain extent and not offend people, if that's what you're looking for. But with autobiographical stuff, I think you tell less of the truth, to be honest, because you're always worried that this is going to offend. ... Unless you're a complete loser and you don't care about hurting people at all.

**GAIMAN:** I think it's also the function of fiction. What is fiction? Fiction is lies that tell true things. It is a metaphor. It is a way of seeing things that you've never seen before, in a way that makes them truer.

**GILBERT:** People have said, "*Love and Rockets* is not realistic enough."

And in a moment of weakness I'll think, "You know what? They're right. I shouldn't draw women this way, or draw this character this way, or have them do this or do that." Then I just came to realize, "Wait a minute! This is all lies! This is art. This is all lies, every bit of it, is a lie!" And it's to, like you said, to bring out the truth somehow. And it's OK to exaggerate as long as you get the feeling that it's real when you're reading it.

**JAIME:** A sense of truth.

**GAIMAN:** It's the underlying truth that is what you have to go for as an artist. It's the point of recognition. It's the point where somebody reads it and knows that "Yes, this is true, and it doesn't matter if it happened or not."

**JAIME:** It was that old Orson Welles thing: "There's nobody in real life like Cagney." Yet there was something so true about his acting, because of his image, the way he carried himself, it just brought out so much truth.

**GILBERT:** Yeah, you sissy autobiographical cartoonists. Take that.

**GAIMAN:** Have you ever had the urge to do an autobiographical —

**GILBERT:** Oh, sure! As a matter of fact, coming up in issue #49 of *Love and Rockets*, I'm going to do autobiographical stories just because I want to try my hand at it — instead of keep putting it down the way I have been! [*Laughs.*] I'm going to try it and try to have fun with it. That may be just an experiment like *Birdland* was, I don't know. I'll do it just for fun, to get away from the regular ... Because actually this comes ... I guess, for the record, we can say that issue #50 will be the last *Love and Rockets* magazine.

**GAIMAN:** I heard rumors that you were going to go over to a comic.

**JAIME:** Yes, but even that's not definite. The only definite is that #50 ends the magazine.

**GILBERT:** We could keep doing it, there's nothing stopping us, but we just felt like a change for ourselves, as well as for the readers. It has nothing to do with quality: It's just a different format. I would like to do different characters.

**GAIMAN:** Are you going to change the name?

Jaime's "To Be Announced" (1998) is reprinted in Penny Century.

**GILBERT:** It would be a shame to drop the name only because, well, I just still think it's a good name, and people recognize it immediately. But at the same time I wouldn't want it to be an albatross, I wouldn't want, automatically we start thinking, "Let's do a comic-book size *Love and Rockets* and then just go right back to what we were doing." At least not entirely. We're thinking of color or partial color.

**GAIMAN:** If you're going to do it for color, I assume you're going to set out to do it for color, as opposed to those horrible colored *Mechanics*, whoo!!

**GILBERT:** They looked colorized. The Penny Century backup looked OK to me, though.

**JAIME:** The printing was off, and there was a whole issue that was just blue and yellow. It just looked really bad. And if I wanted a color comic, I would draw it for color. There is a difference. When they wanted to do it, I was just so wrapped up in the actual *Love and Rockets*, that the *Mechanics* thing was just another thing to worry about, so I didn't really give it as much care as I should have. But then it was mostly reprints, and reprints are reprints. That's stuff that's already done. I don't care much about it.

**GAIMAN:** Would this be both of you working in the same comic together? That may be a silly question ...

**GILBERT:** If it's *Love and Rockets*, yeah, we'll still split up the book. I don't know about Jaime, but I would definitely emphasize different characters, maybe a few that I've already done, or have just introduced recently. But I probably, if we do *Love and Rockets* still, will not go back to Palomar. That might be a mistake in the long run, I don't know. We'll see.

**GAIMAN:** Is there a level on which having an end, or knowing that you have an end to the magazine, keeps you going? I find it easier, knowing when something ends, as if there is a point in the creation of any work of art, where you might as well be building a wall or digging a ditch.

**GILBERT:** In my case, yeah, I do have an end. I know what the last Palomar story is about. I know what happens to the characters. And whether we continue *Love and Rockets* or not, I do have plans for a couple of the characters, just because I recently introduced some of them.

**GAIMAN:** And which characters, if any?

**JAIME:** Maggie, if any. I would just put her in a whole different background. I'm going to follow her until I can't do it no more. Maggie exists no matter what — no matter if they like her or not! [*Laughter.*]

## MOVIES

**GAIMAN:** So let's talk about Hollywood Hell. [*Laughter.*] Partly because I'm fascinated by it, and partly because I assume you guys must have been going through it for the last decade.

**GILBERT:** As in *Love and Rockets* getting made as a film? Or just Hollywood in general?

**GAIMAN:** Both of them.

**JAIME:** It's all the same thing!

**GAIMAN:** Yeah, I was going to say, as a phenomenon, it's the same thing. And also partly one of the reasons I wanted to ask you about this is I've been seeing all the ads for the *Tank Girl* movie. My take on *Tank Girl* is that it's a sweet little comic which is so severely post-Hopey, as to be ... I don't think it would be entirely fair to call it a rip-off of *Love and Rockets*, but, without *Love and Rockets* it would never have existed. I don't think that Jamie Hewlett's style in that way would have existed, and *Tank Girl* definitely wouldn't have looked like young Hopey. I think these are fair statements. There are going to be letters to *The Comics Journal* ...

**JAIME:** [*Laughs.*] Well, as long as you said it.

**GAIMAN:** Well, that's one reason why I'm saying it. If you say it, it's going to sound like sour grapes at this point. But I'm perfectly happy to sit here and say it.

**GILBERT:** Well, the influence is there, but like you said, it's a mixture of Hopey and the early Maggie character, mechanics, rockets and all that stuff. Nothing wrong with stealing from good material, I guess.

Gaiman calls Tank Girl *"Post-Hopey."* This panel is from Tank Girl: The Odyssey #4 (October 1995), written by Peter Milligan and drawn by Jamie Hewlett.

**GAIMAN:** No, it's fine and that's where it comes from. But, I'm sure that if they had wanted to make a simple-minded *Mechanics* movie, you know, "She's a spunky gal with a toolbox! She can fix anything except the human heart." They must have come to you, they must have asked you for films like that.

**GILBERT:** Oh yeah, in the beginning.

**JAIME:** In the beginning we got called up, got taken to lunch, went through the whole thing. Half of them said, "I don't know what the hell *Love and Rockets* is, but I'm sure we could do something with it." The other half said, "I really like this comic, so I'm trying to talk with the people upstairs, talk them into doing a good movie, because we *really believe in this*." For a while, sometimes I would start believing it too, that they really believed that we could really get this done, and it would be small enough ... But they never tell you that they have to answer to 50 people above them — and you know where *that's* going to lead. So we went through that for years, until we started narrowing it down, and started to be able to pick up what they wanted in the first minute, so we just sat there for the rest of the lunch, eating their food —

**GILBERT:** — Nodding and smiling.

**JAIME:** And thinking, "Oh boy, I can't wait to get out of here!"

**GILBERT:** But to be fair, we also weren't really sure what we wanted a *Love and Rockets* movie to be either. So that's where problems came up too. We knew what we *didn't* want it to be: a crummy, Hollywood piece of junk that they pump out a hundred times a year. So we thought, "What *do* we really want it to be? Well, what we started the comic book out to be: something personal, characters that the audience could identify with ..." And obviously Hollywood isn't interested in that, in the way of comic books.

**GAIMAN:** That's the bit I don't understand about this country. You've got a country that's huge enough that it feels like you ought to be able to do anything and have it find its audience.

**GILBERT:** I guess this is leading to: Yes, there will be a *Love and Rockets* movie, and it will be live action. We have written the script. The only way this movie is not going to be made is if we give up.

**GAIMAN:** You've finished a script that you like.

**GILBERT:** Pretty much. There are still some final touches on it, to make it slicker — the sixth revision! [*Laughs.*]

**GAIMAN:** It's a Maggie and Hopey script?

**GILBERT:** It's a *Love and Rockets* script; it's got both worlds in it.

**GAIMAN:** Good. Is anybody actually waiting on this script?

**GILBERT:** No, you're one of the few people who we've talked to about it, just because we wanted as little outside influence as possible that would attempt to change our mind. We went through the Hollywood thing, and if you really want to get something done, you're thinking compromises one right after the other, and that's not a good thing. That was before we had a script. Now we're going to go in with a script, which we're not really going to change.

**GAIMAN:** So there is going to be a movie.

**GILBERT:** Yes. Any Maggie and Luba look-alikes, send your 8" X 10"s to ... We're directing it. There's no reason why we couldn't. We're completely confident that we can direct a film. The way technology is and the way things are now ...

**GAIMAN:** Are you going to be raising the money yourselves for it?

**GILBERT:** We're working with some people, a producer and his partner who will do the dirty job.

**GAIMAN:** So do you have any kind of idea of what kind of timeline this is on?

**GILBERT:** We'd like to see something get started next year, but who knows? I don't know how long it takes to raise money.

**JAIME:** Yeah, I don't know anything about that stuff. I just know I'm ready to make it!

**GAIMAN:** OK. Let me ask you another question.

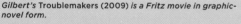

*Gilbert's* Troublemakers (2009) *is a Fritz movie in graphic-novel form.*

You've got the comic. The comic is remarkable. So, why do a movie?

**JAIME:** Because our lives were created on comics, rock 'n' roll and movies.

**GILBERT:** It's the next plateau, Neil! [*Laughter.*]

## RIGHT NOW

**GAIMAN:** What are you up to now?

**GILBERT:** Number 47 should be out when this interview comes out.

**GAIMAN:** How frequently are they shipping now?

**JAIME:** Four times a year. Should be more, but …

**GILBERT:** But you know what? We've only ever done this at the most five times a year, I don't know, it comes out when it comes out. We do our best.

**GAIMAN:** So we're what? A year away from the end?

**JAIME:** I'd say so.

**GILBERT:** The end of *Love and Rockets*, the magazine. … The eight-track, the album, the black-and-white …

**GAIMAN:** So we're now in the VHS, the laser disk, the CD, the DAT tape, the mini-disk version of *Love and Rockets*.

**GILBERT:** Right. *If* we continue it.

**GAIMAN:** Do you see what you do as being about the magazine, or about the collections?

**GILBERT:** I think of them as graphic novels. Even if I try to avoid that — to focus on the magazine more — that's what it turned out to be.

**GAIMAN:** Why was "Human Diastrophism" collected as *Blood of Palomar*? I love the title *Human Diastrophism*.

**GILBERT:** Because nobody could pronounce it. I come up with a lot of names that people can't pronounce.

**GAIMAN:** You spell it out phonetically all the time.

**GILBERT:** Yeah, but on the cover you've got: *Human Diastrophism*. What the heck is human diastrophism? But *Blood of Palomar*, that's like "Blood of Dracula" or something. [*Laughter.*] I don't know.

I think it was just an easier sell. I always make things difficult for myself. I can't have a comic book called *Pipo*, because people would say, "Pipe-o," or "Pippo." People are going to run screaming for the *Joe* or *Andy* comics.

I chose a simple title for *Poison River*, because I knew I would not have to change it! [*Laughs.*]

**GAIMAN:** The other problem, as I see it anyway, of the *Wigwam Bam*, *Poison River* period, is that most of the longtime readers will be fine, will hang in there. But I can't imagine people hopping on at that point.

**GILBERT:** No, not at all.

**JAIME:** We've suffered for that.

**GAIMAN:** And if you're losing by attrition anyway, losing a reader here, a reader there, then if new ones simply can't come on board —

**GILBERT:** This could have been just a coincidence, but a lot of people were getting into books like *Eightball* and *Hate* at that time. They were relatively new books and they were rolling along … I'm not saying they are the same audience, but maybe if somebody was interested in these new comics, *Hate* and *Eightball*, and then when they saw *Love and Rockets*, they might say, "This is the one I don't get."

**GAIMAN:** I think that's definitely something that could have happened around that time period. Because it was always easy to jump on. It was like a slow-moving carousel or bus. I thought of myself as somebody who came to *Love and Rockets* really late. Looking back on it, #7 or #8 was my first.

**GILBERT:** 1984.

**GAIMAN:** Right. And I thought I was late. I always felt vaguely late, like I had missed the first half of the party. I can just imagine trying to jump on in the #30s.

**JAIME:** The first seven issues were only read by professionals in this case anyway! [*Laughter.*] We didn't have our big readership until —

**GILBERT:** Our following didn't start until around issue #10.

**GAIMAN:** I think you need to be around for a while; you need to build up some critical mass. And you need to get to the point where there are enough people reading, that they can tell other people: "I like this. Look at this, I think you'll like it too."

What kind of stuff do you guys like? Across the board.

**GILBERT:** What's coming out now, you mean?

**GAIMAN:** Let's start off with comics. This is always the hard one because this is the one where you go home, and in the car on the way home you think, "Oh fuck, I never mentioned so-and-so, and they're going to kill me."

**GILBERT:** OK, *Doofus* by Rick Altergott. [*Laughter.*] Boy, there are all these names fighting their way out of my head, and don't seem to be getting through ...

**GAIMAN:** Did you see the Chris Ware *Acme Novelty Library* stuff or whatever it's called? I thought that was very strange, and very odd, and I think I like it. I definitely plan to continue reading them.

**GILBERT:** Yeah, I must be getting old or something, but I just have a hard time figuring out his compositions.

**GAIMAN:** Those teeny-tiny —

**JAIME:** Yeah, and every issue is a different package.

**GILBERT:** Yeah, but it's definitely there. There's definitely some form of genius there. And his stories about Superman that were in *Raw*, I guess it was, where Superman is an asshole, and leaves the kid stranded on an island — that was great.

**GAIMAN:** In that Crumb comic, I enjoyed the Aline stuff as much as I enjoyed the Crumb stuff, which, I think is a first for me. It was a strange double vision. I actually found her stuff, in some ways, almost more engaging.

**GILBERT:** Well, it is more personal, I suppose. I mean, in the way her feelings are all out there. Crumb basically describes his reactions, and hers are, like that one panel where she says, "This is me when I get up in the morning" — That was probably the most hideous, self-loathing drawing I've ever seen a woman do. [*Laughter.*]

No, really! But I laughed my head off!

I thought, "Oh this poor woman, I love you!" I mean, look at her, how could you not love the person who drew that? And it's interesting how — Jaime's wife brought this up — how [Aline] draws herself as

a hideous creature, and then Crumb will draw her really sweet. Because that's his perception of her.

## KID STUFF

**GAIMAN:** One of the things I love about what both of you did during a similar period was the kids in your comics. Again, incredibly good-natured — except when they get scared, and even then they would recover their equilibrium incredibly fast. They're like a little force of nature, going into little packs of children. And occasionally it's counterpoint to the adult thing: occasionally it's almost heartbreaking.

**GILBERT:** Knowing what they're going to turn out to be, you mean? [*Laughs.*]

**GAIMAN:** Yes, I suppose I do! But the sheer good nature of the kids, as contrasted to the adult world of confusion ... Is that the way you two see kids?

**JAIME:** I guess I would have to say that's how I *like* to see kids. I was telling Gilbert the other day [*laughs*], how he will take the time to show some pretty rotten kids — or, maybe not so rotten kids, but just difficult-to-handle kids — and I don't want anything to do with them. [*Laughter.*] And I think I'm cheating as an artist by *not* doing that, if I want to put kids in there. That's why I don't do as many kids as he does, because I just don't have the strength!

**GILBERT:** Also the children thing is: We're also trying to remind ourselves of the good things about being kids. Because there are obviously good things about it, and there are rotten things, but it seems the thing nowadays is to remember the rotten things that happened to you when you were a kid. Yeah, there were a lot of rotten things, but there were good things too.

**JAIME:** We went through this big stretch when we were younger of doing kids comics, being influenced by *Peanuts* and *Dennis the Menace*. So we did that a lot — in fact, I think we did more kids' comics than superhero grown-up comics. I pretty much tell [the stories] the same way I did then.

**GAIMAN:** I noticed particularly with your children, that they are very often *Peanuts* characters. You will draw them in a completely different style, even if they're in the same frame as an adult.

**JAIME:** Yeah. That style of how I draw those kids, I've been drawing that since I was a kid myself, so I do it blindfolded. I just decided that I have more fun drawing that way instead of trying to do it realistically. So a lot more comes out of it, more personality in the characters. It's fun to do it that way because that's how I did it for years, as a youngster.

**GAIMAN:** It definitely comes across. Have you guys ever had the urge to do more moonlighting from *L&R*?

**GILBERT:** You mean outside projects?

**GAIMAN:** Yeah, I've seen a few album covers, but very little else ...

**JAIME:** In my case, I'd say that's because comics is what I do best. And it's what I like to do the best.

And also I had this thing that *Love and Rockets* was going to be something that was important. In other words, it wasn't the first step to something better, like a movie. I just kept serious about it, that this is important.

**GAIMAN:** That I have no problem understanding. But why wouldn't you just do a kids' comic for once, just as something to do?

**JAIME:** I had planned to do a kids' comic as opposed to *Birdland*. That was going to be the first comic that children could read of mine! [*Laughs.*] But the more I had ideas for that, the more I wanted to draw chicks! [*Laughter.*] I just can't get away from drawing women. I mean, grown, fully fleshed, beautiful women. That's the one thing that will always bring me back. That's the only thing keeping me going.

**GAIMAN:** Do either of your wives ever get jealous of your relationship with women on the page?

**GILBERT:** We just have to remind them that they're Number One and they're for real.

Gilbert's "Poison River" (1988-1994), reprinted in Beyond Palomar, *is "really about men and how they perceive women."*

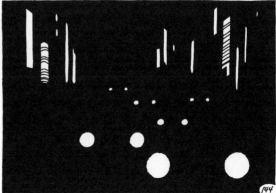

115

*Mario Hernandez drew this ink and crayon portrait, dated 1997.*

**JAIME:** Our wives, he means. [*Much laughter.*]

**GILBERT:** They question it sometimes: *"Gol-ly!!! Look at that!"* But they recognize it's just lines on paper.

**GAIMAN:** [*Laughs.*] Yes, I've met both of your wives and they both seem to have their feet on the ground to know the difference between lines on paper. ... But one of the things *Love and Rockets* is certainly about is women. You see your women from the inside; and the men we tend to know by their actions.

**GILBERT:** That's interesting, because I was thinking as you were saying that, that *Poison River* was basically my first major story that was about men. Yes, it was about Luba and her mother and their relationship, but it was really about men and how they perceive women. You'll notice that both Luba and Maria are used almost as props in the lives of these men. And one of the men who Luba marries has a stroke and realizes, "Oh, I really did love her." He just thought of her as his trophy wife, or whatever. And I was doing the world of men and I was very critical about it, the business sense. ... And I'm wondering if it's because we grew up without

our father, and I have this unconscious animosity toward men. Then again, why do I love *The Wild Bunch* so much?

**GAIMAN:** Both of the comics are incredibly matriarchal. You're looking at matriarchies. I can't think of anything in either of your works that feels like a patriarchy. Whether you're going back through the real family tree or the lady wrestler family tree ...

**GILBERT:** That's another thing that's very important to us. I see now, when I look back at *Love and Rockets* and think, "What did we focus on?" We focused on the family quite a bit. And that means that everything is always linked. People would call it our "soap opera" techniques, and I think that's cheapening it. No, we're just concerned with family, and how families work and don't work, and how families continue and grow. That has always been a focus of our work — the women and the families they are attached to. Jaime's families are more, I think, in the friendship sense.

**GAIMAN:** I think they're more indeterminate. People have brothers and sisters and mother and aunts, but it's the strange extended families of punk, surely.

**JAIME:** Yeah.

**GILBERT:** Whereas I'm doing literal families.

**GAIMAN:** I think both of them work. I assume that wasn't intentional when you set out though.

**JAIME:** Most of the comic just happened the way it happened.

**GILBERT:** Fell into place.

## STYLE

**GAIMAN:** Jaime, your style is seductive, for want of a better word. You look at it and think, "I like these people. I want to be in this world. These people look lovely, I like the way these lines move." It is seductive and enticing, and it grabs you and says, "Hello, come here..."

**GILBERT:** As opposed to Gilbert's ...

**GAIMAN:** As opposed to your style, which doesn't

do that. It's much more — [*Gilbert laughs*] — no, it's not seductive. I find it enormously charming, and capable of, in the end, quite possibly a wider range of things. But it's much more cartoony, and it's not as seductive. It is what it is, and if you don't like it, you don't like it.

**JAIME:** I'm the Paul; you're the John.

**GILBERT:** Yeah, another guy made that Beatles analogy.

**JAIME:** I didn't like it at first, but now it's OK.

**GAIMAN:** Look, you don't get shot!

**GILBERT:** [*Laughs.*] That's right. But look, people make the mistake of thinking that Paul was the weaker Beatle, which is not true. He just decided to go the path of ballads and softer music. That's all. That was his decision because that's what he felt stronger doing. I think the actual rift between Paul and John was that they were equally strong, and John resented that in Paul. He could not eclipse Paul in the Beatles because Paul would always come back with something else. I think there was this real rivalry that just drove John nuts — and maybe McCartney too and he just hid it better, I don't know. But what I'm saying is, I'm defending McCartney because people always think somehow he's the weaker Beatle because he did ballads, and that's not true at all. His strength is there. After the Beatles is another story.

**GAIMAN:** I think that culturally we both like and come down on the easy-to-love. On the Pauls, the things that are —

**JAIME:** I'm user-friendly. [*Laughter.*]

**GAIMAN:** Yes! That's a very good way of putting it. You're more accessible.

**GILBERT:** Carl Barks wasn't the good duck artist because he was *bad*. It was because he was the good duck artist.

**GAIMAN:** He was the good duck artist because you look at his stuff, and it was better than the other duck artists. And it was more friendly. He lured you in.

**GILBERT:** Simple as that. You go through a stack of '60s Marvel, and you think, "Oh, these Ditko and Kirby guys are the good guys. Easily."

**GAIMAN:** What is sad is now we can look at Don Heck and go, "This was a really good '50s Madison Avenue artist in the wrong place, doing the wrong stuff." But he was really good at doing what he did — it just happened to be everything that we hated when we were 7.

**GILBERT:** Yeah, at the time he was not the Good Artist.

**JAIME:** Yeah, but his older stuff, even his monster stuff or the Marvel stuff, you could see an artist there.

**GAIMAN:** Certainly. Also some of the black-and-white reprints of the early Marvel stuff.

**GILBERT:** I think he had a problem with inking. I think that's what really turned people off. He had that weird, scratchy inking. Why did he do that? It

*Jaime and Gilbert "jammed" this 1995* Comics Journal *cover.*

was weird. It was almost like fashion model art. It was very sketchy. But this is why both me and Jaime did this test as kids. We'd always look at artists and think, "This guy is really crummy," then we'd copy line-for-line a drawing they would do and it would come out really well and we'd feel really crummy thinking it was crummy. So yeah, there was an artist in there. Poor Don, he just died.

Don Heck gets into every interview! [*Laughs.*]

## WRAPPING IT UP

**GAIMAN:** So what's going to be on the cover of the *Journal*?

**JAIME:** Women: Do you need to ask?

**GILBERT:** It will be two of my characters and two of Jaime's. Women. After *Poison River* I think I've just gotten rid of the men for the most part for good.

**JAIME:** Poor Adam Hughes, we visited him at one time and Gilbert and I just browbeat him saying, "Why do you think you have to draw guys? You like drawing girls!" And he just had this duty of, "Yes, but —" And we'd say, "You like drawing girls, so draw girls! Forget the guys!" [*Laughter.*] Poor guy. We didn't let up on him.

**GAIMAN:** I don't think anybody should ever put in any kind of character out of guilt. The fun is just creating characters, of making people up who never existed, but ought to. Or sort of live in the back of your head ... Or the one where you see somebody walking down the road and you think, "I wonder what their life is like? I wonder what they'd be like for a ... "

**GILBERT:** Maybe that's what a lot of our detractors feel about us, that we know our characters so well that the readers have come to know them that well and that they're not finding out anything new about them. There is no mystery to a lot of the characters anymore. Of all people, Jerry Seinfeld has been talking about that. He's thinking of canceling his show because of that same reason. They've gone through the characters, you know them, there are no more surprises in them, so why continue it? It's a similar thing for us. For some readers, they just think, "I know Maggie now, and nothing she's going to do will surprise me." People are always looking for something new.

**GAIMAN:** It goes even to, "You guys aren't new anymore."

**GILBERT:** Yeah, but it doesn't mean it's not good, it just means it's not new. And people confuse the two.

**GAIMAN:** Yes. It's the concept of novelty.

**GILBERT:** I imagine that's why a lot of marriages split up: "This isn't new anymore."

**GAIMAN:** Right: "We've done this before, haven't we?"

**GILBERT:** But marriage is supposed to transcend that. That you don't care that it's not new anymore. You're *happy* with this continuation. But people just don't seem to get that far. And being happily married has nothing to do with settling.

**GAIMAN:** In a lot of ways you have more room to maneuver than Jaime does, I would think. You've given yourself various places that you can go; you don't have to stay in Palomar forever. If you leave Palomar for a while, you have L.A., you have the autobiographical stuff, you have something else if you decide it's time to do "Frida Kahlo" or whatever. Whereas you, Jaime, basically have Maggie and Hopey as your points of the compass around which things are going to circle. Do you plan, for example, to keep watching them getting older, to grow them up? I can't quite get my head around the concept of ... I still think of Maggie and Hopey essentially as kids.

**JAIME:** Well if anyone is going to be followed, it's Maggie. She's just the center of the universe that everything happens around — even if she obviously isn't. And wherever she goes, that's where I go. I mean, who knows? With this new comic, it being a different format, I'll have this whole new framework of thinking and how I want to get this thing done.

**GAIMAN:** What about Hopey?

**JAIME:** Hopey? I don't see following her life every step of the way. I can see you seeing her now, in her late 20s (actually by real time she'd be in her 30s), but then not seeing her until she's 50. That's just the way her character always seems to ...

**GAIMAN:** She also has that force-of-nature quality, of people who crash into your life, change it, and then go away. Then five or six years later, just as you've settled down, they crash into it again, like a car running into your house.

**JAIME:** Right. And Maggie I can see growing old with.

**GAIMAN:** I think we're done. Say the last thing.

**GILBERT:** Our mission is to climb the ladder to heaven. And the first rung is dealing with Beauty.

**GAIMAN:** [*Pause.*] Is it yours?

**GILBERT:** Plato, I think.

**GAIMAN:** I was gonna say!

**GILBERT:** [*Laughs.*] It's too good for me, huh? ∎

In the fall of 1982, when the first Fantagraphics-published issue of *Love and Rockets* made its debut, the Southern California punk scene was at its emotional peak, a chaotic, rage-fueled rebellion energized by a do-it-yourself attitude. It was in this microcosmic powder keg of social upheaval that the Hernandez brothers came of age. Thirty years later, punk has been absorbed into the mainstream culture, and its legions of devotees have scattered. Yet *Love and Rockets* is still here, a living monument to punk's enduring legacy.

Like the political climate it reflected, the American comic-book industry of the early '80s was mired in a similar sort of artistic conservatism. Stuck in an endless holding pattern of recycled plots and formulaic stories, the hottest American series in 1982 was *Teen Titans* by Marv Wolfman and George Pérez (winner of the Eagle Award for "Best New Book").

The 2012 comic-book industry is vastly different: hundreds of non-superhero, non-traditional comics are published every year, including everything from handmade, self-published minicomics (a direct descendant of the homemade fanzines which inspired the Hernandez brothers) to book-length cartoon memoirs. Yet, despite all these changes, both personal and cultural, *Love and Rockets* remains avant-garde.

These days, the Hernandez brothers have moved on. Mario has settled into family life in San Francisco, while Gilbert is raising his preteen daughter in Las Vegas. Only Jaime remains in Southern California, and he, too, is now a father. I had the great privilege of reflecting on this milestone in their careers with all three Hernandez brothers in October 2011. Among many topics, we discussed the essential impact of family and fans, the continuing influence of artists and filmmakers and the current state of alternative comics.

—MARC SOBEL, MAY 2012

Ben Horak, Kara Krewer, Anna Pederson and Madisen Semet transcribed this interview; it was copy-edited by the participants.

# MARC SOBEL & THE BROTHERS

*The* Love and Rockets *Companion*

**MARC SOBEL:** Gary [Groth] once said "a lot of artists tend to repeat themselves once they reach a certain age. They really charge through their 20s and reach their apex in their 30s, and then that sense of discovery and freshness is exhausted and they start repeating themselves." How do you keep from falling into repetition after 30 years?

**GILBERT HERNANDEZ:** Well, in my case, I'm doing stuff I didn't do before when I was doing the Palomar stories. Outside *Love and Rockets*, and sometimes in *Love and Rockets*, I'm doing more surreal crime stories. My challenge is to make the readers enjoy those as much as my previous work. But after 30 years, as long as we keep our heads together and stay true to what we always believed in, that's half the battle. The rest is to keep it fresh and to maintain our drawing abilities. We were talking about this the other day. The only thing that would mess us up is if our health started to fail, like if our elbows start to go out, that kind of thing. But as far as our thinking goes and our inspiration, it's the same as it's always been.

**JAIME HERNANDEZ:** When you mentioned how artists get older and start repeating themselves, I couldn't tell you if I am or not. [*Laughs.*] I'm doing this work and it's real personal to me, and I get so inside of it that I have to step outside to see if I am just swimming in a circle or what. And stepping outside helps, but it's still me.

**SOBEL:** How do you step outside of it?

**JAIME:** I think some of it has to do with the way I've always lived my life from the outside looking in. While we were growing up Mexican, we were outsider Mexicans because we were rock 'n' rollers, and most of the Mexican kids we knew liked funk and soul and stuff like that. It was a different world, and then I got into the punk thing and I had my punk friends.

Anyway, to make a long story short, I've always been able to stand on the outside and look at my own culture, my own friends and my own musical tastes because I had different factions of friends that liked different things. I kept it all separate on purpose. For example, I would never invite a certain group of friends to a punk party or, in the beginning, I wouldn't invite my punk friends to a comic-book party: things like that. So it's always been like that, where I'm on the outside looking in at my own life. That's the way I think it is, anyway. [*Laughs.*] I'm not sure if that's really how it is, but I think that's what's helped me. And when I do interviews, I always forget to remind the interviewer that they're talking to two guys here. One guy thinks, "Eh, this is just fun and it's all comics, I don't know what I'm doing!" but then the other side is me taking it very seriously. I'll be both of those guys in the same interview.

**GILBERT:** It actually used to be easier in the old days. When *Love and Rockets* was new, we could go back and read our own work and be surprised that we put things in it that we weren't actually aware of. A lot the stuff was coming from the unconscious. Now I'm a little more aware of everything I'm doing. But in the early days, half of it was just us trying to make fun, cool comics, and our brains were adding something to it that we weren't even aware of as we were doing it.

Keep in mind: We didn't start out as seasoned professionals with *Love and Rockets* #1. That was nothing we'd done before. We didn't go through the usual ranks of drudging through the mainstream, learning our craft and that kind of thing. When I was a kid, I didn't want to do *Spider-Man* or the *Fantastic Four*, as much as I liked them. People were always telling me, "You should do comics. You should go to Marvel ... " But I always said, "No, no, no. I don't want to draw *Spider-Man*. I don't want to do that." I didn't care about that. I liked *Spider-Man*, but my personality doesn't go that way. When I draw, it becomes my own thing.

So we've done our comics on our own all our lives. We literally went from doing amateur comics and sending them to fanzines one day to doing *Love and Rockets* the next. It was all just so new to us that we can look back on our stuff now and think,

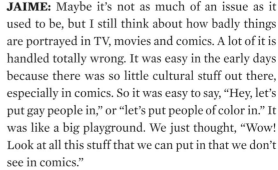

"I did that? I don't remember writing this! Wow, did I write this? Oh yeah!" We surprised ourselves all the time in the early days because, as the cliché goes, the comics wrote themselves, almost. Now it's different, I'm a little more aware of what I'm putting down, what I think the reader might accept and what they might not.

**SOBEL:** In previous interviews, you mentioned that part of the goal of *Love and Rockets* was to fight against the constant barrage of white images and role models in Hollywood and mainstream pop culture, and to depict Latinos in a realistic, humanizing way. With all the changes in American society in the last 30 years, do you still see this as a goal of the comic, and also as an issue in general that needs to be addressed?

**JAIME:** In a way I still do, because even if things have changed, things pretty much look the same. [*Laughs.*] There have been a lot of breakthroughs and things have changed, but when you get down to the bottom line, who is out there? Well, it ain't no Latino.

**GILBERT:** It's changed a little bit, but we were originally talking about pop culture and what is out there in mainstream television and movies. There wasn't any satisfactory representation of Latinos for us. I still don't see any depictions of the Latinos that we see ourselves and continue to put in our comics, even though it's maybe not as obvious as it used to be.

**JAIME:** Maybe it's not as much of an issue as it used to be, but I still think about how badly things are portrayed in TV, movies and comics. A lot of it is handled totally wrong. It was easy in the early days because there was so little cultural stuff out there, especially in comics. So it was easy to say, "Hey, let's put gay people in," or "let's put people of color in." It was like a big playground. We just thought, "Wow! Look at all this stuff that we can put in that we don't see in comics."

**GILBERT:** Comic books were real limited in the sense of multiculturalism. I'm thinking of mainstream comics, which dominated at the time. There might be a book about something real obvious, like South Africa, about the horrible crimes in the barrios. But it was just limited to that, because that's pretty much where the creators and publishers were coming from. That's what they knew, so that's what they exploited. And even though we've had plenty of that type of stuff in our comics, it's still mostly about the characters' lives. The most important thing is the characters' lives and how they respond to things. Humanizing certain characters is still on the top of our list, even if my recent stuff is a little more on the surreal side. But it's still always about that first and foremost.

**SOBEL:** In the last two issues of *New Stories*, it seems like, Jaime, you were looking back at the early days and filling in some of the holes, while, Gilbert, you were looking ahead more. Would you agree with that and is that reflective of where you're each at in terms of the series and the characters?

**JAIME:** For me, yeah, and I was a little worried

*Jaime: "What if this was the last Maggie story I ever did?" From "The Love Bunglers Part 5" (2011) in* Love and Rockets: New Stories #4.

about that [*laughs*], that I was just covering ground that everybody already knew. I was real careful.

**SOBEL:** In terms of what?

**JAIME:** In terms of repeating stuff that people have read for 30 years. I tried to look at it as, "Well, have they seen it from this different angle?" And does it make that much of a difference where it's worth 10 pages? I guess I'm talking about the Letty story ["Return For Me"] more, because most of that information had been shown before, but I just tried to tell it from a different perspective, and hopefully put enough in it where it would feel new enough, where I wasn't just treading water.

As far as the Maggie story ["The Love Bunglers"], I felt it was moving forward, even if it was covering 30 years. It's funny. I did this last issue kind of testing myself, saying, "What if this was the last Maggie story I ever did?" And by the time I was done with it, I was really happy with it, and I said, "Well, if I get hit by a bus tomorrow, then it's cool. It worked."

I set it up just to see what it would look like, but of course it's not the end. No way, she's got to get as old as me; the older I get, she has to catch up. But I think about that a lot when I'm doing new stories, and even if I am covering old ground, I try my best to make it feel new and to give the readers something that they haven't seen, even if it's the same historical moments.

**SOBEL:** You have a unique challenge because you're writing for some fans who have been there since the early '80s and others who have just read pieces of it.

**JAIME:** Yeah, and I admit that with these latest stories, I counted on the 30 years to help it. I was thinking of the people who have been with me for a long time rather than those readers who just picked it up for the first time last year.

So it's always that juggling act, but in this case, I used the strength of its history and all the time that has passed in order to have more of an impact.

**GILBERT:** For me, I'm in a weird position right now because I have the character Killer, who is slowly becoming the focus of my Palomar stories. Now, she's Guadalupe's daughter, which makes

Gilbert's take on a vampire tale: Killer stars in "King Vampire"(2011), a remake of one of Fritz's B movies, in Love and Rockets: New Stories #4.

her Luba's granddaughter, but the plan was that I wasn't going to feature her for eight to 10 years. Now that the comic is yearly, I have a relative plan for the characters as they age, but her character's story didn't come around for about eight years from now. But as I kept making plans, her character kept developing and I thought, "What am I going to do, wait eight years to do this?" [*Laughs.*] So I brought her stories to the forefront right away. The trouble is her story parallels what Fritz is doing with the movie career thing. That bothered me, doing two actresses in the family, because I'm trying to avoid parallels. I've always done it; I've always had two or three characters doing the same thing at the same time, but I'm really trying to avoid that now.

INTERVIEWS

For example, I did a vampire story for *Love and Rockets: New Stories #4* ["King Vampire"]. Now, I'm not looking to do vampire stories, but that one popped in because it was using Killer as an actress, and I thought, "Well, this story wasn't meant to be seen for another eight years," if I was going by my plan, but then I thought, "vampires are hip now and they might not be in eight years." [*Laughs.*] So I thought, "Well, I'll do a vampire story now." Then I thought, "But everybody does a vampire story." Vampire stories are everywhere. Here's where we have to start thinking, "What is *Love and Rockets* really about?" I thought, "Well, they haven't seen a *Love and Rockets* vampire story." So, with that, maybe if I did a vampire story my own way, it would be a little different from everybody else's, and that's what we've always done with the comic. Sometimes we'll run into the problem of doing what everybody else is doing, but part of us knows that we'll just do it a different way.

I just told that little anecdote because that's where my stories are falling right now. They're going back-and-forth within an actual planned structure that I have, but sometimes I'll pull stuff from the beginning or from the end of this plan. It's a juggling act right now. The most important thing is that I just want the stories to be new and for people to be surprised at each comic that I do.

**SOBEL:** Jaime, do you have a similar long-term plan for your characters?

**JAIME:** Not like Gilbert. He's always had his ideas structured better than me. I see mine just as Maggie's got to get to the point where I picture her in the future. I can picture all the characters far away, but I've got to fill in all the in-between stuff from now 'til then. That helps me keep going. The ideas will spring up as I go along, but I don't have it all mapped out.

**GILBERT:** It sounds like I have everything planned, but it's just

basically where the characters are going to be, more or less, not necessarily what the stories are leading up to it. For example, I know that when Fritz is no longer starring in films, her niece's daughter, Killer, takes over and starts remaking her films. That's all I know. The rest I just have to come up with and build up to that. I know who the characters are going to be, generally, but I don't know what the stories are. So that keeps me alert, and hopefully I'll surprise myself along the way, because every once in a while, I still surprise myself.

**SOBEL:** Gilbert, I wanted to ask you about Palomar. In previous interviews, you've said things like you felt "straitjacketed" by it or you'd "outgrown it." Do you have mixed feelings about Palomar at this point?

**GILBERT:** Well, in the old days I felt straitjacketed, because that's all I was doing. It doesn't mean that I felt it was Palomar itself restricting me; it was not being able to goof off with different types of stories. I used to hear from people that Palomar was the norm: that I should do something different, but it has always been the other way around. Palomar is the different thing. One of the reasons I keep going back to Palomar is because the readers like it. And I like it, too, but the main characters' stories are done. I've told all their stories, so to go back to Palomar, I

*Jaime wrote "The Love Bunglers" for his wife "in a roundabout way": Part 5 (2011) is in* Love and Rockets: New Stories #4.

125

have to come up with new stories. But I don't want to necessarily come up with too many new characters because I've got plenty of characters [laughs], and for Palomar, I don't really need that many new ones.

So on one hand, I like Palomar because it's comfortable and I can draw the characters in my sleep and they write themselves. But on the other hand, it's tough to write new stories for old characters or for the old setting of Palomar. That's why I brought in Guadalupe's daughter, Killer. She's learning about Palomar through new eyes. So maybe I can work something new out there.

**SOBEL:** It's been about five years since you've used Luba in a story. Do you feel like her story is done as well?

**GILBERT:** Her vital days are over. Her firebrand days are over. But she's there. I don't want to make her a boring mother hen or anything like that. She's back in issue #5 of Love and Rockets. But, like I said, the stories are no longer about her and that's my challenge. I have to make her interesting in her limited role now.

## FAMILY

**SOBEL:** What roles do your wives play in your creative process?

**JAIME:** I'm mostly left alone. My wife will only comment on what I've been doing lately. Like she'll say, "Oh, I see you ran Maggie through the mill again. If you do that again, I'll never read this comic again." [Laughs.]

I can't take that too seriously, but at the same time, because she had been saying that for a few issues, I honestly wrote "The Love Bunglers," especially the second part, for her in a roundabout way. It's not so much that I'm speaking to her; it's more like, "Maybe you're right. I'll give you what you want for now. But don't bug me for the next 10 issues." [Laughs.] But it worked out. I was very happy with the way the story turned out. I got to keep my integrity as well as give her what she asked for.

**SOBEL:** So she was looking for some kind of resolution to Maggie's love life?

**JAIME:** Yeah, and also she just wanted her to have *something*. I wasn't giving Maggie anything in her eyes. To me, I thought I was: plenty of misery. But her feedback just made me think, and it gave me something to work with at that time. So I think it worked out, and she likes me again. She likes my comics again, too.

**GILBERT:** Well, for me, I usually do Love and Rockets and the Fritz books on my own. My wife never sees them until they're done. But I'm also doing comics for other people like DC, Dark Horse, and now Drawn & Quarterly and even Bongo Comics. Those are the projects that are harder for me to get into because it's harder for me to do a new kind of story for them.

With the other companies, I'm also sometimes dealing with editors that are a little more hands-on. They need to know what I'm doing and to be aware of what I'm working on for the most part, and that's a little different. So it's harder for me to convince myself to do those projects and that's when my wife comes in. She just pretty much encourages me and tells me that it's not that hard. "It's not a problem. You make it a problem; don't make it a problem, it's something you can do."

So she's a pretty good cheerleader, or depending on the project, drill sergeant. [Laughs.] There's stuff I don't want to do and she convinces me to do it.

And I'm usually glad I did it. Just to survive, I have to do outside projects, and the best thing I can do is comics. I'm not asked to do single drawings for $5,000, so I have to do comics to make ends meet. That's why I'm always doing exhaustive projects for other people, but they work out in the end with my cheerleader behind me.

**SOBEL:** You're all fathers now. Mario, you have four kids, right?

**MARIO:** Yeah.

**SOBEL:** And Gilbert and Jaime, you each have one?

**GILBERT:** Yep.

**SOBEL:** How old are your kids?

**JAIME:** Mine is 13.

*Jaime's "Gold Diggers of 1969" ran as a "bottom strip" below the reprinting of his* New York Times *"Maggie La Loca" comic in* Love and Rockets *Vol. II #20 (Summer 2007).*

**GILBERT:** My Natalia is 11, 12 in June.

**MARIO:** My oldest kid is 32 now and my son is 30. They're two years apart. My other daughter is 28 and then I have a daughter at home who is 15.

**SOBEL:** How has the transition into fatherhood impacted your work?

**GILBERT:** There's nothing conscious, other than I have to pay more bills. That's why I do all the comics that I do, because I have to: if people think I'm doing too many comics or there are series or books that they didn't like as much as my other work, I can't help that. I've got to pay the bills. So there's that. It's also made me work more and do more loose-ended stuff. Like I said, I'm doing a zombie comic right now. I would have never done a zombie comic 10 years ago, but I figure, well, if the kids like zombies ... I'm happy with it, but it's not something I normally would let myself do. And like I said, I did a vampire story in the recent *Love and Rockets*. But those are also isolated stories. I'm going to go back to the other stuff soon, but I'm sure as hell not going to do another zombie comic if asked.

Other than that, I have to keep my art away from my daughter. I think she is still too young to read my comics, although she begs me to read them, and I have to say, "You can't. Not 'til you're 16 or so." I don't hide them from her. She could just walk into my room and pull out a book; it's not hidden. I just tell her not to. It's about trust. I tell her, "I don't want you to see this yet" and she's pretty good about it as far as I know. But other than those two things, I haven't consciously

changed anything about the stories. I'm sure she's influenced me quite a bit, but I don't know where.

**JAIME:** I guess that's the same with me. No matter how my lifestyle has changed, I always put a chunk of me aside for the work, so, maybe unconsciously fatherhood has changed me, but I don't know where. I guess I understand the grown-up side of life now, being a responsible parent and all. Maybe that might show through. I'm not sure. Like I said, it's all unconscious.

**MARIO:** With me, my youngest daughter is really heavy into Japanese manga and anime, and a lot of things that are just online. So she gives me a fresh perspective as far as what is going on that I would never search out myself. The older kids are always bringing new stuff home, too, and it inspires me to go, "Wow. I can do this or that now, because I know that some people are doing this weird stuff on this end of the spectrum." It's fascinating because it makes me realize that there is a lot more going on than just tragic biographies or emo comics. When all my kids move away, am I going to go into the opium years where it will be just really dark stories of things from the past, because there won't be anybody to open my eyes to a lot of new stuff? Anyway, that's where all the inspiration for me comes from in terms of being a father — my kids bringing home new and fresh ideas. Not that I use them, but it's inspiring.

**SOBEL:** This might be a silly question, but do you see yourselves in some ways as fathers to your characters?

**JAIME:** Oh yeah! I always refer to my characters as my babies. [*Laughs.*]

I'm so close to my characters, I have dumb conversations with them.

**GILBERT:** I guess I feel that way, too, but not as strongly. It's more that they're part of me, yet at the same time, I'm often their slave. They write the stories themselves. If I have a certain theme with my characters that I repeat over and over, it's not conscious. It's because the characters are doing that by themselves. For example, I'm emphasizing Fritz so much not just because I like drawing her but because I don't know her. I know my other characters, but I don't know her. I've never known her. So I'm compelled to figure her out and that's partly what all these Fritz books are about. They're actually parallels to her life, surreal versions of who she is, but even if there's monsters and gangsters or whatever in the story, it's still a Fritz story, and that's just part of her personality coming through. That's how it is for me. Sometimes I emphasize characters simply to know them, because I don't know them, yet I'm compelled to follow their story.

**SOBEL:** So you feel like you're still getting to know Fritz as a character after all these years?

**GILBERT:** Yeah, and since she's unknowable, that's why I have an inexhaustible supply of stories for her. I have to cut down all the different stories I want to do because there's not enough time for everything. I'll be 90 years old when I'm half done. So I really have to figure out which is the most important story to tell. Those stories of Fritz are pretty much just me trying to figure her out, and at the same time having fun with comics, because since I don't know her, they can be told any way I want. I'm not restricted with Fritz, but it's different with a character like Luba. Luba was Luba from the first frame to the last and I had to follow her path in a naturalistic way. There were very few surprises with Luba after a while, and I think that's what readers liked. She was going to react how she was going to react to a situation and even if it was always the same reaction, they liked it. I hope.

**JAIME:** It's funny because my angle's different. When I do Maggie she takes over everything. None of these big Maggie opuses were meant to be Maggie opuses. Her character just takes over everything and sucks the air out of the room. When I'm writing her and drawing her, I've almost got this crush on her. It's like I'm falling in love with her, and I want to see her go through every aspect of emotion possible.

So it's the opposite of Gilbert. It's the characters I know that I want to explore more, especially someone like Maggie, and after I'm done doing these big, giant stories about her, and I'm running her through the mud and stuff, afterward, I'm like, "Damn, I did it again!" I didn't mean to do this. I wanted to give the other characters something to do, but I just end up putting everything inside of her when I do her. I'm sure a psychologist would have a field day with me about that.

**GILBERT:** My take on you doing Maggie all the time is that she's your ultimate character for self-expression. You are so much yourself doing Maggie that you don't have a reason not to. You don't need a new character, or you're not compelled to write stories about someone else because Maggie speaks for you. So she's there speaking for you.

**JAIME:** That's true.

**GILBERT:** She's all you. All of you. Part of you goes into the other characters, I've noticed, but all of you goes into Maggie. That's why I think Maggie works for you so well and takes over, because it's about you expressing yourself through the story.

**SOBEL:** Gilbert, why has it been so hard for you to get to know Fritz?

**GILBERT:** I don't know. She was actually one of the first serious characters that I ever created, before most of my other characters. This is back in the late '70s. I had created a lot of characters for myself, but they always fell away; they just sort of came and went and were never really defined. Then I did a Fritz story, which was inspired by *Star Wars* of all things. I just wanted to do a *Star Wars*-type comic, but starring a girl.

**SOBEL:** Was this the one that was in the first *Sketchbook*?

**GILBERT:** No. This was the very first story I finished, and the first story I lost in the mail, so I don't have it anymore. It was called "Vacuum Run."

**MARIO:** I got to ink that.

**GILBERT:** Before I created Fritz I was always drawing the same type of girls, and I decided to draw a different type. The way her face was and the eyebrows across her forehead, she just had a different demeanor when I drew her. So I think that's where Fritz comes in. She's different from the other characters I relate to more. All the other characters like Luba and Tonantzín and Pipo, and all the other pretty girls that I've drawn, I know them. But Fritz, for some reason, she was a mystery. I like drawing her for conscious and unconscious reasons. So Fritz went away after she had a tiny part in the first *Love and Rockets*. I just didn't use her anymore. But I kept coming back to her, thinking, "Where can I put this character?" and finally I put her in *Birdland* because I needed an extra character.

I then put her in the Palomar series and from there on, every time I wrote and drew the character, I felt like I just needed to talk about her and show her. But I couldn't ever really get anywhere with her, and, to this day, I'm still doing that.

I finally I figured, well, if that's where I'm going to be, I might as well have fun with it. I put her in B-movie stories where I could obviously have put any other character in, but it's just easier to use her. That's how the recent Fritz stories came about. I could have used different characters, but she was the one I thought would be the thread. I figured I could explore who she is in story after story.

**SOBEL:** Do you still feel compelled to figure her out, or are you satisfied with who she's become at this point?

**GILBERT:** That's the thing; I think this is as far as I'm going to get with her, in terms of knowing her, but since, in all that exploration I've made so many different stories, I thought, "man, just go with it." Like I said, I also just like drawing her. I can change her personality for each story.

At the end of the day, I guess she just became my character that I want to express madness through. It's not a Maggie thing. It's not like I want to express myself as a relatable person. It's more like I want to express myself as a crazy obsessed person. I'm

*This drawing of Fritz is probably from the late '70s: from the Gilbert section in the* Love and Rockets Sketchbook *Vol. 1.*

approximating a crazy artist. I'm actually a pretty average person; it's just that I always loved craziness in comics. Does that make any sense? [*Laughs.*]

**SOBEL:** Yeah.

**GILBERT:** I'm the only one laughing here. I'm scared.

**MARIO:** I'm stunned! [*Laughs.*]

**GILBERT:** And, by the way, if I hear anybody reading this saying, "that's called indulgence," well, it's all indulgence. Palomar was indulgence. Errata Stigmata was indulgence. Expressing yourself in art is indulgent. I've read that [Federico] Fellini believed in that, as does Woody Allen. Critics hate that, heh heh.

## BENT WORLDS

**SOBEL:** I imagine a lot of your fans have only a limited familiarity with B movies and some of the older films you all are into. Could you talk a little about the hobby itself? For example, where do you find the movies that you watch?

**MARIO:** Mostly we just got into it from watching tons of movies as kids. We grew up in a household of "turn on the TV and stay out of the way." So we got to watch a lot of stuff, like all the little scary shows that they used to have on the different channels.

**GILBERT:** I have always been into strange movies, and as a kid, if I had my choice I'd watch a scary movie or a monster movie over a regular film anytime. Regular movies were on TV because our mom watched them, so I learned to like them as well and I learned to like classic films, too, because our TV was always on. Although for her they were just basic entertainment. She didn't seem to care about the artistic difference between a slick Hollywood movie and an art film. She preferred the slicker stuff, the stuff of dreams.

On weekends we'd watch monster movies, which led to gothic mystery movies, and then eventually crime movies. This evolved over the course of several years. In those days foreign movies also fell into that category of strange movies with strange plots. They were supposed to be serious films, but they still had the oddballness of strange American movies, like horror and stuff. Plus, in a foreign movie, you'd probably get to see a naked lady. [*Laughs.*] We were always like, "What the hell? What's going on here? You can't show that on TV." The first sex scene I ever saw was on PBS and it was the violent rape scene in *The Virgin Spring*. Boy, did that send frightening mixed messages to an 11-year-old boy.

So eventually I developed a taste for all kinds of movies and in the last 15 years or so I'm more than ever involved in mysteries and film noir, the dark side of low-budget movies. I avoided horror movies in the '70s and '80s, just because I wasn't interested, but now I am, and I'm catching up on a lot of wacky, creepy shit that came out in those days, usually European. I'm not crazy about super-violence, but a lot of them have that in it, and I basically tolerate it. I guess I just like a bent world, because that's what comic books were like for me. I enjoyed comic books from Marvel and DC, of course, and the kid comics and stuff, but every once in a while I'd read something that was really weird, even if it was in *Classics Illustrated*. Some stories just came off as weird, even though they were supposed to be classic stories. I've always had an interest in that kind of weird stuff.

**SOBEL:** Do you buy DVDs or just watch whatever is on TV?

**GILBERT:** I am a collector. I like to collect two things: movies and comics. There's not much music I collect anymore (although two relatively recent favorites are The Hives and P!NK), but as far as movies and books on comics, especially the reprint collections they've been putting out, I'm addicted. With movies, it's usually DVDs but a lot of times Turner Classic Movies will show some really strange films out of the blue in the middle of the night, usually something I've heard of but never got to see. A lot of the movies I like aren't even available on DVD, at least as far as I know. Of course, things are different now. Everybody else can find this stuff because they know how to work a computer. I don't. I still do it the old-fashioned way by ferreting it out myself.

**MARIO:** I do the same thing. I don't buy as many DVDs as I used to, but I do have a huge collection, and we've all gone through the whole VHS recording-everything phase, before moving into the DVD thing. But it's kind of petered out over the years because of over-saturation. We've got so much stuff but no time to watch it all, even though we try.

**JAIME:** Same with me. I started taping so much stuff that I ran out of time to watch them, and after a while I was just taping stuff and cataloging it and putting it away. Pretty soon I started to run out of shelf space. Then, when DVDs came out, that was a blessing in disguise, because all of my VHS tapes had become obsolete so it was easy for me to let them go. When I started buying DVDs, I was more selective, and I've been more selective, but that's also taken away my adventurous spirit of searching out old things. I'm almost too exhausted to seek the stuff out anymore, but for a while there, I was just taping movie after movie after movie. First some of the channels like TBS would show something

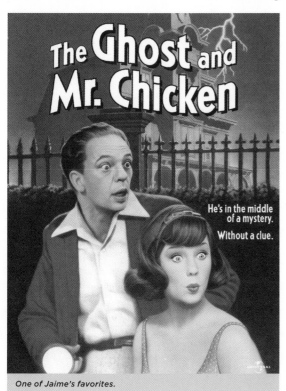

*One of Jaime's favorites.*

old and cool, and then after a while you had AMC and then Turner Classic, and after a while, it just became a racket.

I still love all that old stuff, but the thing I miss is the thrill of watching a movie like that as a kid, and how it was scary or whatever. I also miss that feeling of coming home drunk after a party or something and turning on the TV at 3 in the morning and something I never saw before was on some random local channel. That was a lot of fun.

But the cool thing is every once in a while there's something I missed. Like Gilbert will tell me about this collection that he got of old '70s horror made by this one director of this one company, and it's like, "Where was this? Where were we when this was out?" But that's happening less and less, of course.

**GILBERT:** When you watch a great old movie, especially a foreign movie or something from the '50s or so, you're just reminded how shitty movies are now [*laughs*], because that was just basic entertainment back then. They just wanted to entertain people. It's just so much better than most movies you see now in the theaters.

**MARIO:** It's telling a story you're not familiar with.

**SOBEL:** What are some of your all-time favorites, and maybe some of the ones that found their way — even in a small way — into your work?

**JAIME:** For me, it's hard to say. I've got favorites, but a lot of times they don't relate to my work, because I don't consciously copy them. There's no direct influence; it's just whatever I've soaked up over the years. One of my favorites is *The Ghost and Mr. Chicken*. What the hell does that have to do with my comics? Well, if someone says, "I can see it!" I'll say, "Good," but if they don't see it, that's good too. I don't know. It's all just part of the big package.

**MARIO:** The movies I liked as a kid and even into my later years were stuff like *It's a Mad, Mad, Mad, Mad World* and *The Longest Day*.

They used to be my favorite movies because they were these ensemble things where all these people are connecting into one story. They're all from disparate ends of the spectrum, but they all congregate at the end. Some of the stories that I've done are like that. I like that whole idea of disparate characters that don't know each other who all of a sudden are thrown together. So it has influenced my work in that sense, and *Mad, Mad World*, I have to say, is still one of my favorites.

**GILBERT:** When I'm up against the wall, and I'm asked, "What are your favorite kinds of movies?" I'll be serious. I'll say I like the neorealist Italian movies or great American movies like *How Green Was My Valley* or *A Face in the Crowd*. I'll talk about those in a serious discussion, but if I'm not talking about those kinds of movies, I'll watch anything with Lon Chaney, Jr. He's in some of the worst movies of all time, but I enjoy him like crazy. I just enjoy shabby

movies, and it must be because we watched them as kids like they were serious movies. We weren't the type so much to say, "Oh, that's fake," or "Oh, that's terrible." A lot of people watch those old movies to laugh at them. But when we were kids, we took them fairly seriously.

**MARIO:** And may I say that *Mystery Science Theater 3000,* or whatever the hell it is, has ruined all these movies for me because I like to just watch them and make my own comments. I know people really love it, but watching the original and just wondering what the hell is going on is much better, I think. [*Laughs.*]

**GILBERT:** I was just watching *The Cyclops* starring Lon Chaney, Jr. the other day, and it was like

# ROSALBA FRITZ MARTINEZ' B-MOVIE ROLES

**ROCKIN' THE WAVES 2** Bikini Contest Participant | *Fritz's first movie, a surf documentary in which she appeared for only three seconds.*

**MAD CIRCUS** Bearded Bellydancer

**THE GAMMA LOVERS** Drug Hallucination Demon

**HALLOWED ARE THE SEASONS** Hippy

**KING VAMPIRE** Vampiress | *Original film version.*

**CHANCE IN HELL** Prostitute | *Fritz' first speaking part.*

**THE TROUBLEMAKERS** Grifter | *Fritz' first featured role.*

**SPEAK OF THE DEVIL** Waitress/Serial Killer

**TAME: BLOOD IS THE DRUG** Transvestite/Singer/ Transsexual

**MARIA M.** Mob Wife (in Maria M.) | *Biography of Fritz' mother.*

**TO LIE IN DARKNESS** Bellydancer | *Unfinished remake of Fritz' mother's one movie.*

**BLACK CAT MOON** Prostitute; Porn Star; Seven Clones

**FOR SINNERS ONLY/SAVAGE WORLD** Average Citizen; Average Wealthy Citizen

**HYPNOTWIST/SCARLET BY STARLIGHT** Average Citizen; Cat Creature

**THE EARTHIANS** Astronette

**LOVE FROM THE SHADOWS** Waitress; Brother and Father

**PROOF THAT THE DEVIL LOVES YOU** Simple-Minded Wild Woman; Vacationing Gambler; Aging Dancer; Forest Demoness and Actress

**3 MYSTIC EYES** Sorceress; Psychiatrist; Average Citizen and Queen

**THE MIDNIGHT PEOPLE** Cult Mistress | *Also starring Mila.*

**THE MAGIC VOYAGE OF ALADDIN/ 7 BULLETS TO HELL** Sorceress; Prostitute and secret agent | *Also starring Mila.*

**LIE DOWN IN THE DARK** Bellydancer

**KING VAMPIRE** Vampiress; Person in Surreal Dream; Mother | *Three stories featuring Killer, this KING VAMPIRE version is a TV episode where Fritz reprises her role from her own film.*

I was a little kid again. They all go to this strange place in Mexico where animals are growing giant and there's a Cyclops there. It was crazy, but I still watched it like it was a regular movie.

**MARIO:** Plus, now that we've got kids, we're introducing them to all this stuff. Jaime just said they were watching *Night of the Living Dead* with his daughter, and Gilbert shows his daughter movies all the time. I love to introduce my kids to all kinds of new stuff, too. Some of it they get, and a lot of it they wonder, "Why are you showing me this?" [*Laughs.*] But it's fun to see it through their eyes.

I also learn which movies work, and which ones don't, but they're always entertaining at least.

**SOBEL:** So it's part nostalgia, and part some genuine creative energy in these old movies that still resonates?

**GILBERT:** It's just a whole different world to me.

**JAIME:** It's like getting something out of a cheap, old comic book that most people think was just junk. There's something that you can get out of that stuff, something strange that came out of a particular artist. It's the same with movies and actors and stuff like that.

**SOBEL:** Gilbert, do you see your Fritz stories, like *Chance in Hell* and *Troublemakers*, as a straightforward application of that style or are you commenting more subtly on the genre?

**GILBERT:** There's no real comment in them. These are just my versions of those types of movies we're talking about. And since those movies aren't made anymore and they don't make comics like that anymore, I'm just doing that for fun, really. I'm trying to separate what I do in *Love and Rockets* and the Fritz books, but they're overlapping because that's how my brain works. I always tend to start overlapping everything. I just want people to read a fun, nutty comic book that they'll hopefully enjoy or be creeped out by. When was the last time you were creeped out by a comic book that wasn't about real social issues? Yeah, you can read something like Joe Sacco's books reporting on what's going on in the rest of the world, and that'll creep you out because that's reality. But I'm

looking to creep you out simply with the distorted world in these stories. It's not really about politics or reflecting on the human condition. It's sort of like what David Lynch used to do. He'd show you the regular world, but it was off-kilter, and it just creeped you out even if nothing that wild was really going on.

That's all I wanted to do with those B-movie books, but right now, with *Love and Rockets*, our work is being very scrutinized. We get responses that they're happy with Jaime's half of what's going on, but then they're confused or irritated about what I'm doing and how the Fritz books are encroaching on my work in *Love and Rockets*. So there's a lot of confusion that I'm getting, like, "What are you doing here? Why are you doing this? We don't want to see this."

**MARIO:** But the original idea of *Love and Rockets* was, "we're gonna give them what we want them to read." I remember Gilbert saying, "I don't care what their ideas about what they think they want to read are. This is what I'm gonna show them." I don't know, I still think that's a successful outlook because then you're not a slave to fandom trying to dictate what you put on the page.

As far as my work is concerned, and I don't get enough feedback to know, but I try to give the

*Gilbert's "Bread, Love and Maria" (1994) is reprinted in* Human Diastrophism.

# THE NAKED COSMOS

**SOBEL:** Can you describe how you ended up doing *The Naked Cosmos*, and what the experience was like?

**GILBERT:** As a kid, I loved the guys that used to host the horror movies. Every local channel had some nut, like a crazy meteorologist that wore a Frankenstein or a Dracula suit and introduced the movies. Some of them were better than others. We had a guy in L.A. named Seymour and he was so great, I would rather watch him than the movies he showed. He made the movies fun. And in the daytime there were guys who did the same thing for little kids' shows and cartoons. I just really miss that little part of my childhood. There's not much use for it these days, I guess. I mean, Elvira's made a good living with it, and there's Svengoolie, but not much else. I just felt like making a mock local TV show like that.

At first I was just wearing the costume and my wife was filming me with a video camera, but then I started adding a story to it, and it just built into what *The Naked Cosmos* became. I figured there were enough crazy people like me who might think something like that was funny. It was nothing like *Love and Rockets* and comics. It's just me standing in front of a camera performing. I really just did it for fun. As it turns out, it got put together on DVD and has a tiny cult following. I'm being forced to do a second one with better production values. [*Laughs.*]

**SOBEL:** You're doing a *Naked Cosmos* sequel?

**GILBERT:** Yeah, it's been a long time coming. It's been seven years since *Naked Cosmos*. Isn't that weird? But I'm going to do it again because this time I have a guy who really wants to produce it and use real cameras and sound and all that stuff. So I said, "OK, as long as it's fun for everybody."

*Gilbert starred as Quintas, a bizarre children's TV show host, in the four-episode series* The Naked Cosmos. *This is from the 2005 minicomic that accompanied the DVD.*

readers something different every time that they haven't seen yet. If they wonder, "Why is he writing about this, because skateboarding is popular right now? Why isn't he writing about skateboards?"

I'll just go the other way. I'll give them something they're not looking at right now. No zombies or werewolves, just some strange story that will give them a "Huh?" If I can get a "Huh?" out of people, that's good enough for me.

**SOBEL:** Gilbert, can you expand on what you were saying before about people scrutinizing *Love and Rockets*. Do you think they're having a hard time because it's the same characters and they're struggling to see them in different roles?

**GILBERT:** I think that's part of it, but I think the reality is they simply want me to do something else. They just don't want to read those stories. They don't like those B-movie stories and they don't want me to do them. They want me to do something closer to Palomar, something they can relate to more. Like, "Your stories are supposed to be about me. I want to read about me, not about your wacko ideas or off-kilter worlds." [*Laughs.*]

It's basically that.

"We don't want you to do this, Gilbert. Do what *we* want you to do."

That's pretty much it.

My only concern about it is if it affects sales. I do care if the word-of-mouth is "Don't read *Love and Rockets* because Gilbert's ruining it," because Jaime's enjoying a real good resurgence of people really enjoying what he's doing. That's great; that's fantastic, but if I'm there ruining it ... I guess I can't hurt *Love and Rockets*. *Love and Rockets* will be OK, but if I do other projects ... like I did this zombie massacre comic with Dark Horse and I might get the worst reviews I've ever had for that book. I do want to keep that stuff away from *Love and Rockets*, but it encroaches now and again. The next three Fritz books I'm doing outside of *Love and Rockets* might just get clobbered, but I've reconciled myself with that. From now on, my career will be half of the people liking and the other half just hating what I do. The people that like it really

like it. They come up to me and say, "This is great! When are you going to do more? What are you going to do next?"

But it's a minority. They're outspoken, but I don't think there's that many people. I mostly get, "What the fuck are you doing? Do something good!"

Well, sorry, but I want to do both. I am amused when they say, "Gilbert did this crazy story I didn't like, so his career is over."

Idiots say shit like that and some people might listen. That's my only concern: that people listen to someone dismissing my whole career. It's happened to other artists. But I'm going to continue doing comics the way I want to. The only thing that's going to make me stop is if the people paying me tell me, "You can't do this anymore."

**SOBEL:** What you're describing makes me think back to *Human Diastrophism*, where you had Humberto trying to determine his responsibility as an artist. Does he owe something to his audience, or should he do what he wants to do for himself?

**GILBERT:** Well, I don't want to abandon serious comics forever because that is something I can do and like doing. It's just that right now I have much more energy for the crazy stuff. The serious stuff, sure, there's a place for it. I've done it before and I usually get my best response from stories like that. And I do want to do more, it's just, like I said, the energy and the nasty fun I get from the Fritz books and some of the other stuff I'm doing in *Love and Rockets* just energizes me more. I have so many ideas for that stuff; I do have to put a lot of it aside sometimes.

Also, when I look back at that old stuff, like *Human Diastrophism* and *Poison River*, I see the crazy energy in those stories. I've always had this crazy, nervous energy that I can't always control and it got the better of me during those stories. That's why I'm trying to separate the two more now. I'm trying to have crazy energy stories and then two-people-in-a-room-talking kind of stories. I'm Jekyll and Hyde, but these days I'm mostly Hyde.

**SOBEL:** At this point in your careers, do you still go back to any of your favorite artists for inspiration, like Hank Ketcham, Jack Kirby or Robert Crumb? And, if so, which ones?

**GILBERT:** The room I work in, the way it's set up is, I have all my books and collections on the walls around me. Sometimes, just to get away from the drawing board because my neck hurts or something, I'll pull out a Jack Kirby omnibus, for example, and after 10 minutes of looking at Kirby, I am re-energized. He made superheroes worth something. He did such great work. I'm also looking at [Robert] Crumb all the time. I look at their work all the time, just because the books are in front of me.

Before, I had all my comics in boxes and it took a little bit of effort to find things. But now that they've collected all this stuff in books, it's easier. It's harder on my shelves but it's more convenient. I just literally stand up and walk across the room. Right now I'm looking at the *Complete Terry and the Pirates*. I can look at that any time. I'm also looking at the *Peanuts* collections Fantagraphics has been sending me, thankfully. Sometimes I'll just grab that because the lettering on the spine is staring at me.

I don't only look at the comics I liked as a kid, but there's not that much new stuff that I really look at because comics are so fragmented now. There's not a lot of emphasis on old-school drawing in indy comics, which is what inspired me when I was younger. You have to *read* an indy comic to appreciate it; you can't just browse through it so much and pick up what it's about by the drawings, whereas you can get the gist of what a Jack Kirby comic is about by reading it or simply just skimming through it, because the visual impact is so powerful.

**JAIME:** I have the same kind of situation where I need all those books near me, or I'll never go near them. It's the same as when I do research. I could have a picture of a car in the next room, but I won't go look at it in order to draw it. [*Laughs.*] But with all of these archives, I'll just pull out an old collection and skim through it, just like Gilbert. It's like that energy drink, or that blast of coffee to get to work. It's a booster and it just gets me excited to draw, even if I'm not doing a superhero story or something like that. The inspiration lies in just getting me off my ass and wanting to make the best comics I possibly can.

**SOBEL:** Jaime, do you feel the same as Gilbert in terms of the newer stuff?

**JAIME:** I guess I feel the same way pretty much. If you'd known me since I was 5 years old, you'd know that you've got to twist my arm to get me to read. So sometimes a new alternative book is just too much work, especially if it's one of those big, fat 700-page graphic novels. Sometimes I just pass

*In "Human Diastrophism"(1987), reprinted in the eponymous volume, Humberto discovers true artistic freedom.*

THERE ARE MANY PRESENT WHO INDENTIFY HUGH AS THE MERRY ROGUE WHO HAS KEPT THE FORESTS LIVELY FOR LO, THESE MANY YEARS.....HIS TRIAL AND CONVICTION ARE A MATTER OF MINUTES .....THEN, ACCORDING TO ANCIENT CUSTOM, THE KING ASKS;— "IS THERE ANYONE TO SPEAK ON THE PRISONER'S BEHALF?" PRINCE VALIANT, DRIPPING WITH SWEAT AND PANTING, BURSTS INTO THE CIRCLE. "HOLD," HE GASPS, "I WILL BE THIS MAN'S ADVOCATE!"

NEXT WEEK — The Price of One Word.

*This panel is from Hal Foster's September 8, 1946* Prince Valiant *newspaper page: it's reprinted in* Prince Valiant Vol. 5: 1945-1946.

them by because I know "I'm never gonna get to that." [*Laughs.*]

The older I get, I'm just more into something that's really well drawn and well inked. If it's not drawn that well, that's OK, but it's got to be an artist that really has something beneath all those lines. I guess it's not the lines I'm excited about; it's the artists beneath them. That's how I've tried to approach my own work. I hope people are not just looking at these few lines; I hope there is something they're seeing beyond that. I know that with a lot of the newer comics, it's not that important for that kind of approach to comic telling. But the older and crankier I get, that's what I'm looking for because that's what I was raised on, and you go for the stuff that really inspired you from the beginning.

**GILBERT:** Let me just add a little to that. It's been said here and there by certain fans and reviewers of modern indy comics that *Love and Rockets* looks like clip art. It's this idea that actually being able to draw is now a detriment to storytelling.

**SOBEL:** It's hard to believe someone would say that.

**GILBERT:** It's been said. And it's usually a rival cartoonist that can't draw. Well, this is written in stone

in my house: any artist that criticizes another artist for drawing well is just a jealous idiot. [*Laughs.*] I don't care if they think *Prince Valiant* is the worst comic strip they ever saw. If you can't draw as well as Hal Foster and you're criticizing his ability to draw well, then you're just completely full of massive mountains of shit.

Anyway, that said, I just think as generations go by, young people read certain kinds of comics as they grow up and that's their frame of reference. So when you have something very well drawn, like Jaime's Maggie stories, to them, their only frame of reference is clip art. Things are changing now, like we said before, because of all the reprint books. Now there's so much stuff available. And with the Internet, stuff is just everywhere; you can't escape it if you're interested in comics, even though sometimes it feels like people manage to know less now that there's more information out there.

**SOBEL:** Did you see the new Alex Toth book [*Genius, Isolated*] that came out?

**GILBERT:** Oh yeah, sure. I've got so much of that stuff already, though, from collecting over the years.

**SOBEL:** What you're saying, though ... those books are great for people like me. I don't have all those old comics from the '50s.

**GILBERT:** Right, yeah.

**SOBEL:** I knew some of Toth's work. I'd seen some *Zorro* books here and there but that was just a stunning book for me.

**GILBERT:** That's what's great about this new presentation of the old work. More people get to see it now. We're not looking to duplicate those types of stories; that's not the point. The point is, this is what was done back then by a really good artist. Like Jaime said, I don't look at a Kirby comic to do a superhero story; I just look at what he put into it, his personality and sheer inventiveness. It's just all there, and that still impresses me.

**JAIME:** Yeah, and going back to what I was saying about the image I want to see and all that stuff ... when I was a little kid, and my brothers and I were collecting comics, I never actually read the ones that we had. I only went through them; I looked at the drawings and made up my own ideas about what was going on. I didn't read them until, God, I was almost a teenager and I started to wonder, "What are these about anyway?" [*Laughs.*] But I think that that was a huge part of my training. I was looking at all this art and the ones that spoke to me without reading them were the special ones, while the ones that didn't, I just went by them and didn't hold on to them for very long.

I never realized it, but the first thing I'm looking for when I look at a comic, whether it's new or old, is: Does it speak to me visually? I'll worry about the reading later, or sometimes I won't even read it. For the most part, I guess I have to be pleased visually first.

**GILBERT:** I also learned to write that way, by not reading the words but seeing how the stories were told with the images. I would maybe grab a couple of snippets of dialogue or captions, but I was much more interested in how the story was told visually, and then applying my own story to it. I'm talking about when I was very small, because I was 5 years old when I did my first comic.

I guess that was our beginnings and we just never broke the habit. We still look at a lot of comics that way. Even with all of these reprint books, I'll read some of the stories, and some are boring as hell to read, but the art's great. The visual storytelling is there.

Of course, there are certain artists that you can't help but read. For me, it's Robert Crumb. If I pull out a Crumb book, and open up to a page, I can't help but read it. The drawings tell part of the story, but his writing does as well. That's pretty rare for me these days, where I'm just completely compelled to *read* a comic that I've read a dozen times.

Crumb is one of the few artists that still does that to me, although the Bible [*The Book of Genesis Illustrated by R. Crumb*] was hell to get through. But he didn't write that book. [*Laughs.*]

My problem with the Bible was ... there's got to be some beauty in it, and I didn't really see much beauty in Crumb's telling, outside of his great drawing. Spiritual beauty, I'm saying. Faith is supposed to be beautiful, but I didn't really get any sense of that from *Genesis*. I just saw a bunch of people feeling miserable and screwing other people over. God came off as the good guy in the book.

**JAIME:** It's true. Going through that book, I kept thinking, "Boy, is everyone bummed out." Or pissed off.

**SOBEL:** Or scared.

**GILBERT:** Yeah, they were scared, even though they were given all this beautiful stuff. But they just kept fucking it up. And that's the story of man, I guess.

**SOBEL:** I also thought Crumb did some of the best drawing of his career in *Genesis*, but beauty is not in there, at least not in the people in the story.

**JAIME:** It goes back to what Gilbert was saying earlier, about why he can read Crumb so easily. It's because there's a beauty in Crumb's cartooning that couldn't come out in *Genesis* because, like you said, he didn't write it. It didn't move exactly like a Crumb comic, as beautiful as all the images were. You read a Crumb comic, and you're just running with him, and that's the beauty of it. I think he nailed down the perfect way to tell stories visually, to engage the reader in comics, and I'd never thought about that until Gilbert said that right now. I always knew I liked Crumb, and I would sometimes wonder, "Why do I like this better?" Usually I just thought, "Well, it's because it's 'pure comics,'" and I would just end it at that. But when Gilbert just mentioned what he liked about Crumb and reading it at the same time, I think he's right. Crumb is the perfect example of pure comic book storytelling.

**GILBERT:** That's not to say Crumb hasn't done some pretty negative stuff. Some of the things he's drawn and written I completely disagree with.

# AND HE SAID...

*God scolds in* The Book of Genesis Illustrated by R. Crumb.

Some of the supposed parodies of racist and sexist stuff, that's hard to take, and I can't blame women for getting pissed off.

A few people I've known over the years say, "Aw, women are going after Crumb because they don't have a sense of humor, blah blah." But I'll say, "You know what, if Crumb were saying that about you over and over, you'd feel pretty uncomfortable about it, too." Crumb's being honest and venting his demons, but sometimes it's hard to defend. I can't argue with a woman who gets offended because of how Crumb depicted women in a certain story. I can't say, "Oh well, you're dumb. You should learn to take a joke," because it is insulting. Jaime and I are Latino, and we've heard that kind of shit about us. We don't like it either. So why would women like that stuff? I will say, Crumb the artist can

still engage me despite the negative stuff. Maybe Crumb's just being a satirist, but it's hard to say.

**SOBEL**: People look at that stuff and then they look at *Genesis*, and they're trying to make sense of his decision to do a project like that.

**JAIME**: I've heard people talk about how they were so shocked that Crumb would pick the Bible of all things with his track record, but I just look at it from a cartoonist's point of view. It was just another thing to do. [*Laughs.*] It was another comic to do. It didn't seem strange to me, maybe because Crumb has gone that way before when he'd do his blues biographies and things like that. Or even the one-pagers where he decided to play it straight-faced. So I knew he had it in him. It didn't seem that strange to me. The length of it, I thought anyone's crazy who's going to do all that work in one chunk.

**GILBERT**: Yeah, it wasn't a surprise to me, either. You get a couple of the reviewers saying, "Why did Crumb do this?" That's a dumb question. He's an artist. He can take on anything he feels like. And he finished it. He went the distance and did it, because he's an artist. That's what artists do. If it failed, it failed. I don't think it did. It's not my favorite work of his, but he went for it all the way.

**JAIME**: I'm also impressed that from the first to the last panel, he took his time. There's no point where you think, "Oh, he was tired here." [*Laughs.*] He stuck it out.

**GILBERT**: He definitely gave a hundred percent of himself art-wise, that's for sure. If you look at a lot of the cartoonists we've talked about since we've started making comics, they're all pretty much down to earth as far as the way they draw and tell a story. Crumb, Schulz, Kirby, Ketchum and Owen Fitzgerald, all these guys are artists who just got down and drew people in their stories. There was very little superficial technique about it, you know, razzle-dazzle. Well, except for Kirby who was all razzle-dazzle, but it was natural for him. That's just what came out of Kirby. But if you look at 90 percent of the artists we're inspired by, I'd say they're pretty much down to earth. There's not a lot of fancy stuff going on in the actual art. It's just the art telling the story.

**SOBEL:** In *Ten Years of Love and Rockets*, you each talked about your techniques and approach to compositions and laying out pages. Can you talk about what's changed over the years since then in terms of your drawing process, particularly in the last 10 years or so?

**JAIME:** It's much more controlled than it used to be. In the early days, it was just devil-may-care; I put in whatever I felt like. Now a lot of things have come into my life, like deadlines, so what I feel is important to go into the page has changed, too. Now I will put down what I think it needs to move the story along and then after that I will add in what I think it needs to make a pretty page. For example, I might want to put a background in one panel, but maybe I won't need it the next time because there's already enough in the panel to please the eye. So it's organic for me and I just hope it looks OK. [*Laughs.*]

**GILBERT:** For me, with everything about comics, I'm more conscious of not repeating myself and getting it done. I think more on the technical level now. You have this many panels, you have this many close-ups of the character, you have this many long shots, I think about all that stuff more than I used to. It was more stream of consciousness before, whereas now I think of what is going to be easiest for the reader to absorb. I'm really concerned about the reader absorbing my stuff pretty quickly, because in the past I've really made myself muddy, and it was a struggle to get through my work. I've known that for years. I don't even read my old stuff any more. [*Laughs.*]

**SOBEL:** Are you talking about *Love and Rockets X*, for example, stuff from that period?

**GILBERT:** Yeah, around that period. *Poison River*, *Love and Rockets X*, even a little after that. It all became so dense I don't even want to look at it. If I'm forced to for research, maybe I'll be surprised that I handled certain things better than I remembered I did, but I'm not compelled to go back and read them. I get a headache after three panels. [*Laughs.*]

But now I'm much more conscious about making it easier to absorb. I've always admired comic strips like *Peanuts*, and even *Nancy*, where you look at it and you're immediately absorbed into whatever's going on. It goes back to Crumb as well. You can't help but want to read what's going on in the panel, whereas I'm sure my old stuff pushed people away because it was just too dense.

**SOBEL:** Have your working habits changed in terms of how you approach your day?

**GILBERT:** My problem is I've become a workaholic. I work seven days a week now. I shouldn't, because it wears you out, but if I have some free time, it goes into drawing, or at least preparing the next project. I'm trying to back off that now. I will take time off during the week sometimes, but if I'm here in the house, I just end up at the drawing board without even thinking. But I try to devote at least five days a week, five hours a day. That's what I try to do and then back off at night and on the weekends, if I remember to. I have to remind myself to stop doing comics because of what day it is. All the days run together.

I also try to hang out with the family and just be a normal person, because you can turn into a vegetable doing this stuff all the time. I'm not saying I work all day every day, but there are days it's really good to take off an entire day from drawing or writing. When I go on vacations, they're usually just a few days, but I'm reinvigorated when I come back, because I haven't drawn or written a word in those three or four days. I know how good that is to get away from it but I have really bad working habits. I overdo it.

**JAIME:** I try to give myself regular hours while my wife and daughter are at school and work. I try to make it like this is my day job so I use the nights to be a good husband. But if I'm on a roll, and I'm on the downhill of an issue, where I'm just going gangbusters, I'll work in the day and then at night when they go to bed and you can't keep me away from it.

"Poison River" (1988-1994), collected in Beyond Palomar, is a denser work than Birdland (1990-1994).

But a lot of the times I have this cycle that's been going on since I started this comic, which is that after I finish a story, I go dull. I can't just jump into the next one, or it's very rare. I get this kind of post-comic depression where I can't think straight. I can't put the next comic together even if there's an idea there. It just has to form in my brain while I'm not at the drawing board for days. Sometimes it takes weeks, and now that we do a comic only once a year and I put a 110 percent into those 50 pages, and it's almost feverish by the end of it, afterward I just go blank. And because it's one big chunk of an annual comic, it sometimes lasts even longer now. So I just go about my daily routines, sweeping the porch and things like that, but I'm constantly thinking about the comic and what's next. When I get a little germ, for example, I want to do a story about

the Frogmouth, I'll think, "OK, what's she gonna do? What's her purpose? How do I keep her fun? How do I make her not boring? If I put her in this situation, will that ruin her character?" because I like the character the way she is. She's one character I want to keep the same throughout, instead of so much growing like a lot of the other characters. But then I think, "How long can I keep a character like this the same?" And it's all just swimming around in my head, but I'm not at the drawing board, because when I sit at the drawing board it's just a blank canvas.

Since I finished this last one in New Stories #4, I went through this huge, huge blank slate, because I put so much backlog and sewed up so many loose ends on all that old stuff that I had nothing left after it was done. Only now is everything starting to fall into place. I've been writing an actual story again, and I'm like, "Hey! I didn't lose it!" That can be a pretty scary feeling, but after 30 years I know it

141

won't always be that way. I just have to let it happen. It's this weird psychological cycle I go through every issue.

**SOBEL:** Was this something you dealt with even back in the early days?

**JAIME:** I dealt with it, but on a shorter scale. I guess in the very beginning I didn't have that because it was a free-for-all. I was just putting anything in there, and I didn't care about the outcome. But when I started with the continuity and starting to understand that these characters have to work right for me and communicate with the reader, that's when I started to go through this cycle.

Another one I get sometimes is that, in the middle of doing a story, after I've come up with an idea that I'm happy with and I've started to put it down, there'll be a day when I look at it and go, "This is the worst waste of time for everybody, me included." And I have to leave it alone and go away for a while. Then I'll come back and ask, "Am I ready yet? Nope. Still sucks." This is the same material for the most part that will end up in the book, but it's just this thing that I've got, that I've always had. But I just let it happen now because, after 30 years, I know I will get through it. It's just sometimes I ask when.

**SOBEL:** Is that the same for you, Gilbert?

**GILBERT:** I've learned that that happens. For me, it was the same in the beginning where I'd get something started, and I would finally get the inspiration for it and start working the story, then halfway through, I'd start telling myself, "This is the worst thing I've ever done. This is boring. The readers don't deserve this crap." It's just this weird thing that pops into my head halfway through, and I noticed the pattern after a while, so I stopped believing in it. I think to myself, "This is just a negative pattern, so it's something to dismiss. This is not something to take seriously." Eventually, over the years, I've been able to minimize that negativity. I really don't have that problem so much anymore, because I recognize my patterns of depression. Depression is just ... some psychologist on TV said this once and I always remembered it ... it's anything that keeps you from doing something.

**SOBEL:** I remember that line from Fritz in one of the Venus stories.

**GILBERT:** Yeah, because I had just heard it floating in the ether. I don't even think I was looking at the television. It was in the background or something, but I remember a psychologist saying that, and it made sense to me, because you're believing that whatever you can't do is the truth. Or what you're doing wrong is the truth. In other words, what's real and life affirming for you is somehow not the truth. That's depression talking.

Anyway, nowadays I take these sour patterns less seriously. I know that I'm going to finish my comics; I have to. That's the most important thing, not this emotional block I have. The most important thing is getting the books done and trying to enjoy it. I mean, don't get me wrong, it happens sometimes. I still come up to a blank page sometimes. Like right now, I'm supposed to write this Bart Simpson story and I'm completely blank on it. I have absolutely no idea how to write this Bart Simpson story and the thing's been due for a couple weeks.

**SOBEL:** There have been so many of those stories written.

**GILBERT:** Yeah, and they're written a certain way. *The Simpsons* have a certain particular sense of humor that I'm weak at approximating. If I'm

In the first installment of "Letters From Venus" (1995-1996), reprinted in Luba in America, *Fritz quotes something Gilbert overheard.*

‹ WELL, VENUTH, I'M OFF. TELL YOUR MOTHER THE CHECK ITH IN THE MAIL AND YOU TWO REMEMBER THITH :›

DEPRETHION ITH ANYTHING THAT KEEPTH YOU FROM DOING THOMETHING.

‹ OK, TIA. ›

*Gilbert cartooned "Homer Simpson: Chick Magnet" in* Simpson Comics Presents Bart Simpson #52 (February 2010).

working on my own characters and stuff, it's a little easier, because I can actually bluff those in a pinch. What I mean by bluff is that I trick myself into doing the stories, almost. For example, if I don't know what to do with a certain character, I'll just put him in a random setting and kind of bluff it until the story comes together. The only trouble with that is a lot of times I start to put art and lettering to paper and then I've got to change it all if I've made the wrong drawing or story decision.

**SOBEL:** Has 30 years taken a physical toll on you?

**JAIME:** Oh yeah. My body is falling apart.

**GILBERT:** It's wrecked my neck. I go to a chiropractor.

**JAIME:** Also, other than my back, neck and shoulders, lately I've noticed that my hand doesn't want to go certain places. I have to relearn how to hold the pen. But I treat it all like a learning experience. I'm learning how to do things again because I have to do them differently, like the way I hold the pen or the way I angle my body to get a certain line I want down. Stuff like that. I'm only in my early 50s, but if I hold the pen a certain way, I start to do the Charles Schulz squiggle. But that's only at a certain angle so I just have to teach myself to turn the page

in order to make that line go correctly. Every once in a while I think, "My brain will always be here, but my body's not going to let me finish this stuff." It's kind of maddening sometimes.

It's also materials; they're getting cheaper. I put that in the physical category.

**SOBEL:** What's changed?

**JAIME:** As far as materials, ink is cheaper. It's not as black. Also, the nibs are not the same flexibility as they were because they're using a cheaper metal or something. I used to be able to count on getting the same nib every time and using it the same way every time. Now, in each issue I'm using four different types of nibs, just trying to get the one that will put down the line I want.

Paper is getting cheaper, too. I've always tried to use the best quality plate-finished Bristol board, but even the top quality has gotten cheaper. So where can I go from there? All I can do is hope that the next tablet will be better. And it's funny, because this tablet of Bristol board I'm using now is great. It's like, "Oh, this is how the paper used to be!" But the last three issues, boy was I having trouble with the paper. It's just things like that.

**GILBERT:** Here's a weird thing I've discovered in the last few years. The paper I use and the dimensions I use to draw *Love and Rockets* and the Fritz

Gilbert's back cover for Love and Rockets *Vol. II #5 (Summer 2002).*

is it. I'm doomed. I can't do comics anymore." It was still sore a couple days later so I started working on *Love and Rockets* instead and I noticed I got my wind back; I got my edge back. So I started wondering what happened, but I still didn't put two and two together. I couldn't understand it, but it was simply drawing larger and putting more ink on it. There's also a broader stroke of erasing the page than there is with my regular work. I guess it's just that those muscles have atrophied. But it took me a long time to realize it was the size of the art that was taking a toll on me. So I work on those books differently now. I ink them and erase them differently. It's really a simple thing but I just wasn't conscious of it: such an obvious thing to see, too.

**SOBEL:** Do you have any hand pain or stiffness or any of that sort of thing a lot of cartoonists get?

**GILBERT:** Not too bad because I know when to quit now. I've learned the hard way.

**JAIME:** I have different physical problems at different times during the process of doing an issue. Like, if I go to ink something for the first time, sometimes I forgot how to ink. I think, "This is terrible. What's going on here? I can't even make a straight line." Or within an hour, I'll sometimes start to feel really cramped up, like my whole body is shriveling up toward the paper. But that's only because I'm out of practice from the last time. So I have to back off and take more breaks in the beginning. By the end of it everything's cool. My body has adjusted and it's just like skiing downhill. It's beautiful and I feel good and I see the end of it coming, but it's just the relearning every time I start a new comic that's hard.

## THE INDY COMICS GHETTO

**SOBEL:** In your first *Comics Journal* interview, Gary [Groth] asked you guys if you thought "sex in *Love and Rockets* was frivolously portrayed." I'm curious how you would both answer that question now in regards to your more recent work.

**JAIME:** I don't remember Gary saying that, but I'm

books are pretty small. I can work with that size pretty well, although I can't use the same materials I used to, like certain brushes and stuff, because I'm just drawing too small. I use a pen nib more often now than before.

But I realized— and it didn't hit me until much later — that when I do a DC or Dark Horse comic, I have to use their paper and it's very large to me. And I noticed that after I do a few pages, I'm exhausted. I'm completely wiped out. At first I thought, "This doesn't happen with my own work; I don't get it."

I remember one time I finished a DC story and I couldn't figure out why my shoulder was killing me. I'd gone out with my wife and daughter to go bowling, and afterward, my hand and right arm were so screwed up, I was really worried that I'd seriously messed them up. I thought, "Uh-oh, this

always trying to make my characters as close to real life as possible, while also having fun doing them. So along with people's lives, people have sex. Some people do, some people don't, and it is just a part of their lives. I've always treated it that way. I put it in there because that's the way it is. There was never really a big game plan other than: this is another part of life like going to the bathroom or eating dinner. Someone once told me, "you do sex like no other comic ever did."

I said, "Well, what am I doing? Tell *me* about it so I'll know!" [*Laughs.*]

But maybe it's better they didn't tell me. I'll just keep treating it the same way. It just seems like a natural thing to put in there.

**GILBERT:** I think the sex in my comics is even more frivolous. [*Laughs.*] That's funny that you mention that. I don't remember Gary asking us that either. I think he was playing devil's advocate, because, well ... I think sex *is* often frivolous. You do it or you don't do it, you enjoy it or you don't enjoy it. You like looking at naked people or you don't. I've learned the hard way that a lot of people just don't like it. Of course, there's also a smaller group, just as vocal, who do like it.

I guess part of the question is, "Don't you feel responsible for sexually transmitted diseases and stuff?"

Well, I never think of our readers as under 18, even though a lot of them are. I don't think of them as young people who need to be taught responsibility with sex. I know that's a serious issue, of course, especially with younger people, but I just never think about it. I always forget that there's a broader reader-ship, especially for Jaime's stuff.

There are a lot of younger people reading Jaime's stuff, at least in recent years, but I forget about that. I just like to draw sex like it's an action story or a nightmare or something. Good things happen, bad things happen. I don't think about it. I forget that the world's still uptight about it until I'm yelled at.

**SOBEL:** When you say you get yelled at, where are the negative reactions coming from?

**GILBERT:** I think that there's a lot of, especially in my work, this lack of romance and a lack of how sometimes sex fits into a bad relationship. For example, Fritz is obsessed with her ex-husband. He treats her like crap, but she keeps coming back to him and uses sex to get back to him. I've been criticized for that because people don't want to read

In "Another Story Altogether" (2006), reprinted in Luba: Three Daughters, Señor Yorgos *subtly acknowledges some of the criticisms of Gilbert's recent work.*

that story anymore. They say, "OK, we've seen it, all right. Stop doing that story."

I've actually heard that from intelligent people. So I'm not doing that so much anymore, but I think that's the criticism, that there's no romance. Everybody's already naked and they're already doing it, and they act normal afterwards. I've noticed in the past, I guess when we were doing the second volume of *Love and Rockets,* that there were a lot of semi-autobiographical comics by people who depicted stories where they were with girls and the sex was always bad or it somehow screwed up the character's life, and those comics got really good responses. So it's back to the sadness factor again. People would rather read about sadness rather than people having fun. That's my take on it.

**SOBEL:** One of the things I wrote about in the *Love and Rockets Reader* is that *Birdland* is a lot more than just a sex comic: It's a parody and response to Wilhelm Reich's theories, and there's all this other stuff going on. But in every interview I read, you seem to dismiss the book and I was just curious why?

**GILBERT:** Well, *Birdland* was back when I was talking about feeling straitjacketed by the comics I was doing. The stories I was doing at the time were *Love and Rockets X* and *Poison River,* which were heavily written, and did not have much in the way of layouts. So I just wanted to do an action comic, something where everything was physical as far as the characters' activities were concerned. I thought, "Well, everybody does superheroes and action; this is what so many comics are. I can't just go out there and say, 'I'm going to do an adventure comic.'" That's what everybody else does. But they don't do sex comics. So that's what made me start thinking about it at first. So I decided to do a sex action comic where the actual physical activity was over-the-top in a Kirby sense.

That's pretty much it. I was just doing it as a liberating thing, and to thumb my nose at the naysayers and conservatives. But as with my other comics at the time, it became just as dense. That's just where my brain was. *Birdland* became as convoluted and angst-ridden as my other stuff. It was fun to do

at the time, but I probably wouldn't have the energy to do it again. I guess that's why it sounds like I dismiss it. It was just supposed to be this wacky adventure comic that nobody else was doing.

**SOBEL:** Other than *Birdland,* do you see some of your depictions of sex as an effort to break down some of the taboo and conservatism that's out there, or is it more just about realistic portrayal in your eyes?

**JAIME:** I would say it's both of those. It's a realistic portrayal, but I also don't want anyone to tell me not to use my reality. So at the same time as "Look, this is the way people live," it's also "Look, this is the way people live, and you can't tell me not to."

**GILBERT:** For me, it's also part of the climate of the comics industry. Here I go dumping on indy comics again, but there's this sort of PC self-righteousness about them where it's like, "We don't do what the mainstream does." It's kind of a ghetto to me, I hate to say. There's this attitude people have where it's like, "this is what a real comic's supposed to be about, and that icky Britney Spears stuff doesn't exist."

Well guess what? It does. All that stuff out there on the Internet, the way pop star women are portraying themselves, that's all real. Doing comics for me isn't an escape from the mainstream. It's just doing it my way. So I guess that's going back to what Jaime said. This is how I'm going to do it and pretending that people in the real world don't have these desires and fantasies is just nonsense. It irritates me that things get straitjacketed to, "We don't do what those people do."

That sounds like a safety zone ghetto to me.

**SOBEL:** Can you elaborate on what you mean by calling indy comics "a ghetto?"

**GILBERT:** It just means that there's a specific type of comic that people want to read from independent comics, and then the rest is, "Why are you doing that? I don't want to read that."

It's a subtle kind of fascism. I think a lot of people go toward alternative comics, and other indy scenes, like indy music and films, to get away from the mainstream, to get away from the things that offend them. So they go to a place like indy comics because they have the kind of stories they can relate

*Bang Bang, who reappeared in Birdland, made her first appearance in "Music for Monsters Part 1" (1981), reprinted in Amor y Cohetes.*

to, stories that are about them, but any deviation from that, like what I'm doing with the Fritz books and some things in *Love and Rockets* doesn't fit in the box: even though that's how *Love and Rockets* started out, like a Wild West show with all this nuttiness.

I just think the indy scene today has settled into this sort of rigid comfort. They don't want other things because they don't want what's out in the mainstream. So while the rest of the world is going nuts as hell, indy comics are safe, and it's become the opposite of what they started out as. You don't have to compete with the real world; you can be safe being an indy wise-guy. That's how I see it.

Also, like Jaime said, there are not many well-drawn comics. It's all very stylized because the artists never learned how to draw from life, they've learned to draw from their personality, which is fine, there's a lot of good artists that do that, but as far as comparatively representational illustration in indy comics? "It better not exploit my insecurities." Maybe I'm out of it, but I just don't see stuff I'm that interested in. It seems very safe to me.

**JAIME:** I see what Gilbert is talking about but I've also seen a little more of the indy scene because I

know people here in L.A. who are more a part of the younger set, like my friend Jordan Crane. He'll teach me about the new independent artists, so I do see a lot of it. But I do agree with Gilbert in a way, that it's almost become like, "We're going to make our comics serious," and you're not supposed to fuck around with serious. But Gilbert's still fucking around with his comics. But the closer you get to serious, meaning literature, or academics or something like that, for a lot of people it's like, "You've got to be grown-ups. You can't mess around; you can't be foolish; you can't look silly." A lot of indy comics have gone that way. But on the other hand there are people like Eric Haven, for example, who I really like because he's just nuts. He does comics about a guy walking around, and then he sees a vulture girl or something, and she's like "Come with me."

I see that and I say "Yeah! Great! Awesome!"

But for me those kinds of comics are few and far between. I guess that's how it goes with everything. But, in many cases I do see that, as far as being taken seriously, you can't act silly anymore.

**MARIO:** Well, from my perspective looking at it from the outside — and Gilbert and I actually had a heated discussion once (not mad at each other, but mad at the industry) about how, when comics started becoming these big graphic novels that started

©2013 Eric Haven

*Jaime likes Eric Haven's work. In this panel, Dan Clowes and Adrian Tomine meet God in Haven's "I Killed Dan Clowes" from* Tales to Demolish *#2 (2003).*

**GILBERT:** Another thing is that they're telling roughly the same stories about sad people. [*Laughs.*] After a while, I'll look at the stuff and say, "Hey, they're writing about sad people. I just wrote a story about sad people. Jaime just wrote a story about sad people. Hmmm ... I think I'm sad peopled out right now." [*Laughs.*] That's what happens. You get an overload of sad people stories. Somehow, that's turned into the truth for so many people. Well, sure, it happens to people sometimes, but not always, and not to everybody. I remember having great times growing up.

But I also want to add to what I said before; this is called "covering your ass time." I will admit I don't see a lot of indy comics. I see very few, just what comes to me. So if there is all this great stuff out there, I wish people would let me know about it because I don't see it when I go out or when someone shows me their favorite books.

PRECONCEIVED NOTIONS

**SOBEL:** Back in the '80s I think we all wanted comics that were literate and would attract a wide audience and people would buy in bookstores. It seems now like it's almost swung too far in that direction.

**GILBERT:** That might be, but like I said, I don't see a lot of them. It might also just be that a lot of cartoonists can't handle the big books, that they're stronger doing short stories. But we know that doing short stories from a selling point is suicide.

**SOBEL:** There is the financial aspect of a 200-page book.

**GILBERT:** Actually the new Craig Thompson book, *Habibi*, looks good. His art has progressed to new heights, but I look at it, and it's fighting me. It tells me, "Do not read this. Just look at me."

**SOBEL:** It's been sitting on my shelf for months, and I pull it out every few days and think, "God, this is beautiful," but I haven't read it yet.

**JAIME:** Yeah, he outdid himself art-wise, but I'm afraid to buy it. Part of the reason is because it's

selling in the book stores, like *Blankets*, which was drawn beautifully although I've never read it, all of a sudden you started seeing a lot more books like that. Gilbert was calling them "tragic biographies" and I hadn't noticed that that's what they were. Every best-selling thing, like *Persepolis* and all that stuff, was somebody's biography, and that was the only kind of comics that were coming out in big bulky books. I thought, well, gee, nobody is doing an adventure book like *The Troublemakers*, or a sleazy novel, or a detective story or something like that. They were just doing these long autobiographies because that's what the big publishers want. So far that's basically all I've seen, and, I'm sorry to say, I just don't buy it.

just too big and it's going to take me forever to get through. I almost miss the days where you could buy a ... what do they call them now, floppies? I'm missing that, where you could buy one and read it, and then you were done. I'm not going to complain that it took me 10 minutes to read, because if it's good enough, it's going to last me longer than that 10 minutes.

Also, these days they're collecting all the old strips and comics I've always loved in these big, fat volumes. So, going into the comic store and seeing the new collection of something like *Dick Tracy*, I'm like, "Oh my God, I waited 40 years for this." But then another one comes out, and another one, and I don't have the capacity to soak it all in anymore. So a lot of them sit on my shelf untouched. Two years later I might pull it down and go, "Hey, I never looked at this," and it'll be fresh and cool, but ... sheesh ... I guess my dream became my nightmare.

**SOBEL:** Most of those old strips weren't even meant to be read that way. For example, they published *The Complete Calvin and Hobbes*, which was one of my childhood favorites, but it doesn't have the same impact when you read 100 pages in one sitting.

**JAIME:** Sure. It's like in the *Peanuts* collections, I

*Gilbert on Craig Thompson's* Habibi: *"His art has progressed to new heights, but I look at it, and it's fighting me."*

©2011 Craig Thompson

recently read a favorite story that I originally read in the newspaper strip when I was a teenager about when Charlie Brown starts to grow baseball stitches on his head, and then he becomes Mr. Sack and puts a bag over his head. I remember reading the single strip every day in the paper and I couldn't wait 'til the next one. When I got this collection, I read it in two seconds, the whole saga. It just wasn't the same. So it's true, this stuff wasn't meant to be read all together.

**SOBEL:** Do you think *Love and Rockets* suffers from this?

**JAIME:** Sometimes I wonder about that. For example, I think about someone who's never read *Love and Rockets* before and someone else kept bugging them for years, "You gotta read this! You gotta read this!" and then they finally did, and they spent a weekend reading my whole career. I mean, if you go through the complete *Love and Rockets* in one weekend, or one month, some people might think, "Well, these characters are nice, but I don't feel like I really lived with them."

Well, that's because you only lived with them for that short amount of time. So I can't blame them if they said, "Well, it's cool. It was a great read, but I don't know, the characters are OK," because they didn't *live* with them.

I could be hanging myself right now, but some things were just meant to be spread out, like you were saying.

**GILBERT:** If you read the classic adventure strips like *Dick Tracy* or *Rip Kirby,* or even *Secret Agent X-9*, the modern reader doesn't relate to them so much because, like Jaime said, you're reading something that was supposed to be read once a day. You're supposed to get caught up in the rhythm of it, like, I hate to say it, a soap opera or something. If you break down a *Dick Tracy* sequence, it's an epic where each day you were just slowly building up to this climax of Dick Tracy chasing some crazy maniac. There was all this anticipation and suspense when you read those over time. Now, you can just skim through it and finish it in one sitting. It's the same thing with *Love and Rockets*. Now people can read our entire careers in one weekend.

**SOBEL:** Have you gotten mixed or negative reactions because of the presentation in the new collections?

**JAIME:** Not a lot, and not to my face, but I hear them secondhand. I remember I got this review by some guy saying, "I got this big *Locas* book so I could finally figure out what this Maggie and Hopey thing is about. And what I found out is that they don't do anything." He said, "I guess you had to be there," and I went, "Dammit!"

**GILBERT:** One guy really went after Hopey once, saying, "She's this, she's that, she's this, she's that," and I thought, "You just said what was good about her, but you hated it. That's who the character is, but you're telling everyone they should not like her." That's what I'm running into with my Fritz stuff. This one guy just described everything that happened in *Love from the Shadows* and then he said, "This is terrible. Gilbert's become [Steve] Ditko. He's crazy."

But I thought, "Wait! You've just described what was good about it!"

So I guess it just depends on what your point of view is. It's the old saying: two people can look at the same thing, and one person loves it while the other person hates it. It just turns out that the reviewers with the biggest mouths are the ones who don't like things and love to talk about what they don't like.

**MARIO:** There's a movie reviewer here in San Francisco whose opinion I don't care for, but he said one time that people would write him letters asking, "What is so great about *Citizen Kane*? I saw it the other day and I didn't see anything so big about it." So he said, "Well, it's been built up over the years as the greatest thing since sliced bread, so everybody thinks it's going to be sliced bread, but it's not. It's going to be a different piece of toast for everybody." I think *Love and Rockets* has the same problem sometimes, in terms of preconceived notions.

**JAIME:** Yeah, preconceived notions are killers. That movie *Citizen Kane* isn't that good? No, it is that good, you're just mad at those people who told you it was that good. The film itself is great; it's just the reputation you're arguing with more than the film.

**GILBERT:** What's also odd is, now that they're reprinting a lot of the stuff we've been talking about for years, newer, younger readers are finally seeing what we were talking about. You've got collections of Dick Briefer's *Frankenstein* now, *Nancy and Sluggo*, *Little Lulu* ...

**MARIO:** It's like that Art Spiegelman book, the one with all the kids' comics [*The Toon Treasury of Classic Children's Comics*]; I thought there were a lot of good choices in there, but to us they were just normal stuff we have in our collections. And *Art Out of Time* and its sequel, half of those comics we have, too. They were just normal comics to us, but now they're wacko, space-cadet-type "art" comics. I'm still glad that they're being put out there, so the younger readers can see what that stuff was about, though, because these people were just crazy. To me, that's what I've always liked to see, comic books that look like they were made by crazy people. Even though they were just kindly old men with families whipping out these comics for publishers because they were getting 20 dollars a page.

**JAIME:** A lot of the comic companies back in the '40s and '50s were just following the genres that sold, and they were forcing their artists and writers to fit into that, but a lot of them were never into that stuff so their versions were just crazier than the genre itself because it was their naïve take on it. That's what gave them that crazy quality which made them so much better.

## ANTHOLOGIES

**SOBEL:** Speaking of old comics, I wanted to ask you about *Measles*, your kids' anthology series. Can you describe how that came to life?

**GILBERT:** That was something I came up with. I wanted to get a bunch of the cartoonists that I knew to do short stories for kids, because there weren't really kids' comics out there like the type that we grew up with. It was supposed to be a grab bag of different styles and different types of kids' stories.

Ernie Bushmiller pokes fun at modern art in this October 3, 1944 Nancy newspaper strip.

What happened, though, was that it was really hard for people to switch gears to do kids' stories. Some people were bringing in stuff that was just too harsh, and I'd say, "Hey, you've got to tone this down," but they didn't know how. A lot of people who are cartoonists today have never read a kid's comic. So it was hard. It eventually went away because we couldn't get enough money for the artists to justify spending their time doing it. It was such a low-selling comic.

**SOBEL:** Do you have any sense of whether you were able to reach younger fans?

**GILBERT:** After a couple of issues I realized it was going nowhere; this is not how it used to be. It was a life lesson for me that the past is over; the way comic books use to be read is over. It's different now. Indy comics readers aren't interested in this kind of comic and kids don't read comics like they used to.

**SOBEL:** Especially black-and-white ones.

**GILBERT:** Yeah, a black-and-white comic that was written and drawn by half-crazed cartoonists. I just thought, "Let's have a fun, little, light kid's comic," but it just came off too dark, and there was no audience for it. It's as simple as that. That's why it went away.

**SOBEL:** Mario, can you give some background context for your story, "The Legend of Celestra," from the second issue?

**MARIO:** This is where I came in with my idea of what I thought *Measles* could be like. I don't know if you're familiar with the old *Treasure Chest* comics that the Catholic Church used to put out. I'm seeing them a lot now in the bins at cons and stuff, and

people are really getting into them because they had a lot of cool illustrators, like Reed Crandall and a bunch of others. They would have these "lives of the saints" stories in them, which I loved. So I had this idea about that bell in the bell tower, which, in fact, was part of the fever dreams I used to have when I was sick as a kid. So for years, the idea was stuck in my mind, but I never had any chance to use it until this came up, and I thought, let me do a fake life-of-the-saints thing. I've actually fooled a few people. People come up to me and say, "Hey, where is that legend from? I've never read that anywhere before." I say, "Well, I made it up," and they're shocked. They actually thought I was writing about something real.

**JAIME:** There's a compliment!

**MARIO:** Yeah, I fooled 'em.

**GILBERT:** But here's the problem. I thought that was a terrific story even if the pages were printed in the wrong order.

**SOBEL:** What happened?

**GILBERT:** The pages are out of order. Even if Mario drew the largest page numbers I've ever seen on a comics page, they still printed them out of order. [*Laughs.*] But other than that, the story was great, and I thought, like I said, people just didn't have a frame of reference for reading a story like that. They didn't understand why a story like that existed.

**MARIO:** Yeah, and why is it in what's supposed to be this funny kid's comic?

**GILBERT:** We've been asked that question since we started drawing comics. Why are you doing this story? For example, I did a story on the different uses of a corpse's hand, because in history, out of superstition, they would use corpse's hands for

From Mario's "The Legend of Celestra: The Maiden of Mud"(1999) in Measles #2 (Easter 1999).

different things, like healing and cursing people and stuff. So I just did this one page thing in a comic and I got so many questions, like "Why did you do that story? Why do I have to know that information? Why are you doing this? Do what you do normally! Don't do this!" [*Laughs.*]

I've been getting that stuff from the beginning, and I'm getting even more now. I'm scratching my head, because when we read comics as kids, you just opened up the comic and that's what it was about. You didn't ask why. We knew a romance comic was a romance comic. We just knew that. We didn't have to ask why it existed.

But since the '70s, comics fans became so rigid in their reading of superhero comics that that became the norm. Most people were just so embedded in Marvel and DC in the '70s that that's what comics became after that. It wasn't until the new alternative books like *Raw*, *Weirdo*, *Love and Rockets*, and *Eightball* took off and shook that up that things began to change. Up until then, superheroes had such a grip on what the perception of American comics were, that we'd always get asked questions like "Why did you do that story? Why did you do a story about a bell in a church?"

Even today we sometimes still hear that stuff and I just shake my head. It's a story, and that's it. It's a different kind of story.

**JAIME:** I remember also when people would ask me, "Why are you doing this? I wish you would go back to this." But I think that's also what has given us a lot of our positive response, because we give them things they're not always familiar with and most people embrace that. But there are also a few who just don't get it.

**SOBEL:** What about *Goody Good Comics*? What was your original vision there and why did it end after the first issue?

**GILBERT:** That was just my little break back when I was trying to get away from doing the type of stuff I was doing in *Love and Rockets*, the relatively serious stuff. I just wanted to do a crazy comic book, but it sold so poorly because nobody wanted to read that 15 years ago. It was going to be a *Measles* for adults, where in later issues new artists could come in, like *Zap*, and write and draw the craziest comics that they could think of. I launched it with a long story to make sure it got done. I intended to make it like *Heavy Metal* magazine for good comics, but it failed. Both *Measles* and *Goody Good* even more so, nobody wanted them. I worked really hard to make a fun comic and my peers were amused. Other artists liked it because they thought it was funny and crazy, and they got it, but that's only like 12 people. I'm just always trying to do stuff that nobody wants. [*Laughs.*] Both comics would have grown by now. They could have really been something, but with no one getting paid much, forget it.

**JAIME:** I've heard from a lot of artists and people in alternative comics who started anthology books, and they've always ended up almost heartbroken because either sales were really poor or the artists were not cooperating, or it turned out to be something they didn't plan in the first place, or they felt really guilty about rejecting a lot of the work because they wanted to include everybody and they felt bad about having to take a lot of it out. So the

*This page is from "Extend the Hand of Love to All Who Can Use It" (2000) in* Goody Good Comics #1 *(June 2000), reprinted in* Fear of Comics.

anthology thing drives a lot of people crazy. That's the way it seems to me.

**MARIO:** Look at *Mome. Mome* was a book that Eric Reynolds was editing. It was a pretty good book and it was gaining momentum but he had to cancel it. Anthologies just don't last very long.

**GILBERT:** It was a great place for young cartoonists, too. There were a couple guys I saw in there who I haven't seen before or after, because there's not many other places for them.

**SOBEL:** Speaking of anthologies, Mario, I wanted to ask you about *Brain Capers*. These were stories you did for books like *Real Girl* and *Buzzard*. Can you talk about some of these series and how you became associated with them?

**MARIO:** I'm in San Francisco and I got here in the late '80s when there was still a big community of cartoonists. Steve Lafler was here and a lot of the old underground guys were still around. We'd all hang around together and have barbeques and stuff and every once in a while someone would ask me, "You're not with *Love and Rockets* anymore, what're you doing? Where can I find your stuff?" I'd say, "Well, I've got a thing in *Rip-Off* and I've got a thing in *Buzzard*" and I'd just get these blank stares. Most people don't know anything about those books.

So I decided to do a book with all my stories together in one place so I could say, "Here, now you can read my stuff." [*Laughs.*] It was a greedy little thing that I didn't want to do myself so I had Fantagraphics do it, thank you. I just wanted to have a book together of all the things I'd done so when people asked, I could just hand them *Brain Capers* and say, "here."

**GILBERT:** The sad thing is when people ask me, "What've you been doing lately? Are you still doing comics?" and I say, "Yeah, I've been doing this and this," and talk about the last 10 years and what I've been doing, sometimes they have this look of hurt [*laughs*], like "I'm sorry I asked."

I guess they want to hear that I'm a failure, that I'm not doing anything or that I'm pushing a broom, but I say "No, I've been doing comics all this time."

153

...I KNOW THOSE PLACES ARE A WASTE OF TIME— BUT A GUY'S GOTTA DO SOMETHING, Y'KNOW. I JUST WANT SOMEONE...

WHY DO YOU FIND IT SO IMPORTANT TO HAVE SOMEONE SO SOON? BESIDES THE OBVIOUS...

MMMM...

...THEN, THERE'S ALWAYS THERAPY

*This panel is from Mario's "Big Windows" (1990), reprinted in Brain Capers #1 (1993).*

And now and again you'll get somebody [who'll] yawn and lean back and say, "I haven't read *Love and Rockets* in 20 years," like they're proud of it.

"Oh, so you're illiterate, you bastard?" [*Laughs.*]

**MARIO:** Yeah, people can be rude sometimes. I know I've gotten those kinds of responses. People say "Oh, I didn't read that one" or "I didn't like that last story you did because ... blah blah blah." One guy even said, "Get a job," and I'm like, "OK fine, whatever."

**GILBERT:** Ask me something else I can get mad at.

**JAIME:** I haven't been pissed off yet. [*Laughs.*]

## THE FUTURE OF COMICS

**SOBEL:** As artists who've worked in comics for three decades, what are your impressions about where the medium's going and how it's changing, and what does that mean for you personally?

**JAIME:** I think people will always draw comics, I just don't know how they're going to reach people. It's hard to say because I've lost that competitive edge with the rest of the industry, so I'm out of the loop. I don't know where comics are going, and part of me doesn't really care because I just want to draw my comics and get them out there, and hopefully they will sit on the shelf and not get pushed out. So I don't know. I know there are plenty of people out there like me who love drawing comics and telling stories in comic form. But how they're going to get out there, I don't know. Hopefully we can still print books, but who knows?

**GILBERT:** I imagine there's going to be more Internet comics, because people are reading less and less books. There always could be a weird backlash where people want to look at books again, but right now it looks like people are getting lazier. It's also easier to self-publish on the Internet right now, and pretty soon it's going to be a lot easier. That's what I suspect. I don't see the steamroller of the Internet ever weakening, especially with all the toy technology, because that's basically what iPads are. They're cool toys that are tools as well.

**JAIME:** As far as alternative comics, I've noticed that there are more people out there doing comics their own way than I think in the history of comics ever. So I think that's a good sign that somewhere along those lines it will survive. Every day I hear about a different cartoonist that I didn't know about that's doing their own thing, and it doesn't look like anyone else. I find that really amazing, and it just gives me hope that comics are going to survive, but I don't know how.

**GILBERT:** We're screwed, that's all.

**SOBEL:** [*Laughs.*] Screwed?

**GILBERT:** Well, Jaime and I are, because we like pencil, paper and ink.

**JAIME:** But I'm meeting a lot more people who are still like that, because some of the alternative artists have let this old guy in, and I'm seeing that no matter what certain artists can do, like someone who does silkscreen prints and stuff like that, every single time I talk to them, they say, "Oh my God. I wish I could just do comics." They just want to do comics. They've got all this technical know-how to make other kinds of art but all they want to do is draw comics. So that makes me happy because that's all I want to do, too.

**SOBEL:** Do you ever envision a time when *Love and Rockets* will be published digitally?

**JAIME:** You mean solely?

**SOBEL:** I guess you could look at it both ways: taking all 30 years worth of your work and putting it out on the Internet, and releasing the new books in a digital format.

**JAIME:** Isn't there a company that's doing that? I just got a check from that one company that reproduced all our body of work. See, I don't even know the name of the company.

**GILBERT:** Is it the American Press people [*Alexander Street Press*], or something like that?

**JAIME:** Yeah. We did it through Groth, that's why I'm not that up on it. Yeah, it's out there. You can download whatever you want from our catalog. But I'm so out of it Internet-wise that I can't give you any more details than that.

**SOBEL:** Well, you're on Twitter.

**JAIME:** Yeah, I entered the 20th century. Not the 21st, but the 20th.

**GILBERT:** My wife came across somebody — I guess their blog or whatever — who put the entire issue of the recent *Love and Rockets* out on it. You can just download it.

**SOBEL:** For free?

**GILBERT:** Yeah, like somebody just tore the pages out; scanned them and put it up on the screen. You can read the whole issue.

**SOBEL:** That's a huge problem for a lot of creators. I'm sure you have heard of this. People are scanning all the new books onto the Internet and fans are downloading them illegally.

**GILBERT:** People want to read it that way. Once in a while we'll catch someone and send them a cease-and-desist letter, and they always remove it, but there're just so many people out there that you don't know about.

**SOBEL:** Is piracy something that Fantagraphics is actively fighting against?

**JAIME:** Oh, gee. I don't know.

**GILBERT:** I don't know if they can. There's just so much. It's the Wild West out there. On one hand that's good because there's all that freedom, but on the other hand, you can't stop people from messing you up really badly. Another kid killed himself last week for being bullied on the Internet. It's gotten nasty out there.

**SOBEL:** Has *Love and Rockets* experienced any decline in sales from illegal downloads?

**GILBERT:** I'm not sure. There's always a slight decline in sales for every issue, but that's fairly normal. That's usually an initial print run thing, because our books have a really long shelf life. As long as there are bookstores out there, we're OK, because our books sell all year long, which is pretty nice.

**JAIME:** In my case, I stopped thinking about numbers a long time ago. All I do is wait for them to tell me that I can't do this anymore. It's all I can do; I just hope that I can keep doing it. That's how I look at it. It may be immature, and it may be naïve, but I

*Gilbert's "Neuterbrank Primer" is the back cover of* Love and Rockets *Vol. II #3 (Fall 2001).*

really like being left alone to do my comics without worrying about stuff like that.

**SOBEL:** Mario and Gilbert, you've collaborated over the years on a number of projects from Errata Stigmata [stories] to *Citizen Rex*. Who does what and how do you guys work together?

**GILBERT:** Mario does all the work, and I take all the money. [*Laughs.*]

**MARIO:** What? There was money involved? [*Laughs.*] No, I'm always flattered when Gilbert asks me to do something with him. I'm also thrilled because somebody else will be drawing something that I don't want to draw. A lot of times, Gilbert will just come to me out of the blue and say that he has a project he wants to fill up. Usually it's because he's writing so many things that there are just no more ideas filling up the creation cup, so he says, "Look, I've got this many pages. Can we do something?" Or "Somebody's gonna let us do a comic for Dark Horse," and I'm like, "Yeah, what do you want to do?" Then we just discuss what we'd like to do.

As far as the stuff in *Love and Rockets* that we were doing, like "Me for the Unknown," I'm baffled that that even happened. And that we let it go on as long as it did. But Gilbert was willing to take a chance on me doing a long story. Plus, he added some really cool violence and other things to it. With *Citizen Rex*, I wrote all the narrative and the story and gave him the layouts and stuff like that. He tweaked them a little bit and threw some things out that were a little repetitive. But the one thing that kills me every time, working with Gilbert, is that I'll write this dialogue and it's like my ears are bleeding from trying to make it sound just right and then he'll turn around and add something that seems off-the-cuff, but it's better than everything I wrote in the 10 pages before. It just kills me. [*Laughs.*] But it's also like, thank you!

**GILBERT:** Well, I actually learned that from Stan Lee. Stan Lee was great at taking Jack Kirby's stories and Steve Ditko's stories and making them into something special. Kirby would write a bunch of stuff, and Stan Lee would write a few jokes in there to lighten up certain things, and they're funny. It just worked perfectly. His strengths really came out with those great artists. If those stories had been left to Kirby and Ditko to write, they probably wouldn't be that well loved, even though the art's great and the storytelling is great. But Stan put his two cents in and made it work, and Marvel still lives off that today.

Anyway, that's what I'm thinking of, more or less, when I'm working with Mario. I just think, "OK, what would Stan Lee do?" Where would he put the humor, and where would he pull back? Where does something fit that might be missing? But it has to be integrated with what Mario's written, too. I'm not saying it's always successful. I've probably made quite a few blunders, but sometimes it feels right just to add something.

**MARIO:** Most of the time I'm just saying, "Wow, thank you for clearing that up." [*Laughs.*]

**GILBERT:** Also I like to work with Mario because, like he said, I have too many things on my plate, and I'm just out of ideas as far as concepts or stories. Most of the comics I've done with different writers, I did because those were people I already knew had written well. For example, I did *Yeah!* with Peter Bagge because he wrote good comics like *Neat Stuff* and *Hate*. I knew that so I didn't have any problem with collaborating.

*Birds of Prey*, on the other hand, I wrote myself and another artist, Casey Jones, drew it. It was a disaster on my part I think, not Casey's. I just didn't know how to write a superhero comic. I always thought I did until I actually did one. I also drew an issue for Michael Allred's *I, Zombie*, but, again, I did that because I know Mike and I like his stories. It's really hard for me to collaborate with somebody I don't know, but I'll do it if the money's good and it's quick.

**SOBEL:** Mario, are you writing or drawing anything right now?

**MARIO:** Well, after *Citizen Rex*, which I'm still

milking to this day, I've recently talked to Gary [Groth] about doing a graphic novel. I've had all these ideas over the years that I submitted to *Love and Rockets*, but they were going to be too long or they were just not right for the book, which is fine. The book is wonderful the way it is as far as I'm concerned. It's going along just fine without me. But right now I've got three different ideas, and we'll see which one sticks. I'm going to be drawing some pages and stuff to pitch, to see which one will work the best for a 100-page graphic novel.

I've also been practicing drawing again, actually. I'm going through this career change right now. For the last 10 years I was self-employed, and that takes a lot out of you. Comics just were not very interesting to me. *Citizen Rex* was a cool thing to fill the time and keep my hand in it, and I'm grateful for it because it kept my juices flowing, but I had no strength for drawing or anything after that. I was just too burnt out. But now I've got a regular 9 to 5 job which leaves me a nice chunk of time in the evening where I don't have to sweat trying to figure out what I'm going to be doing the next day. So, it's freed me up, and I'll hopefully be able to do more stuff.

our ability to maintain doing the type of comics we want to do for 30 years. That finally pushed the nay-sayers back, but like Jaime said, for a while they were looking for something new, something more hip, something closer to what their basic lifestyle is about.

See, that's the thing about indy comics. It's the same with indy films too. Fans want the comics or films or music to reflect who they are in a direct sense. When *Love and Rockets* goes away from that a little bit now and again, they start looking for something else to cover that area.

**SOBEL:** When Jaime was in New York recently, I had one fan admit to me that he had "known" Maggie and Hopey and Luba and her family longer than any of his real friends and he cared about them just as deeply. You have such emotionally invested fans, perhaps unique within all of comics. How has that kind of devotion impacted you?

**JAIME:** It's cool. It allows me to do more and to keep on. It's like I'm on the right track. It's the track I wanted to be on, and when I have that kind of support, it's pretty special. It's almost like they're letting me do what I want to do. I'm a kid in a candy store.

## LEGACY

**SOBEL:** There was a period back in the '80s and '90s where a lot of people looked at *Love and Rockets* as the "carrier of the torch" in terms of bringing respectability and intellectual acceptance to the medium. Do you still feel that responsibility, or has that faded over the years?

**JAIME:** I think, just because we're old, people are seeing us that way again. But there was a time through the '90s where we fell out of favor and we weren't the cool kids on the block any more.

**SOBEL:** This was after the first series?

**JAIME:** No, this was during the first 50 issues, but it was the late '80s, early '90s, when they found cooler people to follow.

**GILBERT:** I think they appreciate our longevity and

Mario wrote, and Gilbert drew, Citizen Rex. *This panel is from the first issue (July 2009), and has been collected in the eponymous graphic novel.*

**GILBERT:** Right away it went way beyond what we were hoping. We wanted to make comics that readers could relate to, that readers would want to come back to and enjoy on the simplest level. We also wanted them to understand and enjoy what we enjoyed about growing up and reading comics, but we also wanted to bring something new that hadn't been done before. Like, making Latino characters that were human and making that accessible to readers. We weren't looking for a Latino readership in particular; we were just looking for a general readership. And since it was new, we just thought the newness of it would be enough, but like you said, when our readers became so devoted to it and so supportive, and really, really connected to it, that was better than what we had hoped. Like Jaime said, it puts us on the right track; it keeps us grounded in terms of where we want to go with our stories.

**SOBEL:** Do you feel pressured by that loyalty?

**GILBERT:** Pressured only by the length of time and of how many comics that we've already done. That's the only real pressure. We've done so many different angles on the same types of stories and we've done the characters over and over. The challenge is to make new stories for old characters and keep the readers happy and engaged. We always have to keep pushing ourselves.

**SOBEL:** The last *Comics Journal* interview you did was in '95, and at that point you talked about how the readership was starting to erode after *Poison River* and *Wigwam Bam*. Since then you've gone through a solo period, *Love and Rockets* relaunched, and now you've got the annual graphic novels, and I was just wondering how your audience has responded to each of those iterations.

**JAIME:** I haven't gotten much response along those lines. What I'm hoping for is that no matter which format the comic comes out in, the material will always be there, and that's what people respond to. And I'm happy with that. People ask me what I think about changing formats and all that stuff. I stopped arguing with the market years ago because I have to survive. If I want to do this for a big chunk of my life, then it's got to pay off somehow or I can't

do it. I'd have to get a real job. So if they're going to tell me, "Well, you're going to do it once a year and it's going to have a fat spine so we can also go into bookstores and that will help your sales," then I'm all for it.

As long as they leave my art alone and just let me do my comics. You can publish it any way you want, as long as it will help me survive to do this another 10 or 20 years.

**GILBERT:** The important thing for me is to keep the title of the books *Love and Rockets*. We found that out the hard way with the solo books like *Luba* and *Luba's Comics and Stories*, *Penny Century* and even *Maggie and Hopey Color Fun*. They just did not get the same response as the *Love and Rockets* comics. It's the same material, and some of it's our better material, but it just didn't get noticed without *Love and Rockets* in the title. So keeping it under the *Love and Rockets* banner, whatever the format, is critical.

**SOBEL:** There's something magical about that title.

**GILBERT:** Yeah, it worked too well, which is good for us now. It's perfect now. Anything under the title will get read. But that's why it's harder to do outside projects. Jaime's always talking about doing an outside thing, but then we realize that the readers are going to go to *Love and Rockets* first to look for our new material. They'll go to the other stuff second, maybe. So that's always a consideration.

**SOBEL:** How would you characterize *Love and Rockets*' legacy?

**GILBERT:** We're happy to have broken down a roadblock with the kind of comics that we wanted to do, which was mixing our American influences, a little bit of European influence and a little bit of underground comix influence.

*Love and Rockets* became, though it was not necessarily planned as, the comic you read after you got tired of superhero comics. At that time, there really weren't many comics to read after you outgrew superheroes. They kept coming up with superhero comics that were for adults, but they were still dependent on readers having a sense of superhero history, whereas we were lucky to have people read *Love and Rockets* who had never read a superhero comic before, but liked comics and enjoyed our stories right off the bat. So *Love and Rockets* knocked down that barrier and allowed so many other artists like us to go down that road and do their own comics. Thankfully Fantagraphics felt the same way, too. They were happy that there were other cartoonists going down that same road and wanting to do new, different kinds of comics. Right after us at Fantagraphics came Pete Bagge and then Dan Clowes, etc.

It was also helpful that we were able to produce comic after comic. In the old days, the underground guys couldn't really do that. They did a couple of comics here and there, but since we had mainstream backgrounds, we knew that putting out comic after comic was just better if we were going to stick around. And guys like Pete Bagge and Dan Clowes were able to do that as well. They blossomed into their own artists, and then so many other people after them. So I'm pretty proud of the fact that something as simple as doing our own kind of comic inspired and opened up doors for so many other people. It's pretty cool.

**MARIO:** The thing that just kills me the most is when I read a comics history or a newer article about comics, and it says, "Here we have Will Eisner, Harvey Kurtzman, Jack Kirby, Jaime, or Gilbert, or the Hernandez Brothers." It's like, OK, I can die now. I knew these guys had it in them, and I'm glad that it's all happened the way it has. I wish they'd get more money, but the fact that we're in the freaking history books, man! You can't erase that very easily. There's not too many books still coming out that have kept the quality up, as far as I'm concerned. I mean, if you've read Jaime for the last 10 years, or even five, the quality has just come right up and stayed where it was supposed to. And Gilbert's stuff is just plain freaking weird, and I'm glad he's pissing people off [*laughs*] and that he can still do that.

**GILBERT:** It is pretty weird to think of 30 years. It doesn't feel like it. I don't remember doing a lot of the stories I did. I know the stories and I remember liking doing them and struggling with them and all that, but I don't remember the 30 years. It

This sequence is from "Yeah! Goes to War" in #8 (May 2000), written by Peter Bagge and drawn by Gilbert. It's been reprinted in the graphic novel Yeah!

©2013 Peter Bagge

just seems like we're in the middle of it, like we're always in the middle. We just finished an issue and now we have to get the next one out. The fact that it still gets such a good response from enough people is way more than we could ever ask for.

**JAIME:** I hope that it's just a chunk of the best comics that we've ever had. It's not for me to say, but I hope. It would just be really cool to be on the shelf next to a *Peanuts* book. It's not for me to measure greatness or anything like that, but that's a pretty cool dream, to be next to Charlie Brown, or next to *Archie*. Or the *Fantastic Four*. I don't know. It's all comics, and it's all good to me. ∎

**G**ary Groth's decision to publish *Love and Rockets* not only changed the fate of his company Fantagraphics Books, Inc. — at that time best known for *The Comics Journal*, a comics criticism and journalism periodical — but the history of the medium. With Groth's advocacy and guidance, *Love and Rockets* pioneered the "graphic novel" format, while the Hernandez brothers challenged the narrative and aesthetic boundaries of comics. Together, they ushered in an artistic renaissance unlike anything in the medium's history. Three decades later, despite economic recessions and the slow-motion collapse of print media, comic books are comparatively vital and healthy, and *Love and Rockets* remains one of the industry's most celebrated "alternative" series.

Groth and I spoke by phone and then followed-up over e-mail in April and May 2012. It was a privilege to reflect back on all that has happened in the comics industry since *Love and Rockets* made its auspicious debut in 1981, and to look ahead to the future.

— MARC SOBEL, JUNE 2012

*Madisen Semet transcribed this interview; it was copy-edited by the participants.*

# MARC SOBEL & GARY GROTH

*The* Love and Rockets *Companion*

**MARC SOBEL:** I wanted to start by going back to the beginning, in 1981, and have you describe how well established Fantagraphics was as a publisher. Obviously you had *The Comics Journal* ...

**GARY GROTH:** We weren't established at all as a publisher. We had only started publishing *The Comics Journal* in 1976. By 1981, we had only published a couple of comics before we published *Love and Rockets*. One was Milton Knight's *Hugo*: We published two or three issues of that.

I think this might've been as early as 1979 — we published this crazy sci-fi comic called *The Flames of Gyro* by a Golden Age comic-book artist by the name of Jay Disbrow. I forget how we hooked up ... I might've met him at a convention. He was, to me, an older guy at the time, although he probably

wasn't much older than I am right now. He was a distinguished older guy who smoked a pipe, and he was interested in doing the first comic he'd done in years, because he had worked in comics in the '40s and maybe into the '50s. So we were open to this, although I'm not sure why, but we were. So he drove up to our office/home in Connecticut and literally dropped off the pages. And the pages were huge; they must have been a foot and a half wide by two feet tall. They were absolutely enormous! They were the size the artists in the Golden Age worked at. The size of original art diminished sometime in the late '50s, I think, but the Golden Age art was just huge. So he dropped these pages off and even though it wasn't the kind of comics that I saw myself publishing, I think we were just interested in the whole process of publishing a comic. So we published *The Flames of Gyro* I think as early as 1979.

We also published a couple collections of Don Rosa's work. The titles of those were *Don Rosa's Comics and Stories*. So we were dipping our toes into comics publishing I guess as early as 1979-1980. Then, I think in maybe late 1981 or early 1982, we published Jack Jackson's graphic novel, *Los Tejanos*, which was an historical recreation of the Texas-Mexican War. But we still didn't see ourselves as comics publishers, per se. We saw ourselves as primarily publishing *The Comics Journal* and just dabbling in comics.

**SOBEL:** I've read your review of the self-published *Love and Rockets* issue, but when and where did you actually first meet the Hernandez brothers in person?

**GROTH:** It must've been at a convention on the West Coast. My guess is it was at a Creation Con in Los Angeles. I'm almost sure that's the case. It probably would have been in '82, shortly after we published *Love and Rockets #1*. I know we wanted to give it a big push. I remember I was showing it around at a convention. What I was doing was

Golden Age cartoonist Jay Disbrow is one of the earliest Fantagraphics creators. This sequence is from his one-shot The Flames of Gyro (1979).

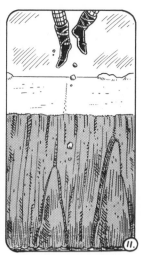

©2013 Don Rosa

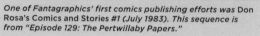
*One of Fantagraphics' first comics publishing efforts was Don Rosa's Comics and Stories #1 (July 1983). This sequence is from "Episode 129: The Pertwillaby Papers."*

showing the cover around, showing it off, basically. I wonder if I met Gilbert, Jaime and Mario before it was actually published, though? I'm not sure about that. But I'm sure I met them at a Creation Convention in Los Angeles.

We were all in our 20s. Jaime might have been 19, I forget, but I met them there at the convention and I think we hit it off, personally. I don't remember specifically what we did, but I remember hanging out at the convention and feeling that we were this oasis at this awful convention — which I often feel. You know, a certain kinship among us and probably a few other artists that I was hanging out with at the time. I think we probably had a table there, too, so we were selling *The Comics Journal* and the few other comics we published and possibly *Love and Rockets* if we had printed it by then. I think *Love and Rockets* #1 came out ... did that come in July of '82?

**SOBEL:** I think it was in the fall.

**GROTH:** That sounds more accurate. So we were probably selling *Love and Rockets* at the convention, too, and they were signing. That's about all I can remember.

**SOBEL:** What do you remember about putting together the first issue?

**GROTH:** Well, we got their self-published comic and I reviewed it in the *Journal* and my brilliant idea was to double the size of it because their self-published comic was 32 pages. So I asked them if they could add to the content of it and if they added 32 pages, we would have our first issue comprising 64 pages and they did that. I'm trying to remember the first issue ... it had Beto's really long "BEM" story, "How to Kill A ... "

**SOBEL:** And Jaime's "Mechan-X" and "Locas Tambien." I guess I wrote a short intro to the book because I was so excited about it. I thought it was such a landmark piece of work that I felt compelled to tout it. But otherwise there was very little production work to do because they sent the work camera-ready. We did not muck with it. We thought it was perfect as it was, so all we did was assemble it.

**SOBEL:** Did you guys have any kind of celebration after it was printed?

**GROTH:** [*Laughs*]. I don't think we had a celebration per se, but we were in a celebratory mood when the box of advanced copies arrived from the printer. Even though we'd published a handful of comics prior to that, somehow I recognized *Love and Rockets* and what they were doing in it ... well, it was the kind of work that we were championing in the *Comics Journal* but that didn't exist at the time.

So, in a weird way, it was this perfect realization of what we were championing without ever having seen it. I remember in particular being

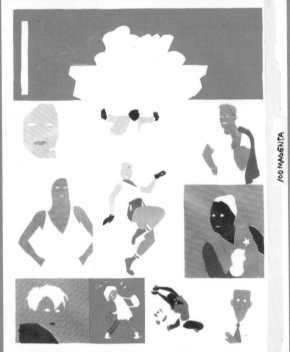

100 MAGENTA

 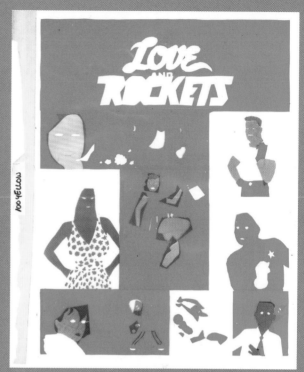

**GROTH:** Preston White cut the overlays for Jaime's cover ... We had to cut overlays for the covers because that's how we did production work back then. Do you know what overlays are?

**SOBEL:** A quick explanation would be great.

**GROTH:** Well, back then they actually had to photograph the artwork. They used what you call a Stat camera. The printer would actually photograph the artwork and create a negative from which they then created a plate, which they put on the press. And in order to do color work, you had to have four different negatives for each color, for each primary color: black, magenta, cyan and yellow. And there were two kinds of color, one was full-color, which was a painting, which they would photograph one way and then separate the color out through the camera. The other way was to do what's called mechanical separations, where you would have an overlay that was called Rubylith. It was a sheet of plastic with a red covering

on it that was actually stuck onto the plastic. So what you would do is put that over the artwork and cut out with an X-Acto knife the red Rubylith for the parts of the artwork that you wanted to photograph that color.

So you had four overlays ... well, you had three overlays because you had the base overlay of black, and you had to cut each overlay based on where you wanted the color to go, but you basically had to guess at the percentages of the color because you might want 50 percent magenta combined with 100 percent yellow and you didn't quite know what that would look like. You could make a pretty good guess, but you didn't quite know for sure, so you'd have to do all this guess work in terms of how the color was going to come out.

The brothers didn't know how to do that and we did, so we cut the overlays for both covers. And really, that was all the production work there was to do.

'BERT '79

*This Hank Ketcham/Elvis Costello mash-up spot illustration originally ran in* The Comics Journal #59 (October 1980). *It is collected in the* Love and Rockets Sketchbook *Vol. 1.*

excited by that, seeing the vision of what we saw comics as capable of doing being so fully realized. I think that's what struck me when we got their self-printed comic and I read it. Because it wasn't like underground comics, it was the next generation, and, in that sense, it was revolutionary because nothing had been done like it before. I think that's what excited me enough to write a review of it. I wish I remembered if I asked Jaime and Gilbert if we could publish it before or after I wrote that review but I don't remember. I'm thinking it was after because I think I got the book and I liked it so much that I just went to the typewriter and wrote a review of it immediately. I also think both of them, but certainly Gilbert, was doing illustrations for *The Comics Journal.*

**SOBEL:** They both were.

**GROTH:** So I guess I'd been in touch with them before that. This is going to sound like I have Alzheimer's or something, but I don't remember if I put two and two together and actually realized ... because a lot of people did spot illustrations for the *Journal* and I wouldn't necessarily communicate a lot with them. We would get the illustrations in and I would maybe drop them a note saying, "Thanks, this is great, we're gonna use it," but I didn't strike up any real relationships or friendships based on that. It was pretty perfunctory. And I'm not entirely sure that I made the connection that the guys who produced this comic were the same guys who were throwing spot illustrations my way.

**SOBEL:** Can you describe your typical responsibilities as editor of the series?

**GROTH:** I can tell you that pretty quickly. They were to talk to the brothers about deadlines.

**SOBEL:** You had deadlines for each issue?

**GROTH:** Well, alleged deadlines. We had deadlines for when we wanted it. It was supposed to be a quarterly book initially, and for the first two or three issues, it's possible it was, or at least close to it. But it became obvious that that was just too much work for the two of them because I think they probably both had jobs. I know that Jaime was working, if not full-time at least part-time, when he was doing very early *Love and Rockets*. So he just didn't have time to produce that much work.

I think I had this vague idea that we should publish this as frequently as possible and that it was my job as an editor, and of course I'd never been an editor on a comic before so I didn't know what I was doing, but it was my job to basically bug them. I thought it was my responsibility to light a fire under them because this was such great work and I wanted as much of it as I could get.

So that was part of my job. Another part was to proofread the work. Now, in the early days, once in a while, they would even ask me an editorial question, such as, "Does this page flow?" or "Is this ambiguous?" or "Is something clear enough?" and I would offer them my advice, but that ended pretty quickly because they certainly knew more about what they were doing than I did.

So I proofread it and made a handful of corrections in terms of spelling or punctuation, but really my main job was to step out of the way and not muck it up. The work was pretty much fully realized from the beginning. There was no editing per se, no editorial conferences, and there were never instances where I would call them up and say, "I think this story is pretty good but you could probably add something here and add something there and change this."

I actually did do a little bit of that in the first couple issues but then I simply stopped because it just seemed ridiculous. They just became so masterful and their vision was so fully realized that I felt completely apart from that. There was no way I could enter that world and think that I had any expertise to offer them.

## BREAKING IN TO BOOKSTORES

**SOBEL:** *Love and Rockets* was one of the first alternative comics to really penetrate the bookstore market. Can you describe how that evolved in the early years and what the hurdles were?

**GROTH:** We published the first *Love and Rockets* collection in 1987. But we didn't have bookstore distribution until approximately '87 or '88 when a huge firm, which may or may not still be in business, called Berkeley Books offered to distribute us. This was around the time of *Maus*. They took on three or four different publishers: us, Eclipse, First Comics and Kitchen Sink. They smelled money and they thought that graphic novels were going to take off, which they weren't at that time. But, at any rate, we finally had what we thought was bookstore distribution and I think we published a couple of *Love and Rockets* collections up to that point but since we had bookstore distribution, we were thinking how can we package *Love and Rockets* so it would sell specifically in the book trade to people who weren't necessarily comics fans. So in order to do that, we devised a format that was a trade paperback format. It was 6 1/2" x 9" to accommodate the format of their art.

*Dale Crain art-directed the covers for* Love and Rockets' *first foray into the bookstore market, circa 1987.*

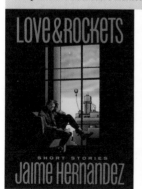 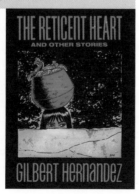 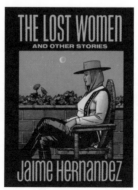 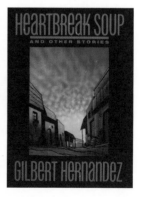

So we repackaged all the work that they'd done up to that point and we actually published four of these books. They had book flaps, their design was a little bit more sophisticated and, of course, the size was all-important because they could fit on the shelves of bookstores and book-buyers would be more welcoming. So we published four of those; two by Gilbert and two by Jaime, and they were really pretty attractive books for that period.

**SOBEL:** How did they do?

**GROTH:** I think they did all right. They didn't do great, because no graphic novel back then did particularly well, unless it was called *Maus*. Getting *Love and Rockets* into the book trade was a very slow and arduous process. Our relationship with Berkeley Books pretty much ended probably within about two years. They just realized they weren't selling enough graphic novels. The time for graphic novels had not yet come. But because we had been in bookstores, we looked around for another distributor and we found a succession of them that kept going out of business. It was like having horses shot out underneath you. [*Sobel laughs.*]

In the mid-late '80s we were in the book trade, but pretty badly. Throughout the '90s we were always being distributed by smaller distributors, and we had a minuscule presence in the book trade, although we were still always trying to push books into the book trade, because our dream was to sell graphic novels outside of the direct sales market, outside the comics market, and outside the small circle of comic-book fans. We wanted to reach readers who weren't necessarily comic-book readers. We finally succeeded in doing that when we hooked up with W.W. Norton, which I think was in 2001. Since then we've sold a hell of a lot more *Love and Rockets* collections in the book trade. As you know, we reformatted all the books.

**SOBEL:** In 2007.

**GROTH:** Yeah, into the smaller manga format that we thought would be better in bookstores. So in a weird way we've come full circle, because we published those smaller format *Love and Rockets*

collections in '87, and we've done several very similar books over the last few years. I hadn't thought about that.

**SOBEL:** What about the original series of reprints, the 15 volumes that made up …

**GROTH:** The complete *Love and Rockets*.

**SOBEL:** The first 50 issues.

**GROTH:** We published those 15 volumes between about '86 and '96 or '97, and then we realized that those weren't as suitable for the book trade.

We were always trying to get the Hernandez brothers into the book trade because I really thought that if any artist had breakout potential, they did. Maybe one of the things I liked so much about *Love and Rockets* and why it was so exciting to me to see the first four issues come out, was that I had this dream that comics ought to be, or were capable of, being the equivalent of mainstream fiction, which I read a lot of, and that they were a literary form capable of sitting on the shelves next to literary fiction. I saw *Love and Rockets* as the comics and visual equivalent of literary fiction. So I always had this confidence that *Love and Rockets* could make it in the book trade among literate readers who weren't necessarily comic readers.

I'm not sure if, to this day, I've fully succeeded in that, but I think we've gone a long way towards succeeding, in terms of persuading ordinary, literate book readers that there's a lot going on there.

**SOBEL:** So would you attribute the long-term success of the series to those reprints or to the direct market fan base, or a combination?

**GROTH:** Well, it's certainly a combination. I think we've sold over 100,000 copies of *Love and Rockets*, although it's hard to break this down, because we've published it in so many different formats. But let's say the first four or five or six issues of the original *Love and Rockets* comic, I'm sure we've printed and sold 100,000 copies of that material in various formats. So I think getting it out into the book trade and getting it reviewed and noticed by people who care about literature and art was instrumental in the growing success of *Love and Rockets*.

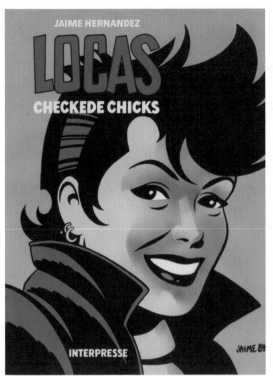

*Here is a selection of* Love and Rockets *foreign edition covers.*

**SOBEL:** I wanted to ask you also about the foreign editions because *Love and Rockets* was one of the first American alternative comics to be translated and exported.

Can you talk about how that worked and how you were able to publish the book outside the U.S., and also what kind of reaction the Brothers' work received overseas?

**GROTH:** We didn't publish any books overseas. We licensed the work to other publishers.

I think the secret to that was that the work was simply more palatable to European sensibilities, and, to a lesser extent, South American sensibilities. I'm pretty sure that we sold *Love and Rockets* very early to French publishers. There was a guy named Fershid Bharucha who was one of those guys who's been involved in French comics publishing forever, even longer than I think I have been involved in American comics publishing. And he was with one of the major houses, but he always had his antennae tuned to alternative work, and I'm pretty sure that he brought *Love and Rockets* over there. I think we also sold it to Spain, and maybe Germany. But I think the work itself was just so much more palatable to European sensibilities. They were way ahead of the curve and doing work like this themselves, so they just immediately latched onto it. God knows how many different countries and formats they've been published in by now, a lot over the years.

By the way, Jaime and I were invited to a convention in Lucca ... this was in 1984. We were both young, but I'm a few years older than Jaime. Now, for some crazy reason they invited both of us. Jaime was feted in Lucca and people loved his work. We must have had 10 or 12 issues out by then, maybe a few more, and he was a big hit. People loved his work over there.

**SOBEL:** Was Gilbert there, too, or just Jaime?

**GROTH:** No, just Jaime. I think they might've given him an award. Jaime would probably remember that. [Jaime received the prestigious Yellow Kid Award in 1984, his first major award in comics.]

So, we went to Lucca, Italy. It was a wonderful convention; they take over the city. Lucca is this beautiful walled city, so it's small-ish and it has great history. They treated us very well and we had a ball. After the show, we took a train from Lucca to Paris, just Jaime and I, both in our 20s. And we spent a few days in Paris. Jaime had never been out of the country before, so this was a pretty huge thing for him.

**SOBEL:** Sure. What did you do in Paris?

**GROTH:** We just hung out. I guess we hung out the entire time together. It was just the two of us.

**SOBEL:** You got along well, obviously.

**GROTH:** We had a great time. It was wonderful. We got to know each other. We also got thrown off a train at gunpoint.

**SOBEL:** [*Laughs.*] What happened?

**GROTH:** It was in Italy. We boarded a train in Lucca. Now, neither one of us spoke Italian. So we boarded a train in Italy to go to Paris, and, of course, this was all my idea. I put together the whole agenda. So I bought the tickets, we get on the train and I go to find our seats. When I found the conductor, I'm waving my tickets at him, unable to speak the language, and he basically just keeps telling me "No" and shaking his head.

Of course I have no idea what this means. So we put our luggage at the end of one of the train cars in the space between the last seat and the bathroom by the doors to the next train. So I tell Jaime, "Wait here, I have to find out what's going on."

He's sitting on our luggage and I finally find someone who can speak English and Italian and I have this person translate for me to the conductor and it turns out ... and to this day I have no fucking clue how I did this ... but they told me I bought a ticket to get on the train but I didn't buy a seat. [*Sobel laughs.*] How that is even possible, I have no idea. I figured it

*This photo, courtesy of Gary Groth, was taken during a European train ride in which Groth and Jaime were threatened at gunpoint.*

was some sort of scam, but anyway, we didn't have a goddamn seat.

Somebody offered to sell me a seat and I said, "I have a friend with me, so we need two seats," and she said, "Well, I only have one seat," and I said, "Well, I can't buy one seat. I'm not gonna leave him."

So I go back and Jaime and I are just sitting there on the floor with our luggage piled up behind us, and I'm feeling terrible because I'm the one who engineered this disaster. Plus, every 20 minutes or so the conductor would walk past us and scream at us in Italian. We had no idea what he was saying, but figured he was probably telling us to get the hell up. But I also didn't give a shit, so I just ignored him.

Then we stopped in a city — I think it was Genovese — and this conductor walked over to us while we were stopped. He screamed at us again and I just waved him off, and then he walked away and said something like "Policia," which I didn't quite catch.

But Jaime turned to me, because Italian is close to Spanish, and he said, "You know, I think he just said something about the police."

I said, "Really? Eh, well, whatever."

So about five minutes later these two cops, literally with submachine guns, walked up, and because we were sitting in front of the door to the train, they were on the platform, and they pointed their guns at us and pointed to the platform. They literally moved their guns from us to the platform and said something, which I think was like "Get the fuck off the train."

[*Sobel laughs.*]

Which we proceeded to do.

So we were stranded in this city of Genovese. I remember this so vividly ... we were like three stories underneath the street and we kept walking up these endless stairs. We never thought we'd reach the top, but we finally made it out and grabbed the first cab we could find. Somehow we conveyed to the cab driver that we wanted to go to a hotel and so he took us to a hotel. We didn't know what we were doing; we'd never been to this town before. So Jaime and I spent the night there and the next day I somehow figured out how to buy plane tickets and we flew to Paris. And that was our adventure on the train. I have a great photo of me and Jaime sitting on our luggage in that train. We're looking like death. I think we'd been up for 24 hours for some reason. We were just looking like shit. Pathetic, confused Americans sitting on our luggage on a train.

**SOBEL:** And I know how much Jaime loves police, too.

**GROTH:** In retrospect it's hilarious, but at the time Jaime and I were just freaking out. We didn't know what was going on.

I felt very responsible because I was the one who set all this up. Jaime had never been out of the country before; he didn't know what the hell we were doing. I barely knew what we were doing, either. I do remember having a great time in Paris, though. I have no idea what we actually did. We saw the *Supergirl* movie.

**SOBEL:** Oh God, really?

**GROTH:** It sounds horrendous but it was the only American movie playing.

**SOBEL:** Was it in English?

**GROTH:** Yeah, it was the only movie we could actually understand. So you have to picture me and Jaime sitting in a Parisian theater, watching *Supergirl*. It's pretty grotesque.

**SOBEL:** [*Laughs.*] There's something so perfect about that though.

## X'ED OUT

**SOBEL:** Switching gears, I wanted to ask you how you felt about the Brothers doing *Mister X* back in '84. I'm aware of what happened and how they didn't get paid right away and all that.

**GROTH:** Yeah, I lived through that. That was pretty horrible, but it was also funny, because Bill Marks was such a scam artist. Mostly that's what I remember. I remember them doing the work, but I'm not sure they really talked to me that much

*Paul Rivoche "colorized"* Love and Rockets: *from Jaime's* Mechanics #3 (December 1985).

about it. I'm sure they told me, "We got this offer to do this paying gig" and I think that's it.

They did it primarily because, of course, they needed money. They couldn't live on income from just *Love and Rockets*, and Marks offered them a page rate and more or less gave them carte blanche, and told them you can do what you want, I'll pay you a hundred dollars a page. It sounded like a good gig. And they did four issues, but all I remember hearing is how they kept sending him pages and he kept not sending them money, and how they would keep asking him for the money, and he'd say, "I'll pay you the next time you send the pages."

It just seemed like this endless cycle of bullshit. They would send him 10 pages, he would pay for three, and then they'd send him another 10, and he'd pay them for three, and then tell them that he'd pay them more money when they sent more pages. It was just always behind and getting farther behind every month.

I remember them being incredibly frustrated and then, ultimately, pretty goddamn pissed off about it. Finally they just ended the relationship because they weren't getting anything out of it. I

don't know, you probably know this better than I do, but I'm not sure they were ever fully paid.

**SOBEL:** It took a year or two but they did eventually get paid.

**GROTH:** Yeah, well obviously that was an unhappy experience, which they did not want to repeat. It was work-for-hire and they were doing the best they could but you could see they didn't quite have their heart in *Mister X* the way they did in *Love and Rockets*.

The thing about the Hernandez brothers is, and this is particularly true, I think, of Jaime, is that they're just not built for work-for-hire. They're just not built for that. They really have an inner need to do their own work.

**SOBEL:** You mentioned that Bill Marks offered them a page rate. What was the arrangement you had with them in terms of payment for *Love and Rockets*?

**GROTH:** It was always a royalty. I can't remember if I paid them in advance, but they would get paid based on how many copies the book sold, which is the way the book trade functions and the way we pay everybody now. I think it's the way underground comics paid their artists, so we just picked it up from them. The more copies we sold, the more they got paid. If I remember correctly, and they should correct me if I'm wrong, but I think we paid them pretty promptly.

## IN LIVING COLOR

**SOBEL:** I also wanted to ask you about the color *Mechanics* miniseries that you did.

**GROTH:** Well, that was another attempt to a) make Jaime more money and b) get his work out into the mainstream more. That was [in 1985] before we had bookstore distribution. We just had a lot of confidence that if we could only get the Bros.' work in front of people's faces we would be able to sell it. We had such supreme confidence in that, and always have. So that was a way of appealing to comics readers who were turned off by black-and-white comics and the whole alternative persona, basically the fans who were essentially captive to Marvel and DC.

**SOBEL:** It was even the standard size.

**GROTH:** Right. And even if we could only get 5 percent of the readers who read garbage like *Spider-Man* or *X-Men* or whatever was being published at the time, if we could get a percentage of those readers, that would be helpful. So that was just one more desperate attempt to do that.

Paul Rivoche [colored those] under Jaime's supervision. Or at least Jaime consulted with him. I think Jaime was reasonably happy with that, although I still get the impression that it was a bit of a compromise to color that story. It was obviously done for black-and-white reproduction. But that was a pretty snazzy little three-issue series.

**SOBEL:** Did you ever think about doing something with "Heartbreak Soup" along the same line?

**GROTH:** I can't remember. I guess we didn't, and we must've had a reason for not doing that, but I just don't remember what that was. I guess the only reason we would have is that we just didn't think it would sell well enough. Jaime has the advantage of having all the pretty chicks and the color series we did, if I remember correctly, had that science-fiction angle to it, that great "Mechanics" story.

I think probably we just did not think "Heartbreak Soup," which was Gilbert's best work at that point, would fly in that format, or would have that same crossover appeal with superhero fans. We probably thought Jaime's would barely have it and Gilbert's wouldn't at all.

*Jaime's "100 Rooms" (1983), reprinted in* Maggie the Mechanic, *reminded Groth of comedies from the '30s and '40s.*

> YEAH, AND YOU KNOW THAT WHEN IT STARTS TO FADE, SOMETHING ALWAYS HAS TO FILL THE VACUUM, WHETHER IT'S AN ACTOR OR A BAND OR WHATEVER, THERE HAS TO BE SOMEONE TO FILL THAT HOLE, WHETHER THERE HAPPENS TO BE ANYONE TALENTED AROUND AT THAT PARTICULAR MOMENT OR NOT.

> ALSO THOSE SAME CORPORATE INTERESTS ARE LOCKED INTO PANDERING TO THE YOUTH CULTURE; THAT'S PROBABLY ANOTHER ASPECT OF WHY THINGS ARE AS CRETINOUS AS THEY ARE.

> YEAH. THE WHOLE IDEA OF GEARING THE CULTURE DOWN TOWARDS TEENAGERS HAS HAD A LOT TO DO WITH IT, DEFINITELY.

> RIGHT...WELL, BOY, DON'T WE SOUND LIKE A COUPLE OF OLD FARTS!

> BETO/97

*Gilbert drew "Are the Kids All Right?": words excerpted from a Seth interview conducted by Gary Groth. It ran in* New Love #4 *(June 1997) and is reprinted in* Fear of Comics.

## "SEX REALLY DOES SELL, I GUESS"

**SOBEL:** Can you talk a little bit about Eros Comix, what the original vision was for that imprint, and how *Birdland* evolved out of that?

**GROTH:** The original vision of Eros Comix was to save our asses.

**SOBEL:** You mean financially?

**GROTH:** The whole reason we started Eros was because we were losing ground every month. So we started Eros. Frank Thorne was among the earliest artists that we published, and at some point I saw it as an opportunity to make money for artists whose work we loved and respected and could use the money. And to that end, I'm sure I just talked to Gilbert. I might've talked to Jaime about it too, but I definitely talked to Gilbert and said, "Do you want to do an X-rated comic, because we think it'll sell like crazy."

*Birdland* might've sold as well or even better than *Love and Rockets*. I think it was a lot easier for Gilbert to do. He just had fun with it, whereas with *Love and Rockets* he really had to focus intensely on it and it was just harder work. *Birdland* I think he really just had a lot of fun with. So he could spend less time on it and make more money.

We would make this offer to artists whose work we were publishing but who were as desperate for money as we were. It was an easy way to make money if they wanted to do it. And that's pretty much it. *Birdland* sold really well. We sold it as a three- or four- issue comic, and then compiled it into a graphic novel and it sold very well for years and years.

**SOBEL:** Was the Eros line as a whole successful?

**GROTH:** Oh, it was incredibly successful. It literally pulled us out of a hole in nine months. Nine months after starting *Eros* we were solvent.

**SOBEL:** Sex really does sell, I guess. It's true.

**GROTH:** Who knew? [*Sobel laughs.*] We were behind the eightball by a substantial amount of money. So, Eros did work, and it worked for a number of years. It was a very important revenue stream for us for many, many years. It's negligible now, though. We only publish a handful of books a year, but in the '90s it really saved us. And I was glad that it could make some dough for Gilbert, too.

## PLAYING FAVORITES

**SOBEL:** Do you want to cite any personal favorite stories, or would you rather leave that alone?

**GROTH:** God, there's so many. "The Whispering Tree." There're just too many stories; I'd have to whittle it down. I mean, everyone has the period

This panel, cartooned circa 2006-2007, is from Jaime's Gods and Science, *which collects the expanded "Ti-Girls" storyline.*

that they like the most, but especially with Jaime, I like every period for different reasons. One of my favorite stories is "100 Rooms," but tomorrow it could be another story. It depends on my mood, because so many of the stories are just so brilliantly executed. And you never know if one of your favorite stories is your favorite because of some sort of nostalgic angle to it or not. But I remember being just blown away by "100 Rooms."

I was already being blown away continuously, but then that came in and I thought that was ... and again, that story was something so new to comics. The rhythm and the pacing of it was something I'd never seen in comics before. I remember thinking that it reminded me of comedies from the '30s and '40s. Like a great comedy like *Holiday* had that. It also had that double-bottomed sense to it of being funny and dramatic at the same time, and he juggled those elements so perfectly.

And then, as you no doubt know, Jaime went in and added panels to it for the book version. I think he added something like nine pages. I'm still just utterly amazed at his ability to do that and make it seamless.

**SOBEL:** Both brothers have a knack for that.

**GROTH:** Yeah, it's just uncanny. It just goes to show you how organic their work is, which is another aspect to it that I love.

**SOBEL:** How did you feel, at the time, about the Brothers' decision to end the first series?

**GROTH:** It was entirely their decision and I was fine with it. They needed a break. They both went on to do new solo comics, then came roaring back with a new edition of *Love and Rockets* when they were ready. In a way, I think it rejuvenated them.

**SOBEL:** This is obscure, but can you talk about the genesis of "The Kids Are All Right," that one-page strip you co-wrote with Seth, that Gilbert illustrated in *New Love* #4?

**GROTH:** I had nothing to do with it! It's a transcript of a portion of my interview with Seth from *The Comics Journal*. I think the exchange just tickled Gilbert and inspired him to turn it into a short strip. It was a pretty funny excerpt, I must say. I just spent three hours in a bar with Seth that was essentially the same conversation.

## THE FUTURE IS NOW

**SOBEL:** Gilbert's post-Palomar stories, and, to a lesser extent, some of Jaime's recent stories like "Ti-Girls Adventures," have received mixed reactions, and I was curious to hear your impressions on why that is?

**GROTH:** I don't think there's any one reason. It may be because any time an artist breaks from the kind of work he's known for and for which he's received plaudits, some readers are going to be skeptical or disturbed that he's not doing what the reader is fond of. Change is difficult to accept or embrace. I'm sure it's an honest appraisal on some people's part. But, artists have to go where they have to go. One may not like the various tangents Gilbert and Jaime have taken, but I also think it's smart and necessary for artists to push themselves into different modes of expression, different tonalities, different subject matter.

I for one loved Jaime's "superhero" story: thought it was brilliant, in fact. It's loving and playful and funny, and eschews all that earnestness and idiotic seriousness that began to infect superheroes, beginning with *Watchmen* in the '80s. As for Gilbert, his stories are more and more coming from some deep, unmediated place and crafted with an intuitive narrative sense.

**SOBEL:** Could you clarify what Fantagraphics' digital strategy is for *Love and Rockets*?

**GROTH:** It's the same as it is with all our other books, which is that sometime in 2012, all of the books for which the artists agree will be available as e-books on various platforms. We're actually beginning with *Love and Rockets*, and then rolling out the rest of our current titles and backlist.

**SOBEL:** Some people were surprised to learn that Gilbert's new book, *Marble Season*, will be published by Drawn & Quarterly. Can you talk about how that decision arose?

**GROTH:** I don't know much about it, to tell you the truth. I believe D&Q pursued Gilbert and made him an offer for a specific type of book.

**SOBEL:** Looking back on the series' three decades, and the evolution of the medium in general over that period, do you think you've accomplished what you set out to do with Fantagraphics and *The Comics Journal*?

**GROTH:** Gulp. I am more at ease being an apostle of failure than of success, but I'd have to say that, yes, we have gone a long way toward accomplishing our mission. Comics (in the newly marketable form of "graphic novels," which I have grudgingly accepted) has become a part of mainstream culture, is appreciated by literate readers who aren't first and foremost comics fanatics, are written and debated about among intelligent circles of readers, and the form itself is as vital as it's ever been.

**SOBEL:** How would you characterize *Love and Rockets'* legacy?

**GROTH:** I don't think there's any question that it's a pivotal series and a pivotal body of work in the history of the medium. R. Crumb had his predecessors in the underground comics movement, but you could truly cite Crumb's work and his fellow underground cartoonists who followed as a landmark in the aesthetic history of comics; and I think one

day Jaime and Gilbert's work will be recognized as the next aesthetic landmark, in the wake of which followed the next generation of alternative or literary cartoonists (for want of any better identity). They're quintessential cartoonists who distilled the language of cartooning into a strikingly original dramatic maturity. ∎

# TIMELINES

# TIMELINE:
# LOCAS

**DISCLAIMER FROM JAIME:** If you, dear readers, have any argument with any of the info here in this timeline, I take full responsibility. I know I have screwed up with my history here and there in the past and I fully thank Marc Sobel and everybody for putting this together, because I wouldn't wanna go near this thing if I were anybody.

*Ed. Note: An asterisk (*) indicates a "guestimate."*

| Year | Description | Story Reference |
|------|-------------|-----------------|
| 1919 | *H.R. Costigan born. | Nobody? So ... |
| 1926 | The Galindo house is constructed. | Maggie: Part 9 |
| 1935 | *Rena Titañon born. | Mechanics |
| 1938 | Nacho Chascarrillo (Maggie's father) born. | Mechanics |
| 1940 | El Diablo Blanco born. | Mechanics |
| 1943 | Quina (Maggie's mother) born. | Mechanics |
| 1947 | *Vicki Chascarrillo (aka Vicki Glori) born. | Camp Vicki |
|  | The Galindo house is physically moved to Hoppers from Crown Road. | Maggie: Part 10 |
| 1949 | Rena Titañon becomes a professional wrestler at age 14. | Mechanics |
| 1950 | Del Chimney born. |  |
| 1952 | Rena slams her rival Bull Marie through the mat. | Toyo's Request |
| 1955 | *Alejandra (Maggie's stepmother) born. | Angelitas |
| 1957 | Rena defeats Tiger Rosa to become world champion at age 22. | Mechanics |
|  | Rena returned to her hometown of Caraxico (in Zymbodia) to wrestle a man; however, when he refused to wrestle a woman, Rena led an angry mob to his house and body-slammed him down a well, cementing her legend. | Who Is Rena Titañon? |
|  | Mrs. Galindo becomes crippled. | Maggie: Part 10 |

| Year | Description | Story Reference |
|------|-------------|-----------------|
| 1958 | *Isabel ("Izzy") Maria Oritz (later Ruebens) born. | Locos |
|  | Rena starts dating Royal Don Rains. | House of Raging Women |
| 1961 | *Beatriz Garcia ("Penny Century") born. | ¡Inquiritis! |
|  | Sal Galindo dies and leaves his garage business to Harvey and Louis. | Maggie: Part 10 |
| 1962 | *Ray Dominguez born. | Maggie: Part 10 |
|  | *Doyle Blackburn born. | Spring 1982 |
| 1963 | *Theresa Leeanne ("Terry") Downe born. | Spring 1982 |
| 1964 | *Esperanza Leticia ("Hopey") Glass born. |  |
|  | Letty Chavez born on Leap Day. | Wigwam Bam |
|  | Rena fulfills Toyo Hibonales' final request and confronts her old rival, Bull Marie. | Toyo's Request |
| 1965 | *Margarita Luisa ("Maggie") Chascarrillo born. | Wigwam Bam |
|  | Vicki Chascarrillo graduates high school, decides to become a wrestler. | Camp Vicki |
|  | Beatriz Garcia meets H.R. Costigan for the first time at Chester Square. | Bay of Threes |
| 1966 | *Joey Glass (Hopey's brother) born. | Maggie and Hopey Color Fun |
|  | Izzy starts baby-sitting Maggie. | Home School |
| 1967 | *Eulalio ("Speedy") Ortiz born. | We Want the World and We Want it Bald |

181

| Year | Description | Story Reference |
|------|-------------|-----------------|
| 1967 | Danita Lincoln born. | We Want the World and We Want it Bald |
| | Rena is looking for a tag-team partner and chooses Vicki Glori. | Camp Vicki |
| | Rena saves her friend and fellow wrestler, India Chala, from Crusher Gaines. | The Little Monster |
| | Hopey's family moves to Hollywood and her mother tries to get her and Joey into child acting. | Wigwam Bam/Maggie and Hopey Color Fun |
| | Louis gives Margarita the nickname "Maggie." | Maggie: Part 10 |
| 1968 | *Daphne ("Daffy") Matsumoto born. | Maggie: Part 10 |
| | Maggie (age 3) and Letty (age 4) go to Knott's Berry Farm for Letty's birthday. | Wigwam Bam |
| 1969 | Rena and Vicki, tag-team champions, lose their title to the Hogg Sisters, and their bitter feud is ignited. | Camp Vicki |
| | Rena arrests Sharkey Horwitz before he can cross the U.S.-Mexican border. | Queen Rena: Life at 34 |
| | Hopey gets a spanking from both the school principal and her father for sneaking out of school. | Day By Day with Hopey: Monday |
| | Esther Chascarrillo born. | The Death of Speedy Ortiz/ Gold Diggers of 1969 |
| | While Nacho is away, Quina, Maggie and baby Esther spend the day wandering around, hiding from the bill collector. | Gold Diggers of 1969 |
| 1970 | Duke Morales introduces Rena to Bernie Carbo. | Mechanics |
| | Rena beats Bull Marie (age 55) who retires after the match. | House of Raging Women |
| | Hopey's parents get divorced and she and Joey move to Hoppers with their mother. | Wigwam Bam/Maggie and Hopey Color Fun |
| | Calvin Chascarrillo (Maggie's brother) born. | Gold Diggers of 1969/ Browntown |
| | Xochitl Nava born. | Whoa Nellie! |

| Year | Description | Story Reference |
|------|-------------|-----------------|
| 1972 | Maggie (age 7) and Letty (age 8) have a sleepover and go to Disneyland for Letty's birthday. | Wigwam Bam |
| | The Birmingham Lady Bashers become tag-team champions. | Whoa Nellie! |
| | H.R. Costigan and Norma get divorced. | Penny Century: On the Road Ag'in |
| 1973 | The infamous title match between Vicki and Rena, where Vicki "used the ropes" to become champion. | Camp Vicki |
| | After losing to Vicki and learning she was pregnant, Rena retired. | Little Monster |
| | Manuel Chascarrillo (Maggie's brother) born. | Browntown |
| 1974 | Rena's son Tony born. | Bob Richardson |
| | Beatriz Garcia moves from Texas to California and meets her future husband, H.R. Costigan, for the second time. | Bay of Threes |
| 1975 | Angel Chascarrillo (Maggie's brother) born. | Browntown |
| | Maggie (age 10) moves with her family from Hoppers to Cadezza. | Locos/Browntown |
| | Maggie's father, Nacho, begins an affair with his secretary, Alejandra. | Browntown |
| | An older neighborhood boy molests Calvin Chascarrillo (age 6). | Browntown |
| | The Saturn Stiletto is shot down and stranded in the jungle of Zymbodia. | Mechanics |
| 1976 | Izzy arrested on her 18th birthday for urinating on a lawn. She is stabbed while in jail. | Locos |
| | Maggie (age 11) visits Letty in Hoppers for her 12th birthday and discovers the song "Wig-Wam Bam" by Sweet. | Wigwam Bam |
| 1977 | Ray takes part in a few burglaries with 'Litos and Big Eddie. | Look Out |
| 1978 | Ruben Chascarrillo born. | Browntown |
| | Maggie's parents split up. | Browntown |

| Year | Description | Story Reference |
|---|---|---|
| 1978 | Maggie (age 13) moves back to Hoppers with her mother, sister and brothers. Calvin stays in Cadezza with his father. | Locos/Wigwam Bam/Browntown |
| | Maggie gets a job working with Harvey and Louis at Sal's Garage. | Return For Me |
| | Letty introduces Maggie to punk music. | Wigwam Bam |
| | Maggie's mother moves to Montoya (Dairytown). Maggie stays behind and lives with her aunt Vicki so she can continue working at Sal's Garage. | Return For Me |
| | Letty Chavez is killed in an automobile accident (age 14). | Young Locas/Wigwam Bam/Return For Me |
| | Izzy goes to college on a teaching scholarship. | Locos |
| | Ray nearly witnesses a race riot with his brothers in Hoppers. | The KKK Comes to Hoppers |
| | Big Eddie's wedding. | The Death of Speedy Ortiz |
| | Gina Bravo born. | Whoa Nellie! |
| | In an effort to find Beatriz, H.R. Costigan tours high schools on the West Coast, giving speeches about staying in school. He finally finds her in Hoppers. | Bay of Threes |
| 1979 | Terry runs away and moves into Del Chimney's punk flophouse in Hoppers. | Tear It Up, Terry Downe |
| | Terry and Hopey start dating. Terry gets Hopey into punk. | Tear It Up, Terry Downe |
| | Terry and Hopey beat up Julie Wree. | The Secrets of Life and Death Vol. 5 |
| | Izzy introduces Maggie and Hopey for the first time. | Locas Tambien |
| | Izzy marries Jack Ruebens, her college English professor. They honeymoon in France. | Locos/The Secrets of Life and Death Vol. 5 |
| | Maggie and Hopey first meet Beatriz in high school and nickname her "Penny Century." | All This and Penny, Too ... |

| Year | Description | Story Reference |
|---|---|---|
| 1979 | Penny Century graduates high school and moves to New Keops, where she works as a waitress at the Bumble Bee and meets Rand Race. She also hooks up with H.R. Costigan, her future husband, for the first time. | Amor y Cohetes/Bay of Threes |
| 1980 | Izzy and Jack Ruebens separate; Izzy has an abortion and attempts suicide. | Locos/Flies on the Ceiling |
| | Izzy suffers from writer's block/nightmares. | "How to Kill A ... " By Isabel Ruebens |
| | Izzy flees to Mexico and becomes involved with Beto and his father. | Flies on the Ceiling |
| | Maggie and Hopey hook up for the first time. | The Return of Ray D. |
| | Maggie (age 15) meets Tony "Top Cat" Chase, her future ex-husband, in an alley outside a punk show in L.A. Later, he is the first man she sleeps with. | Everybody Loves Me, Baby |
| | Penny briefly dates Rand Race. | Amor y Cohetes |
| 1981 | Penny gets fired from her factory job for daydreaming she is Atoma, a superheroine. | "Penny Century, You're Fired" |
| | Maggie, Hopey, Terry, Mary and Daffy attend a Black Flag concert in L.A. and after-party at Lois' house. | Wigwam Bam |
| | Nacho Chascarrillo marries Alejandra. | Angelitas |
| 1982 | Hopey briefly considers dating Henry, but the relationship never gets off the ground. | A Date With Hopey |
| | Hopey, Maggie and Joey get kicked out of the library and visit Izzy, who lectures them about the nails in her bookshelf. | Locas Tambien |
| | Ray Dominguez leaves Hoppers for college on the East Coast. | Spring 1982 |
| | Doyle lives with his girlfriend Stacy and her roommate, Lily Rivera, and works as their bodyguard for their private strip shows. | Spring 1982 |

| Year | Description | Story Reference |
|------|-------------|-----------------|
| 1982 | Maggie graduates high school and briefly works as a waitress at Bumper's, but quits because she doesn't want to strip. | Return of the Butt Sisters |
| | Maggie gets a job as a prosolar mechanic working with Rand Race. | Mechan-X |
| | Maggie goes to Zhato with the prosolar crew to fix the legendary *Saturn Stilletto*; meets Rena for the first time. | Mechanics |
| 1983 | Maggie, Hopey, Izzy and Penny spend a few weeks at Costigan's manor; Maggie hooks up and breaks up with Casey. | 100 Rooms |
| | Penny's misadventures in Zhato with Bomber Bones. | Penny Century: On the Road Ag'in |
| 1984 | Maggie goes to Rio Frio with the mechanics crew, gets lost with Rena on the island of Chepan. | Las Mujeres Perdidas |
| | Fearing Maggie died in Chepan, Hopey moves into Izzy's house. | Las Mujeres Perdidas |
| | Maggie returns to Hoppers, quits her mechanic job and gets a job at Vandy's fast-food restaurant. She moves in with Hopey and Izzy. | Locas |
| | Joe Van Nuys tells Rena about the death of India Chala. | Little Monster |
| | Rena (age 48) announces she is coming out of retirement to reclaim the championship from Vicki Glori. | Little Monster |
| | Hopey's band (the Missiles of October with Terry, Monica and Zero) plays a big gig, but Maggie parties with Speedy and misses the show. | Locas en las Cabezas |
| | Officer Sado arrests Hopey and Izzy for vandalism, while Maggie passes out at a party with Speedy. | Locas Starring Hopey |
| | *Negra Costigan born. | Election Day |

| Year | Description | Story Reference |
|------|-------------|-----------------|
| 1985 | Maggie fixes Mr. Lopez's truck and meets the Garcia brothers (Enero, Febrero and Miercoles) and their cousin, Correo. | Locas At the Beach |
| | Rena (age 49) attempts a comeback with her new partner, Pepper Martinez, but her rage gets her disqualified. Mrs. Minder prevents her from seeing her son, Tony, after the match. | House of Raging Women |
| | *Elias (Danita's son) born. | The Return of Ray D. |
| | Joey and Doyle search for their missing Ape Sex album. | Locas vs. Locos |
| | Maggie, Hopey and Izzy get evicted from their house. | Locas vs. Locos |
| | Penny marries H.R. Costigan. | Locas 8:01 am |
| | Mrs. Galindo dies. Maggie, Hopey and Penny attend her wake. Izzy inherits her house. | Locas 8:01 am/Home School |
| | Doyle helps Maggie and Hopey move into Terry's house temporarily. | Locas 8:01 am |
| | Vicki loses her title to Straska the Russian Wind and is so upset she begs Maggie to move back in with her. | Locas 8:01 am |
| | Ray Dominguez returns to Hoppers. | The Return of Ray D. |
| | Hopey and Terry leave Hoppers for a road tour with their band (La Llorona) without telling Maggie. | The Return of Ray D. |
| | Maggie quits her job at Vandy's and celebrates with Danita Lincoln. | The Return of Ray D. |
| | Esther (Maggie's sister) sparks a gang war by dating Speedy Ortiz and Rojo at the same time. | The Death of Speedy Ortiz |
| | Izzy suffers a nervous breakdown over the escalating violence. | The Death of Speedy Ortiz |
| | Speedy commits suicide. | The Death of Speedy Ortiz |
| | Two weeks after Speedy's death, Maggie retreats to her father's house in Texas. | Wigwam Bam |

| Year | Description | Story Reference |
|------|-------------|-----------------|
| | Maggie returns to Hoppers and gets a job photocopying papers for an insurance company. | Ninety-Three Million Miles From the Sun |
| | Xochitl (age 13) starts baby-sitting her next-door neighbor, Gina Bravo. | Whoa Nellie! |
| 1987 | Bickering, tension and lack of funds plague the La Llorona tour. | Jerusalem Crickets 1987 |
| | La Llorona breaks up; Terry joins 40 Thieves and Zero and Monica return to Hoppers. Hopey is stranded with Tex in Badgeport. | Jerry Slum and the Crickettes |
| | Maggie and Ray hook up for the first time. | A Mess of Skin |
| | Hopey and Tex visit Penny at Costigan's Manor East. | All This and Penny Too |
| | Tex impregnates both Penny and Hopey. | All This and Penny Too |
| | Vicki reclaims the women's wrestling championship belt. | In the Valley of the Polar Bears |
| | Vicki drags Maggie on the road as her "personal accountant" in an attempt to help her grow up. | In the Valley of the Polar Bears |
| | After a fight with her aunt, Maggie flees to the East Coast with Bo Bunyan in search of Hopey. | In the Valley of the Polar Bears |
| | Vicki is stripped of her title for excessive violence and kicked out of wrestling. | In the Valley of the Polar Bears |
| | Vicki marries Big Cash Watkins and moves to Japan. | In the Valley of the Polar Bears |
| | Unsuccessful in her search, Maggie returns to Hoppers and moves in with Ray. | In the Valley of the Polar Bears |
| 1988 | *Clarita born (Penny and Tex's daughter). | Ninety-Three Million Miles From the Sun |
| | Hopey has a miscarriage. | Ninety-Three Million Miles From the Sun |
| | Hopey and Tex briefly live with Mary Christmas, but get kicked out after a fight. | Ninety-Three Million Miles From the Sun |

| Year | Description | Story Reference |
|------|-------------|-----------------|
| | Ray paints Maggie's portrait. Danita replaces her as Ray's model. | Boxer, Bikini or Brief |
| 1988 | Doyle and Ray hang out with their old friend, Lar' Dog, who gets beat up repeatedly by bouncers. | Lar' Dog: Boys Night Out #1398 |
| | Some young punks promote their new album, "Hopey Monsters," with Hopey's missing picture. | Gonna Make You My Man ... |
| 1989 | Hopey and Tex briefly live with some crack dealers. | Ninety-Three Million Miles From the Sun |
| | Penny invites Maggie and Ray to Costigan's East Coast mansion, where she reunites Maggie and Hopey after four years apart. | Ninety-Three Million Miles From the Sun |
| | Maggie and Hopey meet Ray's ex-girlfriend, Maya, at an art gallery. | Las Monjas Asesinas |
| | Ray begins to date Danita Lincoln. | Below My Window Lurks My Head |
| | Hopey discovers her picture on the milk carton "missing" ads. | Below My Window Lurks My Head |
| 1990 | After a racist incident at an East Coast hipster party, Maggie and Hopey have a falling-out and Maggie leaves Badgeport. | Wigwam Bam |
| | After leaving Badgeport, Maggie has two experiences with prostitution. | Chester Square/Maggie the Mechanic or Perla the Prostitute |
| | Hopey gets drawn into Nan Tucker's strange world of sexual fetishism. | Wigwam Bam |
| | Ray and Danita move in together. | Wigwam Bam |
| | Ray is mistakenly beaten up by a group of teenagers. | Wigwam Bam |
| | Bumper's closes. | Wigwam Bam |
| | Lily and Doyle break up. | Wigwam Bam |
| | Doyle hooks up with Nami (Daffy's little sister). | Wigwam Bam |
| | Izzy's frantic search for Maggie and Hopey ends in Texas after she reads Maggie's private diaries. | Wigwam Bam |
| | Penny Century gets pregnant again by her ex-bodyguard, Pete. | Wigwam Bam |

| Year | Description | Story Reference |
| --- | --- | --- |
| 1990 | Nan Tucker's goons rough up Hopey and Tex. | Wigwam Bam |
| | Ray hooks up with Penny Century for the first time. | Penny Century |
| | Doyle leaves Hoppers and drifts around the country before settling in Phoenix and befriending Sid Doan. | Wigwam Bam/Maggie: Part 8 |
| | Vicki Glori opens her wrestling training camp in East Texas. | Whoa Nellie! |
| | Xochitl Nava (age 18) begins training to be a professional wrestler. | Whoa Nellie! |
| | Maggie arrives in East Texas at her aunt's training camp. | Camp Vicki |
| | Maggie reunites with Penny, who is also living in East Texas, and her cousin Xochitl. | Perla and Beatriz |
| | Gina develops a crush on Maggie; Maggie struggles to find work in Texas. | Maggie the Mechanic or Perla the Prostitute |
| | Esther, who is engaged to Alvaro but suffering cold feet, arrives in Texas and moves in with Maggie. | It's Not That Big a Deal |
| | Maggie and friends return to Chester Square; Ruby stabs Gina. | It's Not That Big a Deal |
| 1991-1992 | Hopey returns to Hoppers for the first time in six years and spends the day with Janet Polo, her brother's girlfriend. | We Want the World and We Want it Bald |
| | Danita and Elias move to East Texas. | Son of Butt Sisters |
| | El Diablo Blanco (Rena's brother) asks Maggie out, but they never connect. | Hester Square |
| | Rena returns to Texas to reunite with her son, Tony. | Hester Square |
| | Maggie accidentally starts a false rumor that she is getting married. | Bob Richardson |
| | Danita marries El Diablo Blanco. | Bob Richardson |
| | Esther marries Alvaro. | Bob Richardson |
| | Maggie and Hopey are reunited in Texas while being arrested (end of the first series). | Bob Richardson |

| Year | Description | Story Reference |
| --- | --- | --- |
| 1993 | Xocthitl and Gina decide to become a tag team. | Whoa Nellie! |
| 1996 | Xochitl is voted the Texas Women's Champion after Claudia Casey (the current champion) announces she is pregnant. | Whoa Nellie! |
| | Gina Bravo graduates high school. | Whoa Nellie! |
| | A week after being voted in as chamption, Xochitl loses her belt to Katy Hawk. | Whoa Nellie! |
| | Vicki Glori retires from wrestling and closes her training camp. | Whoa Nellie! |
| 1997 | Maggie, Hopey, Joey and Janet attend Negra Costigan's birthday party; Joey gets kicked out for fighting. | Maggie and Hopey Color Fun |
| | Joey Glass and Janet Polo get married in Las Vegas. | Maggie and Hopey Color Fun |
| | Ray is single and moves to L.A. | Penny Century |
| | Maggie is working for Norma Costigan, doing odd jobs like balancing her shopping budget and driving Negra around. | Locas |
| | Maggie runs into Tony Chase outside one of Norma's pool parties and he asks her out. | Everybody Loves Me, Baby |
| | Guy Goforth, one of Hopey's co-workers, asks her out on a date. | Hopey Hop Sock |
| | Ray's new apartment in L.A. gets broken into. | Look Out |
| | Maggie has a panic attack while driving home from Hoppers on "the horror highway." | Chiller! |
| | Maggie and Tony Chase get married in Las Vegas; Daffy is the maid of honor. | Everybody Loves Me, Baby |
| 1998 | Izzy's book The Secrets of Life and Death is published, but Izzy suffers debilitating stage fright over a public reading, which causes her to grow huge. | Locas |

| Year | Description | Story Reference |
|---|---|---|
| 1998 | Hiding out from the hoopla surrounding her husband's illness, Penny seeks refuge at Izzy's house in Hoppers. | ¡Inquiritis! |
| | Ray sees Vivian Solis at a strip club and starts fantasizing about her. | One More Ladies' Man |
| | Hopey goes on a date with Guy Goforth. | One More Ladies' Man |
| | H.R. Costigan dies. | Nobody? So … |
| | Hopey goes to Costigan's funeral in Colorado by herself. | Election Day |
| | Hopey volunteers at the California polls on Election Day. | Election Day |
| | Norma kidnaps her daughter, Negra, and is later arrested in Texas. | Election Day |
| | Maggie and Tony Chase get divorced. | Everybody Loves Me, Baby |
| 2001-2002 | Maggie manages the Capri Apartments complex in the San Fernando Valley. | Maggie: Part 1 |
| | Julie Wree invites Izzy to appear on her cable access TV show. Maggie meets Vivian Solis, "the Frogmouth," on the set. | Maggie: Part 1 |
| | After her TV appearance, Izzy refuses to return to her house in Hoppers. | Maggie: Part 1 |
| | Hopey is working at an office job and as a part-time bartender at Elmo's Nite Spot. | Maggie: Part 2 |
| | Maggie witnesses Sid Doan pull a knife on Vivian in an alleyway. | Maggie: Part 2 |
| | Vivian lures Maggie to a non-existent pool party at Sid's house and tries to seduce her into a threesome with Reno Banks. | Maggie: Part 3 |
| | Vivian makes a present to Maggie of a Mexican folk-art statue that she'd stolen from Sid. | Maggie: Part 3 |
| | Doyle and Ray reunite at an L.A. adult bookstore. | The Frogmouth |
| | After a fight with Sid Doan's gang, Doyle gives Ray "a hummer" in an alleyway behind the bar. | The Frogmouth |

| Year | Description | Story Reference |
|---|---|---|
| 2001-2002 | Maggie finally takes Izzy back to Hoppers. | Maggie: Part 6 |
| | Maggie hooks up with Vivian for the first time. | Maggie: Part 6 |
| | Maggie and Vivian go to Izzy's house in Hoppers to retrieve the Mexican folk art statue. | Maggie: Part 7 |
| | After a fight, Vivian gets fired from Julie Wree's TV show. | Maggie: Part 8 |
| | Maggie goes to a family reunion/retirement party for her mother in Montoya. | Maggie: Part 9 |
| | After the party, Maggie drives to Hoppers to check on Izzy and discovers her house ablaze. | Maggie: Part 9 |
| | Izzy's house burns down; Izzy disappears. Maggie is drugged by some kids. | Maggie: Part 10 |
| 2005-2006 | Ray sees Maggie at a bar for the first time since their break-up, but doesn't speak to her. | Life Through Whispers |
| | Sid Doan is murdered. | Life Through Whispers |
| | Ray sleeps on Vivian's couch, but nothing sexual happens. | 2 'R's, 2 'L's |
| | Doyle beats up Borneo. | Hagler and Hearns |
| | Ray runs into Maggie at a comic-book convention and finally talks to her. | Near Mint |
| | Ray and Vivian hook up for the first time. | Near Mint |
| | Ray goes to a comic con afterparty at Mike Varan's house and runs into Maggie again. Vivian finally learns of Sid's death, gets into a fight, and gets kicked out of the party. | Fine to Very Fine |
| | Hopey has eye surgery, gets glasses. | Day By Day with Hopey: Tuesday |
| | Hopey's last day of work/going-away lunch. | Day By Day with Hopey: Wednesday |
| | Hopey visits Maggie at her apartment and they witness Alarma jump off the roof in her superhero costume. | Day By Day with Hopey: Friday |

187

| Year | Description | Story Reference |
| --- | --- | --- |
| 2005-2006 | Hopey attends an orientation meeting at Palmetto School. That night she fails to see Terry's new band in concert. | Day By Day with Hopey: Saturday |
| | Hopey and Rosie break up. Rosie moves out. | Day By Day with Hopey: Sunday |
| | Hopey's first official day as a teaching assistant. | Day By Day with Hopey: Monday |
| | After reuniting with Tse Tse in L.A., Maggie goes to visit Rena Titañon at her private tropical island estate. | La Maggie, La Loca |
| | While visiting Rena, Maggie nearly drowns and is attacked on her 40th birthday. | La Maggie, La Loca |
| | Vivian makes Ray escort her to Elmer's house; Elmer beats her up. | Trampas Pero No Trampan |
| | At the wake for Sid Doan, Elmer is strangled to death by a corrupt cop while purportedly resisting arrest. | Male Torso Found in the L.A. River |
| | Maggie attends Ray's art show opening. Reno also has a painting in the show. | The Love Bunglers: Part One |
| | Maggie and Ray have their first date in 17 years. | The Love Bunglers: Part Two |
| | Maggie tries to buy a garage with her old Mechanics friend, Yax Haxley, but it falls through. | The Love Bunglers: Part Three |
| | Maggie and Reno go to a party at Mike Varan's house, where Maggie gets into a fight with Vivian. | The Love Bunglers: Part Four |
| | Angel graduates high school and leaves for college in El Paso, Texas. | The Love Bunglers: Part Five |
| | Calvin suffers a psychotic flashback and bashes Ray's head in with a brick. | The Love Bunglers: Part Five |
| 2008 | Maggie finally learns what happened to Ray and visits him at his sister's home in Hoppers. | The Love Bunglers: Part Five |
| | Maggie starts a small mechanics business with Yax thanks to a loan from Hopey. | The Love Bunglers: Part Five |

| Year | Description | Story Reference |
| --- | --- | --- |
| 2011 | Maggie owns her own garage and lives with Ray. | The Love Bunglers: Part Five |
| | Hopey works as a teacher and lives with her partner and son. | The Love Bunglers: Part Five |
| 2012 | Vivian's half-sister, Tonta, pays a visit. | Tonta, Crime Raiders International Mobsters and Executioners |
| | Doyle and Ray hang out, and Vivian stops by. Maggie picks Ray up and they argue about Reno Banks. | Uh … Oh Yeah |

*Ed. Note: Marc Sobel assembled this timeline with Gilbert's input; however, according to Gilbert, there is no "official" Palomar timeline. An asterisk (*) indicates a "guestimate."*

| Year | Description | Story Reference |
|------|-------------|-----------------|
| 1884 | *"Papa" Pito Cienfuego (Gorgo's father) born. | Another Mysterious Tree |
| 1908 | *Gorgo Cienfuego born. | Another Mysterious Tree |
| 1914 | *Peter Rio born. | Poison River |
| 1927 | Gorgo killed three mobsters in Chicago and saved his father's life. | Another Mysterious Tree |
|      | After the Mysterious Tree revealed itself to Gorgo, his father's sexual impotence was cured. | Another Mysterious Tree |
| 1931 | *Maria Inclan (mother of Luba, Fritz and Petra) born. | Poison River |
| 1937 | *Chelo born. | Another Mysterious Tree |
|      | *Ofelia Beltran born. | Poison River |
| 1943 | A great fire destroyed Palomar, but the town was rebuilt. | Another Mysterious Tree |
| 1948 | Maria came in eighth place in the Miss Ionosfera beauty pageant. | Poison River |
|      | Maria met Hector Martinez after the Miss Luminosa beauty pageant. | Bread, Love and Maria |
|      | Gorgo was beaten, tied to a giant wheel and rolled down a hill by a group of women gangsters. | The Gorgo Wheel |

| Year | Description | Story Reference |
|------|-------------|-----------------|
|      | Maria had a brief affair with a young scientist, who worked on experimental government aircraft. | The Gorgo Wheel |
|      | *Manuel born. | Heartbreak Soup |
| 1952 | Maria seduced Eduardo, a hired hand on "El Señor's" estate and became pregnant (with Luba). | The Gorgo Wheel |
| 1953 | *Luba born. | Act of Contrition/Poison River |
|      | "El Señor" realized that Luba was not his child and threw Maria, Eduardo and Luba off his property. | Poison River |
|      | Maria, Eduardo and Luba briefly lived together in Colonia. | Poison River |
|      | Eduardo was attacked and robbed by Juan Nuñez, a fellow laborer. | Poison River |
|      | Due to his injuries, Eduardo lost his job. | Poison River |
|      | Maria abandoned Eduardo and Luba. | Poison River |
| 1954 | Eduardo carried Luba 900 kilometers to his home, the Central American village of Isleta. | Poison River |

| Year | Description | Story Reference |
|------|-------------|-----------------|
| 1955 | Eduardo and Luba arrived in Isleta, where responsibility for Luba fell to her aunt Hilda and her cousin Ofelia. | Poison River |
| | Gina, Ruben, Ofelia and Luba attended a Communist rally in Gobos. | Poison River |
| | Eduardo died while attempting to return to Colonia in search of Maria. | Poison River |
| | Gina and Ruben were murdered. Ofelia was raped, shot and left for dead. | Poison River |
| | Ofelia went into hiding. Hilda went to live with her cousin, Alicia, and took Luba with her. | Poison River |
| 1957 | *Gato Reyna born. | Heartbreak Soup/The Children of Palomar |
| | Peter Rio formed the band Los Fritos with Docho, Ricky Boy and Fabio. | Poison River |
| | Peter had an affair with Garza's first wife, Ramona. | Poison River |
| | Peter fell in love with Maria after seeing her crack walnuts with her stomach. | Poison River |
| | Maria had affairs with Fermin, Peter Rio and Garza in the same time period. | Poison River |
| | Peter hired Papa Pito and Gorgo to find Luba. | Poison River |
| | Fermin suspected Maria was cheating on him and beat her up. | Poison River |
| | Peter tried to protect Maria from his father, but she ran away. | Poison River |

| Year | Description | Story Reference |
|------|-------------|-----------------|
| 1957 | Maria disappeared after Gorgo gave her a one-way plane ticket to California. | Poison River |
| 1959 | *Heraclio Calderon born. | Heartbreak Soup |
| | Peter married Isobel, a transvestite dancer, and bought her a house, a sex change and a daughter, Arjelia (on the black market). | Poison River |
| | In L.A., Maria starred in a small exploitation film called *Lie Down in the Dark*. | Venus and You |
| 1960 | *Pipo Jimenez born. | Heartbreak Soup |
| | *Israel and Aurora Diaz born. | Heartbreak Soup |
| | *Satch Garcia, Jesus Angel and Vicente born. | Heartbreak Soup |
| 1962 | Elvira found baby Carmen abandoned at the swap meet and brought her home. | For the Love of Carmen |
| 1963 | Fausto Salas was killed by an angry mob of peasants. | Bread, Love and Maria |
| | Chelo rescued Gato, Pintor and Manuel from some strange scientists in the wastelands on the other side of a huge crevice outside Palomar. | The Children of Palomar |
| 1966 | Israel Diaz's twin sister, Aurora, disappeared during a solar eclipse. | Bullnecks and Bracelets |
| 1968 | Pipo fell off one of the giant statues outside of Palomar and was rescued by Martin el Loco. | A Little Story |
| | Hector Martinez, working as an accountant for the Mexican mafia, was reunited with Maria when he picked her up on the side of the road. | Bread, Love and Maria |
| | Maria and Hector Martinez got married. | Bread, Love and Maria |

| Year | Description | Story Reference |
|---|---|---|
| | Papa Pito died after finally completing his mission to find Luba. | Poison River |
| | Peter Rio met Luba (age 15) when his band played in her town. They hooked up for the first time after the concert. | Poison River/Act of Contrition |
| | Luba was fired from the bathhouse after she attacked Omo with a hammer. | Poison River |
| | Peter ditched his band and married Luba. | Poison River |
| 1969 | *Petra Martinez born. | Bread, Love and Maria |
| | Peter began managing Señor Salas' strip club. | Poison River |
| | When he learned of Peter's marriage to Luba, Fermin returned. | Poison River |
| 1970 | Luba's friends Pepa and Lucy introduced her to heroin. | Poison River |
| | Tipped by a false rumor from Isobel, Garza accused Peter of being a subversive, sparking tensions with Salas. | Poison River |
| | Police Captain Jose Ortiz launched an investigation into Peter's personal affairs. | Poison River |
| | Peter hired Gorgo to protect Luba during the investigation. | Poison River |
| | Luba began having an affair with Captain Ortiz. | Poison River |
| | Luba met Archie Ruiz at the dance clubs in Calentura. | Poison River/Act of Contrition |
| | Luba got pregnant (father, unknown). | Poison River |
| 1970 | Luba gave up heroin and became an alcoholic. | Poison River |
| | Ricky raped Luba. | Poison River |
| | Fermin strangled Isobel. | Poison River |

| Year | Description | Story Reference |
|---|---|---|
| | Salas, Garza and several others were killed in a shootout between rival drug gangs. | Poison River |
| 1971 | *Rosalba "Fritz" Martinez born. | Bread, Love and Maria |
| | *Tonantzín Villaseñor born. | The Children of Palomar |
| | Following the shootout, Peter ascended to the head of the drug trade. | Poison River |
| | Luba overdosed on heroin, triggering early labor. | Poison River |
| | Fermin strangled Chato for selling drugs to Luba. | Poison River |
| | Luba's son (Armondo Jose) was taken by Javier, but died in transit to the U.S. due to drug-related heart failure. | Poison River |
| | Fermin strangled Captain Ortiz. | Poison River |
| | Peter suffered a stroke. | Poison River |
| 1972 | Gorgo arranged for Luba to return to her family. | Poison River |
| | Fermin and Blas took Peter to the U.S. for his protection. | Poison River |
| | Fermin strangled Javier. | Poison River |
| | Peter murdered his father. | Poison River |
| | Luba reunited with her aunt Hilda and her cousin Ofelia. | Poison River |
| | Gorgo went to California to watch over Maria. | Poison River |
| | Luba, Ofelia and Hilda decided to return to their hometown of Isleta. | Poison River |
| 1973 | *Diana Villaseñor born. | The Children of Palomar |
| 1973 | In Isleta, Ofelia slept with Sebastian, who gave her drugs to alleviate her chronic back pain. | Poison River |
| | Luba slept with Antonino and became pregnant with Maricela. | Poison River |

| Year | Description | Story Reference |
|---|---|---|
| | Luba, Ofelia and Hilda briefly moved to "El Pueblo de Kovinick," where Luba set up a bathhouse. | Poison River |
| | *Maricela (Luba's first daughter) born. | Poison River |
| | Aunt Hilda died. | Poison River |
| | Luba was run out of town for seducing young boys. | Poison River |
| | Luba briefly dated a Russian navy officer named Grigoryevich Artzybaschev. | Poison River |
| | Ofelia briefly dated Chango Valdes, a married wrestler. | Poison River |
| | Cilingis, Moises and Flaco were all murdered or disabled by Garza loyalists. | Poison River |
| | Soledad Marquez deflowered Pipo Jimenez seven days after her 13th birthday. | Chelo's Burden |
| | Heraclio Calderon and his family moved to Palomar. | Heartbreak Soup |
| | Toco was molested at a movie theater. | Toco |
| | Gorgo rescued Petra and Fritz from a car accident. | Love Story |
| | Hector and Maria split up. Maria took Fritz and Petra away. Hector went into hiding in Central America. | Bread, Love and Maria |
| 1974 | Luba, Ofelia and Maricela arrived in Palomar and opened a bathhouse. | Poison River/Heartbreak Soup |
| 1974 | Maria discovered a severed head in her refrigerator. | Bread, Love and Maria/Rosalba |
| | After being rejected by Zomba, Tipín Tipín hid underneath his house. Carmen and the gang of boys rescued him. | Heartbreak Soup |

| Year | Description | Story Reference |
|---|---|---|
| | Toco died. | Heartbreak Soup |
| | Manuel (age 26) got Pipo (age 14) pregnant. | Heartbreak Soup |
| | Sheriff Borro arrested both Luba and Chelo, but instead of fighting, they became friends. | Heartbreak Soup |
| | Heraclio lost his virginity to Luba. | The Reticent Heart/For the Love of Carmen |
| | Soledad Marquez murdered Manuel in a jealous rage over Pipo. | Heartbreak Soup |
| | Pipo married Gato Reyna. | Ecce Homo |
| 1975 | *Sergio Jimenez born. | Heartbreak Soup |
| | *Guadalupe (Luba's second daughter) born. | The Reticent Heart |
| | Chelo became the sheriff of Palomar. | Heartbreak Soup |
| | Luba opened a movie theater in Palomar. | Act of Contrition |
| 1977 | Maria left Fritz and Petra home alone for several days. | Mouth Trap |
| | Hector Martinez met Rosa, his second wife. | Bread, Love and Maria |
| | Pipo went to the U.S. for the first time on a holiday with Sergio and Gato. | Kisses For Pipo |
| | After their parents died, Tonantzín and Diana Villaseñor lived on the beach outside Palomar, until Pipo discovered them. | The Children of Palomar |
| | Pipo saved Tonantzín and Diana when they accidentally wandered into a demolition area. | The Children of Palomar |
| 1978 | Heraclio went to college and majored in music. | For the Love of Carmen |
| | Luba met and hooked up with Khamo for the first time while on a business trip to San Fideo and got pregnant (with Doralis). | Human Diastrophism/Poseur |

| Year | Description | Story Reference |
|------|-------------|-----------------|
| | Galgo raised Fortunato, Zanto and Diego to seduce women and break their hearts. | The Fortunato Files |
| | While cruising for women in San Fideo, Satch, Vicente, Heraclio and Jesus found Luba at a gas station and gave her a ride back to Palomar. | The Reticent Heart |
| 1979 | *Doralis (Luba's third daughter) born. | Human Diastrophism |
| | Jesus dropped Luba in a stream. | The Laughing Sun |
| 1982 | Heraclio graduated college, moved back to Palomar and took a job teaching music outside of town. | For the Love of Carmen |
| | Heraclio and Carmen got married. | For the Love of Carmen |
| | *Casimira (Luba's fourth daughter) born. | Human Diastrophism |
| 1984 | A blooter baby haunted Tonantzín. | The Children of Palomar |
| 1985 | *Venus (Petra's daughter) born. | Letters From Venus |
| | Luba reunited with and briefly dated her old friend, Archie Ruiz. | Act of Contrition |
| | The water heater at Luba's bathhouse exploded. | Act of Contrition |
| | Heraclio panicked over a strange bump on his head. | The Mystery Wen |
| | Heraclio had a fight with Carmen, got drunk, and ended up at Luba's house. | Love Bites |
| 1985 | Jesus married Laura Gomez after learning she was pregnant. | The Laughing Sun |
| | After hooking up with Fritz in the woods, Matt had an epileptic seizure and hit his head on a rock. | Petra |
| 1986 | Jesus had an affair with Tonantzín. | Farewell, My Palomar ... |

| Year | Description | Story Reference |
|------|-------------|-----------------|
| | After a fight with his wife that injured their baby, Jesus fled to the mountains outside of Palomar. His old gang reunited and brought him back. | The Laughing Sun |
| | Jesus was sentenced to prison on the island of Ofio. | Holidays in the Sun |
| | Luba and her daughters had a run-in with Isidro Rivas at the beach. | On Isidro's Beach |
| | At the Dia de los Muertos celebration in Palomar, Gato assaulted Pipo. | Ecce Homo |
| | After losing their factory jobs, Vicente and Saturnino struggled to find work in San Fideo. | The Way Things're Going |
| | Howard Miller, an American photo-journalist, visited Palomar to capture images for a new book. | An American in Palomar |
| | Carmen had an affair with Israel Diaz, became pregnant and had an abortion. Israel was so ashamed he left Palomar forever. | For the Love of Carmen |
| | Pipo left Gato and moved back to Palomar. | For the Love of Carmen |
| 1986 | Roberto (Gato's brother) was killed when he fell from a roof while fleeing Sheriff Chelo. He was being arrested for murdering his grandfather. | Duck Feet |
| | A witch cast a plague on Palomar after her baby skull was stolen. | Duck Feet |
| | Geraldo Mejia took Tonantzín hostage, but was arrested and sent to prison. | Duck Feet |

| Year | Description | Story Reference |
| --- | --- | --- |
| 1986 | Israel went on a drug-fueled bender after learning that the psychic he hired to find his missing sister was a fraud. | Bullnecks and Bracelets |
| | Israel attacked Gato and smashed his head through a window. | Bullnecks and Bracelets |
| | A foreign archaeological team began an excavation outside of Palomar. | Human Diastrophism |
| | Archie Ruiz proposed to Luba, but she turned him down and suffered a nervous breakdown. | Human Diastrophism |
| | Luba reunited with Khamo at the excavation site. | Human Diastrophism |
| | Martin el Loco discovered the body of Aldo Munkres. | Human Diastrophism |
| | Tomaso stabbed Chancla and left her for dead in a lake. | Human Diastrophism |
| | Luba seduced Humberto, a troubled young artist. | Human Diastrophism |
| | The severed head of Sven Andersson, an archaeologist, was discovered. | Human Diastrophism |
| | Pipo slept with Khamo. | Human Diastrophism |
| | Luba slept with Borro. | Human Diastrophism |
| | Khamo found Chancla alive. | Human Diastrophism |
| | Luba finally revealed to Heraclio that Guadalupe is his daughter. | Human Diastrophism |
| | Luba slept with Tomaso, the serial killer, and became pregnant (with Socorro). | Human Diastrophism |
| | Maricela and Riri ran away together to the U.S. | Human Diastrophism |
| | Chelo accidentally shot Casimira, causing her to lose her right arm. | Human Diastrophism |

| Year | Description | Story Reference |
| --- | --- | --- |
| | Tomaso was caught and arrested during an attack on Diana. | Human Diastrophism |
| | Luba became the new mayor of Palomar. | Human Diastrophism |
| | Tonantzín killed herself during a political protest. Khamo was severely burned trying to save her. | Human Diastrophism |
| | *Tito Calderon born. | For the Love of Carmen/Human Diastrophism |
| | Pipo took in Diana and cared for her after her sister's death. | Pipo |
| | Luba agreed to pay Khamo's hospital bills if he agreed to marry her. | Poseur |
| | Fritz met Mark Herrera at a lowrider car show in L.A. He was there promoting his first motivational video. | High Soft Lisp |
| | Tish and Delmar introduced Fritz to the joys of guns. | High Soft Lisp |
| | Fritz hooked up with her mother's cop friend. | In Bed With Pipo |
| 1987 | *Socorro (Luba's fifth daughter) born. | Human Diastrophism |
| 1988 | *Joselito (Luba's sixth child and only surviving son) born. | Love & Rockets X |
| | Pipo started a sportswear business in Palomar. | Love & Rockets X/Pipo |
| | Vicente returned to Palomar. | Farewell, My Palomar... |
| | Gato lost his job at the factory. | Farewell, My Palomar... |
| | Fritz began seeing her high school guidance counselor and decided to become a therapist. | Memories of Sweet Youth |
| 1989 | Love & Rockets, the band, practiced in Rex's garage for their debut at a Hollywood party. | Love & Rockets X |

| Year | Description | Story Reference |
|---|---|---|
| | White Aryan Resistance members Carl, Ben and Charlie beat up Malvina Wilson, an elderly black woman. | Love & Rockets X |
| | The party was a bust after Rex kicked out three black kids (Junior Brooks, Erf' Quake and E.T.) | Love & Rockets X |
| | After being rejected by Riri, Steve crashed Gerry's car and retreated to Palomar to recover. | Love & Rockets X |
| | Fritz hooked up with Scotty for the first time. | High Soft Lisp |
| | Mike Niznick seduced Igor. | Love & Rockets X |
| | Carl, Ben and Charlie kidnapped E.T. intending to kill him, but Charlie murdered Carl instead. | Love & Rockets X |
| | Riri and Maricela split up. Riri returned to Palomar. | Love & Rockets X |
| | Pipo and Guadalupe visited the U.S.: Guadalupe as an exchange student and Pipo to research expanding her sportswear business. | Love & Rockets X |
| | Igor and Mike went to Germany to film the fall of the Berlin Wall. | Love & Rockets X |
| | Steve returned to L.A. to care for his crippled Korean neighbor. | Love & Rockets X |
| | At a punk party, Fritz got wasted and slept with both of Scotty's roommates. | High Soft Lisp |
| | Fritz briefly appeared as D'Mentia on the low-budget, right-wing student TV show *Phantom of the Campus*. | Fritz After Dark |
| | Fritz started seeing Jerome, a married black lawyer. | Fritz After Dark |

| Year | Description | Story Reference |
|---|---|---|
| | Fritz met David Vasquez at a shooting gallery. They had a brief sexual encounter before Fritz set him up with Petra. | A Gift For Venus |
| | Lars killed himself on the final episode of *Phantom of the Campus* using Fritz's gun, but Jerome cleared her of all charges. | Fritz After Dark |
| | Fritz appeared in her first movie (*Rockin' the Waves II*), a surfing documentary, though the film was not released until years later. | Fritz After Dark |
| 1990 | David Vasquez and Petra got married. | Letters From Venus: Goddess of Love |
| | *Fritz and Mark Herrera got married. | High Soft Lisp |
| 1991 | Fritz famously appeared wearing a bikini in a TV commercial for Mark's motivational video series. This jump-started her film career. | Fritz After Dark |
| 1992 | Carmen and Heraclio had twin boys. | Be Bop a Luba |
| | *Concepcion ("Conchita," Luba's sixth daughter) born. | Be Bop a Luba |
| 1992 | Maria, Petra, Fritz and Venus went on a vacation to a nudist resort, where an employee stole their good-luck "family thing." | Letters From Venus: That Family Thing |
| | Mark Herrera's career as a motivational speaker reached its apex as he played to crowds of 60,000-plus. | High Soft Lisp |
| | To Mark's displeasure, Fritz started appearing in costume at science-fiction conventions. | High Soft Lisp |

| Year | Description | Story Reference |
|------|-------------|-----------------|
| | Fritz made a porn film (*Untitled*) in which she appeared to sleep with a dog creature in the woods. | Venus and You |
| | Fritz had a miscarriage. | High Soft Lisp |
| | Mark's voyeuristic habits led to jealous rages and began to erode his marriage to Fritz. | High Soft Lisp |
| 1993 | Jesus Angel was released from prison. | Farewell, My Palomar … |
| | Jesus slept with Satch's married daughter before returning to Palomar. | Farewell, My Palomar … |
| | Everyone in Palomar attended the going-away party for Guadalupe, Pipo and Diana. | Farewell, My Palomar… |
| | Pipo opened a small boutique in L.A. | Kisses For Pipo |
| | Pipo had an affair with Fortunato. | Kisses For Pipo |
| | Pipo and Gato officially divorced. Sergio had the best season of his soccer career. | Kisses For Pipo |
| | Guadalupe got pregnant, but refused to reveal the identity of the baby's father. | A Trick of the Unconscious |
| | Doralis married Chester, but after several violent fights, they divorced. | A Trick of the Unconscious |
| | Bruno Goyas was attacked by a raven and lost his eye. | A Trick of the Unconscious |
| | Gato convinced Jesus to move with him to the U.S. Doralis decided to join them. | A Trick of the Unconscious |
| | Diana became an international celebrity bodybuilder. | A Trick of the Unconscious |
| | *Jaime ("Jimmy," Guadalupe's son) born. | The Gorgo Wheel |
| | Fritz graduated college and became a therapist. | High Soft Lisp |

| Year | Description | Story Reference |
|------|-------------|-----------------|
| | Petra had breast reduction surgery. | Love Story |
| | Gorgo revealed to Petra the existence of her half-sister, Luba. | Love Story |
| | Garza loyalists shoot Gorgo outside Petra's house. | Love Story |
| | Doralis had lunch with her grandmother, Maria. | The Gorgo Wheel |
| | Maria died of a brain tumor. | Love Story |
| | Gorgo informed Hector Martinez of Maria's death. | Bread, Love and Maria |
| | Fritz and Petra reconnected with their father. | Bread, Love and Maria |
| | Maricela, Guadalupe and Doralis met their aunts (Fritz and Petra) and their families for the first time. | The Gorgo Wheel |
| | Fritz and Petra traveled to Palomar and met Luba for the first time. | Luba Conquers the World |
| | Doralis replaced Inez Perez as the star of Pipo's TV show. | Luba Conquers the World |
| | Guadalupe briefly dated Igor after he returned to the U.S. | Fuckin' Steve! |
| | Jesus Angel married Tita. | Luba Conquers the World |
| | Guadalupe revealed that her son's father was Gato Reyna and they got married. | Luba Conquers the World |
| | Fritz and Mark divorced. | High Soft Lisp |
| | Fritz appeared in her first official B movie. | Fritz After Dark |
| | Fritz and Scotty got married. | High Soft Lisp |
| | Fritz caught Scotty cheating on her. | High Soft Lisp |

| Year | Description | Story Reference |
|---|---|---|
| | "Scotty the Hog" released his first album, *The High Soft Lisp*, which Fritz financed. | High Soft Lisp |
| | Fritz and Scotty divorced. | High Soft Lisp |
| | Fritz married Aldo. | High Soft Lisp |
| | Aldo died after beating Fritz up in a drunken rage. | High Soft Lisp |
| | Strange "bird scientists" kidnapped Chelo, removed her eye, and left her for dead. | The Children of Palomar |
| 1994 | A massive earthquake struck Palomar. Everyone except Maricela and Israel returned to help clean up. | Chelo's Burden |
| | Jesus and Tita got divorced. | Chelo's Burden |
| | Humberto made statues of some Palomar residents and sank them to the bottom of a lake. | Chelo's Burden |
| | Chelo learned she had been carrying a mummified dead baby inside her since she was a teen. | Chelo's Burden |
| | Chelo, Pipo and Luba foiled an assassination attempt on Gorgo. After the incident, Luba decided to move to America. | Chelo's Burden |
| | Fritz got her first speaking role, playing a whore in the B movie *Chance in Hell*. | Venus and You |
| 1995 | Venus began writing letters to her cousin, Casimira. | Letters From Venus |
| | Sergio dragged Venus around town before finally picking up his mother at an S&M club. | Letters From Venus: Driven by Beauty |

| Year | Description | Story Reference |
|---|---|---|
| | Sergio and Fritz hooked up for the first time during a therapy session. | Mama's Boy |
| | Petra offered herself to Sergio, but her husband David interrupted them. | Mama's Boy |
| | Petra and David split up because of Petra's affairs, and because Fritz told Petra that she had slept with David before Petra and David started dating. | Letters From Venus: Who Cares About Love?/A Gift For Venus |
| | Petra hooked up with Carlos again in the back room of Shredder Records. | Letters From Venus: Who Cares About Love? |
| | Petra and David briefly got back together. | Letters From Venus: Who Cares About Love? |
| | When Carlos broke up with Petra, she trashed the store. | Letters From Venus: Who Cares About Love? |
| | Luba and Gorgo traveled to the U.S., but Khamo was prevented from entering the country due to a past drug-trafficking charge. | Luba in America: Chapter 1 |
| | Luba started an immigration, taxes and beepers business in L.A., primarily to help Khamo with his legal problems. | The Sisters, the Cousins, and the Kids ... |
| 1996-1997 | Fritz, Petra and Venus visited Palomar. | The Sister, the Cousins and the Kids ... |
| | Pipo and Igor started dating. | Fuckin' Steve! |
| | Gorgo was kidnapped while Luba met with Garza's daughter to ensure her family's safety. | Luba in America: Chapter 2 |
| | Fritz continued her affair with Jerome, even though his wife was her therapy patient. | As You Know It |
| | Luba had an affair with Fortunato while waiting for Khamo. | Luba in America: Chapter 3 |

| Year | Description | Story Reference |
| --- | --- | --- |
| | Khamo finally arrived in the U.S. after cutting a deal with the police to help catch his former drug connections. | Luba in America: Chapter 3 |
| | Petra became a born-again Christian. | Memories of Sweet Youth |
| | Doralis came out of the closet during her TV show. | El Show Super Duper Sensacional de Doralis |
| | Socorro got accepted into a special school after showing signs of a photographic memory. | Remember Me/Luba |
| | Luba began to suspect that Ofelia was writing a book about her. | Luba |
| | Boots Pina arrived in the U.S. to replace Gato as Pipo's accountant. | Spot Marks the Ex |
| | Socorro and Joselito stole a car to check up on Luba after her fight with Khamo, but they crashed it and had to sneak into the back of Jason's truck to get home. | Snail Trail |
| | Fritz met and hooked up with Hector Rivera several times. | Meeting Cute, Fucking Cuter |
| | Fritz set up Petra with Hector, but lied to her about their past sexual relationship. | Meeting Cute, Fucking Cuter |
| | David, Petra's ex-husband, remarried. | The Goddess and the Goof |
| | Hector went on his first date with Petra. | The Goddess and the Goof |
| | For their second date, Petra took Hector away for the weekend to a romantic beach resort. | The Goddess and the Goof |
| | Guadalupe began training as a bellydancer. | Boots Takes the Case |
| | Pipo confessed her love for Fritz, but Fritz rejected her. | Boots Takes the Case |

| Year | Description | Story Reference |
| --- | --- | --- |
| | L.A. tabloids trashed Pipo and her TV show after Gato fed them rumors that Pipo was bisexual. | The Tao of Doralis/Boots Takes the Case |
| | Pipo's TV show was officially canceled. Afterward, Doralis and Pipo had a falling-out. | The Tao of Doralis |
| | Pipo and Fritz spent a wild, sex-crazed week together in Paris. | In Bed With Pipo |
| | Sergio was suspended from soccer after colliding with a referee. | In Bed With Pipo |
| | Khamo helped some suspicious men posing as cops take down his former drug connections. | Luba |
| | Scotty recruited Steve to help him get back together with Fritz. | The Beloved and the Damned |
| | When Petra learned that Fritz gave Scotty $20,000, she bought a man's costume and beat him up. | The Beloved and the Damned |
| | Some strange men posing as cops molested Khamo. | Luba's Science Lesson |
| | La Valda, Hector's ex-fiancée, had a restraining order placed on him after a fight. Petra was so upset she beat her up. | And Justice For Some |
| | Doralis slept with Fortunato. | The Tao of Doralis |
| | After partying with Petra, Hector went to pick up Luba at a restaurant, but he was so stoned he lost the car. | Hector |
| | Luba and Ofelia got into a fight, but Khamo broke it up. | Luba Again |
| | Maricela reconnected with Ofelia. | But the Little Girls Understand |
| | Sergio begged Guadalupe to run away with him, but she refused. | Fritz and Pipo, Sittin' in a Tree |

| Year | Description | Story Reference |
| --- | --- | --- |
| | Fritz broke up with Sergio. | Fritz and Pipo, Sittin' in a Tree |
| | Pipo broke up with Igor. | Fritz and Pipo, Sittin' in a Tree |
| 1999 | Fritz went to her ten-year high school reunion and fell for Enrique Escobar. | High Soft Lisp |
| 2000 | Fritz decided to marry Enrique while also starting a relationship with Pipo. | Fritz and Pipo, Sittin' in a Tree |
| | After learning of their new relationship, Petra, in disguise, beat up Pipo. | Fritz and Pipo, Sittin' in a Tree |
| | Fritz called off her wedding to Enrique, but they stayed together. | Fritz After Dark |
| | Ofelia suffered a minor heart attack. | God Willing |
| | Doralis returned to Palomar and dedicated herself to helping starving children. | Luba |
| | Luba and Maricela were reunited. | Luba |
| | Guadalupe discovered that Gato wrote a book called Guadalupe and Sergio: A Love Story. | Luba |
| | Reunited with her old boyfriend, Rico, Ofelia finally left Luba to travel the world. | Luba |
| | Gato and Sergio kidnapped and brutally murdered Fortunato. | Luba |
| | Khamo left Luba and returned to Palomar with Doralis. | Luba |
| | Luba and her kids (Casimira, Joselito and Conchita) moved in with Maricela. | Luba |
| | Petra broke up with Hector after Fritz confessed about her previous sexual encounter with him. | Luba |

| Year | Description | Story Reference |
| --- | --- | --- |
| | Sergio and Gato died in a car crash. | Luba |
| | Venus and Yoshio produced a movie starring Petra, Fritz and Enrique as superheroes. | The Big Picture |
| | Guadalupe had a one-night stand with Hector and became pregnant (with Killer). | Down in Heaven |
| 2001 | *Killer (Dora Rivera) born. | Down in Heaven |
| | Doralis wrote a screenplay based on her grandmother's life (Maria M.) | Luba in America 2 |
| | Petra, Fritz and Luba stopped speaking to each other after Fritz accepted the starring role in Maria M. | Another Story Altogether |
| | After falling out with her sisters, Fritz became an alcoholic. | Another Story Altogether |
| 2007 | Hector married Sandra Bobo. | Down in Heaven |
| | At Pipo's urging, Guadalupe slept with Señor Yorgos. | Another Story Altogether |
| | Doralis died from a brain tumor. | Luba in America 2 |
| | Killer appeared in a movie with her aunt Fritz. | Killer * Sad Girl * Star |
| 2014 | Mark Herrera tried to revive his flagging career by searching for the legendary Sea Hog. | Song of the Sea Hog |
| | Venus wrote a script that was nominated, but lost, for Best Screenplay. | Baby Talk |
| | Mark Herrera and his sixth wife, Mila, visited his parents and siblings. | Where the Heart Is |
| | While shooting a movie, Fritz, Mila, Mark and Pipo were led to a fortress where Blas and Flaco forced Fritz to belly dance for Peter Rio. | On a Gut Level |

| Year | Description | Story Reference |
|---|---|---|
| | Fritz accused her father of molesting her as a child, but he denied it. | Blackouting |
| | Mark Herrera's brief comeback was quashed after he was invited to, and then kicked out of, the Elusive Exclusive Club. | God's Eye View |
| | Fritz was fired from a film sequel due to her heavy drinking. | God's Eye View |
| 2015 | Fritz and Mila co-starred in a couple of B movies. | Pattern for Living |
| | Fritz briefly remarried Scott, but he left her again and took most of her money. | Pattern for Living |
| | After her film career took off, Mila left Mark, who ended up penniless and alone, living on the streets. | Pattern for Living |
| 2016 | Fritz directed her first film, *Lie Down in the Dark*, a remake of an exploitation film her mother had starred in. | Venus and You |
| | Luba and Khamo got divorced. | Venus and You |
| | Fritz and Pipo got married. | Venus and You |
| 2018 | Killer performed in a low-budget movie, but never got paid for it. | Sad Girl |
| 2019 | Killer starred in the sequel to Fritz's *Scarlet By Starlight*. | Killer * Sad Girl * Star |
| | Killer witnessed two gay men murder a female cop. | Killer * Sad Girl * Star |
| | Killer remade several more of Fritz's B movies. | Killer * Sad Girl * Star/King Vampire |

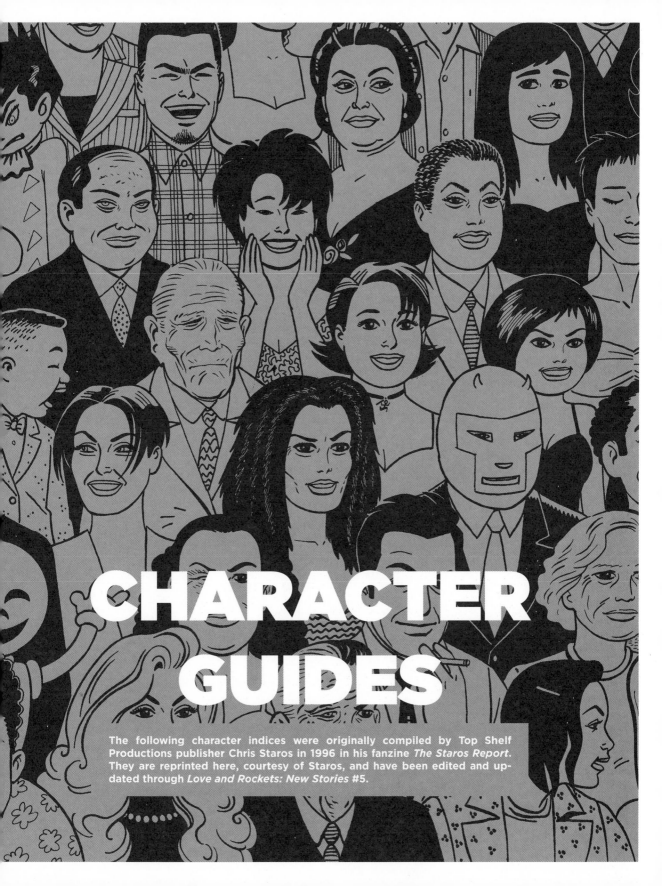

# CHARACTER GUIDES

The following character indices were originally compiled by Top Shelf Productions publisher Chris Staros in 1996 in his fanzine *The Staros Report*. They are reprinted here, courtesy of Staros, and have been edited and updated through *Love and Rockets: New Stories* #5.

| Name | Description | First Appearance |
|------|-------------|------------------|
| A.B. | A religious former co-worker of Hopey's who has two prosthetic arms. | Day By Day with Hopey: Wednesday |
| AL | Vivian, Tonta and Muñeca's stepfather. | Tonta |
| ALARMA KRAKTOVILOVA | One of Maggie's tenants at the Capri Apartments who moonlights as a superhero. In "Ti-Girls Adventures," she was a former member of the Fenomenons who quit to join the latest incarnation of the Ti-Girls. | Maggie: Part 4 |
| ALEJANDRA VARGAS | Nacho's current wife. They have two daughters: Sofia and Maribel. | Angelitas |
| ALVARO HERNANDEZ | Esther's husband, Maggie's brother-in-law. | Bob Richardson |
| ANGEL ALTERGOTT | A woman wrestler from Columbus, Ohio (named after fellow cartoonist Rick Altergott). | Whoa, Nellie! #2 |
| ANGEL CHASCARRILLO | Maggie's brother. | Bob Richardson |
| ANGEL ROSE RIVERA ("ANGEL OF TARZANA") | A high school girl who's into many different sports and briefly lives with Maggie. | Angel of Tarzana |
| ANGEL'S FATHER | Angel Rivera's father, owner of Rivera Construction. | Angels of Tarzana |
| ANTONIO (TONY) | Rena's son with Royal Don Rains who was raised by foster parents when he was a baby. As an adult, he's a masked luchador. | House of Raging Women (mentioned)/ Hester Square (first actual appearance) |

| Name | Description | First Appearance |
|------|-------------|------------------|
| ARACELI | One of Nan Tucker's personal attendants. | Wigwam Bam |
| ARLENE | The yard lady from Hopey's childhood who catches her sneaking out of school. | Day By Day with Hopey: Monday |
| ARTURO ("BIG 'TURO") | Detective hired by H.R. Costigan to find Penny Century. | Penny Century: On the Road Ag'in |
| ATENAS | A flight attendant who brought Maggie to Rena's private island. | La Maggie La Loca |
| ATOMA | Penny Century's fictional superhero identity. Later referred to as Atomica. | "Penny Century, You're Fired" |
| AZTLANA | The superhero identity of Angel Rivera's mother. Angel later took up her mantle and abandoned her Boot Angel persona. | Ti-Girls Adventures Number 34 Part Four: Mothers of Mercy |
| MR. BAKERS | Cheetah Torpeda's comedic sidekick and a former employee of Rongo Ragney. | Rocky's Birthday Surprise |
| BARB | Izzy's old college friend who looks like Maggie. | Wigwam Bam |
| DR. BEAKY | DECEASED. The tyrant owner of the island of Chepan. A vicious and eccentric competitor of H. R. Costigan. | Las Mujeres Perdidas |
| BEN RUBEN | A village wrestler in Zhato. | Mechanics |

| Name | Description | First Appearance |
|------|-------------|------------------|
| BENNY | A drummer in Hopey's band, the Damachers. | Wigwam Bam |
| BENNY THE BALL | A punk friend of Tony Chase's who spread a false rumor that he had slept with Maggie. | Everybody Loves Me, Baby |
| BENNY DOMINGUEZ | Ray's older brother. | Li'l Ray |
| BENSO | Chepan businessman, owner of the robot warehouse. | Las Mujeres Perdidas |
| BERNIE CARBO | Rena Titañon's ex-fiancé; pilot of the Saturn Stiletto. | Mechanics |
| BETO'S FATHER | Izzy's ex-boyfriend in Mexico. | Flies on the Ceiling |
| BETO | The young boy Izzy helped care for in Mexico. | Flies on the Ceiling |
| "BIG BOOBS" BLANCA RIZO | Maggie's rival/enemy since junior high school. She had a relationship with Speedy before he died. | Locas 8:01 am |
| BIRMINGHAM LADY BASHERS | "Beautiful" Bev Davis and "Darling" Doris Roberts. Former women's tag team champions in the '70s. | Whoa, Nellie! |
| BLACK BOMBER | The Weeper's partner in the fight in Plaster City. | Ti-Girls Adventures Number 34 Part One: The Search for Penny Century |

| Name | Description | First Appearance |
|---|---|---|
| BLANDINA DOMINGUEZ | Ray's sister. | The Return of Ray D. |
| BO BUNYAN | A wrestler friend who accompanied Maggie to the East Coast to look for Hopey. | In the Valley of the Polar Bears |
| BOLANI | Norma Costigan's eccentric, alcoholic boyfriend. | C'mon Mom! |
| BOMBER BONES | Detective hired by H.R. Costigan to find Penny Century after her adventures in Zhato. | Penny Century: On the Road Ag'in |
| BOOT ANGEL | The superhero identity of Angel Rivera, the newest member of the newest (third) incarnation of the Ti-Girls. | Ti-Girls Adventures Number 34 Part One: The Search for Penny Century |
| BORNEO | A black man who was part of the crew that murdered Sid Doan. | The Frogmouth |
| BOXHEAD NELSO | Friend of Doyle's. A local Hoppers punk who later worked with Julie Wree. | Ninety-Three Million Miles From the Sun |
| BOYD | A bartender at Little Luigi's Restaurant who was part of a gang that tried to kidnap Rena Titañon. | Hester Square |
| BUBBLES | Negra Costigan's school friend. | La Pantera Negra |
| BULL MARIE | An aging wrestler who retired after losing her last match with Rena. | Toyo's Request |

| | Name | Description | First Appearance |
|---|---|---|---|
| | BUTO | An overweight thug who helped try to kidnap Rena Titañon when she returned to the U.S. | Bob Richardson |
| | CALVIN CHASCARRILLO | Maggie's troubled younger brother. The victim of childhood sexual abuse, Calvin is mentally unstable as an adult. He has a daughter (Linda) whom he fathered at age 16, but has never met her. | The Love Bunglers: Part One |
| | CARLOS | Speedy's friend. | Locos |
| | CARLOS | 'Litos' son. | Below My Window Lurks My Head |
| | CARLOS | Captain of the cargo ship that rescued Rena and Maggie in Chepan. | Las Mujeres Perdidas |
| | CARLOS | One of Hopey's young students. She helps him on her first day as a teacher's assistant. | Day By Day with Hopey: Monday |
| | CASEY | Fugitive who was Maggie's captor, then lover, at Costigan's manor. | 100 Rooms |
| | "BIG" CASH WATKINS | Vicki's husband. A former wrestler. Cash and Vicki have an adopted Japanese son named Hiroshi. | Las Mujeres Perdidas |
| | CHABELA ORTIZ | Izzy's older sister. | Home School |
| | CHABELA'S HUSBAND | Izzy's brother-in-law. | Home School |

| | Name | Description | First Appearance |
|---|---|---|---|
| | CHATA | Tonta's friend. | Tonta |
| | CHEETAH TORPEDA | In "Ti-Girls Adventures" she was Dr. Kwan Ho Lee, an android superhero. | The He That Walks (in *Vortex #7*) |
| | CHEPA | Izzy's cousin. David and Laura's mother. | The Death of Speedy Ortiz |
| | CHIEF | Native who lives on property near Rena's mansion. | La Toña |
| | CHINESS | One of the twin slave girls of Dr. Beaky. The other is Machi. | Las Mujeres Perdidas |
| | CHINO | An old friend of Maggie's mother (Quina) who used to work with her in the packing houses in Huerta. | Browntown |
| | CHIQUITA | Rocky's daughter in the Locas stories. Chiquita is friends with Laura, David and Elias. | Wigwam Bam |
| | CHITO | One of the "braceros," a group of Mexican day laborers who hang out drinking at Chester Square most nights. | Chester Square |
| | CHIVITA | Blanca Rizo's friend / co-worker at El Gallo Restaurant. | The Death of Speedy Ortiz |
| | CHIVITA DOMINGUEZ | Ray's mother. | The Death of Speedy Ortiz |

| Name | Description | First Appearance |
|------|-------------|------------------|
| CHUCHO | Old, conservative Mexican man in the barrio who warns Maggie and Hopey to settle down and get married. | Locas |
| CHUY | Childhood friend of Ray Dominguez and Eddie Ortiz. | 6 Degrees of Ray D. Ation (in Maggie and Hopey Color Fun) |
| CLARITA | The daughter of Penny and Tex. | Below My Window Lurks My Head |
| CLAUDIA CASEY | A young, black wrestler in training at Vicki's camp who became the Texas Women's Champion. | Camp Vicki |
| CLEO | A stripper at Bumper's. | Wigwam Bam |
| CLON | A thug that tried to kidnap Rena Titañon. | Bob Richardson |
| CONNIE | Hopey's stepmother. | Wigwam Bam |
| CORNELIUS EDWARDS | DECEASED. Elias' father; Danita's ex-boyfriend. A dangerous criminal who was killed in jail. | Below My Window Lurks My Head |
| CORREO | The Garcia brothers' cousin who briefly flirted with Maggie. | Locas at the Beach |
| CRAIG | A local Hoppers kid who takes sadistic pleasure in the destruction of Izzy's house. He drugs Maggie. | Maggie: Part 10 |

| Name | Description | First Appearance |
|---|---|---|
| CREAKY | A stripper at Bumper's in the early '80s. | Return of the Butt Sisters |
| CRUSHER GAINES | Drunken wrestler who tried to kill India Chala in New Keops before Rena stopped him. | Little Monster |
| CRYSTAL | Hopey's friend on the East Coast; a young woman hired by Nan Tucker to dress like a schoolgirl. | Wigwam Bam |
| CRYSTAL | Muñeca's best friend. | Tonta |
| CUCA | A former high school classmate of Vivian's who fights her and gets arrested. | Maggie: Part 2 |
| "DAFFY" (DAPHNE MATSUMOTO) | Maggie and Hopey's friend. Noel and Nami's sister. A young Japanese punk who went to college. | Mechanics |
| MAYOR DALGANG | Sleazy politician who hires Stacy and Lily for a private strip show. | Spring 1982 |
| DANITA LINCOLN | Maggie's black co-worker at Vandy's who became a close friend. Elias's mother. Rocky's friend (of the Rocky and Fumble stories). She dated Ray Dominguez for a while and then moved with Elias to Texas, where she married El Diablo Blanco. | Locas 8:01 am |
| DANITA'S MOTHER | Elias' grandmother. | Wigwam Bam |
| DARLEEN YBAÑEZ | Larry's wife. | Lar' Dog: Boys Night Out #1398 |

| | Name | Description | First Appearance |
|---|---|---|---|
| | DAVID | Chepa's young son. Laura's brother. Elias' friend. | Wigwam Bam |
| | DEL CHIMNEY | DECEASED. A Hoppers punk who dealt drugs and owned a popular flophouse. His real name was Porfirio Diaz Rubinski. | 100 Rooms (mentioned) |
| | DELFINO | A local boy who brought Maggie to Rena's private island by boat. | La Maggie, La Loca |
| | DEMOÑA | Former sidekick to Ultimax, later H.R. Costigan's personal bodyguard. | Maggie vs. Maniakk |
| | DICK BAIN | Ladies' wrestling commissioner. | House of Raging Women |
| | DINO AND DICK | Wrestling announcers whom Rena attacked in a blind rage. | House of Raging Women |
| | DIX | H.R. Costigan's limo driver. | Bay of Threes |
| | DOLORES MANTEGAS | Penny's high school friend and old roommate. | Locas 8:01 am |
| | DOT WINKS | A celebrity columnist who had a crush on Rand Race. | Las Mujeres Perdidas |
| | DOYLE BLACKBURN | Ray's best friend. Stacy's and Lily Rivera's ex-boyfriend. He previously served two years in jail. He became homosexual after leaving Hoppers, briefly lived and worked with Sid Doan in Phoenix, and moved back to L.A. He is also a cancer survivor. | Locas vs. Locos |

| | Name | Description | First Appearance |
|---|---|---|---|
| | DUDU | One of Nan Tucker's personal attendants. | Wigwam Bam |
| | "DUKE" (MANUEL MORALES) | The boss of Maggie's prosolar Mechanics crew. Rena's friend. | Mechan-X |
| | "DYNAMITE" PAM JONES | A woman wrestler from San Diego, Calif. | Whoa, Nellie! #1 |
| | EDDIE BRAVO | Nami's ex-boyfriend who confronts Doyle and gets beat up in the process. | Wigwam Bam |
| | BIG EDDIE ORTIZ | Izzy's older brother, Ray's childhood friend. | The Death of Speedy Ortiz |
| | EL CID | Doorman/bouncer on the punk scene. | The Night Ape Sex Came Home to Play |
| | EL DIABLO BLANCO | Rena's little brother. Danita's husband. A masked wrestler in Texas. | Return of the Butt Sisters |
| | ELIAS LINCOLN | Danita's young son. His father, Cornelius, was stabbed and killed in prison. | The Return of Ray D. |
| | ELMER SELMA | DECEASED. Sid Doan's main homeboy. After making a scene at Sid's wake, he was killed by a corrupt policeman after resisting arrest for Sid's murder. | Trampas Pero No Trampan |
| | ELVA | Owner and manager of the Chester Square Motel and Laundromat. | Chester Square |

| | Name | Description | First Appearance |
|---|---|---|---|
| | EME | One of the "braceros," a group of Mexican day laborers who hang out drinking at Chester Square most nights. | Chester Square |
| | ENERO GARCIA | Maggie's friend. One of the Garcia brothers. He lived in a Texas apartment building near Maggie and tried unsuccessfully to date her. One of the "braceros." | Locas at the Beach |
| | ERIC AND DANTE | School friends of Rocky and Fumble who discovered the dimensional space portal. | Rocket Rhodes |
| | ERIC LOPEZ | Singer for a punk band and Frank Lopez's brother. | Tonta |
| | ERNESTO | A janitor/handyman at the Capri Apartments. | Maggie: Part 8 |
| | ESPECTRA | The superhero identity of Xochitl Nava. She was working as a maid for Space Queen before coming out of retirement to lead the newest (third) incarnation of the Ti-Girls. She was also a member of the All New Ti-Girls and was known as Fuerza. | Ti-Girls Adventures Number 34 Part One: The Search for Penny Century |
| | ESPECTRA NEGRA | The evil half of Fuerza (Xo) that was split off and sent into the past by Dr. Blitz's time portal. | Ti-Girls Adventures Number 34 Part Two: Penny is Found |
| | ESTHER HERNANDEZ | Maggie's sister (formerly Esther Chascarrillo). The daughter of Nacho and Quina Chascarrillo. Raised by Quina in Montoya (Dairytown) with her brothers (but not Maggie). Dated Speedy and Rojo for a short time, sparking a gang war. As an adult, she married Alvaro Hernandez and has twin daughters, Yolanda and Lupe (Maggie's nieces and goddaughters). | The Return of Ray D. |
| | EVA BANCHINI | H.R. Costigan's former secretary. | Penny Century: On the Road Ag'in |
| | FEBRERO GARCIA | Brother of Enero and Miercoles. | Locas at the Beach |

| Name | Description | First Appearance |
|---|---|---|
| THE FENOMENONS | The third female superhero group formed by Doctor Zolar, featuring: Alarma (a former member who quit and joined the third version of the Ti-Girls); Sun Swan (briefly married to and later divorced Doctor Zolar); plus two others (unnamed). | Ti-Girls Adventures Number 34 Part One: The Search for Penny Century |
| FINA | Maggie's aunt. Jake's wife. Xochitl's mother. | Angelitas |
| FLACO | Chepan rebel, friend of Rena's. | Las Mujeres Perdidas |
| FRANCIS | Maya's and Mary's friend. | Wigwam Bam |
| FRANCO | Newspaper editor, Dot Winks' boss. | Las Mujeres Perdidas |
| FRANK LOPEZ | Tonta's on-and-off-again boyfriend and Eric Lopez's brother. | Tonta |
| FUMBLE | Rocky's robot sidekick and best friend. | Out O' Space |
| MRS. GABRIE | Long-time elderly neighbor of the Chascarrillo family in Montoya. | Maggie: Part 9 |
| MRS. GALINDO | DECEASED. Sal's widow (of Sal's Garage), an old crippled alcoholic who left her haunted house in Hoppers to Izzy. | Locas vs. Locos |
| MRS. GARCIA | Penny's elderly mother who lives in West Texas, near Chester Square. | It's Not That Big a Deal |

| Name | Description | First Appearance |
|---|---|---|
| GENERAL MATAPOLAS | Dr. Beaky's army chief in Rio Frio. | Las Mujeres Perdidas |
| GIGGLES GALORE | Maggie's acquaintance. | Maggie vs. Maniakk |
| GINA BRAVO | Xochitl's friend and tag-team partner. A lesbian wrestler in Texas. | Camp Vicki |
| MRS. GLASS | Hopey's estranged mother. Born in Colombia in 1944. | Locas Starring Hopey |
| MR. RICHARD GLASS | Hopey's estranged father. He is of Scottish descent. | Locas vs. Locos |
| GOLDEN GIRL | The superhero identity of Mini Rivero. | Ti-Girls Adventures Number 34 Part One: The Search for Penny Century |
| GOLDMAN | Rand Race's lawyer wife. | Maggie the Mechanic or Perla the Prostitute |
| GORRO | One of the Hoppers Locos; friends with 'Litos and Speedy. | The Death of Speedy Ortiz |
| GRACE | Hopey's friend. A lesbian with whom she casually hooks up occasionally. | Day By Day with Hopey: Tuesday |
| GRETCHEN | Tonta's friend and tutor. | Tonta |

| Name | Description | First Appearance |
|---|---|---|
| GUY GOFORTH | Hopey's former co-worker who asked her out on a date. | Loser Leave Oxnard/Election Day |
| HELEN | The lunch lady at Maggie's school. Reno painted a portrait of her, hairnet and all. | The Love Bunglers: Part One |
| HARVEY | Maggie's co-worker at Sal's Garage. | Young Locas |
| HENRY | A punk friend of Maggie and Hopey. He had a crush on Hopey. | A Date With Hopey |
| HENRY | A musician in the punk band Catechism 13 who taught Terry how to play guitar. | Locas 8:01 am |
| HERV ROVICK (H.R.) COSTIGAN | DECEASED. A horned, eccentric billionaire, though he died penniless and alone. Penny Century's husband. Negra's father (with his ex-wife Norma). | "Penny Century, You're Fired" |
| HIROSHI | The adopted Japanese son of Vicki Glori and Cash Watkins. | Angelitas |
| THE HOGG SISTERS | The tag team that dethroned Vicki and Rena. Vicki refused to wrestle and after that match, she and Rena became bitter rivals. | Mechanics |
| HONEST JOE | An old man who hangs out every night at Elmo's, the bar where Hopey works. | Day By Day with Hopey: Thursday |
| "HOPEY" (ESPERANZA LETICIA GLASS) | Maggie's best friend and occasional lover. Joey's sister. Lesbian punk of Scottish-Colombian descent. Plays bass guitar poorly in several bands (La Llorona, Missiles of October, Soul Train Line, Tivoli Nights, The Ronkies, the Damachers, etc.). A part-time bartender at Elmo's, she later became a teacher's assistant at an elementary school. | Mechan-X |

| Name | Description | First Appearance |
|---|---|---|
| INDIA CHALA | DECEASED. "The Little Monster." A dwarf wrestler and friend of Rena's. | The Little Monster |
| ISH | A mobster who works for Mel Spropp. He keeps the peace at Sid Doan's wake. | Male Torso Found in the L.A. River |
| ITSUKI YETO | Daffy's gossipy friend and former punk. | Locas vs. Locos |
| ITZY AND BITZY KAZINAFEK | Texas women's tag-team partners (named after R. Crumb's underground characters). | Whoa, Nellie! |
| IVAT | Maya's friend. Merced's friend and partner. A pretentious "art fag" who offends Maggie with a racist comment about Mexicans. | Wigwam Bam |
| "IZZY" (ISABEL MARIA ORTIZ RUEBENS) | Maggie's childhood friend and baby-sitter. Speedy's older sister. She was the one who introduced Maggie to Hopey (after Letty died). She married and divorced her English professor, Jack Ruebens, had an abortion, and fled to Mexico. She also attempted suicide and spent time in an asylum. | "How to Kill A" By Isabel Ruebens |
| JACK RUEBENS | Izzy's ex-husband. An English professor. | Locos |
| JAKE | Maggie's Uncle. Fina's husband. Xochitl's father. | Angelitas |
| JANET POLO | Hopey's sister-in-law. Joey Glass' wife. | Wigwam Bam |
| JENNY | One of the young women who acted in Nan Tucker's private schoolgirl fetish. Mrs. Watkins attacked her for being "insolent." | Wigwam Bam |

| | Name | Description | First Appearance |
|---|---|---|---|
| | JEWEL TUCKER | Nan Tucker's daughter. Hopey lived with her on the East Coast for a while. | Wigwam Bam |
| | JOCKO | Bernie Carbo's prison cellmate. | Toyo's Request |
| | JOE | Ferryboat driver between Rio Frio and Chepan. Chepan rebel. | Las Mujeres Perdidas |
| | JOE | Ray's co-worker and friend in L.A. | One More Ladies' Man |
| | JOE VAN NUYS | Rena's friend on the wrestling circuit who brought her the news of India Chala's passing. | Little Monster |
| | JOEY GLASS | Hopey's younger brother. Janet's husband. | Locas Tambien |
| | JOHN RHODES | Rocky's father. | Retro Rocky |
| | JOJO | A thug who helped try to kidnap Rena Titañon when she returned to the U.S. | Bob Richardson |
| | JOY | Hopey's former co-worker. | Day By Day with Hopey: Wednesday |
| | JUANA ORTIZ | Izzy, Chabela, Eddie and Speedy's mother. | Locos |

| Name | Description | First Appearance |
|---|---|---|
| JULIE WREE | Hopey's former best friend. A rich West End girl who is now bitter enemies with Maggie and Hopey. She also hosts and produces a public access TV show. | Locas |
| JUMBO NISHIMORI | A woman wrestler from Osaka, Japan. | Whoa, Nellie! #3 |
| JUNIOR NAVA | The son of Xochitl and Mario. The brother of Oscar and Mariposa. | The Navas of Hazel Court |
| KALAMITY JANE BURKESKOVA | A Russian cowboy supervillain; Alarma's former partner. | Ti-Girls Adventures Number 34 Part Three: Daughters of Doom |
| KARLA VON HESS | A woman wrestler from Stuttgart, West Germany. | Whoa, Nellie! |
| KATIE | Friend of Craig's. A local Hoppers kid who takes sadistic pleasure in the destruction of Izzy's house. | Maggie: Part 10 |
| KATY HAWK | The wrestler who beat Xo to win the Texas Women's Championship belt. | Whoa, Nellie! |
| KEBRA | Sid Doan's ex-fiancée. A friend of Julie Wree's. She attacked Vivian in a bar after learning of Sid's affair, injuring Hopey's eye in the process. | Maggie: Part 1 |
| KIKO KURIHARA | Daffy's friend. | Locas vs. Locos |
| KITTY KATZ | Two-time Texas Women's Wrestling champion. | Whoa, Nellie! |

| | Name | Description | First Appearance |
|---|---|---|---|
| | LA VIBORA | Masked wrestler who fought and lost to Vicki. | House of Raging Women |
| | LALO | A young neighborhood boy who hangs out with David, Laura and Elias. | Wigwam Bam |
| | LARRY DEARE | A character with a speaking part in "Wigwam Bam" that had no name. Rick Altergott liked this character, so he and Jaime gave him a name as a joke. | Wigwam Bam |
| | LARRY YBAÑEZ | High school friend of Ray and Doyle's; a drunken deadbeat of a father. | Lar' Dog: Boys Night Out #1398 |
| | LAURA | Chepa's young daughter. David's sister. Elias' friend. | Wigwam Bam |
| | LEE | Mary's boyfriend. A painter. | Wigwam Bam |
| | LELAND | Lee's brother. A pretentious writer who lives on the East Coast. | Wigwam Bam |
| | LENCHO AND ROSALBA LOPEZ | Hopey's neighbors in Hoppers. Maggie repaired their fruit truck in "Locas at the Beach." They tragically lost their baby. | Barrio Huerta |
| | LESTER | A guitarist who was briefly in a band with Hopey and Tex on the East Coast. | Wigwam Bam |
| | LETTY CHAVEZ | DECEASED. Maggie's childhood best friend. She died in a car accident. | Young Locas |

| Name | Description | First Appearance |
|---|---|---|
| LICHA RODRIGUEZ | Maggie's cousin. Leader of the Widows, a female gang in Hoppers. | Locas Starring Hopey |
| LILY RIVERA | A stripper. Doyle's ex-girlfriend. Stacy's former roommate. | A Mess of Skin |
| LINDA | Maggie's niece and realtor. Calvin's estranged daughter. | The Love Bunglers: Part Three |
| 'LITOS CARRANZA | Ray and Speedy's friend. A gangster with sunglasses who mellowed out after losing an eye to a bullet. Carlos' father. | Locas Tambien |
| LOIS | A ferocious bisexual punk whose infamous line was "who wants to fuck?" | Wigwam Bam |
| LORETTA COX | A woman who wrestles in Texas. | Whoa, Nellie! |
| LOUIE | The cousin of Ray's co-worker, Joe. | Life Through Whispers |
| LOUIS | Margarita's co-worker at Sal's Garage, who gave her the nickname "Maggie." | Young Locas |
| LOUIS | Ray's childhood friend. | The Death of Speedy Ortiz |
| LU | A stripper at Bumper's. | Wigwam Bam |

| Name | Description | First Appearance |
|------|-------------|------------------|
| LULA | Rosie's (Hopey's ex-girlfriend) sister. | Day By Day with Hopey: Sunday |
| LUPE | Maggie's niece and goddaughter. Yolanda's twin sister. Daughter of Esther and Alvaro Hernandez. | Maggie: Part 9 |
| LUPE | Quina's friend in Cadezza. | Browntown |
| MRS. LUNBY | One of the tenants at the Capri Apartments. | Maggie: Part 6 |
| LUTHOR | Vagabond who met Maggie and Rena in the sewer tunnels in Chepan. | Las Mujeres Perdidas |
| LUIGI | The owner of the restaurant in Texas where Rena was attacked. | Hester Square |
| LUZ | A waitress Maggie and Penny worked with for a couple hours in Texas. | Maggie the Mechanic or Perla the Prostitute |
| MACHI | One of the twin slave girls of Dr. Beaky. The other is Chiness. | Las Mujeres Perdidas |
| MAD DOCTOR BLITZ | One of Pravda's arch foes; he was responsible for splitting Fuerza (Xo) into Espectra and Espectra Negra, using his time portal. | Ti-Girls Adventures Number 34 Part Two: Penny is Found |
| MAD MALA | Wrestler from Marzipan whom Rena defeated in a title match. | Little Monster |

| | Name | Description | First Appearance |
|---|---|---|---|
| | MAD PATRICK | A rock alien who battled Rocky and Fumble over an asteroid they both claimed. | Out O' Space |
| | MADISON | Co-host on Julie Wree's public access TV show. | Maggie: Part 1 |
| | "MAGGIE" (MARGARITA LUISA CHASCARRILLO) | The daughter of Nacho and Quina Chascarrillo. The sister of Esther, Calvin, Manuel, Angel and Ruben. Hopey's best friend and occasional lover. A bisexual and mechanically inclined woman. In the early "mechanic" stories, Maggie was the co-worker of Rand, Yax and Duke. Aunt Vicki raised Maggie in "Hoppers" (separated from her brothers, sister and mother). She was Ray's girlfriend for a while and was recently reunited with him. She sometimes goes by the nicknames Perla or Perlita. | Mechan-X |
| | MAITE | Penny Century's third daughter. A superhero. | Ti-Girls Adventures Number 34 Part One: The Search for Penny Century |
| | MANDO | Ray's childhood friend. | The Death of Speedy Ortiz |
| | MANIAKK | Supervillain. | Maggie vs. Maniakk |
| | MANUEL CHASCARRILLO | Maggie's brother. | Bob Richardson |
| | MAPY | El Diablo Blanco's personal secretary. | Bob Richardson |
| | MARIA BRAVO | The wrestler that Rena Titañon beat to win the title. | Mechanics |
| | MARIBEL | Maggie's half-sister. The daughter of Nacho and Alejandra. Sofia's sister. | Angelitas |

| Name | Description | First Appearance |
|---|---|---|
| MARIO NAVA | Xochitl's husband. They have three children: Mariposa, Oscar and Junior. | The Navas of Hazel Court |
| MARIPOSA NAVA | The daughter of Xochitl and Mario. The sister of Oscar and Junior. | The Navas of Hazel Court |
| MARY CHRISTMAS | An old friend of Maggie and Hopey. Lee's ex-girlfriend. Hopey and Maggie stayed with her briefly while on the East Coast. She co-hosts a public access TV show with Julie Wree. | Las Monjas Asesinas |
| MATILDA | Maya's ex-lover and roommate. Maya kicked her out so that Hopey could move in. | Wigwam Bam |
| MAYA | Ray's college ex-girlfriend who also had a brief affair with Hopey. Hopey lived with her for a while on the East Coast. | Ninety Three Million Miles From the Sun |
| MR. MAYNEZ | Angel's great-uncle. One of Maggie's upstairs tenants at the Capri Apartments. | Maggie: Part 3 |
| THE MECHANIC | Masked luchador named Ralph. | House of Raging Women |
| MEL SPROPP | A mobster associated with Sid Doan's family. | Male Torso Found in the LA River |
| MRS. MEL SPROPP | Mel Spropp's wife. | Crime Raiders International Mobsters and Executioners |
| MELBA RHODES | Rocky's mother. | Retro Rocky |

| | Name | Description | First Appearance |
|---|---|---|---|
| | MELINDA | Manager and bartender at Bumper's strip club. | Wigwam Bam |
| | MERCED | Ivat's friend and partner. A pretentious "art fag" who offends Maggie with a racist comment about Mexicans. | Wigwam Bam |
| | MIERCOLES GARCIA | Brother of Enero and Febrero. | Locas at the Beach |
| | MIKE | The singer for Blamed Youth whom Daffy had a crush on. | In the Valley of the Polar Bears |
| | MIKE TRAN | Known to his friends as "Mike the Viet Cong." School friend of Ray and Doyle and fellow punk. | The Secrets of Life and Death Vol. 5 |
| | MIKE VARAN | An old friend of Ray's. Vivian's ex-boyfriend. A Hollywood memorabilia dealer. | Near Mint |
| | MIKEY VARAN | Mike's son. A high school friend of Angel Rivera's. | The Love Bunglers: Part Three |
| | MILENA LOZNIKA | Vivian's Serbian friend and an actress on the variety show *Nopales, Nopales.* | Trampas Pero No Trampan |
| | MRS. MINDER | The legal gatekeeper of Rena's son (Antonio) when he was a boy. | House of Raging Women |
| | MINI RIVERO | A pint-sized (4' 2") celebrity and the star of the variety show *Cocktail Hour* from 1953 to 1964. In "Ti-Girls Adventures" she was the superhero Golden Girl. | Cocktail Hour with Mini Rivero (in Maggie and Hopey Color Fun) |

| Name | Description | First Appearance |
|---|---|---|
| MODESTA | Angel Rivera's little sister. | Ti-Girls Adventures Number 34 Part Three: Daughters of Doom |
| MONICA MIRANDA ZANDINSKI | The ex-singer of Hopey's band (La Llorona). She had a sex change and is now a man named Marco. In the early '80s, she was a stripper at Bumper's. | Las Mujeres Perdidas |
| MOON | Leader of an incompetent gang of thugs who tried to kidnap Rena Titañon. | Bob Richardson |
| MORA | Brusque backstage manager for the Texas Women's Wrestling League who works with El Diablo Blanco. | Hester Square |
| MUÑECA | Vivian and Tonta's younger half-sister. | Tonta |
| "THE MUGS" | Two of Nan Tucker's hired thugs who beat up Hopey and Tex. | Wigwam Bam |
| MYRT | A volunteer pollster whom Hopey works with. | Election Day |
| NACHO CHASCARRILLO | Maggie's father. He divorced Quina (Maggie's mother) and now lives in Texas with his new wife, Alejandra, and their two daughters, Sofia and Maribel (Maggie's half-sisters). | Wigwam Bam |
| NAMI MATSUMOTO | The sister of Daffy and Noel. She liked Doyle for a while and also dated Eddie Bravo. | Locas vs. Locos |
| NAN TUCKER | Jewel's mother. A former TV sitcom comedienne with a fetish for young grown women dressed as little girls. | Wigwam Bam |

| | Name | Description | First Appearance |
|---|---|---|---|
| | NEEDRA | Rocky's niece, Rhoda's daughter. | Rocky's Birthday Surprise |
| | NEGRA COSTIGAN | Her full name is Luz Negra Costigan. H.R. Costigan's only child and heir, though she never knew her father. Norma's daughter. | Maggie and Hopey Color Fun |
| | NOEL MATSUMOTO | The sister of Nami and Daffy. | Locas vs. Locos |
| | NORMA LUNA | H.R. Costigan's fourth ex-wife. | Penny Century: On the Road Ag'in |
| | OJOS | A young neighborhood boy who hangs out with David, Laura and Elias. | Wigwam Bam |
| | OSCAR NAVA | The son of Xochitl and Mario. The brother of Mariposa and Junior. | The Navas of Hazel Court |
| | PAT | A female bartender who hosted a large hipster party that Hopey and Maggie attended on the East Coast. | Wigwam Bam |
| | PATSY | Nami's friend. | Wigwam Bam |
| | MR. AND MRS. GAYLORD PATTY | The couple attacked by Norma Luna when she kidnapped her daughter. | Election Day |
| | PEACHES | Negra Costigan's school friend. | La Pantera Negra |

| Name | Description | First Appearance |
|---|---|---|
| PEDERO RODRIGUEZ SAN JO | Zymbodian dictator Sancho Conrado San Jo's lecherous son. | Mechanics |
| PENNY CENTURY (BEATRÍZ GARCIA) | H.R. "Herv" Costigan's widow. She previously dated Rand Race and aborted his child. She has a daughter, Clarita (whose father is Tex), and another child (whose father is her ex-bodyguard, Pete). Penny grew up around Chester Square in Texas and her mother still lives there. | Mechan-X |
| PEPPER MARTINEZ | Puerto Rican wrestler who became Rena's new partner during her comeback. Their tag team was called The Dark Angels. | House of Raging Women |
| PETE | Penny's ex-bodyguard. The father of Penny's second child, though he already had a wife and kids. A weightlifter. | Wigwam Bam |
| "PAPA" POCHENCHO | Maggie's grandfather. The father of Vicki and Nacho Chascarrillo. | Camp Vicki |
| PRAVDA THE RED TRUTH | Alarma's mother, a retired Russian superhero. | Ti-Girls Adventures Number 34 Part Two: Penny is Found |
| QUINA CHASCARRILLO | Maggie's mother. Divorced Nacho (Maggie's father) after he had an affair with Alejanda. Lives in Montoya with her sons. | The Return of Ray D. |
| RALPH | A thug who helped try to kidnap Rena Titañon when she returned to the U.S. | Bob Richardson |
| RAND RACE | A prosolar mechanic and co-worker of Maggie, Yax and Duke in the early days. He previously dated Penny and got her pregnant (but the child was aborted). Maggie, at one time, had a crush on him. Rand is now married to his lawyer, Goldman. | Mechan-X |
| RAY DOMINGUEZ | Maggie's partner. Doyle's best friend. The brother of Benny, Blandina and three other unnamed brothers. He grew up with 'Litos' gang and went away to college, but spent most of his time painting and partying. He came back to Hoppers and dated Maggie, Danita, Penny and Vivian. | The Return of Ray D. |

| Name | Description | First Appearance |
|---|---|---|
| RAYMOND GARCIA | The garbage man who gave Fumble the Radaron robot to Rocky. | Retro Rocky |
| RENA TITAÑON | Also known as "La Toña," or "Queen Rena." A famous wrestling champion and revolutionary. She won the title from Maria Bravo at age 22 and was tag-team partners with Vicki Glori before they split and became bitter rivals. Bernie Carbo was her past lover. El Diablo Blanco is her brother. Antonio (Tony) is her only son. | Mechanics |
| RENO BANKS | Friend of Maggie and Hopey from the Hoppers punk scene. An amateur painter. | Las Mujeres Perdidas |
| RHODA | Rocky's older sister who lives in a city, Needra's mother. | Rocky's Birthday Surprise |
| RICH | Usually called by his nickname, "Fifi." A guitarist in Hopey's short-lived East Coast band. | Wigwam Bam |
| RICK SOLE | Wrestling announcer in Texas. | Whoa, Nellie! |
| ROBBIE GARCIA | One of the 15-year-old boys who mistakenly beat up Ray. | Wigwam Bam |
| ROBERT | A childhood friend of Speedy's in Hoppers. | Return For Me |
| ROCKY | Rocket Rhodes. Fumble's best friend. A teenage adventuress who mostly appeared in early stories outside the "Locas" continuity, but later briefly appeared as Danita's cousin. | Out O' Space (with Fumble)/ Wigwam Bam |
| ROJO | Esther's ex-boyfriend; leader of the Dairytown gang. | The Death of Speedy Ortiz |

| Name | Description | First Appearance |
|---|---|---|
| RONGO RAGNEY | The villainous "man who hates robots." He kidnapped Fumble on the planet Blotos. | Rocky's Birthday Surprise |
| RONNIE | Maggie's co-worker at Vandy's who also worked at Sal's Garage. | Locas 8:01 am |
| ROSA | A brusque East Coast lesbian who had the hots for Maggie. | Wigwam Bam |
| ROSA RICO | Pepper Martinez's mother. A former wrestler known as "La Pantera Negra," one of Rena's early rivals. | House of Raging Women |
| ROSE RAMELLI | Woman who was robbed and beaten up by Sharkey Horwitz. | Queen Rena: Life at 34 |
| ROSENDO | One of the "braceros," a group of Mexican day laborers who hang out drinking at Chester Square most nights. | Chester Square |
| ROSENDO | One of the assistant mechanics at Maggie's Garage. | The Love Bunglers Part Five |
| ROSIE | Hopey's former co-worker, ex-girlfriend and ex-roommate. | Election Day |
| ROY COWBOY | Recurring cartoon character in the Locas universe. | La Chota |
| ROYAL DON RAINS | Rena's ex-boyfriend and the father of Antonio. A former wrestler. | House of Raging Women |

| | Name | Description | First Appearance |
|---|---|---|---|
| | RUBEN CHASCARRILLO | Maggie's brother. | Bob Richardson |
| | RUBY | The prostitute who beat up Maggie and stabbed Gina at Chester Square. | Chester Square |
| | RUDY | Hopey's former co-worker. | Day By Day with Hopey: Wednesday |
| | SGT. SADO | Officer who busted Hopey for spray-painting graffiti. | Locas Starring Hopey |
| | SANCHO CONRADO SAN JO | DECEASED. Billionaire drug lord who controlled the corrupt Zymbodian government. | Mechanics |
| | SANDRA | Duke's wife. | House of Raging Women |
| | SANTIAGO | A neighbor who lived downstairs from Maggie and Esther in their Texas apartment building. | Angelitas Dos |
| | SARA | Blanca Rizo's co-worker at El Gallo Restaurant. | The Death of Speedy Ortiz |
| | SARA | Owner and manager of a restaurant and newsstand at Chester Square. | Chester Square |
| | MRS. SASANCHI | One of Maggie's tenants at the Capri Apartments. | The Love Bunglers Part One |

| | Name | Description | First Appearance |
|---|---|---|---|
| | SCHWARTZ | H.R. Costigan's advisor. | 100 Rooms |
| | SHIRLEY | The teacher who Hopey assists at the Palmetto Elementary School. | Day By Day with Hopey: Saturday |
| | SID "THE KNIFE" DOAN | DECEASED. Doyle's former friend, lover, roommate and business partner who was murdered. He was engaged to Kebra but having an affair with Vivian (the Frogmouth). He was the co-producer of Julie Wree's public access TV show in its early days, before becoming "a wannabe mobster." | Maggie: Part 2 |
| | SIGI | Singer for the band Hopey Monsters, a group of young girls who idolized Hopey and, as a joke, got her picture put on milk cartons (as a missing person) to promote their album. | Gonna Make You My Man ... |
| | SISTER SIN | A masked woman wrestler in Texas. | Whoa, Nellie! |
| | SOFIA | Maggie's half-sister. The daughter of Nacho and Alejandra. Maribel's sister. | Angelitas |
| | SHARKEY HORWITZ | Zymbodian thug. | Toyo's Request |
| | DETECTIVE SLOBINSKI | A corrupt police detective who arrested Elmer Selma for the murder of Sid Doan. | Male Torso Found in the L.A. River |
| | SNOW PATTERSON | A woman wrestler. | Whoa, Nellie! |
| | SPACE QUEEN | Also known as Space Girl. A stuck-up former superhero who works solo. | I Am Cheetah Torpeda |

| | Name | Description | First Appearance |
|---|---|---|---|
| | SPARKY | A friend of Ricky's; a guy Negra was interested in. | La Pantera Negra |
| | "SPEEDY" ORTIZ (EULALIO ORTIZ) | DECEASED. Izzy's younger brother. 'Litos' friend. He loved Maggie, dated Esther for a short time and then killed himself. | Locas Tambien |
| ? | SPOOKY THE SMOKEY | Weird guy who lives alone in a haunted house on Cooper Road in Hoppers. | Locas Tambien |
| | STACY | Doyle's ex-girlfriend. Lily's former roommate. A stripper. | Spring 1982 |
| | STEVIE TV | Terry's mentor. | Tear It Up, Terry Downe |
| ? | STRASKA THE RUSSIAN WIND | The wrestler who finally dethroned Vicki Glori and became champion. | Locas 8:01 am |
| | SUGAR BEAR | Friend of Reno's. | Crime Raiders International Mobsters and Executioners |
| | THE SUGAR TWINS | Sunny and Summer Danisch. The duo that Rena and Pepper Martinez battled for the ladies' tag-team championship during Rena's comeback. | House of Raging Women |
| | LOS SUPERSONICOS | A comical superhero family who appeared in a few short children's strips. | Measles #3 |
| | TALL TRACKER | Interplanetary villain who attacked Maggie but was subdued by Rand Race. | Mechan-X |

| | Name | Description | First Appearance |
|---|---|---|---|
| | TECHO | Delfino's friend who saved Maggie's life, then attacked her and stole her passport during her visit to Rena's estate. | La Maggie, La Loca |
| | "TERRY" (THERESA LEEANN DOWNE) | Hopey's ex-girlfriend. The guitar player in La Llorona (Hopey's band) and later 40 Thieves. She went solo for a while, then joined the band Bootcut Jean. | Mechanics |
| | "TEX" (ANTONIO MCTEAR) | Hopey's friend. A heavy black drummer with glasses. He got both Hopey and Penny pregnant. Penny gave birth to his daughter, Clarita, while Hopey miscarried. | Jerry Slum and the Crickettes |
| | TEXAS TONI BELLE | A woman wrestler. | Whoa, Nellie! |
| | THEODORE "TEDDY" JUNIOR | President and owner of Lips, Inc., the stripper service that Doyle briefly worked for. | Spring 1982 |
| | THIMBELINA | Penny Century's fourth daughter. A one-inch tall superhero baby. | Ti-Girls Adventures Number 34 Part One: The Search for Penny Century |
| | THE ORIGINAL TI-GIRLS | The first female superhero group formed by Doctor Zolar, featuring: Titan Girl (married and later divorced Doctor Zolar); Madam Time; Tiger Woman; Miss Micro (later changed her name to Tiny Taylor). | Ti-Girls Adventures Number 34 Part One: The Search for Penny Century |
| | THE ALL NEW TI-GIRLS | The second female superhero group formed by Doctor Zolar, featuring: Saturna (DECEASED. A former Ti-Girl who died of diabetes); Falcona (a retired alcoholic former hero); Fuerza (Xo's alter ego. Later became Espectra, who married and divorced Doctor Zolar); Golden Girl (Mini Rivero's alter ego); The Weeper (Rocket Rhodes' alter ego). | Ti-Girls Adventures Number 34 Part One: The Search for Penny Century |
| | TIGER ROSA | Women's wrestling champion who was Rena's trainer and tag-team partner. | Mechanics |
| | TITO | Friend of Reno's. | Crime Raiders International Mobsters and Executioners |

| | Name | Description | First Appearance |
|---|---|---|---|
| | TITO JR. | A 19-year-old substitute security guard at Chester Square whom Maggie slept with for money. | Chester Square |
| | TITO SR. | Security guard at Chester Square. Father of Tito Jr. | Chester Square |
| | TOM TOM | A young punk girl with rich parents who had a crush on Joey Glass. | Locas vs. Locos |
| | TONTA (ANOUSH AGAJANIAN) | Vivian Solis' younger half-sister. | Tonta |
| | TONY BELLE | Joey's friend. A skinhead punk who later worked for Julie Wree's TV show. | Locas Tambien |
| | TONY "TOP CAT" CHASE | Maggie's ex-husband. | The Race |
| | TOVAH | Hopey's former co-worker. | Day By Day with Hopey: Wednesday |
| | TOYO HIBONALES | DECEASED. Cared for Rena as a child. | Toyo's Request |
| | "TSE TSE" (ROSA COLORES ARRIAGA BANUELOS) | Rena's companion. The translator/guide for the Mechanics crew in the jungle of Zhato. Later, Tse Tse became a celebrated lecturer and scholar. | Mechanics |
| | TWYLA | The guitar player in Hopey's band, the Damachers. | Wigwam Bam |

| Name | Description | First Appearance |
|---|---|---|
| ULTIMAX | Retired superhero. | Maggie vs. Maniakk |
| VAKKA BOOME | An evil has-been sorcerer who gave Penny Century her superpowers in exchange for her daughter. | Ti-Girls Adventures Number 34 Part One: The Search for Penny Century |
| VENETIA VENDETTA | Maggie's acquaintance. | Maggie vs. Maniakk |
| VICKI CHASCARRILLO | Also known as "Vicki Glori" or "Cowgirl Vicki Lane." Maggie's aunt. Nacho's sister. Cash's wife. She has an adopted Japanese son, Hiroshi. An ex-wrestling champion and one time tag-team partner of Rena. She later defeated Rena by "using the ropes," lost her title and regained it again. She was eventually expelled from the WWW for being too brutal. | 100 Rooms |
| VIVIAN KOSELLI | Wrestler who Bull Marie defeated in 1935. | House of Raging Women |
| VIVIAN SOLIS "THE FROGMOUTH" | An aggressive, loudmouth struggling actress and stripper. The former "ringcard girl" for Julie Wree's TV show. She was the one-time lover or girlfriend to Maggie, Ray, Doyle, Reno, Mike Varan and Sid Doan, among others. | One More Ladies' Man |
| MRS. WATKINS | An elderly woman with a fetish for young girls. She attacked and injured Jenny. | Wigwam Bam |
| WEBSTER | H.R. Costigan's butler. | 100 Rooms |
| THE WEEPER | The superhero identity of Rocket Rhodes. | Ti-Girls Adventures Number 34 Part One: The Search for Penny Century |
| WILLIAM COX | One of Hopey's childhood classmates that got in trouble for sneaking out of school. | Day By Day with Hopey: Monday |

| | Name | Description | First Appearance |
|---|---|---|---|
| | "XO" XOCHITL NAVA | Maggie's cousin. Mario's wife. Has three children: Mariposa, Oscar and Junior. The daughter of Jake and Fina (Maggie's uncle and aunt). Gina's tag-team partner. Xo was briefly the Texas Women's Champion and is known as "Xochitl la Teríble." | Camp Vicki |
| | YAX HAXLEY | A prosolar mechanic and co-worker of Rand, Duke and Maggie in the early years. Later, he became Maggie's business partner. | Mechan-X |
| | YOLANDA | Maggie's niece and goddaughter. Twin sister of Lupe. Daughter of Esther and Alvaro Hernandez. | Maggie Part 9 |
| | YUKI | Toyo's granddaughter. | Toyo's Request |
| | ZACK AND TED | Part of the trio of down-on-their-luck actors hired to play villains in Penny's superhero fantasy at Costigan's manor. | All This and Penny, Too ... |
| | "ZERO" (CHARLES JOSEPH GRAVETTE) | The drummer of Hopey's band (La Llorona). | Mechanics |
| | DOCTOR ZOLAR | DECEASED. Founder and former leader of several female superhero teams, including the original Ti-Girls, the All New Ti-Girls, the Fenomenons and the Zolars. | Ti-Girls Adventures Number 34 Part One: The Search for Penny Century |
| | THE ZOLARS | The fourth female superhero group formed by Doctor Zolar, featuring: Kimmy Misters (aka Perfect Ten); Tasha and Tisha Zolar. | Ti-Girls Adventures Number 34 Part One: The Search for Penny Century |
| | ZONO HIBONALES | DECEASED. Toyo's wayward husband, killed during a confrontation with Rena. | Toyo's Request |

| | Name | Description | First Appearance |
|---|---|---|---|
| **?** | MR. ABRAHMS | María's unseen benefactor late in her life. He bought her a lavish house instead of leaving his wife. | Bread, Love and María (mentioned) |
| | ABU | Steve Stranski's Asian co-worker at Lou's Liquor store. | Love and Rockets X |
| | EL ALCALDE JESÚS (CHUY) BERNAL | DECEASED. The ex-mayor of Palomar. Both he and his wife, Marlena, were murdered by Tomaso. They were also Errata Stigmata's parents. | Human Diastrophism |
| | ALDO | DECEASED. Fritz' third ex-husband. A former boxer and neurologist. He beat Fritz up and then suffered a heart attack. | High Soft Lisp |
| | ALDO MUNKRES | DECEASED. A Palomar resident who was Tomaso's first murder victim. | Human Diastrophism |
| | ALFREDO | A teenage boy that Luba seduced in Isleta. | Poison River |
| | ALICIA | DECEASED. Hilda's cousin who took care of her and Luba after Ofelia's attack. She died of natural causes. | Poison River |
| | ALPHONSO | A filmmaker in the U.S. and Mike Niznick's occasional lover. He was also an actor who played a clown on Pipo's TV show. | Love and Rockets X |
| | AMBER | Kristen Niznick's friend. | Love and Rockets X |
| | ANACLETO | Heráclio's friend from Felix who visited Palomar in search of a girlfriend. | Boys Will Be Boys |

| Name | Description | First Appearance |
|---|---|---|
| ANTONINO | Maricela's father. A soldier that Luba slept with in Isleta. | Human Diastrophism |
| ARCHIE RUIZ | Luba's old friend and ex-boyfriend. A mortician. | Act of Contrition |
| ARJELIA | The black-market daughter of Peter and Isobel. She was later adopted by Docho and his wife. | Poison River |
| ARMANDO JOSÉ | DECEASED. Luba's first son (his father's identity was never confirmed) who was sold on the black-market by Peter and died of heart failure while being transported to the United States. | Human Diastrophism (mentioned) Poison River |
| ARNOLFO | A giant toddler whom Killer and Jimmy baby-sat. His mother abandoned him. | The Kid Stuff Kids |
| ARTURO | A friend of Guero, Manuel and Soledád in Palomar. | Heartbreak Soup |
| AUGUSTÍN JIMÉNEZ | The brother of Pipo, Lucía and Carmen (though Carmen was adopted). Elvira's son. Humberto's friend. | Heartbreak Soup |
| AURORA DÍAZ | Israel's twin sister. She disappeared as a child during a solar eclipse. | Bullnecks and Bracelets |
| BABE | Leonor's unnamed boyfriend. | BEM |
| SEÑOR BACA | A local landlord in Palomar. | Heartbreak Soup |

| | Name | Description | First Appearance |
|---|---|---|---|
| | BAMBI DIBBLE | Carl's girlfriend. Wanda's best friend. An aggressive headbanger who also had a crush on Sean Ogata. | Love and Rockets X |
| | BANG BANG | Inez' friend and partner. She originally was featured in a trio of stories outside Palomar continuity ("Music for Monsters") and later appeared in *Birdland* as a stripper. | Music for Monsters I |
| | BEM | DECEASED. "The Horror." A giant bug-eyed monster and criminal mastermind that escaped and was pursued by Luba, Castle Radium and others. | BEM |
| | BEN | A friend of Carl and Charlie. A self-appointed White Aryan Resistance member who participated in the beating of an elderly black woman. | Love and Rockets X |
| | BERNIE | A Jewish boy who tried to hook up with Fritz in high school. Joel's friend. | High Soft Lisp |
| | BETH | Howard Miller's editor at *Geographic Monthly* magazine. | An American in Palomar |
| | BLACKIE OKAMATO | A Japanese man who is Hector Rivera's childhood friend. | Meeting Cute, Fucking Cuter |
| | BLAS | A gay man and former sax player in Peter Rio's band Los Fritos. He got into the drug trade with Peter and became Salas' lover. He cared for Peter after his stroke and took him to the U.S. | Poison River |
| | SEÑORA BLIVITZ | A phony psychic whom Israel Díaz hired to find his missing sister. | Bullnecks and Bracelets |
| | BLOOTER BABY | An imaginary ghost baby that haunted Tonantzín and Venus. | Children of Palomar |

| | Name | Description | First Appearance |
|---|---|---|---|
| | BOB | Errata Stigmata's ex-boyfriend. | Le Contretemps |
| | BOB ZITZ | An odd, airplane-headed clown who was scared off by the news of BEM's escape. | BEM |
| | BOBBY | A Chicano teen that antagonized Igor about his mixed ethnicity. | Love and Rockets X |
| | BOBBY | Venus' father. Tanya's husband. A line cook who dated Tanya while also sleeping with Petra in high school. | Memories of Sweet Youth |
| | BONER AND KIKO | Friends of Archie Ruiz in San Fideo. | Act of Contrition |
| | BOOKER COURT SLATER | A jock that Fritz hooked up with in high school. | Fritz After Dark |
| | BOOTS PIÑA | Chancla and Concha's sister. Theo's friend. She stole a baby skull from a traveling witch, causing a plague to be cast on Palomar. Later, she moved to the U.S. and replaced Gato as Pipo's accountant. | Duck Feet |
| | BORRO | The brutish ex-sheriff of Palomar. As a detective in the neighboring town of Felix, he investigated the murders in Palomar and slept with Luba. | Heartbreak Soup |
| | BRENDA | Fritz' overweight friend in high school. | High Soft Lisp |
| | BRUCE | An archaeologist who worked on the excavation outside Palomar. | Human Diastrophism |

| | Name | Description | First Appearance |
|---|---|---|---|
| | LA BRUJA | A traveling witch who cursed Palomar after her baby skull was stolen. | Duck Feet |
| | BRUNO GOYAS | Casimira's friend in Palomar whose eye was plucked out by a bird. | A Trick of the Unconscious |
| | BUBBA | A rich American schoolgirl with a huge attitude. A fan of the New Kids on the Block. | Love and Rockets X |
| | BUBBLES | DECEASED. Errata Stigmata's old friend. | Radio Zero |
| | CANDACE | Doralís' American girlfriend. Doralís introduced her to Luba by coming out during one of her TV shows. | El Show Super Duper Sensacional de Doralís |
| | CARL DAVIS | DECEASED. Bambi's boyfriend. A friend of Ben and Charlie. A self-appointed White Aryan Resistance member. He was the ringleader in the beating of the elderly black woman, Malvina Wilson. He was shot and killed by Charlie. | Love and Rockets X |
| | CARLOS | One of Jesús' fellow prisoners. | Holidays in the Sun |
| | CARLOS | One of Petra's ex-lovers. An employee at Shredder Records where Venus buys her comic books. | Letters From Venus |
| | CARMEN CALDERÓN | Heráclio's wife. Tito and the twin's mother. Elvira's adopted daughter. Pipo, Agustín and Lucía's adopted sister. She was found abandoned at a swap meet with a sign that read "good riddance." No one knows how old she is. She was close with Tonantzín Villaseñor. | Heartbreak Soup |
| | CASIMIRA DE LOS SANTOS | The daughter of Luba and Khamo. The sister of Maricela (half-sister), Guadalupe (half-sister), Doralís, Joselito, Socorro and Concepción. She eventually lost an arm after Chelo accidentally shot her out of a tree. | Act of Contrition |

| | Name | Description | First Appearance |
|---|---|---|---|
| | CASTLE RADIUM | A superhero detective. He was BEM's sworn enemy who became possessed by "the horror" when it escaped from prison. | BEM |
| | CATHY | Howard Miller's girlfriend who witnessed Tonantzín's suicide on TV. | Human Diastrophism |
| | CHA CHA CHARLIE | DECEASED. A "two-bit stooge turned gonzo killer" who wore the Golem suit and impersonated BEM, but was defeated by Castle Radium. He died trying to escape. | BEM |
| | CHANCLA PIÑA | The sister of Concha and Boots. She liked Martin el Loco. She was stabbed by Tomaso, but survived. | Act of Contrition |
| | CHANGO VALDES | Ofelia's ex-lover. A retired masked wrestler. He visited Palomar on an archaeological work detail with Khamo and Tomaso. | Human Diastrophism |
| | CHARLIE | A friend of Carl and Ben. A self-appointed White Aryan Resistance member, who participated in the beating of an elderly black woman. He shot and killed Carl. | Love and Rockets X |
| | CHATA | A transvestite stripper at Salas' Club Venus. | Poison River |
| | CHATO | DECEASED. A drug dealer who worked for Cilingis. He sold drugs to Pepa that she, Lucy and Luba all used. Fermín strangled him. | Poison River |
| | CHELA | DECEASED. A desperate homeless woman who watched baby Luba while Eduardo tried to find work. She murdered her three children by throwing them in traffic and then killed herself. | Poison River |
| | CHELO | A former midwife, bañadora ("bather") and Sheriff of Palomar. The daughter of Emil and Irma. When she was young, her father beat her so badly she became infertile. | Heartbreak Soup |

| | Name | Description | First Appearance |
|---|---|---|---|
| | CHESTER | Doralís' ex-husband. | A Trick of the Unconscious |
| | CHIEF | DECEASED. Ringleader of the black-market baby trade. | Poison River |
| | CILINGIS | DECEASED. A skinny drug dealer with large glasses who worked for Salas. Garza loyalists murdered him. | Poison River |
| | CINDY WALKER | Rex's anorexic mother. She hosted the Hollywood party where the band Love and Rockets was supposed to make its debut. Riri briefly worked as her cleaning lady. | Love and Rockets X |
| | CLAY | Steve Stranski's mother's boyfriend. A former coke dealer who served eight years in prison. | Love and Rockets X |
| ? | COLOMBIA CHACON | A Palomar resident who loaned Luba shoes for her date with Archie. | Act of Contrition |
| | CONCEPCIÓN ("CONCHITA") | Luba's eighth and youngest child. The daughter of Luba and Khamo. The sister of Maricela (half-sister), Guadalupe (half-sister), Doralís, Casimira, Joselito and Socorro. | Love and Rockets X |
| | CONCHA PIÑA | The sister of Chancla and Boots. Riri's friend. | Act of Contrition |
| ? | SEÑOR CORTEZ | A colleague of Salas' in the drug trade. | Poison River |
| | CUCA VERTUDES | A woman Archie Ruiz was engaged to and had a child with. | Act of Contrition (mentioned) Poison River |

| | Name | Description | First Appearance |
|---|---|---|---|
| | SEÑORA DAGABERTA | Woman in Palomar who raises orphans. She took in Tonantzín and Diana as young girls. | Children of Palomar |
| | DAISY GARCÍA | A mean girl whom Petra beat up in high school at a car show. | High Soft Lisp |
| | DALIA | Manuel's mother. One of Chelo's first midwife patients. | Chelo's Burden |
| | DANNY CHULO | Fritz' boyfriend and manager. He used to run her fan website. | Pattern for Living |
| | DARLEEN | DECEASED. David Vásquez' first wife. The mother of Rogelio and Joey Vásquez. | A Gift for Venus |
| | DR. D. DAVID SCHULZ | Errata Stigmata's doctor. | Tears From Heaven |
| | DAVID VÁSQUEZ | Petra's ex-husband. Venus' ex-stepfather. He had two sons, Rogelio and Joey, from a previous marriage. He also had a daughter with Petra (Yolanda Marie). | Love Story |
| | DEBBIE | An archaeologist who worked on the excavation outside Palomar. | Human Diastrophism |
| | DELMAR | Fritz' redneck friend in high school. Tish's boyfriend. He introduced Fritz to the joys of firing guns. | High Soft Lisp |
| | DIANA VILLASEÑOR | Tonantzín's little sister. A sprinter who later became a celebrity bodybuilder. Gregory's wife. Tina's mother. | The Laughing Sun (mentioned) Ecce Homo |

| | Name | Description | First Appearance |
|---|---|---|---|
| | DIEGO | Fortunato's "brother" who was also raised by Galgo as an instrument of revenge against women; however, he fell in love and disappeared. | The Fortunato Files |
| | DOCHO | Guitar player in Peter Rio's band Los Fritos. | Poison River |
| | DOCTOR | Obstetrician who sold babies, including Luba and Peter's son, Armando José, into the black market. | Poison River |
| | DORALÍS DE LOS SANTOS | DECEASED. The lesbian daughter of Luba and Khamo. The sister of Maricela (half-sister), Guadalupe (half-sister), Casimira, Joselito, Socorro and Concepción. Chester's ex-wife. She was the star of Pipo's TV variety show and later wrote several of Fritz' films. She died of cancer. | Act of Contrition |
| | DROMUNDO | A guard at Jesús' island prison. | Holidays in the Sun |
| | DULCE | Petra's high school friend. A teenage mother. | Memories of Sweet Youth |
| | E.T. (ELVIN) | Jerome's father. A black teenager who worked as a pizza delivery driver. Friends with Junior Brooks and Erf'Quake. He was kidnapped by Carl, Ben and Charlie, but escaped after Charlie killed Carl instead. | Love and Rockets X |
| | E.T.'S MOTHER | Jerome's grandmother. | Love and Rockets X |
| | ECHO | Precocious newspaper boy who taunted Castle Radium. | BEM |
| | ED | A cop friend of María's who hooked up with Fritz in a graveyard while she was in high school. | Memories of Sweet Youth |

| | Name | Description | First Appearance |
|---|---|---|---|
| | EDUARDO | DECEASED. Luba's father (with María). Hilda's brother. Ofelia's uncle. He was a poor Indian migrant laborer. He and María lived together for a while after her husband kicked her out. Eduardo was later hit on the head and robbed by Juan Nuñez and lost his job. María left him and he eventually died on a beach. | Poison River |
| | EDWINA | Bubbles' mother. | Radio Zero |
| | EFREN | One of the residents of Palomar who chose Luba over Chelo for a bath. | Heartbreak Soup |
| | EL CLAVO ("SPIKE") | A masked wrestler that Tonantzín had a one-night stand with. | Slug Fest |
| | EL FONTANEL | His full name is Juevencio Fontanel Spinoza. The drummer of the defunct Love and Rockets band. Starfire's boyfriend. | Love and Rockets X |
| ? | ELISSA DÍAZ | The mother of Israel and Aurora. Juan Díaz' wife. | Chelo's Burden |
| | ELVIRA JIMÉNEZ | The mother of Pipo, Augustín and Lucía. She adopted Carmen when she was a baby. Her husband was killed in prison. | Chelo's Burden |
| | EMICO | A 17-year-old science policewoman in the dystopian city of New Hiroshima. | Twitch City |
| | EMIL | Chelo's father. Irma's husband. He beat Chelo so viciously that she became infertile. | Chelo's Burden |
| | DR. EMIL | The Belgian man with two penises whom Fritz and Pipo slept with. | In Bed With Pipo |

| | Name | Description | First Appearance |
|---|---|---|---|
| **?** | ENGELBERTA | DECEASED. Tipín Tipín's wife. | Love Bites |
| | ENRIQUE ESCOBAR | Fritz' ex-boyfriend: They were engaged but never got married. He met Fritz in high school, but they didn't get together until their 10-year reunion. He was a professional model and later became a computer programmer and moved back east. | Kidney Stoned Again |
| | ERRATA STIGMATA | A girl afflicted with stigmatic bleeding from the hands and feet. The daughter of the former mayor of Palomar. Witnessing the murder of her parents by Tomaso formed part of her "stigmata." She was sent to live with her Aunt Zephie and Uncle Ira, but Ira killed Zephie and then himself. She usually appears outside of the "Palomar" continuity. Radio Zero is her ex-boyfriend. | Radio Zero |
| | ERF'QUAKE | A black kid who is part of a small posse with Junior Brooks and E.T. Friends with Steve Stranski. | Love and Rockets X |
| | ESTHER | A woman Archie once bought a drink for in San Fideo. | Act of Contrition |
| | FABIO | Bass player in Peter Rio's band Los Fritos. | Poison River |
| | FAUSTO SALAS | DECEASED. Leader of an international drug cartel. Señor Salas' father. He was butchered by an angry mob of peasants in 1963. | Poison River |
| | FERMÍN RIO | DECEASED. Peter's father. He was a singer and conga player who was heavily involved in the illegal drug business. He was a vicious murderer who strangled a number of people to death. Had affairs with María and Isobel, but his son eventually stole both of them away. Peter killed him. | Poison River |
| | FLACO | A drug dealer who worked for Salas. Unidentified Garza loyalists cut off his arms and legs. | Poison River |
| | FLOR | A paranoid resident of Isleta who claimed she saw aliens. | The Book of Ofelia |

| | Name | Description | First Appearance |
|---|---|---|---|
| | FORTUNATO | DECEASED. "The man that no woman can resist." As a child, he was rescued off the coast of Sicily and was named for his "good fortune." Later he was purchased by Galgo and raised to seduce women and break their hearts. As an adult, he was a mysterious blond "player"; Luba, Fritz, Pipo and several other characters had affairs with him. He was beaten to death by Sergio. | Luba in America – Chapter 3 |
| | FRANKY OBREGON | Lars and Fritz' college friend. He was the co-star of *Phantom of the Campus*, a low-budget right-wing TV show on a university station. | Fritz After Dark |
| | FRITZ (ROSALBA FRITZI MARTÍNEZ) | The daughter of María and Hector. Petra's little sister and Luba's half-sister. Mark Herrera's fourth wife. She also married Aldo and Scotty the Hog. She was engaged to Enrique Escobar, but called it off. She dated Pipo's son, Sergio, and is currently married to Pipo. She speaks with a "high soft lisp" and worked as a therapist before starring in cult B movies. She also appeared in *Birdland*. | Music for Monsters I |
| | GA GA | Kristen Niznick's friend. | Love and Rockets X |
| ? | GABRIELA | Vicente's mother. | Chelo's Burden |
| | GABY | One of Pipo's employees on her early TV show *El Show de Inez*. | A Trick of the Unconscious |
| | GALGO | DECEASED. An embittered businessman who bought Fortunato, Diego and Zanto as boys and raised them as instruments of revenge against women. Zanto murdered him. | The Fortunato Files |
| | GAMBOA FAMILY | Old friends of Hilda's whom she, Luba and Ofelia briefly stayed with upon their return to Isleta. | Poison River |
| | GARZA | DECEASED. A rival drug lord that did business with Señor Salas. He had an affair with María. Salas' gang killed him in a shootout. | Poison River |
| | GATO REYNA | DECEASED. Pipo's ex-husband. Sergio's adoptive father. Guadalupe's husband. Jimmy's father. Gato had a love/hate relationship with Pipo throughout his life. When he was laid off, Pipo left him. He later helped his ex-wife with her business affairs. When she fired him, he fed rumors to the tabloids about her relationship with Fritz. He died in a car crash with Sergio. | Heartbreak Soup |

| Name | Description | First Appearance |
|---|---|---|
| GATO'S GRANDFATHER | DECEASED. A tyrannical alcoholic ex-military officer who relentlessly abused Gato. Gato's brother Roberto murdered him. | Heartbreak Soup |
| GERALDO MEJIA | Gato and Roberto's cousin. A criminal who went to jail for cocaine possession and assaulting Tonantzín. He was born again in prison and sent political letters to Tonantzín. | Duck Feet |
| GERRY | Steve Stranski's best friend. One of the surfer dudes who visited Palomar. | Human Diastrophism |
| GINA | DECEASED. A friend of Ofelia's when Luba was a toddler. Ruben's girlfriend. A communist supporter. She was raped and murdered by government loyalists. | Poison River |
| GLINDA GONZALEZ | Venus and Yoshi's friend. | Letters From Venus: Who Cares About Love? |
| GLORIA | A fellow teacher who gave Heráclio periodic rides back to Palomar, discussing literary classics along the way. | Love Bites |
| GÓMEZ | A government loyalist and childhood friend of Ruben's. | Poison River |
| GORGO CIENFUEGO | Papa Pito's son. A former enforcer for the drug mob. He followed and protected María, searched out and found Luba and saved the lives of Fritz and Petra. He reunited Petra and Fritz with their older half-sister, Luba, in Palomar. He was kidnapped and is presumed dead. | Poison River |
| GREG | One of Fritz' boyfriends. A cop. | As You Know It |
| GREGORY | Diana's husband. Tina's father. | A Trick of the Unconscious |

| | Name | Description | First Appearance |
|---|---|---|---|
| | GRIGORYEVICH ARTZYBASCHEV | A Russian navy officer whom Luba briefly dated before moving to Palomar. | An American in Palomar (mentioned) Poison River |
| | GUADALUPE REYNA | The daughter of Luba and Heráclio. The half-sister of Maricela, Doralís, Casimira, Joselito, Socorro and Concepción. She moved to the U.S. as an exchange student and had a son (Jimmy) with Gato Reyna, whom she married. After Gato died, she slept with Hector Rivera, which resulted in their daughter, Dora (Killer). She is a grade-school teacher and performs and teaches bellydancing. | Act of Contrition |
| | GUERO | A blond, light-skinned friend of Arturo, Manuel and Soledád's in Palomar. | Heartbreak Soup |
| | SEÑOR GUY | One of the residents of Palomar who chose Luba over Chelo for a bath. | Heartbreak Soup |
| | HANS | Chelo's stepfather. A German truck driver. Irma married him after Emil left Palomar. | Chelo's Burden |
| | HAROLD PENIS | A bizarre man who went in search of BEM. | BEM |
| ? | HECTOR | Riri's younger brother. | Human Diastrophism |
| | HECTOR MARTÍNEZ | Fritz and Petra's father. María's second husband (divorced). Hector worked for the mob, and to protect his daughters, he had to leave the U.S. and promise never to contact them. María told them he was dead, but they eventually found out that he was alive. He later married Rosa. Fritz accused him of molesting her when she was a toddler. | Bread, Love and María |
| | HECTOR RIVERA | Killer's father. Fritz' ex-lover and Petra's ex-boyfriend. La Valda's ex-fiancé. He works at World Express delivering packages. He helped Socorro and Joselito get home safely after their car accident. He had a one-night stand with Guadalupe that resulted in their daughter Dora (Killer). He married Sandra Bobo. | Snail Trail |
| | HERÁCLIO CALDERÓN | Carmen's husband. The father of Tito and the twins (with Carmen) and Guadalupe (with Luba). His best friends are Satch, Vicente, Israel and Jesús. He went to college and teaches music at a school near Palomar. He has three older sisters and his parents live in Colombia. | Heartbreak Soup |

| Name | Description | First Appearance |
|---|---|---|
| HILDA BELTRAN | DECEASED. Luba's aunt. Eduardo's sister. Ofelia's blind mother. She helped raise Luba as a girl. | Poison River |
| HOWARD MILLER | An American photojournalist who visited Palomar. | An American in Palomar |
| HUMBERTO | A young artist in Palomar. He witnessed Tomaso in the act of murder, but refused to tell anyone, preferring to let his artwork speak for itself. He was banned from creating art, but secretly made sculptures of many Palomar residents, which he sank to the bottom of a lake. | Human Diastrophism |
| IGOR VALDEZ | Wanda's ex-boyfriend. He is half black, half Latino. He used to work at Mr. Pekarman's hubcap shop, but left the U.S. and went to Germany with Mike Niznick to shoot a documentary film. He later returned to the U.S. and briefly dated Pipo. | Love and Rockets X |
| INEZ PEREZ | Bang Bang's partner. She originally was featured in a trio of short stories outside Palomar continuity ("Music for Monsters") and later appeared in *Birdland* as a stripper. In Palomar continuity, she was briefly the host of Pipo's morning exercise TV show before Doralís replaced her. She was also a news reporter on the local Spanish channel in the U.S. | Music for Monsters I |
| INGRID CASTILLO | Hector Martínez' ex-girlfriend. The third runner-up in the Miss Luminosa pageant of 1948. | Bread, Love and María |
| IRA | DECEASED. Errata Stigmata's wealthy uncle. He killed his wife, Zephie and then himself. | Tears From Heaven |
| IRMA | Chelo's mother. Emil's wife. A midwife. She later married Hans, a German truck driver. | Chelo's Burden |
| ISIDRO RIVAS | A former fishmonger whose wife left him after his business went bankrupt. He now lives on the beach outside Palomar. | On Isidro's Beach |
| ÍSOBEL | DECEASED. Peter's ex-wife. A transsexual exotic dancer that Peter financed a sex change for. She was originally Fermín's lover. Peter also got her a daughter on the black-market (Arjelia). Fermín strangled her for betraying Peter to Garza. | Poison River |

| | Name | Description | First Appearance |
|---|---|---|---|
| | ISRAEL DÍAZ | The son of Elisa and Juan Díaz. Aurora's twin brother. The childhood friend of Satch, Vicente, Heráclio and Jesús. A bisexual, decadent bodybuilder whose sister disappeared during a solar eclipse when they were children. | Heartbreak Soup |
| | SEÑOR ITO | A man who saved Emico's life and later slept with her. | Twitch City |
| | JAIME ("JIMMY") | Guadalupe and Gato's son. Killer's older brother. One of the "Kids Stuff Kids." | The Gorgo Wheel |
| | JAN | A personal trainer who slept with her client, Enrique Escobar. | Fritz After Dark |
| | JANUS | Pipo's French lover. A male stripper. | In Bed With Pipo |
| | JASON STERLING | Hector's friend with a pickup truck. | Snail Trail |
| | JAVIER | DECEASED. Blas' homosexual ex-lover. Zenen's business partner in the black-market baby trade. Fermín strangled him to death for taking Luba's son. | Poison River |
| | JAXON | The owner of a punk rock art club, The Polka Parade, where Tyrone Bone had a showing. | The Beloved and the Damned |
| | JENNA CHONG | Mark Herrera's third ex-wife. A professional figure skater. | Dumb Solitaire |
| | JEROME | E.T.'s young son. | Love and Rockets X |

| | Name | Description | First Appearance |
|---|---|---|---|
| | JEROME | A black man married to a white woman who had an ongoing affair with Fritz over the years. They first met in college when he was the lawyer who represented Lars Mucklebus regarding their TV show, *Phantom of the Campus*. | As You Know It |
| | JEROME'S WIFE | A white woman who was Fritz' therapy patient. Her husband cheated on her with Fritz. | As You Know It |
| | JESSE | One of the residents of Palomar who chose Luba over Chelo for a bath. | Heartbreak Soup |
| | JESÚS ÁNGEL | A childhood friend of Satch, Vicente, Israel and Heráclio. Toco's older brother. Laura's ex-husband. He was sent to prison for accidentally hurting his child. He had a lover in prison named Marcos (amongst others). After he was released from prison, he slept with Satch's married daughter, moved to the U.S. with Gato, married and divorced Tita, then disappeared. | Heartbreak Soup |
| | JO JO | Trix' daughter. Steve Stranski's niece. | Love and Rockets X |
| | JOE | A punk drug user with whom Petra fooled around in high school. | Memories of Sweet Youth |
| | JOEL MAYER | DECEASED. A Jewish boy who hooked up with Petra in high school. Bernie's friend. | High Soft Lisp |
| ? | JOEY REYNA | Gato's brother. | Duck Feet (mentioned) |
| | JOEY VÁSQUEZ | David's son. Petra's ex-stepson. Venus' ex-stepbrother. Rogelio's little brother. | Letters From Venus: Goddess of Love |
| | JOEY SALDAÑA | Archie Ruiz' colleague at the mortuary. | Act of Contrition |

| | Name | Description | First Appearance |
|---|---|---|---|
| | JORGE | Israel's ex-boyfriend who is married to Mimi. | Bullnecks and Bracelets |
| | JOSÉ ORTIZ | DECEASED. A corrupt police captain associated with Señor Salas and Peter's drug mob. Fermín strangled him for having an affair with Luba. | Poison River |
| | JOSELITO | The son of Luba and Khamo. The brother of Maricela (half-brother), Guadalupe (half-brother), Doralís, Casimira, Socorro and Concepción. | Love and Rockets X |
| | JOSÉ VALDEZ | Igor's father. An Exxon gas station employee. | Love and Rockets X |
| | JOSH | A boy Petra hooked up with in high school. | Petra |
| | JUAN | Peter and Luba's servant who helped Luba escape back to her family. | Poison River |
| ? | JUAN COBOS | A resident of Palomar whose car was stolen by Jesús Ángel after his fight with his wife. | The Laughing Sun (mentioned) |
| ? | JUAN DÍAZ | The father of Israel and Aurora. Elisa's husband. | Chelo's Burden |
| | JUAN NUÑEZ | A migrant laborer with five children who lost his job and, in desperation, beat up and robbed Eduardo in Colonia. | Poison River |
| | JUNIOR BROOKS | A black kid who is the leader of a small posse with E.T. and Erf'Quake. He is an amateur artist. | Love and Rockets X |

| | Name | Description | First Appearance |
|---|---|---|---|
| | MR. KANG | A Korean man with missing limbs who rents the shed behind Steve Stranski's mother's house. | Love and Rockets X |
| | KARLA | One of Israel Díaz' lovers. | Bullnecks and Bracelets |
| | KARLOTA | María's former maid at El Señor's estate. She briefly lived with Eduardo and María in Colonia, but later ran away. | Poison River |
| | KAT | Carlos' girlfriend. | Letters From Venus: Who Cares About Love? |
| | KATY | Luba's teenage friend who slept with Docho. | Poison River |
| | "KILLER" (DORA RIVERA) | Jimmy's little sister. Guadalupe's daughter, conceived during a one-night stand with Hector Rivera. Like Fritz, she grew up and became a B-movie actress. She was named Dora after her departed aunt Doralís. | The Kid Stuff Kids Starring in: Down in Heaven |
| | KIP | DECEASED. Hector Martínez' childhood friend and Army buddy. They went to the Miss Luminosa pageant in 1948 together. He was captured and tortured to death by North Korean soldiers. | Bread, Love and María |
| | THE KEWPIES | A strange group of racist, eccentric women who watched Venus and redid her hairdo while Sergio was taking care of his mother. | Mama's Boy |
| | KHAMO (SANTIAGO KHAMO DE LOS SANTOS) | Luba's ex-husband. The father of Doralís, Casimira, Joselito and Concepción (all with Luba). He also had an affair with Pipo. He left Palomar with Tonantzín and was badly burned trying to save her. He came back to Palomar and married Luba. They moved to the U.S., where he helped prosecute his former drug connections in exchange for amnesty. They eventually divorced. | Human Diastrophism |
| | KRISTA ST. JOHN | Mark Herrera's fifth ex-wife. A personal trainer to the stars. | Dumb Solitaire |

| | Name | Description | First Appearance |
|---|---|---|---|
| | KRISTEN NIZNICK | Mike Niznick's daughter. An attractive bulimic teen. She lived with her father and had a crush on Sean Ogata, but eventually left the U.S. and went to live with her mother in Iraq. Maricela had a crush on her. | Love and Rockets X |
| | LALI | Owner of the only bar in Palomar. | The Mystery Wen |
| | LARS MUCKLEBUS | DECEASED. The star, writer and director of *Phantom of the Campus* (he played the lead character, Phanto), a low-budget right-wing TV horror show on a university station. Fritz had a small non-speaking role on the show, which ended when Lars killed himself in the final episode. | Fritz After Dark |
| | LA VALDA DANE | Mark Herrera's second ex-wife. An exotic dancer. She was also Hector Rivera's ex-fiancée, who was shot in the belly while eight months pregnant and lost the baby. She originally appeared in *Birdland* as Mark's ex-wife. | Birdland |
| | LAURA GÓMEZ | Jesús Ángel's ex-wife. They had a daughter together. | The Laughing Sun |
| | LEONOR | A clairvoyant woman haunted by dreams about BEM. | BEM |
| ? | LICHA MÁRQUEZ | Soledád's mother. One of Chelo's first midwife patients. | Chelo's Burden |
| | DETECTIVE LINDA | Part of the team from Felix sent to investigate the murders in Palomar. | Human Diastrophism |
| ? | LITA | Vicente's ex-girlfriend. | Heartbreak Soup |
| ? | LITTLE JOE | An American drug dealer whose father was an associate of Khamo's before he went to prison. | Luba |

| | Name | Description | First Appearance |
|---|---|---|---|
| **?** | MR. LORENZANO | Luba's neighbor in the U.S. Joselito and Socorro stole his car and crashed it. | Snail Trail (mentioned) |
| | LORRAINA | One of the children in Palomar who stole the bruja's baby skull: a childhood friend of Doralís. | Duck Feet |
| | LUBA (LUBA DE LOS SANTOS) | Daughter of María and Eduardo. The mother of Maricela, Guadalupe, Doralís, Casimira, Joselito Socorro, and Concepción. Ofelia's cousin. Peter Rio's and Khamo's ex-wife. Older half-sister of Fritz and Petra. In Palomar, Luba was a bañadora, owned a movie theater, and later became Mayor. In the U.S., she owns an immigration, taxes and beeper business. | BEM |
| | LUCÍA JIMÉNEZ | The younger sister of Pipo, Augustín and Carmen (adopted). Elvira's daughter. | Heartbreak Soup |
| | LUCY | A friend of Luba and Pepa. She was addicted to heroin. Baltazar's wife. | Poison River |
| | MALVINA WILSON | The elderly black woman who was attacked by Carl, Ben and Charlie behind a neighborhood grocery store. | Love and Rockets X |
| | MANUEL | DECEASED. Dalia's son. Sergio's father (with Pipo). He had an affair with Pipo as a teen. Soledád Márquez killed him in a jealous rage. | Heartbreak Soup |
| | MARCOS | A gay friend of Israel's. Jesús' fellow prisoner and occasional lover. He met Jesús when he was released from prison. | Holidays in the Sun |
| | MARÍA INCLÁN | DECEASED. Luba's mother. She married a rich man ("El Señor") but he kicked her out after he found out that Luba wasn't his child. She had affairs with Garza, Fermín and Peter Rio. She had two more daughters (Fritz and Petra) with her second husband, Hector Martínez. She divorced Hector in the early '70s and moved to the U.S. with her daughters. She died of a brain tumor at the age of 62. | Poison River |
| | MARICELA | Luba's oldest child. The daughter of Luba and Antonino. The half-sister of Guadalupe, Doralís, Casimira, Joselito, Socorro and Concepción. She is a lesbian who ran away with her lover, Riri, to live in the U.S., but they broke up. She lives in the U.S. and works as a librarian. | Heartbreak Soup |

| | Name | Description | First Appearance |
|---|---|---|---|
| | MARK HERRERA | Fritz' ex-husband. A former motivational speaker who subsequently went on a failed search for the legendary Sea Hog. He originally appeared in *Birdland* as Fritz' husband and lover. | Birdland |
| | MARK HERRERA'S PARENTS AND SIBLINGS | Mark's father was a Vietnam veteran. He has two brothers and a sister, all of whom treat him and his wife, Mila, with hostility and jealousy. | Where the Heart Is |
| **?** | MARLENA BERNAL | DECEASED. Errata Stigmata's mother. The wife of Palomar's Mayor Jesús (Chuy) Bernal. Tomaso murdered her. | Human Diastrophism (mentioned) |
| | MARTA GARCÍA | Satch's wife. | The Laughing Sun |
| | MARTÍN EL LOCO | A young, wealthy boy in Palomar known as the town crazy. He had a crush on Chancla, and gave a lot of his money away to the town *curandera* (Xiohmara) to heal Chancla after Tomaso stabbed her. | Act of Contrition |
| | MATT | A boy Fritz hooked up with in high school. Afterward, he had an epileptic seizure and hit his head on a rock. | Petra |
| | MELVIN | A Jewish drug dealer who was one of Petra's high school friends and her occasional lover. | Memories of Sweet Youth |
| | MEME | Mistress who owns a brothel on the outskirts of Palomar. | Duck Feet |
| **?** | SEÑORA MEZA | DECEASED. The mother of an old friend of Archie Ruiz. | Act of Contrition |
| | MIGUEL MENDOZA | A cute boy whom Venus had a crush on. | The New Adventures of Venus |

| | Name | Description | First Appearance |
|---|---|---|---|
| | MIGUEL RAMOS | Chelo's ex-lover. | The Reticent Heart |
| | MILA CASTELLON | Mark Herrera's sixth wife. A professional model and actress. | Dumb Solitaire |
| | MILLIE VALDEZ | Igor's mother. Juan's wife. | Love and Rockets X |
| | MIKE NIZNICK | Kristen's father. A Vietnam veteran and ex-hippie who now writes and produces documentary films. He is Jewish and was briefly married to a Muslim woman from Iraq. They had one daughter, Kristen, then separated. After the divorce, he came out of the closet. | Love and Rockets X |
| | MITCHELL | An employee at the nude resort who stole Petra's "family thing" statue. After he won the lottery, he returned it in the mail. | Letters From Venus: That Family Thing |
| | MOISES MORAGA | DECEASED. A drug dealer who worked for Salas. He was brutally killed by Garza loyalists. | Poison River |
| | NENA GARCÍA | Satch's mother. Olaf's wife. | Heartbreak Soup |
| | OBREGON | DECEASED. Jesús' troubled fellow prisoner who committed suicide. | Holidays in the Sun |
| | OFELIA BELTRAN | Luba's older cousin. Hilda's daughter. For many years, she lived with Luba in Palomar, then in California, helping raise her children. Ofelia was a communist sympathizer and was raped and shot by government supporters. She survived, but her back was badly injured and she became sterile. She eventually left Luba to travel the world with her old boyfriend, Rico. | Heartbreak Soup |
| ? | OLAF GARCÍA | Satch's father. Nena's husband. | Chelo's Burden |

| Name | Description | First Appearance |
| --- | --- | --- |
| THE OLD MAN | One of Israel Díaz' lovers; an older wealthy gentleman. | Bullnecks and Bracelets |
| OMO | A bathhouse patron whom Luba attacked with a hammer when she was a teenager, injuring his eye. | Poison River |
| OONA | Errata Stigmata's friend; a fellow stigmatic. | Tears From Heaven |
| PADRE PACO | Palomar's local clergy. | Heartbreak Soup |
| PAM | Gerry's friend. | Love and Rockets X |
| PAT | Fritz' friend. | Rosalba |
| PATRICE | Luba's sworn enemy, a black woman who wanted to seduce BEM with a bizarre ritual. | BEM |
| PAULO P. PIÑATA | A mad scientist and professor who hoped to capture BEM, but was possessed by the creature. | BEM |
| PAULO PINZON | A man Pipo slept with. | Mama's Boy |
| SEÑOR PAZ | DECEASED. A businessman whom Fermín strangled, under orders of Fausto Salas, for suspicions of supporting Communism. | Poison River |

| Name | Description | First Appearance |
|---|---|---|
| PEDRO PACOTILLA | The ubiquitous ethnic cartoon character whose beaming visage is used in everything from comic books to soft drink advertisements. Once a racist character, he's since evolved into a less insulting-looking hand puppet. | Poison River |
| PEE WEE | A bouncer at Stinky's strip club where La Valda danced. | Birdland |
| MR. PEKARMAN | The Jewish owner of a hubcap shop where Igor and Scott worked. Inspired by the legendary comics scribe Harvey Pekar. | Love and Rockets X |
| PEPA | A friend of Lucy and Luba. She was addicted to heroin. | Poison River |
| PEPO | Heráclio's friend and drinking buddy. | The Mystery Wen |
| PETER RIO | Fermín's son. Luba's first husband. A musician who worked for Señor Salas in the drug trade. He had an affair with María and promised her that he would find her daughter. Later, when he found Luba, he married her, but he also had another wife and daughter (Isobel and Arjelia, respectively). He suffered a stroke and Blas took him to the U.S. He murdered his father. | BEM |
| PETRA MARTÍNEZ | The older daughter of María and Hector Martínez. Fritz' sister and Luba's half-sister. Venus' mother (with Bobby). She married and divorced David Vásquez. They had a daughter (Yolanda Marie). She dated Hector Rivera for a while, and eventually became a born-again Christian. She is currently married to Vic. She also appeared in *Birdland*, where she had an affair with Mark Herrera. | Birdland |
| PINO | Luba's first boyfriend. She broke up with him after she met Peter. | Poison River |
| PINTÓR SALCEDO | DECEASED. A boy who died in Palomar after being accidentally pinned under a car. His ghost is sometimes seen at Pintór's Tree. | Heartbreak Soup |
| PIPO JIMÉNEZ | Elvira's daughter. The sister of Augustín, Lucía and Carmen (adopted). Sergio's mother. She lost her virginity to Soledád at 13, had an affair with Manuel and got pregnant. After Manuel was killed, she married Gato. She divorced Gato and had an affair with Khamo. After starting a sportswear business, she moved to the U.S. and became a very successful producer. She briefly dated Igor, and married Fritz. | Heartbreak Soup |

| | Name | Description | First Appearance |
|---|---|---|---|
| **?** | PITO | DECEASED. Hilda's late husband. | Poison River (mentioned) |
| | PAPA PITO CIENFUEGO | DECEASED. Gorgo's father. A private investigator known for his ability to locate missing women. He died of natural causes after finding Luba for Peter. | Poison River |
| | THE PROFESSOR | Mark Herrera's colleague and rival. A famous motivational speaker on the East Coast. | Baby Talk |
| **?** | RADIO ZERO | Errata Stigmata's ex-boyfriend. | Radio Zero (mentioned) |
| | RAJ | A high school football player whom Fritz hooked up with. | High Soft Lisp |
| | DR. RAMIREZ | One of the trio of suspicious visitors who arrived in Palomar after the earthquake to assassinate Gorgo. | Chelo's Burden |
| | RAMONA GARZA | DECEASED. Garza's first wife who was also Peter Rio's lover. She died of leukemia in 1967. | Poison River |
| **?** | RAÚL | Gato's ex-business partner whom Pipo had an affair with. | Pipo (mentioned) |
| | REX WALKER | Cindy's racist, spoiled son. An ex-member (bassist) of the defunct Love and Rockets band. | Love and Rockets X |
| | RICKY BOY | An ex-member (organist) of Peter Rio's band, Los Fritos. He raped Luba. | Poison River |

| | Name | Description | First Appearance |
|---|---|---|---|
| | RICO ("OOLI") | Ofelia's boyfriend in Isleta whom she dated when Luba was a baby. They were reunited years later and left to travel the world together. | Poison River |
| | RIRI | Maricela's ex-lover. They ran away to live in the U.S., but she eventually left Maricela, went back to Palomar and had a child. | Act of Contrition |
| ? | RITA | Jesús and Toco's mother. | Chelo's Burden |
| | RITA MANKOVICH | Mark Herrera's first ex-wife. A former TV news reporter for a right-wing station, she later became a celebrated author of children's books. | Dumb Solitaire |
| | ROBERTO REYNA | DECEASED. Gato's older brother who murdered his grandfather. He died when he fell from a roof trying to escape from Chelo. | Duck Feet |
| | ROGELIO VÁSQUEZ | DECEASED. David's son. Petra's ex-stepson. Venus's ex-stepbrother. Joey's big brother. He died of the same illness that claimed his mother. | Letters From Venus: Goddess of Love |
| | ROMERO | A man who was protecting Riri and Maricela from the immigration police and helping them get fake legal papers. | Love and Rockets X |
| | ROSA | Hector Martínez' second wife. She revealed to him the secret of the crosses inside the fish. | Bread, Love and María |
| | ROXANNE | Paulo's partner who tried to seduce BEM. | BEM |
| | RUBEN | DECEASED. He was a friend of Ofelia's when Luba was a baby. Gina's boyfriend. A Communist sympathizer who was sodomized and murdered by government loyalists. | Poison River |

| Name | Description | First Appearance |
|------|-------------|------------------|
| RUDY | A friend of Archie's who used to hit on Luba when she was a teen in Calentura. | Act of Contrition |
| MRS. RUIZ | Archie's mother. | Act of Contrition |
| SEÑOR SALAS | DECEASED. The homosexual son of Fausto Salas who inherited his father's narcotics business. Garza's rival clan killed him in a shootout. He was Peter Rio's boss and Blas' lover. | Poison River |
| SANDRA BOBO | Hector's wife. Guadalupe's friend and fellow bellydancer. Guadalupe set her up with Hector and they got married three days later. | Down in Heaven |
| SANTIAGO | María's ex-boyfriend whom she briefly lived with after leaving Hector Martínez. | Bread, Love and María |
| SANTOS | DECEASED. Chelo's unborn son who died in utero and was preserved inside her as a mummified fetus. | Chelo's Burden |
| SATCH (SAKAHAFTKEWA GARCÍA) | A childhood friend of Heráclio, Vicente, Israel and Jesús. The son of Nena and Olaf. He lives in Felix with Marta, his wife, and their seven children. | Heartbreak Soup |
| SATURNINO | Vicente's down-on-his-luck friend and roommate in San Fideo. | The Way Things're Going |
| SCOTT | "Scotty the Hog." Fritz' second ex-husband (they were married and divorced twice). The obese ex-lead singer of the defunct Love and Rockets band. He later released a solo album called *High Soft Lisp*, which Fritz paid for. | Love and Rockets X |
| SEAN OGATA | The Japanese ex-guitar player of the defunct Love and Rockets band. | Love and Rockets X |

| Name | Description | First Appearance |
|---|---|---|
| SEBASTIAN | Ofelia's ex-lover. They met in Isleta when he gave her drugs to help with her chronic back pain. | Poison River |
| MR. SANCHEZ | Mark Herrera involved Mr. Sanchez in his and his wife Fritz' fetishistic sex life. | High Soft Lisp |
| "EL SEÑOR" | María's unnamed billionaire ex-husband who kicked her out when he realized Luba was not his daughter. | Poison River |
| SERAFINA | Peter and Luba's maid who helped Luba escape back to her family. | Poison River |
| SERGIO JIMÉNEZ REYNA | DECEASED. The son of Pipo and Gato (his real father was Manuel). He was an international soccer superstar. He dated Fritz but was in love with Guadalupe. He died in a car crash with Gato. | Ecce Homo |
| SIMON HERRERA | Mark Herrera's brother. | Birdland |
| MR. SMITH | A therapy patient whom Fritz slept with. | Birdland |
| SOCORRO | Luba's fifth daughter (with Tomaso, the convicted murderer). The half-sister of Maricela, Guadalupe, Doralís, Casimira, Joselito and Concepción. She is a genius with a photographic memory. | Love and Rockets X |
| SOFIA | One of Israel Díaz' ex-lovers; a transsexual. | Bullnecks and Bracelets |
| SOFRONIO | Guadalupe's ex-boyfriend. | Luba Conquers the World |

| Name | Description | First Appearance |
|------|-------------|------------------|
| SOLEDÁD MÁRQUEZ | Licha's son. Manuel's best childhood friend. He was Pipo's first lover and later killed Manuel. | Heartbreak Soup |
| STARFIRE | El Fontanel's girlfriend. | Love and Rockets X |
| STEÑA | A woman whose soul was the subject of a battle between Death, God and the Devil. | A Folk Tale |
| STEVE STRANSKI | A surfer dude and dope fiend with glasses and long blond hair who lives in the U.S. Gerry's best friend and everybody's pal. He visited Palomar in search of the perfect wave and again after he crashed Gerry's car following his embarrassing encounter with Riri. He is secretly in love with Guadalupe. | Human Diastrophism |
| STUMBO | A surfer and bodybuilder who bullied Matt and Scott on the beach. He later became a punk and dated Fritz. | Petra |
| SVEN ANDERSSON | DECEASED. A Swedish archaeologist who worked on the excavation outside Palomar. Tomaso murdered him. | Human Diastrophism |
| TANYA | A waitress who dated Bobby. Bobby was cheating on her with Petra in high school. Bobby and Tanya got married, making her Venus' stepmother. | Memories of Sweet Youth |
| SEÑOR TATA | Palomar resident who rented his house to Howard Miller. | An American in Palomar (mentioned) |
| TCUC | A native local boy in Isleta. | Poison River |
| TERRIBLE BULLY | A bully at Venus' school. | The New Adventures of Venus |

| | Name | Description | First Appearance |
|---|---|---|---|
| | THEO | A young boy in Palomar who helped Tonantzín gather babosas to fry up and sell on the street. | Slug Fest |
| | MRS. TIBURCIA | A widow in Palomar who was born again after her husband's death. | Boys Will Be Boys |
| | TINA | The daughter of Diana and Gregory. | A Trick of the Unconscious |
| | TIPÍN TIPÍN | A depressive Palomar widower who was befriended by Carmen and others. | BEM |
| ? | MISS TIPPY | Hector and Blackie's 11th-grade home economics teacher, who was rumored to have given Hector a blowjob. | Hector (mentioned) |
| | TISH | Fritz' high school friend. Delmar's girlfriend. | High Soft Lisp |
| | TITA | Jesús Ángel's second ex-wife. | Luba Conquers the World |
| | TITI | Gato's secretary at his old factory job near Palomar. | Bullnecks and Bracelets |
| | TITO PHOEBUS-APOLLO CALDERÓN | The oldest son of Heráclio and Carmen. He has twin siblings. | Human Diastrophism (mentioned) Be Bop a Luba |
| | TOCO | DECEASED. Jesús' wacky little brother. He died of an illness as a young boy. | Heartbreak Soup |

| Name | Description | First Appearance |
|------|-------------|------------------|
| TODD | A loathsome Hollywood movie producer whom Mike Niznick tried to network with. | Love and Rockets X |
| TOMÁS | One of Luba's employees at her immigration, taxes and beepers business in the U.S. | El Show Super Duper Sensacional de Doralís |
| TOMASO MARÍN | A convicted serial murderer. Socorro's father (with Luba). Tomaso was a migrant worker who was born in Palomar, where he killed his mother. After being away for several years, he returned on an archaeological work detail and committed several murders before he was arrested. | Human Diastrophism |
| TOMOKO ITO | One of Venus' fellow students and soccer teammates. | The New Adventures of Venus |
| TONANSÍN CAROLONGAS | A young woman who briefly dated Manuel and was with him the night he was murdered. | Heartbreak Soup |
| TONANTZÍN VILLASEÑOR | DECEASED. Diana's big sister. A promiscuous young woman who gathered and sold fried babosas on the streets of Palomar. She left town with Khamo and died after she set herself on fire at a political protest. | The Mystery Wen |
| TONYA | A friend of Venus amd Yoshio's. | Letters from Venus |
| TRASCA | A thug who was part of a gang that attacked Sergio and stole his leather jacket. | Mama's Boy |
| TRINCHIS | DECEASED. Manuel's aunt. | Heartbreak Soup |
| TRIX STRANSKI | Steve Stranski's sister. | Love and Rockets X |

| | Name | Description | First Appearance |
|---|---|---|---|
| | TYRONE BONE ("T BONE") | Leticia's boyfriend. A black punk artist who is friends with Junior Brooks and Steve Stranski. | Love and Rockets X |
| | VELENTIA | Bubbles' ex-girlfriend. | Radio Zero |
| | VENUS | Petra's daughter (with Bobby). Luba and Fritz' niece. A precocious girl who loves comic books and writing. | The Gorgo Wheel |
| | VIC | Petra's new husband. Venus' stepfather. | Venus and You |
| | VICENTE | A childhood friend of Satch, Heráclio, Israel and Jesús. A nice guy who was born with a deformed face. He left Palomar with his friend, Saturnino, for the United States, but never crossed the border. He later moved back to Palomar. | Heartbreak Soup |
| | VICTOR | Hector Martínez' friend. | Bread, Love and María |
| | SEÑOR VU | A Cambodian immigrant who hosted Guadalupe when she first arrived in the U.S. as an exchange student. | Love and Rockets X |
| ? | WALTER VILLASEÑOR | DECEASED. Tonantzín and Diana's father. | Children of Palomar (mentioned) |
| | WANDA | Igor's ex-girlfriend. Bambi's friend. | Love and Rockets X |
| | WILLIE | Petra's cynical co-worker at the medical lab. | Meeting Cute, Fucking Cuter |

| Name | Description | First Appearance |
|---|---|---|
| WINONA | Maricela's spoiled ex-girlfriend whom she briefly dated after breaking up with Riri. | A Trick of the Unconscious |
| XIOHMARA | Palomar's resident faith healer ("curandera"). | The Mystery Wen |
| YOLANDA MARIE VÁSQUEZ | Venus' little stepsister. Nicknamed "Yolie." The daughter of Petra and David. She stayed with Petra after the divorce. | The Sisters, the Cousins, and the Kids… |
| YOLIE GARZA | Garza's second wife. | Poison River |
| SEÑOR YORGOS | A well-hung playboy whom Pipo hired to sleep with Guadalupe. | Another Story Altogether |
| YOSHIO YOSHIKI | Venus' best friend. A well-dressed Japanese boy. | Letters from Venus |
| ZANTO | Fortunato's "brother" who was also raised by Galgo as an instrument of revenge against women. Zanto murdered Galgo to save Fortunato. | The Fortunato Files |
| ZENEN | DECEASED. Javier's partner in the black-market baby trade. | Poison River |
| ZEPHIE | DECEASED. Errata Stigmata's sadistic, overweight aunt. Her husband, Ira, murdered her. | Tears From Heaven |
| ZOMBA | Tipín Tipín's ex-lover. | Heartbreak Soup |

| Name | Description | First Appearance |
|---|---|---|
| ZUMAYA | Found innocent of peeping. | The Book of Ofelia |
| DR. ZUMAYA | The Palomar physician whom Manuel briefly worked for. | Heartbreak Soup |

# LETTER COLUMNS AND BROS.' FAVORITES

# LETTER COLUMN HIGHLIGHTS

The sporadic *Love and Rockets* letters pages were an integral part of the overall experience for long-time fans who followed the series over the course of its first 50 issues. These highlights from the frequently funny, often intelligent and occasionally infuriating letters columns (often written by other comics professionals) represent a lively discussion of the series as it was originally published.

## ISSUE #4

The first published letters page appeared in the fourth issue, and it was immediately clear that Fantagraphics had a breakout hit on its hands. However, the introductory columns by Gary Groth that appeared in the first few issues dismayed David John Carltock, who holds the distinction of writing the first letter published. He complained "how is a person supposed to write about what they find good or bad about any given book, if everything of remarkable interest is itemized for you?"

This elicited the first of the many sarcastic responses that were to appear in the letters pages. Groth wrote:

> Our editorial/explanatory overkill may be a result of our perception of the direct-sales market as controlled by the four-color comics sheep, and of *Love and Rockets* as bucking this trend. Apparently, though, long-winded treatises on the nature of comics as art and blow-by-blow descriptions of *L&R* aren't necessaily the best ways to go bringing about a renaissance. (It's also presumptuous as hell.) Our excitement may have gotten the best of us, and we were wrongly trying to sledgehammer the sheep into understanding what the Hernandezes

are doing with the form that nobody else is doing; wrongly because if you buy *L&R* in the first place, you're likely to be sympathetic to its approach. I happen to think that this kind of advocacy criticism is needed, but I agree that the pages of *L&R* isn't the place for it. The work speaks for itself.

Other highlights from the first letter column include:

"Their stories have a naturalism that I've never seen done in any comics and a ring of truth in all of the situations and characters even when it veers off into fantasy or science fiction or surrealism or satire (all of which they handle beautifully)."

— Steve Leialoha

"After having read Gary's editorial I immersed myself in your story; after finishing your story, I immersed myself in Gary's editorial. Those points which had seemed slightly vague became fully understandable. Your story lived up to Gary's words."

— Scott Hampton

"My feeling right now is that Los Brothers Hernandez are going to get better and better with each successive issue [ ... ]"

— Bhob Stewart

## ISSUE #5

"Other little things keep cropping up in my mind like the clothing of the people, the self-reliance of the female characters, certain new wave elements, [ ... ] environments that aren't squeaky clean, healthy politics, writing that puts people before the plot, people who haven't saved the universe from the dreaded space mucus, and the presence of people whom, if I were to meet them, I would care about."

— Bill Pegler

## ISSUE #6

"I like Jaime's stuff best. I love the contemporary fashion and hair styles. Also, you seem to know women pretty well. What's your secret, man? Eleven sisters, 12 girlfriends, or just hanging out on street corners?"

— Steve Rude [as *Steven O. Rude*]

## ISSUE #7

"He's obviously synthesized a variety of influences and come up with a style that combines the best of Will Eisner and Dan de Carlo, with maybe a touch of Steve Ditko thrown in for good measure. It's a very accessible graphic style, with a kind of bare, unadorned quality. There's no attempt to wow the reader with flash, no extraneous detail, no 'gingerbread.' What you see is what you get. Panels are simple and uncluttered, suggesting a kind of relaxed spaciousness. Compositions are strong and simple, figures clean-limbed and attractive."

— Pete Scott on Jaime's "Locas"

## ISSUE #9

"I believe there is a growing movement in this field toward a new gestalt. Talents emerging in the field like the Hernandez brothers, Scott McCloud, Charles Burns, Rick Geary, and ... I include Marc Hempel and myself ... are establishing the look and feel of a generation of comics. There is a real and accurate reflection of the moods of the world in this work. In years to come we'll be able to look back at the obvious effect the work is having around us and vice versa ... but for now it is still too new and too little for me to clearly define it."

— Mark Wheatley, creator of *Mars*

## ISSUE #10

"Jaime, you have joined Gil Kane, Alex Toth, Wally Wood and Joe Kubert as one of my favorite artists. Your people are gorgeous, you draw clothing better than *anyone*, and you use black and white format to its fullest potential."

— Karl Heitmueller, Jr.

"So, women *do* read *Love & Rockets* — and I'm writing this to prove it."

— Kate Coffee

"As a woman, I wanted to thank you for portraying them as interestingly and believably as you do. [A girlfriend of mine] called the other day, and we talked about how we hate the stereotypical portrayal of women as creatures who need a man to get them out of trouble, and I told her that she had better read *Love and Rockets*."

— Monica Sharp

## ISSUE #11

"I've read that you've derived your various styles from this person or that person. I definitely see the *Archie* influence, but I think I see an influence that no one has yet mentioned: *Little Lulu*."

— Bob Moulton

"I've learned a lot about Hispanic thought, life and feeling from these books. At the same time, you've created characters and situations that are universal [ ... ] And please continue to add the translations for us poor gringos and gringas out here. We need the education."

— Christy Marx

## ISSUE #12

"What does Hopey do while Maggie's off in Chepan, sit around and watch *Wheel of Fortune*, or what?"

— Amy Fairweather

"[ ... ] Gilbert ranks with Wolverton as a visualizer of the grotesque."

— John MacLeod

"Having been involved in the hard-core punk scene since around 1978, I really appreciate the fact that the punks in *Love and Rockets* are portrayed as human beings with gen-yoo-wine personalities, rather than the switchblade-wielding Nazi-vermin we were in the mainstream publications."

— Albert Godot

## ISSUE #13

"One of the greatest strengths of *Love and Rockets* has been that the characters change (and even age!) over time. After witnessing Rena Titañon confront her own mortality in *Love and Rockets* #10, the typically 'ageless' comics hero just seems so incredibly shallow!"

— Charles Van Meter

"The punkified 'Archie-ness' of the 'Locas Tambien' stories really caught my attention. But *ahh* ... I never loved Betty and Veronica the way I love Maggie and Hopey. What an intriguing relationship — Maggie seems almost innocent of the lesbian undertones of her friendship with Hopey. Hopey, however, is all too aware of that sexuality. I can't help but wonder how Hopey is affected by Maggie's fickle crushes."

— David Smay

"But *Cheetah Torpedah*!! Holy frijoles! She is *amaz-ing*! As sublime a character as *Astro Boy*, but a whole lot sexier!"

— Kurt Busiek and Adam Philips

*Love and Rockets 1989 Calendar*

"[ ... ] I feel I really know these characters because Jaime can establish strong characterization via lucid, introspective dialogue in a short number of pages. There are no wordy captions explaining the obvious, a fault that sometimes plagues mainstream comics."

— Billy Ford

## ISSUE #14

"I have come to find more and more that plot is inessential to Jaime's work: I am more interested in one page of Maggie and Hopey talking (or, more likely, arguing) than in 30 pages of leotards and lasers. Of course, to get away with a story that concentrates on character, you have to be good enough to convince the reader that your creations have an essence of reality in them, and are not mere plot ciphers. That Jaime succeeds may well be the underlying reason that his work has an almost inexplicable magic to it."

— Andrew Littlefield on
"Las Mujeres Perdidas"

"Jaime has arrived at the wonderful notion of crossing the moody European feel of Moebius or Pratt, with the excellent opportunities for humor that the Bob Montana style affords. This is not, of course, to suggest that he is one of those hopeless copycat types, as his stuff is a unique delight."

— Andrew Littlefield (again)

"Just the other day I was flipping through an issue of the British weekly *Melody Maker*, and in the independent Top 20 list, #13 happened to be a song called 'Ball of Confusion' by none other than Love

*Love and Rockets 1990 Calendar*

HOPEY, MAGGIE, GORGO AND ERRATA

and Rockets. I totally flipped out. I just had to write and let you guys know."

— Donald Odita

## ISSUE #15

"'*Love and Rockets* is the worst piece of trash ever created in the entire history of the comic book. Nothing would make me happier than to be able to trade my copy of issue #1 for a copy of the latest issue of *Marvel Age*.' I don't really mean what I just said, but I'm pretty sure it's never been said before."

— Gary Dunaler

"[ ... ] Gilbert seems to eschew any reference to mainstream comics (lately, anyway) for stylized realism closer to classic newspaper strips of days gone by. His characters and plotting are of a complexity unheard of in this medium. *Real* people, *real* stories, *real* settings, *real* life, with the twist of the fantastic through his wonderful perspective. Gilbert Hernandez is the Fellini of comics."

— Steve Dovas

## ISSUE #16

"Bert. Lose the brush. Like, now. I mean it. Go back to the pen-nib technique you were using. Whoever told you you could ink with a brush *lied*. Okay?"

— Alan D. Oldham

"I compared the Maggie and Hopey of issue #1 to those of issue #14, and their looks have changed very much, in my opinion; even the art itself has. I am glad I noticed that change, as it tells me that Jaime is growing and expanding as an artist and storyteller just as his characters are also experiencing growth and change."

— Alan Larry

"The stories are mostly charming portrayals of realistically flawed characters trying to cope in a world where good and evil are not always black and white, and the latter does not always triumph over the former."

— Joshua M. Ottenberg

## ISSUE #17

"On issue 15: At first, I thought that Maggie would look much better with some added flesh, but she's gaining it all below the midriff and becoming out of proportion."

— J.L. Paine

"[ ... ] How about restoring Maggie's beautiful 120 pound figure?"

— Coby Stites

"I have come up with several suggestions which, I think, will improve the comic. Jaime: More Locas like '100 Rooms' in *Love and Rockets* #4. None of your successive Locas stories have equaled it. Beto: Another all-encompassing 'Heartbreak Soup' is called for. As you did in your first 'Heartbreak Soup,' feature all the inhabitants of Palomar in one long story."

— Patrick J. Lee

## ISSUE #18

"She has become fat and unattractive, lost the wonderful Mechanics figure she had for so long; she has given up the only thing she truly loved to do, by quitting her mechanic job; and she has given up her pursuit of Rand Race. She is working in a fast food joint, when she could be out traveling to exotic places and having great adventures. Maggie is lost, drifting aimlessly because she has found true happiness and given it up, because deep down inside she wants nothing more than to go back to being a Mechanic, but her pride, her sorrow at apparently losing Race won't let her. Since she has left Duke's crew, she is trying to return to the only other life she knows, the dull barrio life of her youth — but even that is not the same."

— Robert T. Jeschonek on Jaime's
"Locas At the Beach"

"The piece was a dark and deep portrait of Jesus, the exile from Palomar, a man who, because he could not possess the idealized woman Luba, destroyed what happiness he had. Beto, I found this piece quite touching and bleak, a sad collage of regrets and fantasies that gave a long and harsh look into the mind of Jesus. Each page conveyed a sense of sorrow and desolation and silence; the story was told with a minimum of words, relying instead on the gray intensity of the images in Jesus' mind."

— Robert T. Jeschonek on Gilbert's
"Holidays in the Sun"

## ISSUE #19

"And has anyone pointed out how well Gilbert writes about (and draws) children? Most of the writers on the Eng.-Lit. syllabus are conspicuous failures in this area — the kids tend to become mere types, or precocious stand-ins for the author."

— Paul Truster on Gilbert's "Duck Feet"

"One of Jaime's strengths is his ability to sketch his characters just enough so that we delight in their interplay because we know them as our friends, but not so fully that we know them too well. If possible, they are not just barrio archetypes, but more human personalities that we see around us, that we date, that we sleep with, that we shun."

— Charles Yoakum, on Jaime's "Locas"

"I've always admired Beto's work a bit more than Jaime's. The impressionistic play of light and dark, plus the textures he achieves with pen and ink add to his carefully thought stories. The Milt Caniff-Chester Gould influence is definitely there. Ever notice that Heraclio resembles Flat Top?"

— L. Faither Adonis

## ISSUE #20

"We the race of cosmic Latin Americans who are the direct descendants of the ancient astronauts who came to the planet Earth from higher developed planets wish to acknowledge that we fully recognize the outstanding contribution which you have made toward the advancement of making human behavior understood within the science of sociology. By way of your curriculum development program known as *Love and Rockets*, you have reached the dimension of explaining the battle of the brains as related to environmental factors that produce a chain reaction with the end result of why people act as they do."

— "Cisco Drake, Educacion Realistica"

That was what can only be described as the single most bizarre letter ever printed in a comic book. The sender, "Cisco Drake," appears to have either an abnormally twisted sense of humor or some kind of mental disorder, as well as extreme homophobic and racist opinions, which, thankfully, were not quite articulate enough to fully understand. As Gary Groth commented, "We advise our readers to take this with a ton of salt."

## ISSUE #21

"[ ... ] It's hit me how drastically *Love and Rockets* has changed the comic book idiom. Cartooning has always been considered a 'low' art form — even its biggest names like Thomas Nast and Herbert Block are hardly regarded as 'classics.' With *Love and Rockets*, however, the comic book could gain its deserved place in the art world; with *Love and Rockets*, the comic book far surpasses the meager advances toward respectability made in recent years by the comic strip; with *Love and Rockets* it could even eclipse the progress most laudably made by animation/cartoons."

— Stephen Farenza

"Times are rough, but your work gives me a joy that pervades my soul. Your talent will be worshipped years later, but fuck that, keep doin' it now, your way, which with that latest 19th outpouring of the enigma and challenge to be human in an inhuman world makes me feel good and makes me cry."

— Joel Stelt

## ISSUE #22

"So Don Thompson thinks that *Love and Rockets* is 'occasionally sexist.' This from a man who gives the *X-Men* and *X-Factor* both "A's" on the grading scale. Well, just for the record, I've always found

Thompson to be pompous and overbearing, not to mention the epitome of the out-of-touch comics freak who feels like he has to go out of his way to show how intelligent he is. This unbelievable judgment just goes to show you *Love and Rockets* is easily the most realistic book I buy (dinosaurs and spaceships aside). I know people who are just like these characters. I have yet to meet anyone as one-dimensional as any of the *X-Men*."

— Karl Heitmueller

## ISSUE #25

"Speedy Ortiz's death was not seen, was not over-dramatized, was not forced upon the reader, and was not eulogized. But it was felt."

— Doug Schell

"Hopey, in my opinion, is the only kind of woman worth loving. She has the 'X' quality. She is clever and independent — interesting and funny. This is rare in the real world and even if it could be found, what chance does a man have against someone like Maggie?"

— Mark Winston

"[ ... ] 'Human Diastrophism' is scaring the shit out of me because I just don't know what to expect next!"

— C.E. Dinkins

## ISSUE #28

There was no letters column in this issue; however, on the inside front cover, Jaime and Gilbert presented "Comics Highly Recommended by the Bros.!" Their recommendations were:

- *The Fun House* by Lynda Barry
- *Joe's Bar* by José Muñoz & Carlos Sampoyo
- *Weirdo* and *Hup!* by R. Crumb
- *Neat Stuff* by Peter Bagge
- *Yummy Fur* by Chester Brown
- *Lloyd Llewellyn* by Dan Clowes

There were also a few interesting notes regarding the brothers' personal lives:

1) "Contrary to what you may have read in certain rags published by Marvel writers and artists, we do not paint houses for a living." ** 2) "We are no longer selling original art." 3) "We have formed a new band called *Nature Boy*, with Jaime on drums, Gilbert on guitar and vocals, and Carol (Gilbert's wife) on bass."

[** This alludes to a situation Gary Groth explained (in an excerpt from the January 1989 *Comics Journal* issue (#126), which has been cut in this reprint), "*WAP!* is a newsletter for comics freelancers edited by Steve Gerber, Steven Grant, and Frank Miller. In their first issue they printed a story — without making any attempt to confirm it — claiming that the Hernandez brothers were paid so poorly for *Love and Rockets* that they were painting Gary Groth's house to make ends meet." Jaime said, "I thought it was pretty chickenshit. Obviously, it was to get at you [Groth]. Maybe they felt bad about hurting our feelings, but we were never approached to begin with."]

## ISSUE #31

"The themes presented in #29 and #30 have been poor ideas because they're not creative, they're destructive. You're not doing romantic drama here, you're doing studies in deviant behavior."

— Brian Catanzaro on Jaime's "Flies on the Ceiling"

"When you draw children, the Hank Ketcham influence really shows. Those first six panels of 'Ninety-Three Million Miles from the Sun,' I expected Mr. Wilson to come yelling 'DENNIS!' at any moment."

— Charlie Harris

"[ ... ] Do you think you could develop a character whose life *wasn't* pure misfortune? Someone who didn't have a miserable, depressing life? Someone I could really care for but *not* pity?"

— Charlie Harris again, referring to the second chapter of Gilbert's "Poison River." Gilbert's reply to Harris: "None of my characters has had a 'miserable, depressing life.' None. And I don't do requests."

The Hernandezes received a backlash to their

*The first six panels from "Ninety-Three Million Miles from the Sun ... " (1988) are reprinted in* The Girl from H.O.P.P.E.R.S.

answers to the letters in issue #31. Many fans were taken aback by their jagged, irritable tone. In an interview titled "Love Bites" with Robert Young for *The Comics Interpreter* #6 (Winter 2001), Jaime noted: "Actually, the few times we did that we were only trying to match the tone of the questions from those particular letters. Little did we know that everybody else in the world were allowed to be assholes but we weren't. That's the way we saw it, anyway."

## ISSUE #33

This issue featured a single, full-page letter from A.C. Fish of Kalamazoo, Mich., titled simply "Clarify Your Positions."

"I've noticed a recent trend [ ... ] among the Hoppers folks and the citizens of Palomar that I feel needs to be addressed. I've seen few examples of parent-hood and other aspects of life merging success-fully. Child care and a career seem to be mutually exclusive. Family planning issues are sporadic to non-existent; abortion is seen as a shameful but necessary form of birth control. People lose their children or else lose their dreams. This has not been my perception of the reality of parenthood. Are either of you guys parents? Have you never witnessed child caregivers who could also fulfill themselves in other ways? Is this something cultural that I, in my lower-middle-class, ethnocentric way, am missing?"

## ISSUE #34

"[ ... ] I am confident you will disregard ideas such as those expressed by A.C. Fish in the last letters section. So-called liberals like Fish are often the first to trumpet the sanctity of human rights, yet it is evident that they have very little tolerance for anything that fails to completely conform to their own dogmatic views. These Zen fascists are just as terrified at the risks inherent in freedom of choice as the Bible-thumping hillbillies of the Right [ ... ] There is no need for you to 'Clarify Your Positions.' Your readers, hopefully, can think for themselves [ ... ] Avoid the pressure of those who would turn *L&R* into a propaganda tool for their version of acceptable behavior."

— Charles Havenden

"A.C. Fish of Kalamazoo [ ... ] had a bit of an axe to grind on the subject of 'weakness' in female characters [ ... ] Here's the kick. Maggie, Hopey, Izzy, Luba, Carmen — the list is very long — are people, not monuments to any cause. They're all fucked up, all wonderful on their own terms [ ... ] I hate to drag you over the coals, A.C. Fish, but your letter is couched in the terms of a social worker — if only social workers spent so much time on such fucked up urban/rural situations in the Real World [ ... ] A.C. Fish, life isn't tidy; it's a great, dirty shitwad and people get dirty and fuck up everyone they give a shit about."

— Paul Sigerson

## ISSUE #36

"Just thought I'd write and say 'hi.'"

— Evan Dorkin

"I think you both sort of romanticize your characters (the straight ones) by making the majority of them so homo-tolerant. My experience has been a lot different [ ... ] growing up [in] north California [ ... ]

I have to keep it to myself/play along the majority of the time [ ... ] You integrate your gay and straight characters in a way that I've never seen possible."

— Andy Pataky

## ISSUE #43

"I remember it as a sunny, lazy day in June or maybe July in 1986, when I discovered my life, a graphic representation of *my* life, sitting in quiet splendor on the shelves of a comics shop. I was 16 years old, full of self-indulgent teenage angst, lonely, confused, death-obsessed, girl-crazy — I felt myself to be completely marginalized, disenfranchised, on the fringes of society ... this is the kind of pretentious haze I waded through at that time. Man, I was primed and ready, so when I walked into the store that afternoon I literally gasped when I saw the cover to the first *Love and Rockets* collection; the image had the impact of a truck. I'm not exaggerating here; I immediately recognized myself and the people I knew at the time as I flipped through the pages [ ... ]

These days when I look back on the older issues they very much define a very important, very special period of my life. Those days are over, I'm not the boy I was, I'm maturing and learning to become a man, and it's a strange thing, but it seems in many ways the magazine is growing with me. Am I wrong in this assumption? *Love and Rockets* is definitely not the same magazine it was years ago, which is one of the things I've always respected most about you. You've always shown that courage to accept the changes that the characters seem to demand, you've always been seen to acknowledge that a work must constantly be defined and redefined, developed and redeveloped in order to sustain any sort of creative vitality.

That said, I do have *some* reservations about the magazine. I feel that in some ways part of the spirit of experimentation has left the book. It seems to me that both of your drawing styles have, in a sense, stagnated (for lack of a better term). Absolutely, they've deepened, developed, grown more into their own unique entities, but I still feel as though both of you have been drawing the same pictures in the same way for years now. Just once I would like to see Beto draw a story with a pen instead of a brush, [ ... ] or for both of you to try some things in color, or for Jaime to try telling a story using completely different characters."

— Ho Che Anderson

## ISSUE #50

The final issue featured a double-page letters column (the first in nearly three years), including 15 letters (and one Hopey-lookalike photo), as well as a heartfelt thanks from the brothers, which spanned both the inside front and back covers. Fantagraphics also used the inside back cover to announce the Hernandezes' plans to launch three solo series — Gilbert's *New Love*, and Jaime's *Whoa, Nellie!* and *Penny Century*. There was no mention of Gilbert's bizarre superhero fantasy, *Girl Crazy*, published by Dark Horse Comics, the first issue of which preceded issue #50 by a couple of weeks (in May 1996).

"Thank you for all your work and heart. It was a rare treat in a spleen-tweezed world"

— Buz Rico

"I do wish you'd consider an idea: An explicit story about Palomar along the lines of *Birdland*. I'd give my left arm (just my left, I draw with my right) to see someone (preferably me) plow Luba's humongous hooters. What position did Guadalupe get pregnant in? What does Pipo look like giving head? OK, OK, I know I'm a pervert, but I know what I like."

— Clifford McDowell

"Your stories ignited my love of comics, which soon after meant I created my own. 'The Death of Speedy' story 'arc' is my all-time favorite comics work. It was great to the 20-year-old back in '89 and still is to me now."

— Andi Watson

"Your comics are perfect and poignant, like the last day of summer."

— Heather

"Never forget the lasting impact you have made in the comics industry, as well as on countless readers."

— Constant Ng

"I just wanted to say, for me, as I'm sure for many others, you've made a huge difference in my life and I'll carry Palomar and Hoppers and all their inhabitants in my heart for a long, long time."

— Zara Waldeback

"Fourteen years has seemed one long lifetime and a half since I got *Love and Rockets* #1 at the tender age of 14 [ ... ] Thanks to Jaime, Gilberto and Mario for showing the rest of us how damn much something as dumb as a comic can affect your life."

— Marc Arsenault

By Gilbert, Jaime and Mario
From *Love and Rockets* Vol. II #10 (Spring 2004)

## 32 REASONS WHY I DO WHAT I DO AND WHY I DO IT THE WAY I DO IT — Jaime

- *Dennis the Menace Giant Christmas Issues* #10 & #11 — Owen Fitzgerald at his darn finest and funnest.
- *Little Archie* #20 — What can I say: Bob Bolling is the main reason I write stories the way I do.
- *Ghost Stories* #1 — John Stanley scaring little kids on his terms.
- *Classics Illustrated* #124: "The War of the Worlds" — A perfect example of fine storyboarding.
- *Zap Comics* #0 — Crumb covered every form of comic storytelling worth telling in one issue.
- *Herbie* #1 — Whew!
- *Fantastic Four* #1 — The one that started it all before it was ruined forever.
- *Bats* #1 — Monster Comics!!!
- *Blazing Combat* #4, *Eerie* #4 and *Creepy* #10 — Finest collection of the greatest comic-book illustrators at the peaks of their careers.
- *Superman* #202: "Tales of the Bizarro World" — The title says it all.
- *Archie* #123 — Harry Lucey, Harry Lucey, Harry Lucey.
- *Superman* #149: "The Death of Superman" — This should not have been an imaginary story.
- *Marvel Tales Annual* #1 — Everybody's origin when they seemed more like monster comics.
- *Heartbreak Soup & Other Stories* — When Gilbert started to really dust me.
- *You're the Greatest, Charlie Brown* — My favorite Sunday-afternoon *Peanuts* collection.
- *Dell Giant* #51: "Tarzan, King of the Jungle" — A big, fat colorful book of reading pleasure by Jesse Marsh.
- *Stupid Comics* — Bagge at his stupidest.
- *Black Cat* #63 — Linda Turner is my favorite movie star.
- *Weirdo* #20 — Excellent collection of the best alternatives at their best.
- "A Funny Night" from *Ernie Pook's Comeek* — Those four panels made my whole childhood flash before my eyes.
- "Ed the Happy Clown" from *Yummy Fur* — The only comic at the time besides Gilbert's that had me running scared.
- *Mad* #70 — More of the finest illustrators doing what they do best.

- *Tales to Astonish* #30 — I don't even own this comic but I know what's in it.
- "Young Dan Pussey" — Fuckin' Dan'l. [Daniel Clowes]
- *Classics Illustrated Junior* #514: "The Steadfast Tin Soldier" — Pure children's enjoyment.
- *Hot Wheels* #5 — That Alex Toth, showin' off.
- *Showcase* #62: "The Inferior Five" — Don't ask me.
- *Archie Giant Series* #23: "Betty & Veronica Summer Fun" — I can't help it; I love fat summer reading comics.
- *Sgt. Fury and His Howling Commandos* #3: "Midnight on Massacre Mountain" — Can never have enough Kirby. Enough? Wait, what about *Dennis the Menace in Mexico?* What about ... ? Arghh ...

## BETO'S GREATEST HITS

### 10 FAVORITE COMICS OR COMIC STORIES:

- *Charlton Premiere* #2: "Children of Doom" by Denny O'Neil and Pat Boyette — The potential of original graphic novels began here with me, a visionary sci-fi epic.
- *Doofus Omnibus* by Rick Altergott — Along with *Stupid Comics* by Pete Bagge and *Portajohnny* by Johnny Ryan, my favorite fucked-up, funny comics.
- "Ducks Yas Yas" in *Zap Comics* #0 by Robert Crumb — A Zonked-out hippie on the bum. You don't read this masterpiece; you live it.
- *Ghost Stories* #1 by John Stanley and various artists — Mainstream monster stories without gore, but a creepier comic I've never seen.
- *I Never Liked You* by Chester Brown — The first, most fully realized graphic novel.
- *Dell Giant* #50: "Marge's Little Lulu and Witch Hazel Trick 'N' Treat" by John Stanley, others — Captures the eerie beauty of Halloween for a kid.

- *Little Archie* #20: "The Long Walk" by Bob Bolling — The sweetest, most heartbreaking story I've ever read in a comic book. Bob Bolling's sensitivity and storytelling skills in so many *Little Archie* stories make him my favorite cartoonist of all.
- *Showcase* #37: "The Metal Men vs. The Flaming Doom" by Bob Kanigher, Ross Andru and Mike Esposito — I guess I'm into tragic robots. I cared that the robot team were all "killed" saving the world.
- "Nightmare Sublime" by Mario Hernandez — Big brother channeling Richard Sala as a goof and turning out a surreal magnum opus in two pages.
- *The Spirit* "Ten Minutes" by Will Eisner — The last 10 minutes of a tragic punk's life.

### 12 FAVORITE COMICS SERIES:

- Lynda Barry collections — Warm philosophical remembrances of childhood.
- *The Black Cat* — Art by Lee Elias. Sexy superheroics from a student of the Caniff school.
- *Classics Illustrated* and *Classics Illustrated Junior* — by various writers and artists. Simplistic versions of classic stories that nonetheless inspired me.
- *Creepy/Eerie/Blazing Combat* 1964-1967 — by Archie Goodwin and various artists. Monster and war comics in glorious black and white.
- *Dennis the Menace* — strip by Hank Ketcham and comic art by Owen Fitzgerald. My favorite kid character.
- *Donald Duck* by Carl Barks — Gives Disney a good name.
- *Eightball* by Dan Clowes — Haunting. The way I like it.
- *Herbie* by Shane O'Shea and Ogden Whitney — The original haunting funny book. The poor artist even ended up in the laughing house.
- *Locas* by Jaime Hernandez — That rare connection of adult storytelling and virtuoso artistry.
- *Mad magazine* 1960s by the Usual Gang of

Idiots — Inspired satire with amazing black-and-white art.

- *Peanuts* by Charles Schulz — The greatest comic strip of all time? Probably.
- *Spider-Man* by Stan Lee and Steve Ditko — My favorite superhero comic of all time. I never cared more about a guy in a costume. The Thing is up there with him, though.

## 16 FAVORITE COMIC ARTISTS:

- Charles Burns — *Black Hole*, stories in *Raw*.
- Roy Crane — *Wash Tubbs, Buz Sawyer*.
- Dan DeCarlo — *Betty and Veronica, She's Josie*.
- Ramona Fradon — *Metamorpho, Brenda Starr*.
- Chester Gould — *Dick Tracy*.
- Jack Kirby — *Fantastic Four, Fourth World*, Marvel monsters, mostly everything else.
- Warren Kremer — *Hot Stuff, Little Dot*.
- Harry Lucey — *Archie*.
- Jesse Marsh — *Tarzan*.
- Jose Muñoz — *Joe's Bar, Sinner,* stories in *Raw* magazine.
- Bruno Premiani — *Doom Patrol*.
- Richard Sala — *Evil Eye*.
- Mike Sekowsky — *JLA,* romance, and sci-fi comics.
- Seth — *Palookaville*.
- Dick Sprang — *Batman*.
- Osamu Tezuka — *Astro Boy*.

## THE BEST OF THE BEAST – Mario

### MY LIST OF FAVORITE COMICS CREATORS (in no particular order)

- Jack Kirby — For all the obvious reasons, but then look at *X-Men* #2 page 17, panel 4 and be awed at simplicity and style.
- Gene Colan — His wash work for the Warren books made me too ashamed to come out from under the bed.

- Alex Toth — I've always had a love/hate relationship with his work but he's THE master of simple design, dang 'im.
- Joe Kubert — His ragged but concise style has charmed me for years. His *Tarzan* rivals my *Tarzan* fave, which brings me to ...
- Jesse Marsh — OK, so everybody loves Russ Manning's beautiful *Tarzan* work, me too, but ... Marsh did the *Tarzan* books for Dell and Gold Key for nigh-on 30 frickin' years, plus Western books, science fiction, adventure, movie adaptations and who-knows-what-else, all with a deft and sometimes sloppy style that changed sometimes with every issue. A master at mood and composition. I can't get enough.
- Gardner Fox/Bob Kanigher/Bob Haney/etc. — The writers of DC during the Silver Age and beyond had imagination and storytelling up the wazoo. OK, so a good number of Marvel and later DC writers kicked major ass, I bow to them, but these guys wrote in such a vast array of genres. Pick up any of the SF or crime anthologies of the day and see what imagination, economy and precision in storytelling is all about.
- The EC Crowd — For bringing a little class (YES, CLASS!) to comics.
- Stan Lee — For creating comics in the modern age. Love him or hate him, we need at least a couple more like him right now to clean house.
- The Masters of Newspaper Strips — [Allen] Saunders and [William] Overgard (rugged style), Milton Caniff, [Frank] Robbins, [Noel] Sickles (that whole school, that despite kicking and screaming, I learned to love), Roy Crane (swoon), Chester Gould (no sissies need apply), Leonard Starr, Hal Foster, Jim Holdaway, Jose Luis Salinas, Gus Arriola, I could go on forever ...
- Walt Kelly — *Peanuts* is the standard to strive for, but for sheer elegance of rendering and turn of phrase, the guy still hasn't been equaled. He could be a king of minicomics today, but he didn't draw shitty.
- The Original Underground Guys and Newer Alternative Gang — Spain, Crumb, [Gilbert]

Shelton, [Daniel] Clowes, [Peter] Bagge, [Steve] Lafler (for sheer cussidness and love of the medium, my mentor), J.R. Williams.

## MY LIST OF THE BEST/FAVORITE COMICS SERIES:

- *Tarzan* (Dell/Gold Key) — I don't know who wrote these but I can pick up just about any issue and find gems in each one of 'em. Standouts include the cool annuals and stories about Boy with his friend Dombie. (With Jesse Marsh art, natch.)
- Marvel Comics of the '60s and '70s — *FF,* Kirby's *Thor,* Ditko's *Spider-Man.* I got hooked like the rest of the world.
- *Deadman* (DC) — Neal Adams and gang had me hooked from the get-go. These guys were rollin'.
- The Archie Universe in the '60s — I own more of this type comic than anything else in my collection.
- *Love and Rockets* — Yeah, I think my brothers are geniuses, what the fuck you gonna do about it?
- *One Year Affair* (*National Lampoon*) —This series came so uncomfortably close to my friends' and my own life, I developed a crush on the female character. Beautifully rendered by Ralph Reese.
- *Doctor Strange* (Marvel) — I gotta give this one its own recognition because it really is so different from the rest of the Marvel universe. Steve Ditko was on a roll with this. Marie Severin stepped up and impressed the hell out of me, and even Gene Colan's vision kept me coming back for more.
- *Mad* magazine, '50s through '60s —All because Xaime looked like Alfred E. Neuman when he was 5, I was hooked and have worn out all my copies.

## MY LIST OF BEST COMIC BOOKS AND STORIES

Things I read as a kid, OK, but still stand up to rereading today: clever, unselfconscious entertainment.

- *Lois Lane* #48: "When Lois Lane Became Cinderella" (DC) — A book-length masterpiece.

Superman gets so fed up with Lois' meddling, trying to find out his secret identity, that he gives her a challenge; he will take her into three different eras in the past (a hot Helen of Troy; Cinderella, complete with Mr. Mxyzptlk as her fairy godmother; and Florence Nightingale, smack in the middle of the Crimean War), then he will disguise himself as a peripheral character and she has to find him out. One of the peaks in storytelling and the best overall issue to me, beautifully realized by the master of Lois, Kurt Schaffenberger.

- *Lady Chatterley's Lover* by Hunt Emerson — Having never read the original, I have only this deliciously hilarious retelling as only Emerson's harebrained genius could tell it. Check out the trembling masturbation and full-page orgasm scenes. A priceless masterpiece.
- *Superman* #149: "The Death of Superman" (DC) — Lex Luthor torturing Superman, who is strapped to a table, writhing under a Kryptonite ray. Luthor on trial like Adolph Eichmann (arrogant until they send his ass to the Phantom Zone). Flower-faced aliens weeping at Superman's funeral. I can barely talk about it (choke) now. A throwaway, book-length imaginary story but it sure kicked my ass. Pass on the new version.
- *Ghost Stories* #1: "The Monster of Dread End … ," "The Werewolf Wasp," "The Door … ," "The Black Stallion" (Dell) — The first two stories, creepily drawn by [Ed Robbins and uncredited], changed the way I felt about slash-and-burn artists. I was always a "pretty image/Alex Raymond school" purist, but this showed me that atmosphere is what makes it good. The shiftily drawn "The Door … " and "Black Stallion" stories rounded out a book that was read and reread and talked about for years at our house.
- *Marge's Little Lulu and Witch Hazel Trick 'N' Treat* (a Dell Giant) — From the first story, "The Little Girl and the Terrible Word," to the last one, "Little Itch's Disappearing Trick" (a story that creeped out me and my 6-year-old), another wonder of [John] Stanley's imaginative storytelling genius.

- *Uncle Scrooge Annual* (a Gold Key Giant) — I picked up a real intense feeling for Carl Barks' genius. Some of his best in a paper-covered over-stuffed annual. A comic I waited three long days to buy at my regular location, closed due to a death in their family. So I waited three days, BFD ... Yeah, you try hanging on to a quarter, 7-8 years old, when that quarter is all the money you'll see for a long while and comics distribution was so shitty, stuff you saw one day at only one location was gone the next and you got other comics and candy, for pity's sake, screamin' atcha from all sides!

- *The Fabulous Furry Freak Brothers* #1 (Rip Off Press) — So they were reprints from somewhere else — who knew, who cared! This is one of the funniest damn comics ever produced. I don't think I've ever recovered from the hernia-inducing laughing I did when I first read it.

# CHECKLIST

| TITLE | No. | STORY TITLE | ARTIST | PUB. DATE | PUBLISHER | NOTES |
|-------|-----|-------------|--------|-----------|-----------|-------|
| **LOVE AND ROCKETS** SERIES (COMIC BOOKS AND SKETCHBOOKS) | | | | | | |
| *Love and Rockets* | 1 | BEM | Gilbert | 1981 | Self-published | |
| - | | Mechan-X | Jaime | | | |
| - | | "How to Kill A ... " By Isabel Ruebens | Jaime | | | |
| - | | Music for Monsters | Gilbert | | | |
| *Love and Rockets* Vol. I | 1 | BEM | Gilbert | Fall 1982 | Fantagraphics | "BEM" expanded from self-published #1 |
| - | | Music for Monsters | Gilbert | | | |
| - | | Mechan-X | Jaime | | | |
| - | | Barrio Huerta | Jaime | | | |
| - | | " ... Penny Century, You're Fired!" | Jaime | | | |
| - | | "How to Kill A ... " By Isabel Ruebens | Jaime | | | |
| - | | Locas Tambien | Jaime | | | |
| - | 2 | Radio Zero | Gilbert | Spring 1983 | | |
| - | | Music for Monsters | Gilbert | | | |
| - | | Mechanics | Jaime | | | |
| - | | Somewhere, in California ... : Part 1 | Mario | | | |
| - | 3 | Sopa De Gran Pena (Heartbreak Soup: Part 1) | Gilbert | Summer 1983 | | |
| - | | Ya Wanna? | Gilbert | | | Renamed "Untitled" — 1 p. surreal strip |
| - | | Locker Room Interviews | Gilbert | | | Renamed "Locker Room" — 1 p. surreal strip |
| - | | Love & Rockets | Jaime | | | |
| - | | Maggie vs. Maniakk | Jaime | | | |

| TITLE | No. | STORY TITLE | ARTIST | PUB. DATE | PUBLISHER | NOTES |
|---|---|---|---|---|---|---|
| *Love and Rockets* Vol. I ...continued | | Locas | Jaime | | | |
| - | | Toyo's Request | Jaime | | | |
| - | | Somewhere, in California ... : Part 2 | Mario | | | |
| - | 4 | Twitch City | Gilbert | Fall 1983 | | |
| - | | Music for Monsters | Gilbert | | | |
| - | | Heartbreak Soup: Part 2 | Gilbert | | | |
| - | | 100 Rooms | Jaime | | | |
| - | | Rocky & Fumble: Out O' Space | Jaime | | | |
| - | 5 | A Fan Letter | Gilbert | March 1984 | | 1st 32 pp. issue |
| - | | Act of Contrition: Part 1 | Gilbert | | | |
| - | | Le Contretemps | Gilbert | | | Errata Stigmata story |
| - | | Locas Starring Hopey | Jaime | | | |
| - | | T42 | Jaime | | | |
| - | | Rocky & Fumble: Retro Rocky | Jaime | | | |
| - | 6 | The Mystery Wen | Gilbert | May 1984 | | |
| - | | Act of Contrition: Part 2 | Gilbert | | | |
| - | | Las Mujeres Perdidas: Part 1 | Jaime | | | |
| - | | Amor y Cohetes | Jaime | | | |
| - | 7 | Act of Contrition: Part 3 | Gilbert | July 1984 | | |
| - | | The Whispering Tree | Gilbert | | | |
| - | | Las Mujeres Perdidas: Part 2 | Jaime | | | |
| - | | Locos | Jaime | | | |
| - | 8 | The Laughing Sun: Part 1 | Gilbert | September 1984 | | |
| - | | On Isidro's Beach | Gilbert | | | |
| - | | Las Mujeres Perdidas: Part 3 | Jaime | | | |
| - | 9 | The Laughing Sun: Part 2 | Gilbert | November 1984 | | |
| - | | Las Mujeres Perdidas: Part 4 | Jaime | | | |

| TITLE | No. | STORY TITLE | ARTIST | PUB. DATE | PUBLISHER | NOTES |
|---|---|---|---|---|---|---|
| *Love and Rockets* Vol. I ...continued | | The Adventures of Rocky and Her Robot Fumble | Jaime | | | |
| - | 10 | Ecce Homo | Gilbert | January 1985 | | 48 pp. issue with 13 pp. excerpt from *Sketchbook* Vol. 1 |
| - | | Ready? Set? Go! | Gilbert | | | 1 p. "thank you" strip |
| - | | Locas | Jaime | | | 1 p. gag strip on inside front cover |
| - | | Las Mujeres Perdidas: Part 5 | Jaime | | | |
| - | 11 | Tears From Heaven | Gilbert | April 1985 | | Errata Stigmata story — written with Mario |
| - | | Las Mujeres Perdidas: Part 6 | Jaime | | | |
| - | | Rocky & Fumble: Where Are We? | Jaime | | | |
| - | 12 | Slug Fest | Gilbert | July 1985 | | |
| | | The Reticent Heart | Gilbert | | | |
| - | | Rocky's Birthday Surprise | Jaime | | | |
| - | 13 | Boys Will Be Boys | Gilbert | September 1985 | | |
| - | | An American in Palomar: Part 1 | Gilbert | | | |
| - | | Locas | Jaime | | | |
| - | | La Toña | Jaime | | | |
| - | | Young Locas | Jaime | | | |
| - | 14 | An American in Palomar: Part 2 | Gilbert | November 1985 | | |
| - | | Locas en las Cabezas | Jaime | | | |
| - | | The Little Monster | Jaime | | | |
| - | 15 | Holidays in the Sun | Gilbert | January 1986 | | |
| - | | Locas At the Beach | Jaime | | | |
| - | | Queen Rena: Life at 34 | Jaime | | | |
| - | 16 | Love Bites | Gilbert | March 1986 | | |
| - | | A True Story | Gilbert | | | Autobiographical story |
| - | | House of Raging Women | Jaime | | | |
| - | 17 | The Way Things're Going | Gilbert | June 1986 | | |

| TITLE | No. | STORY TITLE | ARTIST | PUB. DATE | PUBLISHER | NOTES |
|---|---|---|---|---|---|---|
| *Love and Rockets* Vol. I ...continued | | Duck Feet: Part 1 | Gilbert | | | |
| - | | Locas vs. Locos | Jaime | | | |
| - | | Rocket Rhodes | Jaime | | | |
| - | 18 | Duck Feet: Part 2 | Gilbert | September 1986 | | |
| - | | Locas: 8:01am - 11:15pm | Jaime | | | |
| - | 19 | Bullnecks and Bracelets | Gilbert | January 1987 | | |
| - | | The Secrets of Life and Death Vol. 5 | Jaime | | | |
| - | | Mojado Power! | Jaime | | | |
| - | | Who Says It Never Snows in Zymbodia? | Jaime | | | |
| - | 20 | For the Love of Carmen | Gilbert | April 1987 | | |
| - | | The Return of Ray D. | Jaime | | | |
| - | 21 | Bala | Gilbert | July 1987 | | 1 p. gag strip |
| - | | Human Diastrophism: Part 1 | Gilbert | | | |
| - | | Jerusalem Crickets: 1987 | Jaime | | | |
| - | | Vida Loca: The Death of Speedy Ortiz: Part 1 | Jaime | | | |
| - | 22 | Human Diastrophism: Part 2 | Gilbert | August 1987 | | |
| - | | Jerusalem Crickets | Jaime | | | |
| - | | Vida Loca: The Death of Speedy Ortiz: Part 2 | Jaime | | | |
| - | 23 | Human Diastrophism: Part 3 | Gilbert | October 1987 | | Issue includes the brothers' 15 favorite albums of all time |
| - | | Vida Loca: The Death of Speedy Ortiz: Part 3 | Jaime | | | |
| - | 24 | Human Diastrophism: Part 4 | Gilbert | December 1987 | | |

| TITLE | No. | STORY TITLE | ARTIST | PUB. DATE | PUBLISHER | NOTES |
|---|---|---|---|---|---|---|
| *Love and Rockets* Vol. I ...continued | | The Night Ape Sex Came Home to Play | Jaime | | | |
| - | | Jerry Slum and the Crickettes | Jaime | | | |
| - | | A Mess of Skin ... | Jaime | | | |
| - | 25 | Human Diastrophism: Part 5 | Gilbert | March 1988 | | |
| - | | All This and Penny, Too ... | Jaime | | | |
| - | 26 | Human Diastrophism: Part 6 | Gilbert | June 1988 | | |
| - | | In the Valley of the Polar Bears: Part 1 | Jaime | | | |
| - | 27 | Beep Beep | Gilbert | August 1988 | | 2 pp. surreal strip |
| - | | A Folk Tale | Gilbert | | | |
| - | | In the Valley of the Polar Bears: Part 2 | Jaime | | | |
| - | 28 | Frida | Gilbert | December 1988 | | Biography of painter Frida Kahlo |
| - | | Boxer, Bikini or Brief | Jaime | | | |
| - | | Tear It Up, Terry Downe | Jaime | | | |
| - | | Li'l Ray and the Gang | Jaime | | | |
| - | | Lar' Dog: Boys Night Out #1398 | Jaime | | | |
| - | 29 | Poison River: Part 1 | Gilbert | March 1989 | | |
| - | | Flies on the Ceiling | Jaime | | | |
| - | | El Show de Chota | Jaime | | | Color back cover |
| - | 30 | Poison River: Part 2 | Gilbert | July 1989 | | 48 pp. issue |
| - | | Ninety-Three Million Miles From the Sun ... And Counting | Jaime | | | |
| - | 31 | Poison River: Part 3 | Gilbert | December 1989 | | |
| - | | Love and Rockets X: Part 1 | Gilbert | | | |
| - | | Las Monjas Asesinas | Jaime | | | |
| - | | Spring 1982 | Jaime | | | |
| - | 32 | Poison River: Part 4 | Gilbert | May 1990 | | |

| TITLE | No. | STORY TITLE | ARTIST | PUB. DATE | PUBLISHER | NOTES |
|---|---|---|---|---|---|---|
| *Love and Rockets* Vol. I ...continued | | Love and Rockets X: Part 2 | Gilbert | | | |
| - | | Below My Window Lurks My Head: Part 1 | Jaime | | | |
| - | | ... And In This Corner ... | Jaime | | | |
| - | | Below My Window Lurks My Head: Part 2 | Jaime | | | |
| - | 33 | Poison River: Part 5 | Gilbert | August 1990 | | |
| - | | Love and Rockets X: Part 3 | Gilbert | | | |
| - | | Wigwam Bam: Part 1 | Jaime | | | |
| - | 34 | Poison River: Part 6 | Gilbert | December 1990 | | |
| - | | Love and Rockets X: Part 4 | Gilbert | | | |
| - | | Wigwam Bam: Part 2 | Jaime | | | |
| - | 35 | Poison River: Part 7 | Gilbert | April 1991 | | 40 pp. issue with 6 pp. excerpt from *Sketchbook* Vol. 2 |
| - | | Love and Rockets X: Part 5 | Gilbert | | | |
| - | | Wigwam Bam: Part 3 | Jaime | | | |
| - | 36 | Poison River: Part 8 | Gilbert | November 1991 | | |
| - | | Love and Rockets X: Part 6 | Gilbert | | | |
| - | | Wigwam Bam: Part 4 | Jaime | | | |
| - | 37 | Poison River: Part 9 | Gilbert | February 1992 | | |
| - | | Love and Rockets X: Part 7 | Gilbert | | | |
| - | | Wigwam Bam: Part 5 | Jaime | | | |
| - | 38 | Poison River: Part 10 | Gilbert | June 1992 | | |
| - | | Love and Rockets X: Part 8 | Gilbert | | | |
| - | | Wigwam Bam: Part 6 | Jaime | | | |
| - | | Wigwam Bam: Part 7 | Jaime | | | |

| TITLE | No. | STORY TITLE | ARTIST | PUB. DATE | PUBLISHER | NOTES |
|---|---|---|---|---|---|---|
| *Love and Rockets* Vol. I ...continued | 39 | Poison River: Part 11 | Gilbert | August 1992 | | |
| - | | Love and Rockets X: Part 9 | Gilbert | | | |
| - | | Wigwam Bam: Part 8 | Jaime | | | |
| - | 40 | Poison River: Part 12 | Gilbert | January 1993 | | |
| - | | Somewhere in the Tropics | Mario | | | |
| - | | The Bros Speak | Gilbert, Jaime | | | 1 p. "thank you" strip |
| - | | Chester Square | Jaime | | | |
| - | 41 | Death, God and the Devil Are One | Gilbert | May 1993 | | |
| - | | Another Mysterious Tree | Gilbert | | | |
| - | | Mouth Trap | Gilbert | | | |
| - | | Camp Vicki | Jaime | | | |
| - | 42 | Farewell, My Palomar ... | Gilbert | August 1993 | | |
| - | | Perla and Beatriz | Jaime | | | |
| - | | Easter Hunt | Jaime | | | |
| - | | ... Gonna Make You My Man | Jaime | | | |
| - | 43 | Love Story | Gilbert | December 1993 | | |
| - | | Marilyn Monroe | Gilbert | | | 3 pp. boxing strip |
| - | | Pipo | Gilbert | | | |
| - | | The Navas of Hazel Court | Jaime | | | |
| - | | Our Christmas!!! | Jaime | | | |
| - | | Maggie the Mechanic or Perla the Prostitute | Jaime | | | |
| - | 44 | A Trick of the Unconscious | Gilbert | March 1994 | | |
| - | | It's Not That Big a Deal | Jaime | | | |
| - | 45 | Bread, Love and Maria | Gilbert | July 1994 | | |
| - | | Angelitas | Jaime | | | |
| - | | We Want the World and We Want it Bald ... | Jaime | | | |

| TITLE | No. | STORY TITLE | ARTIST | PUB. DATE | PUBLISHER | NOTES |
|---|---|---|---|---|---|---|
| *Love and Rockets* Vol. I ...continued | | The KKK Comes to Hoppers | Jaime | | | |
| - | | Angelitas Dos | Jaime | | | |
| - | 46 | Hernandez Satyricon | Gilbert | December 1994 | | |
| - | | Carmen | Gilbert | | | Color back cover |
| - | | Butt Sisters | Jaime | | | |
| - | | Son of Butt Sisters | Jaime | | | |
| - | | Return of the Butt Sisters | Jaime | | | |
| - | | War Paint | Jaime | | | Jaime's Palomar story |
| - | 47 | The Gorgo Wheel | Gilbert | April 1995 | | |
| - | | Hester Square | Jaime | | | |
| - | 48 | Luba Conquers the World | Gilbert | August 1995 | | |
| - | | Bob Richardson: Part 1 | Jaime | | | |
| - | 49 | My Love Book | Gilbert | November 1995 | | |
| - | | Bob Richardson: Part 2 | Jaime | | | |
| - | 50 | Chelo's Burden | Gilbert | May 1996 | | 56 pp. final issue |
| - | | Bob Richardson: Part 3 | Jaime | | | |
| - | | Bob Richardson: Part 4 | Jaime | | | |
| - | | Life and Rockets | Mario | | | |
| *Mechanics* | 1 | Penny Century On the Road Ag'in: Part 1 | Jaime | October 1985 | Fantagraphics | Reprints "Mechanics" from *Love and Rockets #2* in color with new .backup stories |
| - | | Hey Hopey | Jaime | | | |
| - | 2 | Penny Century On the Road Ag'in: Part 2 | Jaime | November 1985 | | |
| - | | Meanwhile...Back At the Ranch | Jaime | | | 1 p. interlude to *Mechanics* |
| - | 3 | Locas | Jaime | December 1985 | | 1 p. commentary strip — reprinted in *Bonanza* |
| *Love and Rockets Bonanza* | | Mecanicos | Jaime | March 1989 | Fantagraphics | Two versions featuring Gilbert or Jaime variant covers |
| - | | Welcome to Palomar | Gilbert | | | |

| TITLE | No. | STORY TITLE | ARTIST | PUB. DATE | PUBLISHER | NOTES |
|---|---|---|---|---|---|---|
| *Love and Rockets Bonanza ...continued* | | 24T | Jaime | | | |
| - | | Meanwhile ... Back at the Ranch | Jaime | | | |
| - | | The Goat | Jaime | | | |
| - | | Sugar 'N' Spikes | Gilbert | | | |
| - | | Maggie the Mechanic | Jaime | | | |
| - | | The Many Faces of "Big" Danny Chesterfield | Gilbert | | | |
| - | | Hey Hopey | Jaime | | | |
| - | | A Little Story | Gilbert | | | |
| - | | Locas | Jaime | | | |
| - | | Space Case | Gilbert | | | |
| - | | A Date With Hopey | Jaime | | | |
| *Ten Years Of Love and Rockets* | | Be Bop a Luba | Gilbert | September 1992 | Fantagraphics | Character guide, interviews, short strips |
| - | | Is It Ten Years Already? | Jaime | | | |
| - | | Locas Tambien | Jaime | | | |
| *Love and Rockets Sketchbook* | Vol. 1 | | Gilbert, Jaime | February 1989 | Fantagraphics | |
| - | Vol. 2 | | Gilbert, Jaime | October 1992 | | |
| *Birdland* Vol. 1 | 1 | | Gilbert | October 1990 | Fantagraphics | |
| - | 2 | | Gilbert | February 1991 | | |
| - | 3 | | Gilbert | July 1991 | | |
| *Birdland* Vol. 2 | 1 | | Gilbert | June 1994 | Fantagraphics | |
| *Whoa, Nellie!* | 1 | | Jaime | July 1996 | Fantagraphics | Jaime's first solo series |
| - | 2 | | Jaime | August 1996 | | |
| - | 3 | | Jaime | September 1996 | | |
| *New Love* | 1 | All With a Big Hello | Gilbert | August 1996 | Fantagraphics | |
| - | | Letters From Venus | Gilbert | | | 1st mention of *Grip: The Strange World of Men* |

| TITLE | No. | STORY TITLE | ARTIST | PUB. DATE | PUBLISHER | NOTES |
|---|---|---|---|---|---|---|
| *New Love* ...continued | | Spirit of the Thing | Gilbert | | | Quasi-Palomar "mysterious tree"-themed story |
| - | | Nevermind | Gilbert | | | 1/2 p. Fritz strip |
| - | 2 | Saint Lucy | Gilbert | October 1996 | | 1 p. "Patron Saint" strip |
| - | | Lung of Life | Gilbert | | | 1 p. strip influenced by Joost Swarte's clear line style |
| - | | Letters From Venus: Life on Mars | Gilbert | | | |
| - | | St. Martin de Porres | Gilbert | | | 1 p. "Patron Saint" strip |
| - | | The Fabulous Ones | Gilbert | | | adapts Melville |
| - | | Saint Zita | Gilbert | | | 1 p. "Patron Saint" strip |
| - | | Peripeteia | Gilbert | | | |
| - | | Saint Jude | Gilbert | | | 1 p. "Patron Saint" strip |
| - | 3 | Letters From Venus: Driven by Beauty | Gilbert | March 1997 | | |
| - | | El Show Super Sensacional de Doralis | Gilbert | | | |
| - | | Uncommon Bonds | Gilbert | | | Title changed to "Quackin' in the New Age" |
| - | | Mama's Boy | Gilbert | | | |
| - | | Huh..? Wha..? | Gilbert | | | Parody of Steve Ditko |
| - | 4 | Drink, Fucker! | Gilbert | June 1997 | | |
| - | | Mosquito | Gilbert | | | 1 p. strip — origin of mosquitos |
| - | | Letters From Venus: Who Cares About Love? | Gilbert | | | |
| - | | Equinox, Jr. | Gilbert | | | 1/2 p. strip |
| - | | Father's Day | Gilbert | | | |
| - | | Are the Kids All Right? | Gilbert | | | 3/4 p. "written" by Gary Groth and Seth |
| - | | Roy | Gilbert | | | 1st appearance of Roy and Judith |
| - | | Kidney Stoned Again | Gilbert | | | |

| TITLE | No. | STORY TITLE | ARTIST | PUB. DATE | PUBLISHER | NOTES |
|---|---|---|---|---|---|---|
| *New Love* ...continued | 5 | La Llorna | Gilbert | September 1997 | | |
| - | | Letters From Venus: That Family Thing | Gilbert | | | |
| - | | Heroin | Gilbert | | | 1 p. strip |
| - | | She Sleeps With Anybody But Me | Gilbert | | | |
| - | | Heroin | Gilbert | | | 1 p. strip |
| - | 6 | Letters From Venus: Goddess of Love | Gilbert | December 1997 | | |
| - | | The Slugs of Palomar | Gilbert | | | 1 p. Palomar strip |
| - | | Roy in "Serious Fuckin'" | Gilbert | | | |
| - | | Glorified, Magnified | Gilbert | | | |
| - | | Shout Ramirez | Gilbert | | | |
| - | | Wobbly Buttocks Frenzy | Gilbert | | | Page/panel design experiment |
| - | | Abraxas | Gilbert | | | A follow-up to "Spirit of the Thing" |
| - | | Venus Tells It Like It Is | Gilbert | | | Venus argues in favor of the comic-book medium |
| *Maggie And Hopey Color Fun* | 1 | Maggie and Hopey Color Fun | Jaime | May 1997 | Fantagraphics | Colors by Jeff Johnson, Rhea Patton, Chris Brownrigg and Jaime. Indicia title: *Maggie and Hopey Color Special*, #1 |
| - | | Cocktail Hour with Mini Rivero | Jaime | | | 2 pp. color strip |
| - | | I Am Cheetah Torpeda | Jaime | | | 2 pp. color strip |
| - | | 6 Degrees of Ray D. Ation | Jaime | | | 4 pp. color strip |
| *Penny Century* | 1 | Penny Century | Jaime | December 1997 | Fantagraphics | |
| - | | Fire Water | Jaime | | | 2 pp. gag strip |
| - | | Locas | Jaime | | | |
| - | | La Pantera Negra | Jaime | | | |
| - | | Hopey Hop Sacks | Jaime | | | |
| - | | To Be Announced | Jaime | | | 1 p. color back-cover strip |

| TITLE | No. | STORY TITLE | ARTIST | PUB. DATE | PUBLISHER | NOTES |
|---|---|---|---|---|---|---|
| *Penny Century* ...continued | 2 | Penny Century | Jaime | March 1998 | | |
| - | | Look Out | Jaime | | | |
| - | | To Be Announced | Jaime | | | 1 p. strip |
| - | | Chiller! | Jaime | | | |
| - | | Ya Can't Win 'Em All | Jaime | | | 1 p. strip |
| - | | C'Mon Mom! | Jaime | | | |
| - | | Locas | Jaime | | | Giant Izzy story |
| - | | Space Girl | Jaime | | | 1 p. color back-cover strip |
| - | 3 | Home School | Jaime | September 1998 | | |
| - | | To Be Announced | Jaime | | | 1 p. color back-cover strip |
| - | 4 | Penny Century | Jaime | January 1999 | | |
| - | | Loser Leave Oxnard | Jaime | | | |
| - | | !Inquiritis! | Jaime | | | |
| - | | To Be Announced | Jaime | | | 1 p. strip |
| - | | One More Ladies' Man | Jaime | | | 1st appearance Frogmouth (Vivian Solis) |
| - | | Nobody? So... | Jaime | | | Death of H.R. Costigan |
| - | | Cocktail Hour with Mini Rivero | Jaime | | | 1 p. color back-cover strip |
| - | 5 | Penny Century | Jaime | June 1999 | | |
| - | | Election Day Parts 1 & 2 | Jaime | | | |
| - | | The Littlest Mermaid Princess Doe | Jaime | | | |
| - | | I Am From Earth | Jaime | | | |
| - | | To Be Announced | Jaime | | | 1 p. color back-cover strip |
| - | 6 | The Race | Jaime | November 1999 | | |
| - | | Mag! Look! | Jaime | | | 1 p. color back-cover strip |
| - | 7 | Everybody Loves Me, Baby | Jaime | July 2000 | | Maggie's marriage to Tony Chase |
| - | | Epilogos | Jaime | | | |
| - | | Space Queen | Jaime | | | 1 p. color back-cover strip |

| TITLE | No. | STORY TITLE | ARTIST | PUB. DATE | PUBLISHER | NOTES |
|---|---|---|---|---|---|---|
| *Luba* | 1 | Luba in America: Part 1 | Gilbert | February 1998 | Fantagraphics | |
| - | | The Sisters, the Cousins, and the Kids | Gilbert | | | Khamo's face added to last panel in TPB |
| - | | El Show Super Duper Sensacional de Doralis | Gilbert | | | New page added to TPB |
| - | | That Family Thing Again | Gilbert | | | |
| - | | The Old Man Sets Up! | Gilbert | | | |
| - | | Fuckin' Steve! | Gilbert | | | |
| - | | La Sorpresa | Gilbert | | | |
| - | 2 | Luba in America: Part 2 | Gilbert | July 1998 | | |
| - | | As You Know It | Gilbert | | | New pages (94 and 97) added to TPB |
| - | | Damp and Snuggy | Gilbert | | | |
| - | | All in the Family | Gilbert | | | |
| - | | The Old Man's Touch | Gilbert | | | |
| - | | Pipowear | Gilbert | | | |
| - | 3 | Luba in America: Part 3 | Gilbert | December 1998 | | |
| - | | Poseur | Gilbert | | | Khamo's origin story |
| - | | Luba's Cousin Ofelia | Gilbert | | | |
| - | | A Cada Quien Lo Suyo | Gilbert | | | |
| - | | Spot Marks the Ex | Gilbert | | | Boots arrives in the U.S. |
| - | | Remember Me | Gilbert | | | 1st story in *The Book of Ofelia* |
| - | 4 | El Show Super Duper Sensacional de Doralis | Gilbert | January 2000 | | Doralis comes out to her mother |
| - | | Boots Takes the Case | Gilbert | | | Follow-up to "Spot Marks the Ex" |
| - | | Firstborn | Gilbert | | | |
| - | | Bromear | Gilbert | | | |
| - | 5 | Luba | Gilbert | October 2000 | | |
| - | | Kisses for Pipo | Gilbert | | | |
| - | | Snail Trail | Gilbert | | | |

| TITLE | No. | STORY TITLE | ARTIST | PUB. DATE | PUBLISHER | NOTES |
|---|---|---|---|---|---|---|
| *Luba* ...continued | | El Baile | Gilbert | | | |
| - | 6 | Luba | Gilbert | Spring 2002 | | |
| - | | Meeting Cute, Fucking Cuter | Gilbert | | | |
| - | | El Show Super Duper Sensacional Fantastico de Doralis | Gilbert | | | |
| - | | The Goddess and the Goof | Gilbert | | | |
| - | | Buen Viaje, Socorro | Gilbert | | | |
| - | 7 | The Beloved and the Damned | Gilbert | Summer 2003 | | |
| - | | Luba's Science Lesson | Gilbert | | | |
| - | | And Justice For Some | Gilbert | | | |
| - | | Uno Dos Tres | Gilbert | | | |
| - | 8 | Luba | Gilbert | Summer 2004 | | |
| - | | The Tao of Doralis | Gilbert | | | |
| - | | The Fortunato Files | Gilbert | | | Fortunato's origin story |
| - | | Sergio Rocks | Gilbert | | | |
| - | | Guadalupe | Gilbert | | | |
| - | | Luba Again | Gilbert | | | |
| - | | Click! | Gilbert | | | |
| - | 9 | La Luba | Gilbert | Fall 2004 | | |
| - | | Burning For You | Gilbert | | | |
| - | | Pipo's Burden | Gilbert | | | |
| - | | Of Two Minds | Gilbert | | | |
| - | | But the Little Girls Understand | Gilbert | | | |
| - | | Luba | Gilbert | | | |
| - | | Fritz and Pipo, Sittin' in a Tree... | Gilbert | | | |
| - | | God Willing | Gilbert | | | |
| - | 10 | Luba | Gilbert | Winter 2004/05 | | Sergio and Gato die |
| *Luba's Comics and Stories* | 1 | Memories of Sweet Youth | Gilbert | March 2000 | Fantagraphics | Fritz and Petra issue |
| - | | Venus Gives Us the Lowdown | Gilbert | | | |

| TITLE | No. | STORY TITLE | ARTIST | PUB. DATE | PUBLISHER | NOTES |
|---|---|---|---|---|---|---|
| *Luba's Comics and Stories* ...continued | 2 | In Bed With Pipo | Gilbert | December 2000 | | Pipo issue |
| - | 3 | The Book of Ofelia | Gilbert | December 2002 | | Ofelia and the Little Ones issue |
| - | | Ask Luba | Gilbert | | | |
| - | | The Book of Ofelia 2 | Gilbert | | | |
| - | 4 | The Light of Venus | Gilbert | June 2004 | | Venus issue |
| - | | The Glamorous Life | Gilbert | | | |
| - | | The Big Picture | Gilbert | | | |
| - | 5 | Hector | Gilbert | September 2004 | | Lovers and Hector issue |
| - | | Khamo | Gilbert | | | |
| - | | Fortunato | Gilbert | | | |
| - | | Lovers and Hector | Gilbert | | | |
| - | 6 | Luba | Gilbert | November 2005 | | Petra, Luba and Fritz issue |
| - | | Rosalba | Gilbert | | | |
| - | | Petra | Gilbert | | | |
| - | | Three Daughters | Gilbert | | | |
| - | 7 | Fritz After Dark | Gilbert | January 2006 | | |
| - | 8 | Another Story Altogether | Gilbert | June 2006 | | Guadalupe issue |
| - | | Luba in America 2 | Gilbert | | | Doralis dies |
| *Measles* | 1 | The New Adventures of Venus | Gilbert | December 1998 | Fantagraphics | Kid's anthology with Jaime and Gilbert, Johnny Ryan, Joost Swarte and others |
| - | | Space on the Loose! | Mario | | | |
| - | 2 | The New Adventures of Venus | Gilbert | April 1999 | | Venus and Fritz go to Space Fun |
| - | | Venus | Gilbert | | | |
| - | | The Legend of Celestra | Mario | | | |
| - | | La Blanca | Jaime | | | 2 pp. strip |
| - | 3 | The New Adventures of Venus | Gilbert | Summer 1999 | | Venus' soccer game |
| - | | Los Super Sonicos | Jaime | | | 2 pp. strip |
| - | | Uncle Frankenstein | Mario | | | |

| TITLE | No. | STORY TITLE | ARTIST | PUB. DATE | PUBLISHER | NOTES |
|---|---|---|---|---|---|---|
| *Measles* ...continued | 4 | The New Adventures of Venus: Parts 1 and 2 | Gilbert | Summer 1999 | | Venus makes a comic strip for her sister |
| - | | Los Super Sonicos | Jaime | | | 1 p. color back-cover strip |
| - | 5 | The New Adventures of Venus | Gilbert | Winter 2000 | | Venus celebrates Xmas |
| - | | Santa Claus From Other Planets | Gilbert | | | 1 p. strip |
| - | | Y2K Coloring Page | Gilbert | | | 1 p. strip |
| - | | The Fake Santa Claus | Jaime | | | 2 pp. strip |
| - | | Christmas With Los Super Sonicos | Jaime | | | 1 p. color back-cover strip |
| - | 6 | La Venus | Gilbert | Spring 2000 | | 2 pp. strip |
| - | | Birthday Bash | Mario | | | |
| - | 7 | Venus | Gilbert | January 2001 | | 1 p. strip |
| - | 8 | The New Adventures of Venus | Gilbert | August 2001 | | Surreal tribute to the Measles contributors |
| - | | Los Super Sonicos | Jaime | | | 4 pp. strip |
| *Love and Rockets* Vol. II | 1 | Julio's Day: Part 1 | Gilbert | Spring 2001 | Fantagraphics | |
| - | | Me For the Unknown: Part 1 | Gilbert | | | Written by Mario |
| - | | Buzzin' | Gilbert | | | 1 p. strip |
| - | | Maggie: Part 1 | Jaime | | | |
| - | 2 | Julio's Day: Part 2 | Gilbert | Summer 2001 | | |
| - | | Me For the Unknown: Part 2 | Gilbert | | | Written by Mario |
| - | | Erratic Stigmatic | Gilbert | | | Tears From Heaven follow-up |
| - | | Maggie: Part 2 | Jaime | | | |
| - | 3 | Julio's Day: Part 3 | Gilbert | Fall 2001 | | |
| - | | Me For the Unknown: Part 3 | Gilbert | | | Written by Mario |
| - | | The High Soft Lisp: Part 1 | Gilbert | | | |
| - | | The Neuterbrank Primer | Gilbert | | | Roy color strip — back cover |
| - | | Maggie: Part 3 | Jaime | | | |
| - | 4 | Me For the Unknown: Part 4 | Gilbert | Summer 2002 | | Written by Mario |

| TITLE | No. | STORY TITLE | ARTIST | PUB. DATE | PUBLISHER | NOTES |
|---|---|---|---|---|---|---|
| *Love and Rockets* Vol. II ...continued | | 1 page - Misc strips | Gilbert | | | Use of a Corpse Hand, Roy, etc. |
| - | | The High Soft Lisp: Part 2 | Gilbert | | | |
| - | | Julio's Day: Part 4 | Gilbert | | | |
| - | | Maggie: Part 4 | Jaime | | | |
| - | | Maggie: Part 5 | Jaime | | | |
| - | | The Frogmouth | Jaime | | | |
| - | 5 | Our Return | Gilbert | Summer 2002 | | Surreal strip |
| - | | Roy and Judith | Gilbert | | | Roy strip — 1 p. |
| - | | Me For the Unknown: Part 5 | Gilbert | | | Written by Mario |
| - | | Confirmation | Gilbert | | | Surreal strip |
| - | | The High Soft Lisp: Part 3 | Gilbert | | | |
| - | | Julio's Day: Part 5 | Gilbert | | | 1 p. |
| - | | Bay of Threes | Jaime | | | |
| - | 6 | Toco | Gilbert | Winter 2002/03 | | |
| - | | Kid Stuff | Gilbert | | | |
| - | | Julio's Day: Part 6 | Gilbert | | | 1 p. |
| - | | 30,000 Hours to Kill | Gilbert | | | Roy strip — 4 pp., 55 tiny panels per page |
| - | | Peterson | Gilbert | | | Surreal strip |
| - | | Me For the Unknown: Part 6 | Gilbert | | | Written by Mario |
| - | | Maggie: Part 6 | Jaime | | | |
| - | 7 | Me For the Unknown: Part 7 | Gilbert | Spring 2003 | | Written by Mario |
| - | | The High Soft Lisp: Part 4 | Gilbert | | | |
| - | | Julio's Day: Part 7 | Gilbert | | | 1 p. |
| - | | Maggie: Part 7 | Jaime | | | |
| - | 8 | She's Only Crying | Gilbert | Summer 2003 | | |
| - | | The Little Stunt Boy in "The Art of the Deal" | Gilbert | | | |
| - | | Julio's Day: Part 8 | Gilbert | | | 1 p. |
| - | | The High Soft Lisp: Part 5 | Gilbert | | | |
| - | | Maggie: Part 8 | Jaime | | | |
| - | | Modern Marzipan: 1957 | Mario | | | 1 p. color back-cover strip (unsigned) |

| TITLE | No. | STORY TITLE | ARTIST | PUB. DATE | PUBLISHER | NOTES |
|---|---|---|---|---|---|---|
| *Love and Rockets* Vol. II ...continued | 9 | The High Soft Lisp: Part 6 | Gilbert | Fall 2003 | | |
| - | | Julio's Day: Part 9 | Gilbert | | | 1 p. |
| - | | Me For the Unknown: Part 8 | Gilbert | | | Written by Mario |
| - | | Maggie: Part 9 | Jaime | | | |
| - | 10 | Julio's Day: Part 10 | Gilbert | Spring 2004 | | |
| - | | Whatever Happened to...? | Gilbert | | | |
| - | | Roy and His Pals in "Monsters and Heroes" | Gilbert | | | Roy strip |
| - | | Me For the Unknown: Part 9 | Gilbert | | | Conclusion Written by Mario |
| - | | Reflections the Day After | Gilbert | | | |
| - | | Maggie: Part 10 | Jaime | | | |
| - | 11 | Dumb Solitaire | Gilbert | Fall 2004 | | |
| - | | The Kid Stuff Kids Return in "Intellectual Pursuit" | Gilbert | | | |
| - | | Shindleria Praematurus | Gilbert | | | Surreal strip — written by Mario |
| - | | Julio's Day: Part 11 | Gilbert | | | |
| - | | Stars Sweet Home | Jaime | | | 1 p. strip |
| - | | Life Through Whispers | Jaime | | | |
| - | | Who Is Rena Titañon? | Jaime | | | 4 pp. strip |
| - | 12 | Julio's Day: Part 12 | Gilbert | November 2004 | | |
| - | | A Gift For Venus | Gilbert | | | |
| - | | The Kid Stuff Kids in "Sea Hog Serenade" | Gilbert | | | Back cover to *L&R* Vol. 2 #12 (originally in color, later collected in black and white) |
| - | | 2 'R's, 2 'L's | Jaime | | | |
| - | | Hagler and Hearns | Jaime | | | |
| - | | Day By Day With Hopey: Tuesday is Whose Day? | Jaime | | | |
| - | | Ser O No Ser | Jaime | | | |

| TITLE | No. | STORY TITLE | ARTIST | PUB. DATE | PUBLISHER | NOTES |
|-------|-----|-------------|--------|-----------|-----------|-------|
| *Love and Rockets* Vol. II ...continued | 13 | Song of the Sea Hog | Gilbert | March 2005 | | |
| - | | The Kid Stuff Kids | Gilbert | | | |
| - | | Julio's Day: Part 13 | Gilbert | | | |
| - | | Angel of Tarzana | Jaime | | | |
| - | | Day By Day With Hopey: Wednesday is Bitter Ends Day | Jaime | | | |
| - | | Angel of Tarzana | Jaime | | | |
| - | | Did Ya Get Got? | Jaime | | | |
| - | | Angel of Tarzana | Jaime | | | |
| - | | Cream City | Jaime | | | |
| - | 14 | Baby Talk | Gilbert | July 2005 | | |
| - | | Julio's Day: Part 14 | Gilbert | | | |
| - | | The Kid Stuff Kids | Gilbert | | | |
| - | | Where the Heart Is | Gilbert | | | |
| - | | The Divining Runes of Merro Mosso | Gilbert | | | 1 p. strip — written by Mario |
| - | | Home Sweet Stars | Jaime | | | 2 pp. strip |
| - | | The Divining Runes of Merro Mosso | Mario | | | |
| - | | Day By Day With Hopey: Thursday is Her's Day | Jaime | | | |
| - | | Day By Day With Hopey: Friday is Jai Alai Day | Jaime | | | |
| - | 15 | The Kid Stuff Kids | Gilbert | November 2005 | | |
| - | | On a Gut Level | Gilbert | | | |
| - | | Day By Day With Hopey: Saturday is Shatterday | Jaime | | | |
| - | | Near Mint | Jaime | | | |
| - | | Angels of Tarzana | Jaime | | | |
| - | 16 | The Kid Stuff Kids Starring in "Down in Heaven" | Gilbert | Spring 2006 | | |
| - | | Fine to Very Fine | Jaime | | | |

| TITLE | No. | STORY TITLE | ARTIST | PUB. DATE | PUBLISHER | NOTES |
|---|---|---|---|---|---|---|
| *Love and Rockets* Vol. II ...continued | | Day By Day With Hopey: Sunday is Put That Gun Down Day | Jaime | | | |
| - | 17 | Blackouting | Gilbert | Summer 2006 | | |
| - | | Julio's Day: Part 15 | Gilbert | | | |
| - | | God's Eye View | Gilbert | | | |
| - | | Day By Day With Hopey: Monday is Attila the Hun Day | Jaime | | | |
| - | | Day By Day With Hopey: Tuesday is ... One More Tuesday | Jaime | | | |
| - | 18 | Pattern For Living | Gilbert | Winter 2006/07 | | |
| - | | Julio's Day: Part 16 | Gilbert | | | |
| - | | Yes, God | Gilbert | | | 1 p. strip about God (not reprinted) |
| - | | Trampas Pero No Trampan | Jaime | | | |
| - | 19 | Julio's Day: Part 17-18 | Gilbert | Spring 2007 | | Conclusion |
| - | | Emanon | Gilbert | | | Surreal strip |
| - | | Male Torso Found in L.A. River | Jaime | | | |
| - | | Uk Utirr Tagual Tor Zok | Jaime | | | |
| - | | Rocks Over Rocks | Jaime | | | |
| - | 20 | Venus and You: Parts 1-3 | Gilbert | Summer 2007 | | |
| - | | Untitled | Gilbert | | | |
| - | | You People | Gilbert | | | 1 p. strip |
| - | | The High Road | Gilbert | | | 1 p. strip |
| - | | La Maggie La Loca - Expanded version | Jaime | | | Expanded version of the 2006 *New York Times* "Funny Pages" *Locas* strip |
| - | | Gold Diggers of 1969 | Jaime | | | Unreprinted at press time |
| *New Tales Of Old Palomar* | | The Children of Palomar Part 1 | Gilbert | November 2006 | Fantagraphics | Part of the oversized Ignatz series |
| - | | The Children of Palomar Part 2 | Gilbert | March 2007 | | |
| - | | The Children of Palomar Part 3 | Gilbert | November 2007 | | |

| TITLE | No. | STORY TITLE | ARTIST | PUB. DATE | PUBLISHER | NOTES |
|---|---|---|---|---|---|---|
| *Love and Rockets: New Stories* | 1 | The Funny Papers | Gilbert | Summer 2008 | Fantagraphics | Squarebound annuals |
| - | | Papa | Gilbert | | | |
| - | | The New Adventures of Duke and Sammy | Gilbert | | | |
| - | | Victory Dance | Gilbert | | | Julio's Day tie-in |
| - | | Chiro el Indio | Gilbert | | | Written by Mario |
| - | | Never Say Never | Gilbert | | | Surreal strip |
| - | | ? | Gilbert | | | Surreal strip |
| - | | Ti-Girls Adventures: Part One: The Search for Penny Century | Jaime | | | |
| - | | Ti-Girls Adventures: Part Two: Penny Is Found | Jaime | | | |
| - | 2 | Sad Girl | Gilbert | Summer 2009 | | |
| - | | Hypnotwist | Gilbert | | | Fritz B movie |
| - | | Ti-Girls Adventures: Part Three: Daughters of Doom | Jaime | | | |
| - | | Ti-Girls Adventures: Part Four: Mothers of Mercy | Jaime | | | |
| - | 3 | Scarlet By Starlight | Gilbert | Summer 2010 | | Fritz B movie |
| - | | Killer * Sad Girl * Star | Gilbert | | | |
| - | | The Love Bunglers: Part One | Jaime | | | |
| - | | Browntown | Jaime | | | |
| - | | The Love Bunglers: Part Two | Jaime | | | |
| - | 4 | King Vampire | Gilbert | Summer 2011 | | Fritz B movie |
| - | | And Then Reality Kicks In | Gilbert | | | |
| - | | The Love Bunglers: Part Three | Jaime | | | |
| - | | The Love Bunglers: Part Four | Jaime | | | |
| - | | Return For Me | Jaime | | | |
| - | | The Love Bunglers: Part Five | Jaime | | | |

| TITLE | No. | STORY TITLE | ARTIST | PUB. DATE | PUBLISHER | NOTES |
|---|---|---|---|---|---|---|
| *Love and Rockets: New Stories* ...continued | 5 | Somewhere Outside the U.S. Border | Gilbert | Summer 2012 | | |
| - | | Tonta | Jaime | | | |
| - | | Proof That The Devil Loves You | Gilbert | | | Fritz B movie |
| - | | Crime Raiders International Mobsters and Executioners | Jaime | | | |
| - | | Somewhere in the U.S. | Gilbert | | | |
| - | | Uh...Oh, Yeah | Jaime | | | |
| - | | Shoes | Jaime | | | |
| - | | And Back Again | Gilbert | | | |

# *LOVE AND ROCKETS* REPRINTS
## (COLLECTIONS AND GRAPHIC NOVELS)

| TITLE | No. | STORY TITLE | ARTIST | PUB. DATE | PUBLISHER | NOTES |
|---|---|---|---|---|---|---|
| *The Complete Love and Rockets* Vol. 1: *Music for Mechanics* | | Introduction by Carter Scholz | | September 1985 | Fantagraphics | |
| - | | Mechan-X | Jaime | | | |
| - | | Locas Tambien | Jaime | | | |
| - | | "How to Kill A ... " By Isabel Ruebens | Jaime | | | |
| - | | BEM | Gilbert | | | |
| - | | Barrio Huerta | Jaime | | | |
| - | | " ... Penny Century, You're Fired!" | Jaime | | | |
| - | | Music for Monsters: Part 1 | Gilbert | | | |
| - | | Mecanicos | Jaime | | | |
| - | | Mechanics | Jaime | | | |
| - | | Radio Zero | Gilbert | | | |
| - | | Music for Monsters: Part 2 | Gilbert | | | |
| - | | Somewhere, in California ... : Part 1 | Mario | | | |
| - | | A Little Story | Gilbert | | | |
| - | | Cover Gallery | | | | |

| TITLE | No. | STORY TITLE | ARTIST | PUB. DATE | PUBLISHER | NOTES |
|---|---|---|---|---|---|---|
| *The Complete Love and Rockets* Vol. 2: *Chelo's Burden* | | Preface by Gary Groth | | June 1986 | Fantagraphics | |
| - | | Sopa de Gran Pena | Gilbert | | | |
| - | | Love and Rockets | Jaime | | | |
| - | | Maggie vs. Maniakk | Jaime | | | |
| - | | Music for Monsters: Part 3 | Gilbert | | | |
| - | | Hey Hopey | Jaime | | | |
| - | | Untitled | Gilbert | | | |
| - | | 100 Rooms | Jaime | | | |
| - | | Twitch City | Gilbert | | | |
| - | | Toyo's Request | Jaime | | | |
| - | | Locas Tambien | Jaime | | | |
| - | | Somewhere, in California ... : Part 2 | Mario | | | |
| - | | Out O' Space | Jaime | | | |
| - | | Locker Room | Gilbert | | | |
| - | | Cover Gallery | | | | |
| *Love and Rockets: Short Stories* | | Carter Scholz introduction | | August 1987 | Fantagraphics | repackaged in the hopes of gaining a foothold in the bookstore market |
| - | | 100 Rooms | Jaime | | | |
| - | | Mechan-X | Jaime | | | |
| - | | Locas | Jaime | | | |
| - | | Mechanicos | Jaime | | | |
| - | | Love and the Rocket | Jaime | | | |
| - | | Love and Rockets | Jaime | | | |
| - | | Hey Hopey | Jaime | | | |
| - | | Toyo's Request | Jaime | | | |
| - | | Locas Tambien | Jaime | | | |
| - | | Penny Century: On the Road Ag'in | Jaime | | | |
| - | | Locas Starring Hopey | Jaime | | | |
| - | | T42 | Jaime | | | |

| TITLE | No. | STORY TITLE | ARTIST | PUB. DATE | PUBLISHER | NOTES |
|---|---|---|---|---|---|---|
| *Heartbreak Soup and Other Stories* | | Alan Moore Introduction | | August 1987 | Fantagraphics | Repackaged in the hopes of gaining a foothold in the bookstore market |
| - | | Sopa de Gran Pena | Gilbert | | | |
| - | | The Mystery Wen | Gilbert | | | |
| - | | Radio Zero | Gilbert | | | |
| - | | Twitch City | Gilbert | | | |
| - | | Act of Contrition | Gilbert | | | |
| - | | Fan Letter | Gilbert | | | |
| - | | Untitled | Gilbert | | | |
| - | | Locker Room | Gilbert | | | |
| - | | The Laughing Sun | Gilbert | | | |
| - | | A Little Story | Gilbert | | | |
| *The Complete Love and Rockets Vol. 3: Las Mujeres Perdidas* | | The Lost Women (Las Mujeres Perdidas) | Jaime | August 1987 | Fantagraphics | Originally appeared under the internal series title "Mechanics"; the story arc is collected here as "The Lost Women" ("*Las Mujeres Perdidas*") |
| - | | Fan Letter | Gilbert | | | |
| - | | Cover Gallery | Gilbert, Jaime | | | |
| - | | Act of Contrition | Gilbert | | | |
| - | | Le Contretemps | Gilbert | | | |
| - | | The Whispering Tree | Gilbert | | | |
| - | | The Laughing Sun | Jaime | | | |
| - | | A Date With Hopey | Jaime | | | |
| *The Complete Love and Rockets Vol. 4: Tears from Heaven* | | Tears From Heaven | Gilbert | January 1988 | Fantagraphics | |
| - | | Penny Century: On the Road Ag'in | Jaime | | | |
| - | | Amor y Cohetes | Jaime | | | |
| - | | Isidro's Beach | Gilbert | | | |
| - | | Locas Starring Hopey | Jaime | | | |
| - | | Slug Fest | Gilbert | | | |
| - | | Ready Set Go | Gilbert | | | |

| TITLE | No. | STORY TITLE | ARTIST | PUB. DATE | PUBLISHER | NOTES |
|---|---|---|---|---|---|---|
| *The Complete Love and Rockets* Vol. 4: *Tears from Heaven* ...continued | | Cover Gallery | Gilbert, Jaime, Mario | | | |
| - | | Locas | Jaime | | | |
| - | | Ecce Homo | Gilbert | | | |
| - | | T42 | Jaime | | | |
| - | | Locos | Jaime | | | |
| - | | Retro Rocky | Jaime | | | |
| - | | Rocky: Where Are We? | Jaime | | | |
| - | | Rocky's Birthday | Jaime | | | |
| - | | The Reticent Heart | Gilbert | | | |
| - | | The Many Faces of "Big" Danny Chesterfield | Gilbert | | | |
| *The Lost Women and Other Stories* | | Introduction by Brad Holland | | May 1988 | Fantagraphics | Repackaged in the hopes of gaining a foothold in the bookstore market |
| - | | Young Locas | Jaime | | | |
| - | | The Lost Women | Jaime | | | |
| - | | Locas en Las Cabezas | Jaime | | | |
| - | | The Little Monster | Jaime | | | |
| - | | At the Beach | Jaime | | | |
| - | | Locas | Jaime | | | |
| - | | Queen Rena: Life at 34 | Jaime | | | |
| - | | House of Raging Women | Jaime | | | |
| - | | A Date with Hopey | Jaime | | | |
| *The Reticent Heart and Other Stories* | | Harvey Pekar Introduction | | May 1988 | Fantagraphics | Repackaged in the hopes of gaining a foothold in the bookstore market |
| - | | Sugar 'N' Spikes | Gilbert | | | |
| - | | Isidro's Beach | Gilbert | | | |
| - | | Ecce Homo | Gilbert | | | |
| - | | Space Case | Gilbert | | | |
| - | | Slug Fest | Gilbert | | | |

| TITLE | No. | STORY TITLE | ARTIST | PUB. DATE | PUBLISHER | NOTES |
|---|---|---|---|---|---|---|
| *The Reticent Heart and Other Stories* ...continued | | The Reticent Heart | Gilbert | | | |
| - | | The Way Things're Going | Gilbert | | | |
| - | | The Whispering Tree | Gilbert | | | |
| - | | Love Bites | Gilbert | | | |
| - | | An American in Palomar | Gilbert | | | |
| - | | Holidays in the Sun | Gilbert | | | |
| - | | For the Love of Carmen | Gilbert | | | |
| - | | Tears From Heaven | Gilbert | | | |
| - | | A True Story | Gilbert | | | |
| - | | | | | | |
| *The Complete Love and Rockets* Vol. 5: *House of Raging Women* | | La Tona | Jaime | September 1988 | Fantagraphics | |
| - | | The Little Monster | Jaime | | | |
| - | | Queen Rena Life at 34 | Jaime | | | |
| - | | A True Story | Gilbert | | | |
| - | | An American in Palomar | Gilbert | | | |
| - | | Boys Will Be Boys | Gilbert | | | |
| - | | Young Locas | Jaime | | | |
| - | | Locas | Jaime | | | |
| - | | Locas en las Cabezas | Jaime | | | |
| - | | Locas at the Beach | Jaime | | | |
| - | | House of Raging Women | Jaime | | | |
| - | | Holidays in the Sun | Gilbert | | | |
| - | | Love Bites | Gilbert | | | |
| - | | The Adventures of Maggie the Mechanic | Jaime | | | |
| - | | Cover Gallery | | | | |

| TITLE | No. | STORY TITLE | ARTIST | PUB. DATE | PUBLISHER | NOTES |
|---|---|---|---|---|---|---|
| *The Complete Love and Rockets* Vol. 6: *Duck Feet* | | The Mystery Wen | Gilbert | May 1989 | Fantagraphics | |
| - | | Rocky and Fumble | Jaime | | | |
| - | | The Way Things're Going | Gilbert | | | |
| - | | Locas | Jaime | | | |
| - | | Locas vs. Locos | Jaime | | | |
| - | | Duck Feet | Gilbert | | | |
| - | | Locas | Jaime | | | |
| - | | Secrets of Life and Death | Jaime | | | |
| - | | Bullnecks and Bracelets | Gilbert | | | |
| - | | Mojado Power! | Jaime | | | |
| - | | Rena | Jaime | | | |
| - | | Rocket Rhodes | Jaime | | | |
| - | | For the Love of Carmen | Gilbert | | | |
| - | | Cover Gallery | Gilbert, Jaime | | | |
| *The Complete Love and Rockets* Vol. 7: *The Death of Speedy* | | The Return of Ray D. | Jaime | November 1989 | Fantagraphics | |
| - | | The Death of Speedy Ortiz | Jaime | | | |
| - | | Jerusalem Crickets: 1987 | Jaime | | | |
| - | | Jerusalem Crickets: The Letter | Jaime | | | |
| - | | Jerry Slum and the Crickettes | Jaime | | | |
| - | | The Night Ape Sex Came Home to Play | Jaime | | | |
| - | | A Mess of Skin ... | Jaime | | | |
| - | | All This and Penny, Too ... | Jaime | | | |
| - | | In the Valley of the Polar Bears | Jaime | | | |
| - | | Cover Gallery | Jaime | | | |

| TITLE | No. | STORY TITLE | ARTIST | PUB. DATE | PUBLISHER | NOTES |
|---|---|---|---|---|---|---|
| *The Complete Love and Rockets* Vol. 8: *Blood of Palomar* | | Welcome to Palomar | Gilbert | December 1989 | Fantagraphics | |
| - | | Sugar 'N' Spikes | Gilbert | | | |
| - | | Space Case | Gilbert | | | |
| - | | Heraclio's Burden | Gilbert | | | |
| - | | The Cast of Characters in "Human Diastrophism" | Gilbert | | | |
| - | | Human Diastrophism | Gilbert | | | Substantially altered from its initial appearance in *Love and Rockets* #21-#26 |
| - | | Cover Gallery and Chapter Headings | Gilbert | | | |
| *The Complete Love and Rockets* Vol. 9: *Flies on the Ceiling* | | Flies on the Ceiling | Jaime | October 1991 | Fantagraphics | |
| - | | Bala | Gilbert | | | |
| - | | Boxer, Bikini or Brief | Jaime | | | |
| - | | Tear it Up, Terry Downe | Jaime | | | |
| - | | Li'l Ray | Jaime | | | |
| - | | Frida | Gilbert | | | |
| - | | Lar'dog: Boy's Night Out #1398 | Jaime | | | |
| - | | Ninety-Three Million Miles From the Sun ... And Counting | Jaime | | | |
| - | | Beep Beep | Gilbert | | | |
| - | | Las Monjas Asesinas | Jaime | | | |
| - | | Below My Window Lurks My Head Part 1 | Jaime | | | |
| - | | ... And in This Corner ... | Jaime | | | |
| - | | Below My Window Lurks My Head Part 2 | Jaime | | | |
| - | | A Folk Tale | Gilbert | | | |

| TITLE | No. | STORY TITLE | ARTIST | PUB. DATE | PUBLISHER | NOTES |
|---|---|---|---|---|---|---|
| *The Complete Love and Rockets* Vol. 9: *Flies on the Ceiling* ...continued | | Spring 1982 | Jaime | | | |
| - | | El Show de Chota | Jaime | | | |
| - | | Cover Gallery | Gilbert, Jaime | | | |
| *The Complete Love and Rockets* Vol. 10: *Love and Rockets X* | | Love and Rockets X | Gilbert | May 1993 | Fantagraphics | |
| - | | Cover Gallery and Cast of Characters | Gilbert | | | |
| *Love and Rockets* Vol. 11: *Wigwam Bam* | | Wigwam Bam Parts 1- 8 | Jaime | March 1994 | Fantagraphics | |
| - | | Gonna Make You My Man ... | Jaime | | | |
| - | | Cover Gallery | Jaime | | | |
| *The Complete Love and Rockets* Vol. 12: *Poison River* | | Poison River Parts 1-17 | Gilbert | September 1994 | Fantagraphics | |
| - | | Cover Gallery | Gilbert | | | |
| *The Complete Love and Rockets* Vol. 13: *Chester Square* | | Chester Square | Jaime | July 1996 | Fantagraphics | |
| - | | Camp Vicki | Jaime | | | |
| - | | Perla and Beatriz | Jaime | | | |
| - | | The Navas of Hazel Court | Jaime | | | |
| - | | Maggie the Mechanic or Perla the Prostitute | Jaime | | | |
| - | | It's Not That Big a Deal | Jaime | | | |
| - | | Angelitas | Jaime | | | |
| - | | We Want the World and We Want it Bald ... | Jaime | | | |
| - | | Angelitas Dos | Jaime | | | |
| - | | Butt Sisters | Jaime | | | |

| TITLE | No. | STORY TITLE | ARTIST | PUB. DATE | PUBLISHER | NOTES |
|---|---|---|---|---|---|---|
| *The Complete Love and Rockets* Vol. 13: *Chester Square* ...continued | | Son of Butt Sisters | Jaime | | | |
| - | | Return of the Butt Sisters | Jaime | | | |
| - | | Hester Square | Jaime | | | |
| - | | Bob Richardson | Jaime | | | |
| - | | Cover Gallery | Jaime | | | |
| *The Complete Love and Rockets* Vol. 14: *Luba Conquers the World* | | Be Bop a Luba | Gilbert | December 1996 | Fantagraphics | |
| - | | Character guide | Gilbert | | | |
| - | | Farewell, My Palomar | Gilbert | | | |
| - | | A Trick of the Unconscious | Gilbert | | | |
| - | | The Way Things Went | Gilbert | | | |
| - | | Pipo | Gilbert | | | |
| - | | Carmen | Gilbert | | | |
| - | | Another Mysterious Tree | Gilbert | | | |
| - | | "Gorgo Has Seen the Business of Blood ... " | Gilbert | | | |
| - | | Mouth Trap | Gilbert | | | |
| - | | Love Story | Gilbert | | | |
| - | | Bread, Love and Maria | Gilbert | | | |
| - | | The Gorgo Wheel | Gilbert | | | |
| - | | Luba Conquers the World | Gilbert | | | |
| - | | Chelo's Burden | Gilbert | | | |
| - | | Cover Gallery | Gilbert | | | |
| *The Complete Love and Rockets* Vol. 15: *Hernandez Satyricon* | | Hernandez Satyricon | Gilbert | August 1997 | Fantagraphics | |
| - | | War Paint | Jaime | | | |

| TITLE | No. | STORY TITLE | ARTIST | PUB. DATE | PUBLISHER | NOTES |
|---|---|---|---|---|---|---|
| *The Complete Love and Rockets* Vol. 15: *Hernandez Satyricon* ...continued | | Somewhere in the Tropics | Mario | | | |
| - | | Marilyn Monroe | Gilbert | | | |
| - | | The KKK Comes to Hoppers | Jaime | | | |
| - | | Death, God and the Devil Are One | Gilbert | | | |
| - | | Life and Rockets | Mario | | | |
| - | | My Love Book | Gilbert | | | |
| - | | Our Christmas!!! | Jaime | | | |
| - | | Easter Hunt | Jaime | | | |
| - | | Is It Ten Years Already? | Jaime | | | |
| - | | Through the Years | Gilbert, Jaime | | | Includes a variety of covers and illustrations for mixed media |
| - | | Heartbreak Soup | Gilbert | | | Unpublished, unfinished strip |
| - | | Beto and Carol in "It's Not The Motion, It's The Meat" | Gilbert | | | With wife Carol Kovinick, originally printed in *Weirdo* #25 (1989) |
| - | | Love and Rockets | Gilbert, Jaime | | | Originally appeared in Capital City distributor's catalog 1994 |
| - | | Say, Man ... | Gilbert | | | Originally appeared in *Details* magazine |
| - | | Boy Chick in "Takin' It To The Streets" | Gilbert | | | Originally appeared in *Slant* magazine 1995 |
| - | | Calendar Art | Gilbert, Jaime | | | Illustrations |
| - | | Cover Gallery | Gilbert, Jaime | | | |
| *The Complete Love and Rockets* Vol. 16: *Whoa Nellie!* | | Whoa Nellie! #1-#3 | Jaime | June 2000 | Fantagraphics | |
| - | | pin-ups, Cover Gallery | | | | |

| TITLE | No. | STORY TITLE | ARTIST | PUB. DATE | PUBLISHER | NOTES |
|---|---|---|---|---|---|---|
| *The Complete Love and Rockets* Vol. 17: *Fear of Comics* | | All With a Big Hello | Gilbert | October 2000 | Fantagraphics | Includes comics from *New Love* #1-#6, *Hate*, *Goody Good Comics*, *Zero Zero*, *Vortex* and *UG!3K* |
| - | | The Spirit of the Thing | Gilbert | | | |
| - | | Nevermind | Gilbert | | | |
| - | | Roy | Gilbert | | | |
| - | | The Fabulous Ones | Gilbert | | | |
| - | | Moby Dick | Gilbert | | | |
| - | | A Gallery of Humanitarians and Beloved Martyrs | Gilbert | | | |
| - | | Return of the Tzik | Gilbert | | | Reprinted from *Vortex* #7 |
| - | | Shout Ramiriz | Gilbert | | | |
| - | | Lung of Life | Gilbert | | | |
| - | | Peripeteia | Gilbert | | | |
| - | | Drink, Fucker! | Gilbert | | | |
| - | | Mosquito | Gilbert | | | |
| - | | Equinox Jr. | Gilbert | | | |
| - | | You Don't Change a Person's Mind, He Just Stops Arguing | Gilbert | | | |
| - | | Extinct Animals | Gilbert | | | |
| - | | Father's Day | Gilbert | | | |
| - | | Gilbert "Beto" Hernandez | Gilbert | | | |
| - | | Wilson in "Kidney Stoned" | Gilbert | | | |
| - | | Are the Kids All Right? | Gilbert | | | |
| - | | Twelve-Forty-Two | Gilbert | | | |
| - | | Love Swine | Gilbert | | | |
| - | | "Me" | Gilbert | | | Written by Peter Bagge, reprinted from *Hate* #26 |
| - | | La Llorna | Gilbert | | | |
| - | | She Sleeps with Anybody But Me | Gilbert | | | |
| - | | Abraxas | Gilbert | | | |
| - | | A Piercing Denial | Gilbert | | | From *UG!3K* |
| - | | Glorified, Magnified | Gilbert | | | |

| TITLE | No. | STORY TITLE | ARTIST | PUB. DATE | PUBLISHER | NOTES |
|---|---|---|---|---|---|---|
| *The Complete Love and Rockets* Vol. 17: *Fear of Comics* ...continued | | Wobbly Buttocks Frenzy | Gilbert | | | |
| - | | The Shit Eaters | Gilbert | | | Reprinted from *Zero Zero* |
| - | | Extend the Hand of Love to All | Gilbert | | | A Roy story, reprinted from *Goody Good Comics #1* |
| - | | The Slugs of Palomar | Gilbert | | | |
| - | | Within Reason | Gilbert | | | |
| - | | Heroin 1-3 | Gilbert | | | |
| - | | Roy in "Serious Fuckin'" | Gilbert | | | |
| *The Complete Love and Rockets* Vol. 18: *Locas in Love* | | Maggie and Hopey Color Fun (parts 1-4) | Jaime | October 2000 | Fantagraphics | 26 pp. of color. From *Penny Century #1-#4* and *Maggie and Hopey Color Fun*. "La Blanca" is from *Measles* |
| - | | Cocktail Hour With Mini Rivero: Parts 1 & 2 | Jaime | | | |
| - | | I Am Cheetah Torpedah | Jaime | | | |
| - | | 6 Degrees of Ray D. Ation | Jaime | | | |
| - | | Penny Century 1, 2, 3 | Jaime | | | |
| - | | Fire Water | Jaime | | | |
| - | | Locas | Jaime | | | |
| - | | La Pantera Negra | Jaime | | | |
| - | | Hopey Hop Sacks | Jaime | | | |
| - | | To Be Announced 1, 2, 3 | Jaime | | | |
| - | | Look Out | Jaime | | | |
| - | | Chiller! | Jaime | | | |
| - | | You Can't Win 'Em All | Jaime | | | |
| - | | C'mon Mom! | Jaime | | | |
| - | | Locas | Jaime | | | |
| - | | Space Girl | Jaime | | | |

| TITLE | No. | STORY TITLE | ARTIST | PUB. DATE | PUBLISHER | NOTES |
|---|---|---|---|---|---|---|
| *The Complete Love and Rockets* Vol. 18: *Locas in Love* ...continued | | Loser Leaves Oxnard | Jaime | | | |
| - | | ¡Inquiritis! | Jaime | | | |
| - | | One More Ladies' Man | Jaime | | | |
| - | | Nobody? So ... | Jaime | | | |
| - | | La Blanca | Jaime | | | |
| - | | Home School | Jaime | | | |
| *The Complete Love and Rockets* Vol. 19: *Luba in America* | | El Show de Doralis | Gilbert | 2001 | Fantagraphics | *Luba in America* is the first volume of a trilogy starring Palomar's matriarchal figure. Volume 2 is *Luba: The Book of Ofelia*, and Volume 3 is *Luba: Three Daughters* |
| - | | Letters From Venus | Gilbert | | | |
| - | | Letters From Venus: Life on Mars | Gilbert | | | |
| - | | Venus | Gilbert | | | |
| - | | Letters From Venus: Driven By Beauty | Gilbert | | | |
| - | | El Show Super Sensacional de Doralis | Gilbert | | | |
| - | | Quackin' in the New Age | Gilbert | | | |
| - | | Mama's Boy | Gilbert | | | |
| - | | Driven by Beauty: A Beto Burlesque | Gilbert | | | |
| - | | Letters From Venus: Who Cares About Love? | Gilbert | | | |
| - | | Kidney Stoned Again | Gilbert | | | |
| - | | Letters From Venus: That Family Thing | Gilbert | | | |
| - | | Letters From Venus: Goddess of Love | Gilbert | | | |

| TITLE | No. | STORY TITLE | ARTIST | PUB. DATE | PUBLISHER | NOTES |
|---|---|---|---|---|---|---|
| *The Complete Love and Rockets* Vol. 19: *Luba in America* ...continued | | Luba in America: Chapter One | Gilbert | | | |
| - | | The Sisters, the Cousins, and the Kids | Gilbert | | | |
| - | | El Show Super Duper Sensacional de Doralis | Gilbert | | | |
| - | | That Family Thing Again | Gilbert | | | |
| - | | The Old Man Sets Up | Gilbert | | | |
| - | | Fuckin' Steve! | Gilbert | | | |
| - | | La Sorpresa | Gilbert | | | |
| - | | Luba in America: Chapter Two | Gilbert | | | |
| - | | As You Know It | Gilbert | | | |
| - | | Damp and Snuggy | Gilbert | | | |
| - | | All in the Family | Gilbert | | | |
| - | | Pipowear | Gilbert | | | |
| - | | Luba in America: Chapter Three | Gilbert | | | |
| - | | Poseur | Gilbert | | | |
| - | | Luba's Cousin Ofelia | Gilbert | | | |
| - | | A Cada Quien lo Suyo | Gilbert | | | |
| - | | Memories of Sweet Youth | Gilbert | | | |
| - | | Venus Gives us the Lowdown! | Gilbert | | | |
| - | | El Show Super Duper Sensacional de Doralis | Gilbert | | | |
| - | | Firstborn | Gilbert | | | |
| - | | Venus Tells it Like it is! | Gilbert | | | |
| - | | Cover Gallery and Inside Front Cover Art | Gilbert | | | |

| TITLE | No. | STORY TITLE | ARTIST | PUB. DATE | PUBLISHER | NOTES |
|---|---|---|---|---|---|---|
| *The Complete Love and Rockets* Vol. 20: *Dicks and Deedees* | | Penny Century | Jaime | June 2003 | Fantagraphics | Material originally appeared in *Penny Century* #5-7 and *Love and Rockets* Vol. 2 #4-5 |
| - | | Election Day (Part 1) | Jaime | | | |
| - | | The Little Mermaid Princess Doe | Jaime | | | |
| - | | Election Day (Part 2) | Jaime | | | |
| - | | I Am From Earth | Jaime | | | |
| - | | The Race | Jaime | | | |
| - | | To Be Announced | Jaime | | | |
| - | | Mag Look! | Jaime | | | |
| - | | Everybody Loves Me Baby | Jaime | | | |
| - | | Bay of Threes | Jaime | | | |
| - | | Space Queen | Jaime | | | |
| - | | The Frogmouth | Jaime | | | |
| *The Complete Love and Rockets* Vol. 21: *Luba: The Book of Ofelia* | | Remember Me | Gilbert | December 2005 | Fantagraphics | Material originally appeared in *Luba* #3-#10, *Luba's Comics and Stories* #2-#5, and *Measles* #3 |
| - | | Luba and the Kids | Gilbert | | | |
| - | | Luba | Gilbert | | | |
| - | | The Book of Ofelia | Gilbert | | | |
| - | | Spot Marks the Ex | Gilbert | | | |
| - | | El Show Super Duper Sensacional Fantastico de Doralis | Gilbert | | | |
| - | | Snail Trail | Gilbert | | | |
| - | | Bromear | Gilbert | | | |
| - | | Meeting Cute, Fucking Cuter | Gilbert | | | |
| - | | Buen Viaje Socorro | Gilbert | | | |
| - | | Luba | Gilbert | | | |
| - | | The Fortunato Flies | Gilbert | | | |
| - | | The Goddess and the Goof | Gilbert | | | |
| - | | El Baile | Gilbert | | | |

| TITLE | No. | STORY TITLE | ARTIST | PUB. DATE | PUBLISHER | NOTES |
|---|---|---|---|---|---|---|
| *The Complete Love and Rockets* Vol. 21: *Luba: The Book of Ofelia* ...continued | | The Glamorous Life | Gilbert | | | |
| - | | Boots Takes the Case | Gilbert | | | |
| - | | And So ... | Gilbert | | | |
| - | | Kisses for Pipo | Gilbert | | | |
| - | | In Bed With Pipo | Gilbert | | | |
| - | | Luba | Gilbert | | | |
| - | | Uno Dos Tres | Gilbert | | | |
| - | | The New Adventures of Venus | Gilbert | | | |
| - | | The Beloved and the Damned | Gilbert | | | |
| - | | Luba's Science Lesson | Gilbert | | | |
| - | | And Justice for Some | Gilbert | | | |
| - | | The Tao of Doralis | Gilbert | | | |
| - | | Hector | Gilbert | | | |
| - | | Sergio Rocks | Gilbert | | | |
| - | | Luba Again | Gilbert | | | |
| - | | Click! | Gilbert | | | |
| - | | La Luba | Gilbert | | | |
| - | | Burning for You | Gilbert | | | |
| - | | Pipo's Burden | Gilbert | | | |
| - | | Of Two Minds | Gilbert | | | |
| - | | But the Little Girls Understand | Gilbert | | | |
| - | | Luba | Gilbert | | | |
| - | | Fritz and Pipo Sittin' in a Tree ... | Gilbert | | | |
| - | | God Willing | Gilbert | | | |
| - | | Luba | Gilbert | | | |
| *The Complete Love and Rockets* Vol. 22: *Ghosts of Hoppers* | | Maggie: Parts 1-10 | Jaime | December 2005 | Fantagraphics | Material originally appeared in *Love and Rockets* Vol. 2 #1-4, #6-#10 |

| TITLE | No. | STORY TITLE | ARTIST | PUB. DATE | PUBLISHER | NOTES |
|---|---|---|---|---|---|---|
| *The Complete Love and Rockets Vol. 23: Luba: Three Daughters* | | Ask Luba | Gilbert | November 2006 | Fantagraphics | Material originally appeared in *Luba's Comics and Stories* #3, 4, 6, 8; *Measles* #1; and *Love and Rockets* Vol. 2 #6, #11–#16 |
| - | | The Petra Question | Gilbert | | | 1st appearance of story |
| - | | Mystery of the Sea Hog | Gilbert | | | 1st appearance of story |
| - | | Message from an Ex | Gilbert | | | 1st appearance of story |
| - | | A Gift for Venus | Gilbert | | | |
| - | | The New Adventures of Venus | Gilbert | | | |
| - | | The Light of Venus | Gilbert | | | |
| - | | The Big Picture | Gilbert | | | |
| - | | For Art's Sake | Gilbert | | | 1st appearance of story |
| - | | Luba | Gilbert | | | |
| - | | Petra | Gilbert | | | |
| - | | Rosalba | Gilbert | | | |
| - | | Who the Fuck is Hector? | Gilbert | | | 1st appearance of story |
| - | | Sister, Thithter | Gilbert | | | 1st appearance of story (not reprinted in *Luba* oversized hardcover) |
| - | | Something About Pipo | Gilbert | | | 1st appearance of story |
| - | | Ms. Super Fit USA | Gilbert | | | 1st appearance of story |
| - | | Three Daughters | Gilbert | | | |
| - | | Hector's 2¢ | Gilbert | | | 1st appearance of story |
| - | | Day Job | Gilbert | | | 1st appearance of story |
| - | | Kid Stuff | Gilbert | | | |
| - | | The Kid Stuff Kids in "Sea Hog Serenade" | Gilbert | | | |
| - | | The Kid Stuff Kids Return in "Intellectual Pursuit" | Gilbert | | | |
| - | | The Kid Stuff Kids | Gilbert | | | |

| TITLE | No. | STORY TITLE | ARTIST | PUB. DATE | PUBLISHER | NOTES |
|---|---|---|---|---|---|---|
| *The Complete Love and Rockets Vol. 23: Luba: Three Daughters* ...continued | | The Kid Stuff Kids starring in "Down in Heaven" | Gilbert | | | |
| - | | Luba's Daughter Guadalupe in "Another Story Altogether" | Gilbert | | | |
| - | | Genetically Predisposed | Gilbert | | | 1st appearance of story |
| - | | Luba in America Part 2 | Gilbert | | | |
| - | | | | | | |
| *The Complete Love and Rockets Vol. 24: The Education of Hopey Glass* | | Day by Day with Hopey | Jaime | February 2008 | Fantagraphics | Material originally appeared in *Love and Rockets* Vol. 2 #11-#19 |
| - | | Angel of Tarzana | Jaime | | | |
| - | | Life Through Whispers | Jaime | | | |
| - | | 2 'R's, 2'L's | Jaime | | | |
| - | | Hagler and Hearns | Jaime | | | |
| - | | Ser O No Ser | Jaime | | | |
| - | | Did Ya Get Got? | Jaime | | | |
| - | | Cream City | Jaime | | | |
| - | | Near Mint | Jaime | | | |
| - | | Angels of Tarzana | Jaime | | | |
| - | | Fine to Very Fine | Jaime | | | |
| - | | Trampas Pero No Trampan | Jaime | | | |
| - | | Male Torso Found in L.A. River | Jaime | | | |
| - | | Uk Utirr Tagual Tor Zok | Jaime | | | |
| - | | Rocks Over Rocks | Jaime | | | |
| *The Complete Love and Rockets* Vol. 25: *High Soft Lisp* | | Dumb Solitaire | Gilbert | January 2010 | Fantagraphics | Material originally appeared in *Love and Rockets* Vol. II and *Luba's Comics and Stories* |
| - | | The High Soft Lisp | Gilbert | | | 7 new pp. added to original story |

| TITLE | No. | STORY TITLE | ARTIST | PUB. DATE | PUBLISHER | NOTES |
|---|---|---|---|---|---|---|
| *The Complete Love and Rockets* Vol. 25: *High Soft Lisp* ...continued | | Song of the Sea Hog | Gilbert | | | |
| - | | Where the Heart Is | Gilbert | | | |
| - | | Baby Talk | Gilbert | | | |
| - | | Her Only True Love | Gilbert | | | |
| - | | On a Gut Level | Gilbert | | | |
| - | | Fritz After Dark | Gilbert | | | |
| - | | God's Eye View | Gilbert | | | 2 new pp. added to original story |
| - | | Blackouting | Gilbert | | | 2 new pp. added to original story |
| - | | Pattern for Living | Gilbert | | | 1 new p. added to original story |
| *The Complete Love and Rockets Vol. 26: God and Science: Return of the Ti-Girls* | | Ti-Girls Adventures: Parts 1-5 | Jaime | April 2012 | Fantagraphics | Includes material from Love and Rockets: New Stories Vol. 1 and Vol. 2 plus 30 new pages |
| *Palomar: The Heartbreak Soup Stories* | | Chelo's Burden | Gilbert | August 2003 | Fantagraphics | Oversized hardcover collection |
| - | | Sopa de Gran Pena | Gilbert | | | |
| - | | Act of Contrition | Gilbert | | | |
| - | | Ecce Homo | Gilbert | | | |
| - | | An American in Palomar | Gilbert | | | |
| - | | Love Bites | Gilbert | | | |
| - | | Duck Feet | Gilbert | | | |
| - | | Human Diastrophism | Gilbert | | | |
| - | | Farewell, My Palomar | Gilbert | | | |
| - | | Luba Conquers the World | Gilbert | | | |
| - | | Epilogue: Chelo's Burden. | Gilbert | | | |
| - | | | | | | |

| TITLE | No. | STORY TITLE | ARTIST | PUB. DATE | PUBLISHER | NOTES |
|-------|-----|-------------|--------|-----------|-----------|-------|
| *Luba* | | El Show de Doralís | Gilbert | 2009 | Fantagraphics | Oversized hardcover collecting *Luba in America*, *The Book of Ofelia*, *Three Daughters* and content from *Luba's Comics And Stories* |
| - | | Letters from Venus | Gilbert | | | |
| - | | The New Adventures of Venus | Gilbert | | | |
| - | | Life on Mars | Gilbert | | | |
| - | | Venus | Gilbert | | | |
| - | | Driven by Beauty | Gilbert | | | |
| - | | El Show Super Sensacional de Doralis | Gilbert | | | |
| - | | Quackin' in The New Age | Gilbert | | | |
| - | | Mama's Boy | Gilbert | | | |
| - | | Huh..? Wha.?! | Gilbert | | | From *New Love* |
| - | | Who Cares About Love? | Gilbert | | | |
| - | | Kidney Stoned Again | Gilbert | | | |
| - | | That Family Thing | Gilbert | | | |
| - | | Goddess of Love | Gilbert | | | |
| - | | Luba in America (Chapter One) | Gilbert | | | |
| - | | The Sisters, The Cousins and the Kids ... | Gilbert | | | |
| - | | El Show Super Duper Sensacional de Doralis | Gilbert | | | |
| - | | That Family Thing Again | Gilbert | | | |
| - | | The Old Man Sets Up! | Gilbert | | | |
| - | | Fuckin' Steve! | Gilbert | | | |
| - | | Luba in America (Chapter Two) | Gilbert | | | |
| - | | As You Know It | Gilbert | | | |
| - | | Damp and Snuggy | Gilbert | | | |
| - | | All in the Family | Gilbert | | | |
| - | | Pipowear! | Gilbert | | | |

| TITLE | No. | STORY TITLE | ARTIST | PUB. DATE | PUBLISHER | NOTES |
|---|---|---|---|---|---|---|
| *Luba* ...continued | | Luba in America (Chapter Three) | Gilbert | | | |
| - | | Poseur | Gilbert | | | |
| - | | Luba's Cousin Ofelia | Gilbert | | | |
| - | | A Cada Quien Lo Suyo | Gilbert | | | |
| - | | Memories of Sweet Youth | Gilbert | | | |
| - | | La Sorpresa | Gilbert | | | |
| - | | Venus Gives Us the Lowdown! | Gilbert | | | |
| - | | El Show Super Duper Sensacional de Doralis | Gilbert | | | |
| - | | Firstborn | Gilbert | | | |
| - | | Venus Tells It Like It Is! | Gilbert | | | |
| - | | Remember Me | Gilbert | | | |
| - | | Luba and the Little Ones | Gilbert | | | |
| - | | Luba | Gilbert | | | |
| - | | The Book of Ofelia | Gilbert | | | |
| - | | Spot Marks the Ex | Gilbert | | | |
| - | | El Show Super Duper Sensacional Fantastico de Doralis | Gilbert | | | |
| - | | Snail Trail | Gilbert | | | |
| - | | Bromear | Gilbert | | | |
| - | | Meeting Cute, Fucking Cuter | Gilbert | | | |
| - | | Buen Viaje, Socorro | Gilbert | | | |
| - | | Luba | Gilbert | | | |
| - | | The Fortunato Files | Gilbert | | | |
| - | | The Goddess and the Goof | Gilbert | | | |
| - | | El Baile | Gilbert | | | |
| - | | The Glamorous Life | Gilbert | | | |
| - | | Boots Takes the Case | Gilbert | | | |
| - | | And So ... | Gilbert | | | |
| - | | Kisses for Pipo | Gilbert | | | |

| TITLE | No. | STORY TITLE | ARTIST | PUB. DATE | PUBLISHER | NOTES |
|---|---|---|---|---|---|---|
| *Luba* ...continued | | In Bed With Pipo | Gilbert | | | |
| - | | Luba | Gilbert | | | |
| - | | Uno Dos Tres | Gilbert | | | |
| - | | The New Adventures of Venus | Gilbert | | | |
| - | | The Beloved and the Damned | Gilbert | | | |
| - | | Luba's Science Lesson | Gilbert | | | |
| - | | And Justice for Some | Gilbert | | | |
| - | | The Tao of Doralis | Gilbert | | | |
| - | | Hector | Gilbert | | | |
| - | | Khamo | Gilbert | | | |
| - | | Hector | Gilbert | | | |
| - | | Fortunato | Gilbert | | | |
| - | | Hector | Gilbert | | | |
| - | | Lovers and Hector | Gilbert | | | |
| - | | Click! | Gilbert | | | |
| - | | Sergio Rocks | Gilbert | | | |
| - | | Guadalupe | Gilbert | | | |
| - | | Luba Again | Gilbert | | | |
| - | | La Luba | Gilbert | | | |
| - | | Burning for You | Gilbert | | | |
| - | | Pipo's Burden | Gilbert | | | |
| - | | Of Two Minds | Gilbert | | | |
| - | | But the Little Girls Understand | Gilbert | | | |
| - | | Luba | Gilbert | | | |
| - | | Fritz and Pipo, Sittin' in a Tree | Gilbert | | | |
| - | | God Willing | Gilbert | | | |
| - | | Ofelia | Gilbert | | | |
| - | | Luba | Gilbert | | | |
| - | | Group Portrait | Gilbert | | | |
| - | | Ask Luba | Gilbert | | | |
| - | | The Petra Question | Gilbert | | | |
| - | | Mystery of the Sea Hog | Gilbert | | | |
| - | | Message from an Ex | Gilbert | | | |

| TITLE | No. | STORY TITLE | ARTIST | PUB. DATE | PUBLISHER | NOTES |
|---|---|---|---|---|---|---|
| *Luba* ...continued | | A Gift for Venus | Gilbert | | | |
| - | | The Light of Venus | Gilbert | | | |
| - | | The Big Picture | Gilbert | | | |
| - | | For Art's Sake | Gilbert | | | |
| - | | Luba | Gilbert | | | |
| - | | Petra | Gilbert | | | |
| - | | Rosalba | Gilbert | | | |
| - | | Who the Fuck is Hector? | Gilbert | | | |
| - | | Something About | Gilbert | | | |
| - | | Ms. Super Fit USA | Gilbert | | | |
| - | | Three Daughters | Gilbert | | | |
| - | | Hector's 2¢ | Gilbert | | | |
| - | | Day Job | Gilbert | | | |
| - | | Kid Stuff | Gilbert | | | |
| - | | Sea Hog Serenade | Gilbert | | | |
| - | | Intellectual Pursuits | Gilbert | | | |
| - | | The Kid Stuff Kids 1, 2, 3 | Gilbert | | | |
| - | | Down in Heaven | Gilbert | | | |
| - | | Another Story Altogether | Gilbert | | | |
| - | | Genetically Predisposed | Gilbert | | | |
| - | | Blackouting | Gilbert | | | Previously collected in *High Soft Lisp* |
| - | | Luba in America 2 | Gilbert | | | |
| - | | Doralis | Gilbert | | | |
| - | | Venus and You | Gilbert | | | The final chapter, from *Love and Rockets* Vol. II #20, is previously uncollected. |
| *Locas: The Maggie and Hopey Stories* | | Mechanics | Jaime | September 2004 | Fantagraphics | Oversized hardcover collection |
| - | | Hey Hopey | Jaime | | | |
| - | | Maggie Vs. Maniakk | Jaime | | | |
| - | | Locas Tambien | Jaime | | | |
| - | | 100 Rooms | Jaime | | | |
| - | | Locas Starring Hopey | Jaime | | | |

| TITLE | No. | STORY TITLE | ARTIST | PUB. DATE | PUBLISHER | NOTES |
|---|---|---|---|---|---|---|
| *Locas: The Maggie and Hopey Stories* ...continued | | Locas | Jaime | | | |
| - | | Las Mujeres Perdidas | Jaime | | | |
| - | | Locos | Jaime | | | |
| - | | Young Locas | Jaime | | | |
| - | | Locas en las Cabezas | Jaime | | | |
| - | | Locas at the Beach | Jaime | | | |
| - | | House of Raging Women | Jaime | | | |
| - | | Those Wild and Mixed Up Locas | Jaime | | | |
| - | | Locas vs. Locos | Jaime | | | |
| - | | Locas 8:01 am - 11:15 pm | Jaime | | | |
| - | | The Secrets of Life and Death Vol. 5 | Jaime | | | |
| - | | A Date With Hopey | Jaime | | | |
| - | | The Return of Ray D. | Jaime | | | |
| - | | Jerusalem Crickets | Jaime | | | |
| - | | Vida Loca: The Death of Speedy Ortiz | Jaime | | | |
| - | | The Night Ape Sex Came Home to Play | Jaime | | | |
| - | | Jerry Slum and the Crickettes | Jaime | | | |
| - | | A Mess of Skin ... | Jaime | | | |
| - | | All This and Penny, Too ... | Jaime | | | |
| - | | In the Valley of the Polar Bears | Jaime | | | |
| - | | Boxer, Bikini or Brief | Jaime | | | |
| - | | Tear it Up, Terry Downe | Jaime | | | |
| - | | The Adventures of Maggie the Mechanic | Jaime | | | |

| TITLE | No. | STORY TITLE | ARTIST | PUB. DATE | PUBLISHER | NOTES |
|---|---|---|---|---|---|---|
| *Locas: The Maggie and Hopey Stories* ...continued | | Ninety-Three Million Miles from the Sun ... And Counting | Jaime | | | |
| - | | Las Monjas Asesinas | Jaime | | | |
| - | | Below My Window Lurks My Head (Parts 1 & 2) | Jaime | | | |
| - | | ... And in this Corner ... | Jaime | | | |
| - | | Wigwam Bam | Jaime | | | |
| - | | ... Gonna Make You My Man | Jaime | | | |
| - | | Chester Square | Jaime | | | |
| - | | Camp Vicki | Jaime | | | |
| - | | Perla and Beatriz | Jaime | | | |
| - | | Easter Hunt | Jaime | | | |
| - | | Maggie the Mechanic or Perla the Prostitute | Jaime | | | |
| - | | It's Not That Big a Deal | Jaime | | | |
| - | | Angelitas | Jaime | | | |
| - | | We Want the World and We Want it Bald ... | Jaime | | | |
| - | | Angelitas Dos | Jaime | | | |
| - | | Butt Sisters | Jaime | | | |
| - | | Son of Butt Sisters | Jaime | | | |
| - | | Return of Butt Sisters | Jaime | | | |
| - | | Hester Square | Jaime | | | |
| - | | Bob Richardson | Jaime | | | |
| *Locas II: Maggie, Hopey and Ray* | | Maggie and Hopey Summer Fun | Jaime | June 2009 | Fantagraphics | Oversized hardcover collection |
| - | | Penny Century | Jaime | | | |
| - | | Locas | Jaime | | | |
| - | | La Pantera Negra | Jaime | | | |
| - | | Hopey Hop Sacks | Jaime | | | |
| - | | Look Out | Jaime | | | |
| - | | Chiller! | Jaime | | | |
| - | | C'mon Mom! | Jaime | | | |

| TITLE | No. | STORY TITLE | ARTIST | PUB. DATE | PUBLISHER | NOTES |
|---|---|---|---|---|---|---|
| *Locas II: Maggie, Hopey and Ray ...continued* | | Home School | Jaime | | | |
| - | | To Be Announced | Jaime | | | |
| - | | Loser Leave Oxnard | Jaime | | | |
| - | | ¡Inquiritis! | Jaime | | | |
| - | | One More Ladies' Man | Jaime | | | |
| - | | Nobody? So ... | Jaime | | | |
| - | | Election Day Parts 1 & 2 | Jaime | | | |
| - | | The Littlest Mermaid Princess Doe | Jaime | | | |
| - | | The Race | Jaime | | | |
| - | | Everybody Loves Me, Baby | Jaime | | | |
| - | | Maggie Parts 1-10 | Jaime | | | |
| - | | The Frogmouth | Jaime | | | |
| - | | Bay of Threes | Jaime | | | |
| - | | Life Through Whispers | Jaime | | | |
| - | | 2 'R's, 2 'L's | Jaime | | | |
| - | | Hagler and Hearns | Jaime | | | |
| - | | Day by Day With Hopey: Tuesday Is Whose Day | Jaime | | | |
| - | | Day by Day With Hopey: Wednesday Is Bitter Ends Day | Jaime | | | |
| - | | Day by Day With Hopey: Thursday Is Her's Day | Jaime | | | |
| - | | Day by Day With Hopey: Friday Is Jai Alai Day | Jaime | | | |
| - | | Day by Day With Hopey: Saturday Is Shatterday | Jaime | | | |
| - | | Day by Day With Hopey: Sunday Is Put That Gun Down Day | Jaime | | | |

| TITLE | No. | STORY TITLE | ARTIST | PUB. DATE | PUBLISHER | NOTES |
|---|---|---|---|---|---|---|
| *Locas II: Maggie, Hopey and Ray* ...continued | | Day by Day With Hopey: Monday Is Attila the Hun Day | Jaime | | | |
| - | | Day by Day With Hopey: Tuesday Is ... One More Tuesday | Jaime | | | |
| - | | Ser O No Ser | Jaime | | | |
| - | | Angel of Tarzana | Jaime | | | |
| - | | Did Ya Get Got? | Jaime | | | |
| - | | Cream City | Jaime | | | |
| - | | Near Mint | Jaime | | | |
| - | | Angels of Tarzana | | | | |
| - | | Fine to Very Fine | Jaime | | | |
| - | | Trampas Pero No Trampan | Jaime | | | |
| - | | Male Torso Found in L.A. River | Jaime | | | |
| - | | Uk Utirr Tagual Tor Zok | Jaime | | | |
| - | | Rocks Over Rocks | Jaime | | | |
| *Love and Rockets Library* Vol. 1: *Maggie the Mechanic* | | Mechan-X | Jaime | January 2007 | Fantagraphics | |
| - | | "How to Kill A ... " By Isabel Ruebens | Jaime | | | |
| - | | Locas Tambien | Jaime | | | |
| - | | "... Penny Century, You're Fired!" | Jaime | | | |
| - | | Mecanicos | Jaime | | | |
| - | | Mechanics | Jaime | | | |
| - | | Meanwhile ... Back at the Ranch | Jaime | | | |
| - | | Hey Hopey | Jaime | | | |
| - | | Penny Century On th' Road Ag'in | Jaime | | | |
| - | | Maggie Vs. Maniakk | Jaime | | | |

| TITLE | No. | STORY TITLE | ARTIST | PUB. DATE | PUBLISHER | NOTES |
|---|---|---|---|---|---|---|
| *Love and Rockets Library* Vol. 1: *Maggie the Mechanic* ...continued | | Locas Tambien | Jaime | | | |
| - | | Toyo's Request | Jaime | | | |
| - | | 100 Rooms | Jaime | | | |
| - | | T42 | Jaime | | | |
| - | | Locas Starring Hopey | Jaime | | | |
| - | | Locas | Jaime | | | |
| - | | Las Mujeres Perdidas | Jaime | | | |
| - | | Amor y Cohetes | Jaime | | | |
| - | | T42 | Jaime | | | |
| - | | Locos | Jaime | | | |
| - | | Young Locas | Jaime | | | |
| - | | Locas | Jaime | | | |
| - | | Locas en las Cabezas | Jaime | | | |
| - | | Locas at the Beach | Jaime | | | |
| - | | Those Wild and Mixed-Up Locas | Jaime | | | |
| - | | A Date With Hopey | Jaime | | | |
| *Love and Rockets Library* Vol. 2: *Heartbreak Soup* | | Chelo's Burden | Gilbert | January 2007 | Fantagraphics | |
| - | | Heartbreak Soup | Gilbert | | | |
| - | | A Little Story | Gilbert | | | |
| - | | Toco | Gilbert | | | |
| - | | Act of Contrition | Gilbert | | | |
| - | | The Whispering Tree | Gilbert | | | |
| - | | The Mystery Wen | Gilbert | | | |
| - | | The Laughing Sun | Gilbert | | | |
| - | | On Isidro's Beach | Gilbert | | | |
| - | | Ecce Homo | Gilbert | | | |
| - | | The Reticent Heart | Gilbert | | | |
| - | | Slug Fest | Gilbert | | | |
| - | | An American in Palomar | Gilbert | | | |
| - | | Boys Will Be Boys | Gilbert | | | |

| TITLE | No. | STORY TITLE | ARTIST | PUB. DATE | PUBLISHER | NOTES |
|---|---|---|---|---|---|---|
| *Love and Rockets Library* Vol. 2: *Heartbreak Soup* ...continued | | Holidays in the Sun | Gilbert | | | |
| - | | Love Bites | Gilbert | | | |
| - | | The Way Things're Going | Gilbert | | | |
| - | | For the Love of Carmen | Gilbert | | | |
| - | | Duck Feet | Gilbert | | | |
| - | | Bullnecks and Bracelets | Gilbert | | | |
| *Love and Rockets Library* Vol. 3: *The Girl from H.O.P.P.E.R.S.* | | La Toña | Jaime | July 2007 | Fantagraphics | |
| - | | The Little Monster | Jaime | | | |
| - | | Queen Rena Life At 34 | Jaime | | | |
| - | | House Of Raging Women | Jaime | | | |
| - | | Locas Vs. Locos | Jaime | | | |
| - | | Locas 8:01 A.M. | Jaime | | | |
| - | | Who Says It Never Snows In Zymbodia? | Jaime | | | |
| - | | The Secrets Of Life And Death: Vol. 5 | Jaime | | | |
| - | | The Return Of Ray D. | Jaime | | | |
| - | | Vida Loca: The Death Of Speedy Ortiz | Jaime | | | |
| - | | Jerusalem Crickets: 1987 | Jaime | | | |
| - | | Jerusalem Crickets | Jaime | | | |
| - | | Jerry Slum And The Crickettes | Jaime | | | |
| - | | The Night Ape Sex Came Home To Play | Jaime | | | |
| - | | A Mess Of Skin ... | Jaime | | | |
| - | | All This And Penny, Too ... | Jaime | | | |

| TITLE | No. | STORY TITLE | ARTIST | PUB. DATE | PUBLISHER | NOTES |
|---|---|---|---|---|---|---|
| *Love and Rockets Library* Vol. 3: *The Girl from H.O.P.P.E.R.S.* ...continued | | In The Valley Of The Polar Bears | Jaime | | | |
| - | | Boxer | Jaime | | | |
| - | | Bikini Or Brief | Jaime | | | |
| - | | Tear It Up | Jaime | | | |
| - | | Terry Downe | Jaime | | | |
| - | | Li'l Ray | Jaime | | | |
| - | | The Adventures Of Maggie The Mechanic | Jaime | | | |
| - | | Lar' dog: Boy's Night Out #1398 | Jaime | | | |
| - | | Spring 1982 | Jaime | | | |
| - | | Ninety-Three Million Miles From The Sun ... and Counting | Jaime | | | |
| - | | Las Monjas Asesinas | Jaime | | | |
| - | | Below My Window Lurks My Head: Part 1 | Jaime | | | |
| - | | ... And In This Corner ... | Jaime | | | |
| - | | Below My Window Lurks My Head: Part 2 | Jaime | | | |
| - | | Flies On The Ceiling | Jaime | | | |
| *Love and Rockets Library* Vol. 4: *Human Diastrophism* | | Sugar 'N' Spikes | Gilbert | July 2007 | Fantagraphics | |
| - | | Space Case | Gilbert | | | |
| - | | Heraclio's Burden | Gilbert | | | |
| - | | Human Diastrophism | Gilbert | | | |
| - | | Cast Of "Human Diastrophism" | Gilbert | | | |
| - | | Be Bop A Luba | Gilbert | | | |
| - | | Farewell, My Palomar ... | Gilbert | | | |

| TITLE | No. | STORY TITLE | ARTIST | PUB. DATE | PUBLISHER | NOTES |
|---|---|---|---|---|---|---|
| *Love and Rockets Library* Vol. 4: *Human Diastrophism* ...continued | | A Trick Of The Unconscious | Gilbert | | | |
| - | | The Way Things Went | Gilbert | | | |
| - | | Pipo | Gilbert | | | |
| - | | Carmen | Gilbert | | | |
| - | | Another Mysterious Tree | Gilbert | | | |
| - | | Mouth Trap | Gilbert | | | |
| - | | Love Story | Gilbert | | | |
| - | | Bread | Gilbert | | | |
| - | | Love And Maria | Gilbert | | | |
| - | | The Gorgo Wheel | Gilbert | | | |
| - | | Luba Conquers The World | Gilbert | | | |
| - | | Chelo's Burden | Gilbert | | | |
| *Love and Rockets Library* Vol. 5: *Perla La Loca* | | Wigwam Bam | Jaime | October 2007 | Fantagraphics | |
| - | | ... Gonna Make You My Man | Jaime | | | |
| - | | Chester Square | Jaime | | | |
| - | | Camp Vicki | Jaime | | | |
| - | | Perla and Beatriz | Jaime | | | |
| - | | The Navas of Hazel Court | Jaime | | | |
| - | | Maggie the Mechanic or Perla the Prostitute | Jaime | | | |
| - | | It's Not That Big a Deal | Jaime | | | |
| - | | Angelitas | Jaime | | | |
| - | | We Want the World and We Want it Bald | Jaime | | | |
| - | | Angelitas Dos | Jaime | | | |
| - | | Butt Sisters | Jaime | | | |
| - | | Son of Butt Sisters | Jaime | | | |
| - | | Return of the Butt Sisters | Jaime | | | |

| TITLE | No. | STORY TITLE | ARTIST | PUB. DATE | PUBLISHER | NOTES |
|---|---|---|---|---|---|---|
| *Love and Rockets Library* Vol. 5: *Perla La Loca* ...continued | | Hester Square | Jaime | | | |
| - | | Bob Richardson | Jaime | | | |
| *Love and Rockets Library* Vol. 6: *Beyond Palomar* | | Poison River | Gilbert | October 2007 | Fantagraphics | |
| - | | Love and Rockets X | Gilbert | | | |
| - | | | | | | |
| *Love and Rockets Library* Vol. 7: *Amor y Cohetes* | | Sixto the Dinosaur | Jaime | March 2008 | Fantagraphics | |
| - | | Love and Rockets | Jaime | | | |
| - | | BEM | Gilbert | | | |
| - | | Barrio Huerta | Jaime | | | |
| - | | Music For Monsters | Gilbert | | | |
| - | | Radio Zero | Gilbert | | | |
| - | | Somewhere, in California ... : Part 1 | Mario | | | |
| - | | Untitled | Gilbert | | | |
| - | | Twitch City | Gilbert | | | |
| - | | Somewhere, in California ... : Part 2 | Mario | | | |
| - | | Rocky in: Out o' Space | Jaime | | | |
| - | | Locker Room | Gilbert | | | |
| - | | A Fan Letter | Gilbert | | | |
| - | | Retro Rocky | Jaime | | | |
| - | | Le Contretemps | Gilbert | | | |
| - | | The Adventures of Rocky | Jaime | | | |
| - | | Tears From Heaven | Gilbert | | | |
| - | | Rocky in: Where Are We? | Jaime | | | |
| - | | Big Danny Chesterfield | Gilbert | | | |
| - | | Rocky's Birthday Surprise | Jaime | | | |

| TITLE | No. | STORY TITLE | ARTIST | PUB. DATE | PUBLISHER | NOTES |
|---|---|---|---|---|---|---|
| *Love and Rockets Library* Vol. 7: *Amor y Cohetes* ...continued | | A True Story | Gilbert | | | |
| - | | Bala | Gilbert | | | |
| - | | The Goat | Jaime | | | |
| - | | Frida | Gilbert | | | |
| - | | Rocky in: Rocket Rhodes | Jaime | | | |
| - | | Beep Beep | Gilbert | | | |
| - | | Mojado Power! | Jaime | | | |
| - | | A Folk Tale | Gilbert | | | |
| - | | El Show de Chota | Jaime | | | |
| - | | Hernandez Satyricon | Gilbert | | | |
| - | | War Paint | Jaime | | | |
| - | | Somewhere in the Tropics | Mario | | | |
| - | | Marilyn Monroe | Gilbert | | | |
| - | | The KKK Comes to Hoppers | Jaime | | | |
| - | | Death, God and the Devil Are One | Gilbert | | | |
| - | | Our Christmas!!! | Jaime | | | |
| - | | Life and Rockets | Mario | | | |
| - | | Easter Hunt | Jaime | | | |
| - | | My Love Book | Gilbert | | | |
| - | | Is It Ten Years Already? | Jaime | | | |
| *Love and Rockets Library* Vol. 8: *Penny Century* | | Whoa Nellie! | Jaime | March 2010 | Fantagraphics | |
| - | | Maggie and Hopey Color Fun | Jaime | | | |
| - | | Penny Century | Jaime | | | |
| - | | Locas | Jaime | | | |
| - | | La Pantera Negra | Jaime | | | |

| TITLE | No. | STORY TITLE | ARTIST | PUB. DATE | PUBLISHER | NOTES |
|---|---|---|---|---|---|---|
| *Love and Rockets Library* Vol. 8: *Penny Century* ...continued | | Hopey Hop Sacks | Jaime | | | |
| - | | Look Out | Jaime | | | |
| - | | Chiller! | Jaime | | | |
| - | | C'mon Mom! | Jaime | | | |
| - | | Locas | Jaime | | | |
| - | | Home School | Jaime | | | |
| - | | To Be Announced | Jaime | | | |
| - | | Loser Leave Oxnard | Jaime | | | |
| - | | ¡Inquiritis! | Jaime | | | |
| - | | One More Ladies' Man | Jaime | | | |
| - | | Nobody? So ... | Jaime | | | |
| - | | Election Day | Jaime | | | |
| - | | The Littlest Mermaid Princess Doe | Jaime | | | |
| - | | I Am From Earth | Jaime | | | |
| - | | The Race | Jaime | | | |
| - | | Everybody Loves Me Baby | Jaime | | | |
| - | | Epilogos | Jaime | | | |
| - | | Bay of Threes | Jaime | | | |
| *Love and Rockets Library* Vol. 9: *Esperanza* | | Maggie | Jaime | September 2011 | Fantagraphics | |
| - | | The Frogmouth | Jaime | | | |
| - | | Life Through Whispers | Jaime | | | |
| - | | Day by Day with Hopey | Jaime | | | |
| - | | Angel of Tarzana | Jaime | | | |
| - | | 2 'R's, 2 'L's | Jaime | | | |
| - | | Hagler and Hearns | Jaime | | | |
| - | | Ser O No Ser | Jaime | | | |
| - | | Did Ya Get Got? | Jaime | | | |

| TITLE | No. | STORY TITLE | ARTIST | PUB. DATE | PUBLISHER | NOTES |
|---|---|---|---|---|---|---|
| *Love and Rockets Library* Vol. 9: *Esperanza* ...continued | | Cream City | Jaime | | | |
| - | | Near Mint | Jaime | | | |
| - | | Angels of Tarzana | Jaime | | | |
| - | | Fine to Very Fine | Jaime | | | |
| - | | Trampas Pero No Trampan | Jaime | | | |
| - | | Male Torso Found in L.A. River | Jaime | | | |
| - | | Uk Utirr Tagual Tor Zok | Jaime | | | |
| - | | Rocks Over Rocks | Jaime | | | |

# MAJOR NON-*LOVE AND ROCKETS* PUBLICATIONS

| TITLE | No. | STORY TITLE | ARTIST | PUB. DATE | PUBLISHER | NOTES |
|---|---|---|---|---|---|---|
| *Mister X* | 1-4 | | Gilbert, Jaime, Mario | June 1984-May 1985 | Vortex | Collected in *Mister X: The Archives* by Dark Horse, November 2008 |
| *Return of Mister X* | | | Gilbert, Jaime, Mario | December 1986 | Vortex | Collecting *Mister X #1-4* |
| *Brain Capers* | 1 | A City Story | Mario | August 1993 | Fantagraphics | Collecting previously published Mario stories |
| - | | Waiting For You... | Mario | | | Collecting previously published Mario stories |
| - | | Big Windows | Mario | | | |
| - | | Likes and Lumps of a He-Devil | Mario | | | |
| - | | Fake Foreign Funnies "Yip! Kah-Booom!" | Mario | | | |
| - | | Fake Foreign Funnies "Zd'A'Lik! Bah, Foom Bah!" | Mario | | | |
| - | | Fake Foreign Funnies "Bah Foom Bah!" | Mario | | | |
| - | | Nightmare Sublime | Mario | | | |
| - | | Hey Chucky! | Mario | | | Never reprinted |
| - | | Chalk Artist | Mario | | | |
| *Girl Crazy* | 1-3 | | Gilbert | May-July 1996 | Dark Horse Comics | |

| TITLE | No. | STORY TITLE | ARTIST | PUB. DATE | PUBLISHER | NOTES |
|-------|-----|-------------|--------|-----------|-----------|-------|
| *Yeah!* | 1-9 | | Gilbert | October 1999-June 2000 | DC Comics | Written by Peter Bagge |
| *Goody Good Comics* | 1 | Mike Hayes | Jaime | June 2000 | Fantagraphics | 1 p. color back-cover strip |
| - | | Extend the Hand of Love to All | Gilbert | | | A Roy story |
| *Tales From Shock City* | 1 | | Gilbert, Mario | October 2001 | Fantagraphics | Reprint of Gilbert's backup stories from *Mister X* plus one new story |
| *Grip: The Strange World of Men* | 1-5 | | Gilbert | January-June 2002 | DC Comics / Vertigo | Gilbert's Vertigo debut |
| *Birds of Prey* | 50-55 | | Gilbert | February-July 2003 | DC Comics | Illustrated by Casey Jones |
| *The Naked Cosmos* | | | Gilbert | April 2005 | Bright Red Rocket | One-shot comic and four-episode TV series with Carol Kovinick |
| *Sloth* | | | Gilbert | August 2006 | DC Comics / Vertigo | His first work conceived and executed as a graphic novel |
| *Chance in Hell* | | | Gilbert | March 2007 | Fantagraphics | First of Fritz' B movies. Cover painting by Rick Altergott |
| *Speak of The Devil* | 1-6 | | Gilbert | July 2007-May 2008 | Dark Horse Comics | |
| *The Trouble-makers* | | | Gilbert | July 2009 | Fantagraphics | Second of Fritz' B movies. Cover painting by Rick Altergott |
| *Citizen Rex* | 1-6 | | Gilbert, Mario | July-December 2009 | Dark Horse Comics | Miniseries written by Mario and illustrated by Gilbert |
| *The Art of Jaime Hernandez* | | | Jaime | April 2010 | Abrams ComicArts | Coffee table art book by Todd Hignite |
| *Love From the Shadows* | | | Gilbert | April 2011 | Fantagraphics | Third of Fritz' B movies. Cover painting by Steve Martinez |
| *The Adventures of Venus* | | The World of Venus | Gilbert | May 2012 | Fantagraphics | Includes stories from Measles #2-8 and a new 24-pp. story |
| - | | The New Adventures of Venus | Gilbert | | | |

| TITLE | No. | STORY TITLE | ARTIST | PUB. DATE | PUBLISHER | NOTES |
|---|---|---|---|---|---|---|
| *The Adventures of Venus* ...continued | | Venus | Gilbert | | | |
| - | | The New Adventures of Venus | Gilbert | | | |
| - | | The New Adventures of Venus | Gilbert | | | |
| - | | The New Adventures of Venus | Gilbert | | | |
| - | | La Venus | Gilbert | | | |
| - | | Venus | Gilbert | | | |
| - | | The New Adventures of Venus | Gilbert | | | |
| - | | Santa Claus from Other Planets | Gilbert | | | |
| *Julio's Day* | | | Gilbert | March 2013 | Fantagraphics | |

# OTHER MISCELLANEOUS PUBLICATIONS

| TITLE | No. | STORY TITLE | ARTIST | PUB. DATE | PUBLISHER | NOTES |
|---|---|---|---|---|---|---|
| *AARGH!* | | | Gilbert, Jaime | October 1988 | Mad Love Publishing | Back cover illustration by Jaime and Gilbert |
| *Advance Comics* | 91 | | Jaime | July 1996 | Capital City Distribution | Cover by Jaime, interview with Jaime and Gilbert |
| *All Shook Up* | | Wibble My Soul | Mario | 1990 | Rip Off Press | Anthology about California earthquake |
| - | | It Must Be Jelly, 'Cause Jam Don't Shake Like That | Mario | | | Short story by Rebecka Wright, with illustrations by Mario |
| *Amazing Heroes* | 10 | | Gilbert | April 1982 | Fantagraphics | Gilbert pin-up |
| - | 138 | | Gilbert, Jaime | April 1988 | Fantagraphics | 2nd Annual Swimsuit Special. Miscellaneous pin-ups by Jaime and Gilbert |
| *Amazing Heroes Preview Special* | | | Gilbert, Jaime | 1985 | Fantagraphics | Cover by Jaime, pin-ups by Gilbert and Jaime |
| *American Splendor* | 4 | Today I Am a Mouse | Gilbert | December 2006 | DC Comics/ Vertigo | 6 pp. story written by Harvey Pekar includes Gilbert art and cover |

| TITLE | No. | STORY TITLE | ARTIST | PUB. DATE | PUBLISHER | NOTES |
|---|---|---|---|---|---|---|
| *Anthology of Graphic Fiction, Cartoons and True Stories* | | A Little Story | Gilbert | 2006 | Yale University Press | |
| - | | Flies on the Ceiling | Jaime | | | |
| *Anthology of Graphic Fiction, Cartoons and True Stories Vol. 2* | | Drink, Fucker! | Gilbert | 2008 | Yale University Press | |
| - | | Mosquito | Gilbert | | | |
| - | | She Sleeps with Anybody but Me | Gilbert | | | |
| - | | Jerusalem Crickets | Jaime | | | |
| *Anything Goes!* | 1 | Who's Stronger? | Gilbert | October 1986 | Fantagraphics | Benefit comic for Fantagraphics<br><br>4 pp. story written by Jan Strnad |
| - | 2 | Those Wild and Mixed-Up Locas | Jaime | December 1986 | Fantagraphics | Pencil artwork and rare sketches |
| - | 4 | Space Case | Gilbert | May 1987 | | Anthology includes a 4 pp. color Heartbreak Soup story |
| *Art of BOOM! Studios* | | | Jaime | January 2012 | BOOM! Studios | Includes Jaime pin-up in "music" section |
| *Back Issue* | 3 | | Gilbert, Jaime | March 2004 | TwoMorrows Publishing | Includes article "Rough Stuff: 12 Cartoonists Cut Loose" by David Hamilton |
| *Bart Simpson Comics* | 52 | Homer Simpson: Chick Magnet | Gilbert | February 2010 | Bongo Comics | |
| - | 56 | Lisa Rocks the Party | Gilbert | October 2010 | | |
| *Beasts!* | | | Gilbert, Jaime | February 2007 | Fantagraphics | Includes illustrations by Jaime and Gilbert |
| *Beasts! Book 2* | | | Gilbert, Jaime | October 2008 | | |
| *Best American Comics 2006* | | Day by Day With Hopey: Tuesday is Whose Day? | Jaime | 2006 | Houghton Mifflin | Anthology series |
| *Best American Comics 2007* | | Fritz After Dark | Gilbert | 2007 | Houghton Mifflin | Anthology series |

| TITLE | No. | STORY TITLE | ARTIST | PUB. DATE | PUBLISHER | NOTES |
|---|---|---|---|---|---|---|
| *Best American Comics 2008* | | Gold Diggers of 1969 | Jaime | 2008 | Houghton Mifflin | Anthology series |
| *Best American Comics 2009* | | Papa | Gilbert | 2009 | Houghton Mifflin | Anthology series |
| *Best American Comics 2010* | | Water! Electricity! Meat! | Gilbert, Mario | 2010 | Houghton Mifflin | Anthology series |
| *Best American Comics 2011* | | Browntown | Jaime | 2011 | Houghton Mifflin | Anthology series |
| *Best American Comics 2012* | | The Love Bunglars: Part Four | Jaime | 2012 | Houghton Mifflin | Anthology series |
| *1980-1990: The Best Comics of the Decade* Vol. 2 | | | Gilbert, Jaime | 1990 | Fantagraphics | Jaime and Gilbert cover |
| *Bettie Page Comics* | 1 | | Gilbert, Jaime | March 1996 | Dark Horse Comics | Includes pin-ups by Jaime and Gilbert |
| *Big Mouth* | 6 | Blood and Carpet Don't Mix | Mario | December 1996 | Fantagraphics | Includes 3 pp. autobiographical story written by Mario and illustrated by Pat Moriarty and Eric Reynolds (not reprinted) |
| *Bizarro Comics* | | X-Ray Three | Gilbert | 2001 | DC Comics | Anthology includes 2 pp. spread by Gilbert |
| *Bizarro World* | | The Red Bee Returns | Gilbert | 2005 | DC Comics | Anthology includes Jaime cover |
| *Blab!* | 3 | | Gilbert | 1988 | Kitchen Sink Press | Anthology includes Gilbert commentary on R. Crumb |
| *Book of Changes* | | | Gilbert, Jaime | January 2001 | Fantagraphics | Interview book by Kristine McKenna with portraits by Jaime and Gilbert |
| *Buzzard* | 3 | The Adventures of Bixl! | Mario | March 1991 | Cat Head Comics | not reprinted |
| - | 5 | Fake Foreign Funnies: "Bah Foom Bah!" | Mario | 1992 | | |
| - | 6 | Fake Foreign Funnies: "The Drag Hags" | Mario | August 1992 | | not reprinted |

| TITLE | No. | STORY TITLE | ARTIST | PUB. DATE | PUBLISHER | NOTES |
|---|---|---|---|---|---|---|
| *Buzzard* ...continued | 7 | Fake Foreign Funnies: "Yip! Kah-Booom!" | Mario | February 1993 | | |
| - | 9 | Fake Foreign Funnies: "Dündernöggin und Malletmarx, Those Crazy Pinhead Skinheads!" | Mario | October 1993 | | not reprinted |
| - | 11 | Fake Foreign Funnies: "Bah Foom Bah!" | Mario | 1994 | | |
| - | 12 | Fake Foreign Funnies: "Bah Bah Foom" | Mario | 1994 | | |
| *CBGB* | 1 | | Jaime | July 2010 | | Jaime cover |
| *California Girls* | 8 | | Mario | May 1988 | Eclipse Comics | Trina Robbins *Betty and Veronica*-inspired miniseries includes a dress designed by Mario |
| *Capital City Distributor's Catalog* | | Love & Rockets | Gilbert, Jaime | 1994 | Capital City | 2 pp. strip by Gilbert and Jaime (reprinted in *Love and Rockets* Vol. 15: *Hernandez Satyricon*) |
| *Catwoman: Selina's Big Score* | | | Jaime | August 2003 | DC Comics | Graphic novel by Darwyn Cooke: includes pin-up by Jaime |
| *Centrifugal Bumble-Puppy* | 2 | Homo Eruptus | Gilbert | October 1987 | Fantagraphics | Anthology edited by Joe Sacco |
| - | 4 | | Jaime | December 1987 | | Featuring a cover by Jaime |
| *Clerks: The Comic Book* | 1 | | Gilbert | February 1998 | Oni Press | Alternative cover by Gilbert |
| *Cocktail Comix* | | | Gilbert, Jaime | 1992 | | Rare 8 pp. minicomic from the 1992 Dallas Fantasy Fair with sketches of Richard Gere by both Jaime and Gilbert |
| *Comic Arf* | | | Jaime | 2008 | Fantagraphics | Jaime contributed art to this Craig Yoe-edited anthology |
| *Comic Art Magazine* | 1 | When I Was Little | Jaime | 2002 | Comic Art | |

| TITLE | No. | STORY TITLE | ARTIST | PUB. DATE | PUBLISHER | NOTES |
|---|---|---|---|---|---|---|
| *Comic Art Magazine* ...continued | 9 | | Gilbert | 2007 | Buenaventura Press | Includes "Jesse Marsh: History of His Work in Comics — A Q&A with Gilbert Hernandez" by Ron Goulart and Adrian Tomine |
| *Comic Book Artist* Vol. II | 6 | | Gilbert | November 2005 | TwoMorrows Publishing | Will Eisner tribute issue featured pin-up by Gilbert |
| *Comic Book Confidential* | | | Jaime | January 1989 | Sphinx Productions | 16 pp. free black-and-white movie promo comic from Sphinx Productions, includes art by Jaime |
| *The Comics Go to Hell: A Visual History of the Devil in Comics* | | | Gilbert, Jaime | March 2005 | Fantagraphics | By Fredrik Strömberg, includes Jaime and Gilbert drawings |
| *The Comics Journal* | 63 | | Gilbert, Jaime | May 1981 | Fantagraphics | Miscellaneous early fan art by Jaime and Gilbert |
| - | 72 | | Jaime | May 1982 | | |
| - | 73 | Formula and the Superhero | Gilbert | July 1982 | | With Hal Blythe and Charlie Sweet |
| - | 75 | | Gilbert, Jaime | September 1982 | | Miscellaneous early fan art by Jaime and Gilbert |
| - | 80 | | Jaime | March 1983 | | Cover by Jaime |
| - | 100 | | Jaime | July 1985 | | Cover by Jaime |
| - | 126 | | Gilbert, Jaime | January 1989 | | Cover by Jaime and Gilbert; Jaime, Gilbert and Mario interviewed by Gary Groth, Robert Fiore and Thom Powers |
| - | 167 | | Jaime | April 1994 | | Back cover by Jaime and Joe Sinnott |
| - | 178 | | Gilbert, Jaime | July 1995 | | Cover by Jaime and Gilbert, Jaime and Gilbert interviewed by Neil Gaiman |
| - | 184 | | Jaime | February 1996 | | Cover portrait of Burne Hogarth by Jaime |
| - | 200 | Destroy All Fanboys | Gilbert | December 1997 | | |
| - | | A Life In Comics | Jaime | | | |

| TITLE | No. | STORY TITLE | ARTIST | PUB. DATE | PUBLISHER | NOTES |
|---|---|---|---|---|---|---|
| *The Comics Journal Special Edition* | 1 | Funnybook Folly | Gilbert | Winter 2002 | Fantagraphics | Gilbert's contribution to "Cartoonists on Cartooning" |
| - | | Untitled | Jaime | | | 1 p. Roy comic as part of "Cartoonists on Cartooning" |
| *The Comics Journal Special Edition: Cartoonists on Music* | 2 | They Laughed When I Told Them I Wanted To Rock | Gilbert | Summer 2002 | Fantagraphics | |
| - | | My Dream | Jaime | | | |
| *The Comics Journal Special Edition: Four Generations of Cartoonists* | 4 | Me, Myself and I | Gilbert | Winter 2004 | Fantagraphics | |
| - | | So, When Was It Really | Jaime | | | |
| *Crime Stoppers of America* Vol. 1 | | | Gilbert | 2002 | | Minicomic Gilbert made for Comic-Con International: San Diego. It itemizes 70 "mock" superheroes from the '40s and '50s. |
| *Dallas Fantasy #2 and Best of Dallas Fantasy Comics* | | | | c.1988 | | Rare convention minicomics, 8 pp. each |
| *Dark Horse Presents* | 100 | Los Malcriados | Mario | August 1995 | Dark Horse Comics | |
| *Dark Horse Presents* | 131 | Girl Crazy | Gilbert | April 1998 | Dark Horse Comics | |
| *Death Tales* | 1 | The Ghoul Man | Jaime | 2002 | http://whatthingsdo.com | Jaime's monster minicomic, available online at *What Things Do* (http://whatthingsdo.com/comic/the-ghoul-man/) |
| *Dial M for Monster* | | | Gilbert | September 2003 | IDW Publishing | A collection of Cal McDonald mystery stories by Steve Niles with Gilbert illustrations |

| TITLE | No. | STORY TITLE | ARTIST | PUB. DATE | PUBLISHER | NOTES |
|---|---|---|---|---|---|---|
| *Deadline* | 45-48 | The Death of Speedy Ortiz | Jaime | October 1992-February 1993 | Deadline Publications | U.K. anthology reprint |
| *Different Beat Comics* | 1 | Say, Man ... | Gilbert | March 1994 | Fantagraphics | Rare 3 pp. strip. Reprinted from *Details* magazine (reprinted in *Love and Rockets* Vol. 15: *Hernandez Satyricon*) |
| - | | The He That Walks | Jaime | | | |
| *Dirty Stories* | | | Jaime | 1998 | Fantagraphics | Sex anthology includes Jaime cover |
| *Doris Danger Seeks... Where Giant Monsters Creep and Stomp* | | | Gilbert, Jaime, Mario | February 2006 | Slave Labor Graphics | Series featured pin-ups by all three brothers. |
| *Duplex Planet* card set | | | Jaime | 1996 | Kitchen Sink | Includes Jaime art |
| *Fandom Circus* | 2 | | Jaime | December 1978 | fanzine | Rare pre-*Love and Rockets* fanzine with Jaime's first published story |
| *Fantaco Chronicles* | 1 | | Gilbert | July 1981 | fanzine | '80s fanzine with Gilbert pin-up art in X-Men issue |
| *The Fan's Zine* | 7 | | Gilbert, Jaime | Winter 1978 | fanzine | Comics news and reviews fanzine with early art by Gilbert and Jaime |
| - | 8 | | Gilbert, Jaime | Spring/ Summer 1979 | | |
| *Fantazine* | 5 | | Jaime | 1978 | fanzine | Early pre-*Love and Rockets* fanzine with Jaime story featuring the first published appearance of Maggie. |
| *Free Speeches* | | | Jaime | August 1998 | Oni Press | CBLDF benefit comic includes Jaime illustration |
| *Funny Book* | | | | May 2005 | Fantagraphics | Fantagraphics Free Comic Book Day giveaway |
| *GI Joe* | 164 | | Gilbert | March 2011 | IDW | Gilbert provided an alternate cover |

| TITLE | No. | STORY TITLE | ARTIST | PUB. DATE | PUBLISHER | NOTES |
|---|---|---|---|---|---|---|
| *The Guild: Vork* | 1 | | Gilbert | December 2010 | Dark Horse Comics | Gilbert provided an alternate cover |
| *Hate* | 26 | Me | Gilbert | March 1997 | Fantagraphics | 3 pp. Peter Bagge backup story with Gilbert art. Also includes a 1 p. ad for "Action Suits," Peter Bagge's band, with Gilbert art |
| *Heck!* | | Chalk Artist | Mario | 1989 | Rip Off Press | Anthology with 4 pp. Mario story |
| *Hey!* | | | Gilbert | 1988 | | Underground minicomic — a double-issue flipbook featuring jam pages by Gilbert with several other artists. |
| *History of the DC Universe — Limited Signed HC* | | | Gilbert, Jaime | 1988 | DC Comics | Gilbert and Jaime contributed to a 3 pp. gatefold poster jam with dozens of other artists |
| *House of Mystery* | 14 | | Gilbert | August 2009 | DC Comics/ Vertigo | Featuring Gilbert art |
| *How to Draw Flies* | | | Jaime | 1984 | | Comic-Con International: San Diego minicomic featuring art by Jaime |
| *iZombie* | 12 | | | April 2011 | DC Comics/ Vertigo | Featuring Gilbert art |
| *Janx* | 1 | | Gilbert | 1986 | Emilio Soltero Graphic Productions | Includes Gilbert pin-up |
| *Jay and Silent Bob* | 3 | | Jaime | December 1998 | Oni Press | Jaime provided an alternate cover |
| *John Carter of Mars: The Jesse Marsh Years* | | | | May 2010 | Dark Horse Comics | Featured a foreword by Mario |
| *Kramers Ergot* Vol. 7 | | The Toppers | Jaime | November 2008 | Buenaventura | Oversized hardcover anthology from Buenaventura Press |
| *LA Weekly* Vol. 15 | 20 | | Gilbert, Jaime | April 1993 | Los Angeles Weekly Inc. | Cover by Jaime and Gilbert |
| *Los Angeles CityBeat* Vol. 2 | 51 | | Jaime | December 2004 | David Comden | Cover by Jaime |
| *Loud Mouth Louie* | 1 | | Gilbert | 1997 | Funky Devil Productions | Includes Gilbert pin-up |

| TITLE | No. | STORY TITLE | ARTIST | PUB. DATE | PUBLISHER | NOTES |
|---|---|---|---|---|---|---|
| *Madman Adventures* TPB | | | Mario | 1993 | Kitchen Sink Press | Mario contributed to cover jam |
| *Madman: All New Giant-Sized Super Ginchy Special!* | | | Gilbert | April 2011 | Image | Includes Gilbert pin-up |
| *Madman Picture Exhibition* | 2 | | Gilbert, Jaime, Mario | May 2002 | AAA Pop Comics | Includes pin-ups by all three brothers |
| *Madman Bubble Gum Cards* | | | Mario | 1994 | Dark Horse Comics | Includes Mario art |
| *Masters of the Comic Book Universe Revealed!* | | | Gilbert | 2006 | Chicago Review Press | By Arie Kaplan, includes interview with and original art by Gilbert |
| *McSweeney's Quarterly Concern* | 13 | Julio's Day | Gilbert | 2004 | McSweeney's | Reprints part of "Julio's Day" by Gilbert and "Locas" and "La Blanca" by Jaime |
| - | | Locas | Jaime | | | |
| - | | La Blanca | Jaime | | | |
| *Moebius Legends of Arzach Gallery* Vol. 2 | | | Jaime | December 1993 | Tundra | Includes Jaime art in tribute gallery (Tundra) |
| *Mome* | 19 | Roy | Gilbert | Summer 2010 | Fantagraphics | |
| *Mona* | 1 | | Jaime | 1999 | Kitchen Sink Press | Anthology featured Jaime cover |
| *MySpace Dark Horse Presents* | Vol. 2 | Manga | Gilbert | February 2009 | Dark Horse Comics | |
| *MySpace Dark Horse Presents* | Vol. 4 | Dreamstar | Gilbert | December 2009 | Dark Horse Comics | |
| *MySpace Dark Horse Presents* | Vol. 6 | Las Primas Controla | Jaime | February 2011 | Dark Horse Comics | |
| *Narrative Corpse: A Chain Story by 69 Artists!* | | | Gilbert, Jaime | 1995 | Raw Books / Gates of Heck | Jaime and Gilbert contributed |
| *Negative Burn* | 31 | | Gilbert, Jaime | January-February 1996 | Caliber Press | Includes 4 pp. Jaime sketchbook |
| *New Age Comics* | 1 | | Gilbert, Jaime | 1985 | Renegade Press | Comics news |

| TITLE | No. | STORY TITLE | ARTIST | PUB. DATE | PUBLISHER | NOTES |
|---|---|---|---|---|---|---|
| *The New Comics Anthology* | | Whispering Tree | Gilbert | 1991 | MacMillan Publishing | Anthology edited by Bob Callahan |
| - | | The Goat | Jaime | | | |
| - | | Funslower Feeds | Mario | | | |
| *The New Smithsonian Book of Comic-Book Stories: From Crumb to Clowes* | | Locos | Jaime | 2004 | Smithsonian Institution/ New College Press | |
| - | | Pipo | Gilbert | | | |
| *New York Times Magazine* "The Funny Pages" | | La Maggie La Loca | Jaime | April 2006 | Arthur Ochs Sulzberger, Jr. | Expanded in *Love and Rockets* Vol II #20 |
| *No Sex* | 14 | Inez | Gilbert | 1980-1982 | fanzine | Early pre-*Love and Rockets* sci-fi fanzine edited by David Heath Jr. |
| - | 18 | Penny Century | Jaime | | | |
| *Nursery Rhyme Comics* | | Jack and Jill | Jaime | 2011 | First Second | |
| - | | Humpty Dumpty | Gilbert | | | |
| *Open Season: The Mini Comic* | | | Jaime, Mario | 1989 | | Comic-Con International: San Diego minicomic featured art by Jaime and Mario |
| *Potboiler* | 1 | | Jaime | 1979 | fanzine | Early pre-*Love and Rockets* fanzine with Jaime story featuring the first published appearance of Penny Century and H.R. Costigan. |
| *The Powerpuff Girls* | 25 | | Jaime | May 2002 | DC Comics | Includes Jaime pin-up |
| *Prime Cuts* | 2 | | Gilbert | March 1987 | Fantagraphics | Features Gilbert cover |
| *Private Stash: A pin-up Girl Portfolio by Twenty Artists* | | | Jaime | February 2007 | Buenaventura Press | Includes Jaime pin-up (Buenaventura Press) |

| TITLE | No. | STORY TITLE | ARTIST | PUB. DATE | PUBLISHER | NOTES |
|---|---|---|---|---|---|---|
| *Punk Planet Magazine* | 46 | | Jaime | November 2001 | Ingram Periodicals Inc. | Cover by Jaime, includes interview with Jaime |
| *Purgatory, USA* | 1 | | Gilbert, Jaime | March 1989 | Slave Labor Graphics | Collection of early Ed Brubaker stories featuring a cover by Jaime and Gilbert |
| *Real Girl* | 1 | Likes and Lumps of a He-Devil | Mario | October 1990 | Fantagraphics | |
| - | 2 | Big Windows | Mario | 1991 | | |
| | 3 | After Ten | Mario | March 1992 | | |
| - | 5 | | Jaime | April 1993 | | Cover |
| *Real Schmuck* | 1 | Hot Foot | Mario | April 1993 | Starhead Comix | Anthology featured stories written by Dennis Eichhorn with art by Mario |
| *Real Smut* | 6 | | Gilbert | August 1993 | Fantagraphics | Features Gilbert cover |
| *Real Stuff* | 4 | | Jaime | November 1991 | Fantagraphics | Includes Jaime cover |
| *Renegade Romance* | 1 | Waiting For You... | Mario | 1987-1988 | Renegade Press | Cover by Gilbert |
| - | 2 | | Jaime | 1988 | | Cover |
| *Rip Off Comix* | 28 | Nightmare Sublime | Mario | January 1990 | Rip Off Press | Includes 1 p. pin-up by Jaime and Gilbert |
| *RoadStrips* | | I'm Proud to be An American... | Gilbert | 2005 | Chronicle Books | Anthology includes 2 pp. Gilbert story |
| *The Rocket* | | | Gilbert, Jaime | August 1986 | Bob McChesney Seattle Rocket | Seattle's alternative rock newspaper featured cover by Jaime and Gilbert |
| *The Rocketeer* | | | Jaime | 1985 | Eclipse | Jaime was credited with a "last minute art assist" by Dave Stevens |
| *SPX 2003* | | | Jaime | 2003 | Comic Book Legal Defense Fund | Features Jaime cover |
| *Sexy Stories From World Religions* | 1 | Cleavo Masquerading as the Savior | Mario | 1990 | Last Gasp Eco-Funnies | Never reprinted |
| *Silverheels* | 3 | All My Love, Aliso Road | Jaime | May 1984 | Pacific Comics | Unfinished 8 pp. color backup story |
| *Slant Magazine* | | Boy Chick in "Takin' it to the Streets" | Gilbert | 1995 | Urban Outfitters | 1 p. strip (magazine only lasted 9 issues) |

| TITLE | No. | STORY TITLE | ARTIST | PUB. DATE | PUBLISHER | NOTES |
|---|---|---|---|---|---|---|
| *Spicecapades* | | The Spice Girls Forget The Words | Gilbert | 1999 | Fantagraphics | Tongue-in-cheek 1 p. strip tribute to the Spice Girls |
| *Star Wars Tales* | 20 | Young Lando Calrissian | Gilbert | June 2004 | Dark Horse Comics | 8 pp. short story |
| *Strange Tales II* | 2 | Love and the Space Phantom | Jaime | January 2011 | Marvel | Cover by Jaime |
| *Strange Tales II* | | Old School Rules! | Gilbert | | | |
| *Strip Aids USA* | | Handsome | Jaime | August 1988 | Last Gasp | |
| - | | Tony | Gilbert | | | |
| - | | Get a Clue! Or, Urban Legends We've Known and Loathed | Mario | | | |
| *Street Music* | 6 | | | August 1990 | Fantagraphics | Features Gilbert cover |
| *Superman and Batman: World's Funnest* | | Last Imp Standing | Jaime | 2000 | DC Comics | *Elseworlds Special* written by Evan Dorkin with three pages drawn by Jaime |
| *Supernatural Law: Secretary Mavis* | 4 | | Jaime | January 2003 | Exhibit A Press | Featured Jaime cover |
| *Tarzan: The Jesse Marsh Years* | Vols. 1-3 | | | 2009 | Dark Horse Comics | Vol. 1 includes a foreword by Mario, Vol. 2 includes one by Gilbert and Vol. 3 includes one by Jaime |
| *Tempus Fugitive* | 2 | | Gilbert | July 1990 | DC Comics | Includes Gilbert pin-up |
| *Tom Strong's Terrific Tales* | 1 | Tesla Time | Jaime | January 2002 | DC Comics | 4 pp. story written by Alan Moore |
| *Transmetropolitan* | 31, 32, 33 | | Jaime | March-May 2000 | DC Comics | Includes Jaime covers |
| *Treehouse of Horror* | 14 | Homer Conquers the World | Gilbert | October 2008 | Bongo Comics | |
| *The True North II* | | Tierra de Pajaro | Gilbert | 1991 | Comic Legends Legal Defense Fund | Free speech benefit anthology includes a 1 p. Gilbert story (which was reprinted in the collected edition of *Birdland*) |

| TITLE | No. | STORY TITLE | ARTIST | PUB. DATE | PUBLISHER | NOTES |
|---|---|---|---|---|---|---|
| *UG!3K* | | A Piercing Denial | Gilbert | 1999 | Fogelcomix | Anthology of underground funnies strips by Gilbert, Jaime, Mario |
| - | | Nightmare Sublime | Mario | | | From *Rip Off Comix* #28 |
| - | | Handsome | Jaime | | | From *Strip Aids* |
| *Vortex* | 7 | Return of the Tzik | Gilbert | March 1984 | Vortex Comics | A quasi-sequel to "BEM". Also includes Jaime cover |
| - | 11 | The He That Walks | Jaime | June 1985 | Vortex Comics | Includes Jaime cover |
| *Warped Reality* | 4 | | | 1996 | CBLDF | CBLDF benefit anthology with Gilbert illustrations |
| *Weirdo* | 25 | Beto and Carol | Gilbert | Summer 1989 | Last Gasp | Autobiographical story (reprinted in *Love and Rockets* Vol. 15: *Hernandez Satyricon*) |
| *Who's Who: Definitive Directory of the DC Universe* | 18 | | Jaime | August 1986 | DC Comics | Pin-up of Phantom Girl |
| - | 21 | | Jaime | November 1986 | DC Comics | Pin-up of Shrinking Violet |
| *Zero Zero* | 7 | The Shit Eaters | Gilbert | January-February 1996 | Fantagraphics | Includes 1 p. Gilbert strip |

**Marc Sobel** is a writer and critic whose work has appeared in a variety of publications and websites, including *The Comics Journal*, Sequart Research and Literacy Organization, Comic Book Galaxy, Hooded Utilitarian and elsewhere. He lives in Queens, N.Y., with his wife and two sons.

**Kristy Valenti** has written comics criticism for ComiXology and *The Comics Journal*, which she co-edits. For Fantagraphics, she's edited *Listen, Whitey! The Sights and Sounds of Black Power 1965-75*, *Man of Rock: A Biography of Joe Kubert* and *Most Outrageous*, among other titles. She lives in Seattle, Wash.